Jack

Jack

A Life of
C. S. Lewis

George Sayer

CROSSWAY BOOKS • WHEATON, ILLINOIS
A DIVISION OF GOOD NEWS PUBLISHERS

Jack: A Life of C. S. Lewis.

First edition titled *Jack: C. S. Lewis and His Times*, published in 1988 by Harper & Row.

Second edition published by
Crossway Books
a division of Good News Publishers
1300 Crescent Street
Wheaton, Illinois 60187.

Excerpt from "Love's as warm as tears" in *Poems* by C. S. Lewis, copyright © 1964 by the Executors of the Estate of C. S. Lewis and renewed 1992 by the C. S. Lewis Pte Ltd., reprinted by permission of Harcourt Brace & Company.

Excerpt from *Spirits in Bondage* by C. S. Lewis, edited by Walter Hooper, copyright © 1984 by C. S. Lewis Pte Ltd., reprinted by permission of Harcourt Brace & Company.

Cover design: Russ Peterson

Cover photo: © Hulton Deutsch Collection, Ltd.

Art Direction/Design: Mark Schramm

First printing, Crossway edition, 1994

Printed in the United States of America

Library of Congress Cataloging-in-Publication Data
Sayer, George.
    Jack : a life of C. S. Lewis / George Sayer. — 2nd ed.
       p.   cm.
    Rev. ed. of: Jack: C. S. Lewis and his times. 1st ed. 1988.
    1. Lewis, C. S. (Clive Staples), 1898-1963. 2. Authors,
English—20th century—Biography. I. Title.
PR6023.E926Z88 1994   823'.912—dc20 [B]   93-26860
ISBN 0-89107-761-8

02		01		00		99		98		97		96		95		94
15	14	13	12	11	10	9	8	7	6	5	4	3				

To my wife
Margaret

TABLE OF CONTENTS

ACKNOWLEDGMENTS

I am deeply grateful to many—to Walter Hooper who first suggested that I should write something about C. S. Lewis; to the late Clyde S. Kilby who invited me to give the Wade lecture on Lewis at Wheaton College, put at my disposal the magnificent Wade Collection of Lewis material assembled there and gave me limitless help and hospitality; to his successor, Lyle Dorsett, and to all members of the staff there, especially Marjorie Mead, without whose patience and encouragement I should certainly not have finished this book.

Among other individuals I want to thank Lady Dunbar of Hempriggs and her husband, the late Leonard Blake. I am indebted also to some who are no longer alive—Stephen Schofield, Dom. Bede Griffiths, the Rev. R. H. Head, Dr. R. E. Havard, A. F. Lace, Hugh Sinclair, Sir Donald Hardman, and Sir Alexander Clutterbuck.

Further, I am grateful to:

Messrs Curtis Brown on behalf of the C. S. Lewis Pte Ltd. for permission to quote numerous passages from unpublished and published letters and diaries of C. S. Lewis; to print a short poem by Joy Lewis and to quote from her letters; to quote from *Spirits in Bondage, Essays Presented to Charles Williams,* and *The Personal Heresy.*

Curtis Brown and Macmillan Publishing Company for permission to quote part of a letter from Bill Gresham printed in *And God Came In* by Lyle Dorsett.

HarperCollins for permission to quote from *Surprised by Joy, The Four Loves, Mere Christianity, The Great Divorce, Dymer, They Stand Together, C. S. Lewis: A Biography* by Roger Lancelyn Green and Walter Hooper, and from *The Inklings* by Humphrey Carpenter.

Cambridge University Press for permission to quote from *Studies in Medieval and Renaissance Literature, Selected Literary Essays*, and *An Experiment in Criticism*.

Harcourt Brace Jovanovich for permission to quote from *Spirits in Bondage, That Hideous Strength, Poems, Dymer*, and *Light on C. S. Lewis*.

The Marion E. Wade Collection for permission to quote numerous passages from the letters, diaries, and other writings of Major W. H. Lewis.

Oxford University Press for permission to quote from *The Allegory of Love, English Literature in the Sixteenth Century*, and *A Preface to Paradise Lost*.

The estate of the late Dame Helen Gardner for permission to quote from her British Academy Lecture on C. S. Lewis.

Lady Dunbar of Hempriggs for permission to quote from letters written by her mother.

Shelley Fawcett for permission to quote from a letter by his father, Hugh I'A. Fausset.

I have made every effort to trace the present-day holders of the copyrights to the material that I have used. If the copyright holders will let me know of any errors or omissions, I shall be happy to rectify these in subsequent editions.

FOREWORD

The sustained interest in C. S. Lewis, especially in the United States, and the worldwide sales of his books are not by themselves sufficient justification for another biography when there is a good one by Green and Hooper. But I have been fortunate in having at my disposal materials not available to them. These include the million-word diary kept by C. S. Lewis's brother, Major W. H. Lewis, the material about Joy Davidman collected and presented by Professor Lyle Dorsett, the mass of material assiduously collected by Stephen Schofield and published in *The Canadian C. S. Lewis Journal,* and my own recollections of a relationship that lasted for twenty-nine years.

In most of the biographies that I have read, the early years are the most interesting. I have therefore given far more space than Green and Hooper to this part of Lewis's life. I have similarly given more attention to other aspects, such as his early poetry, his relationship with Mrs. Moore, his life as a university teacher, and his life at the Kilns.

I have also tried to provide something like a miniature critical commentary on his books and to guess at which are likely to be still in print and read at the beginning of the twenty-first century.

NOTE ON THE PRIMARY SOURCES

Much of the material for a biography of C. S. Lewis is easily available to the student. It has been assiduously collected for the Bodleian Library, Oxford, by the Reverend Walter Hooper; and for the Wade Collection, Wheaton College, Illinois, by Professor Clyde Kilby. Thanks to a sharing arrangement, nearly all manuscripts can be consulted in either library. The important exception is the complete text of the diary kept by Major W. H. Lewis, which is at present available only at Wheaton.

The student should be warned that the following sources were edited before reaching these libraries:

The Lewis Papers, 11 volumes (Leeborough Press). This collection of family papers was assembled by Albert Lewis, the father of W. H. and C. S. Lewis, edited and typed by Warren after his father's death, and bound in Oxford. The original documents were then destroyed. Many letters and other documents of great interest, such as C. S. Lewis's school reports, were never included at all. There is reason to suppose that some letters were cut or altered before being included.

Letters of C. S. Lewis, edited with a memoir by W. H. Lewis (Bles, 1966). This is a short version of a manuscript entitled "C. S. Lewis: A Biography" by W. H. Lewis, which was edited and much reduced in size by Christopher Derrick on behalf of the publisher. Even in the original version, some of the letters were considerably edited, often to the extent of altering their meaning.

Now there is a revised and enlarged edition of C. S. Lewis's numerous and excellent letters, edited by Walter Hooper, (Collins, 1988).

All My Road Before Me: The Diary of C. S. Lewis, 1922–1927, edited by Walter Hooper (HarperCollins, 1991), was also helpful.

They Stand Together: The Letters of C. S. Lewis to Arthur Greeves, 1914–1963, edited by Walter Hooper (Collins, 1979). This is a splendid book, quite admirably edited, with the deletions made by Greeves restored. However, not all the letters written by Lewis to Greeves are here. Some were deliberately destroyed by Greeves during his lifetime and by Lisbeth Greeves, a cousin by marriage, after his death.

I am greatly indebted to Green and Hooper's *C. S. Lewis: A Biography* (Harcourt Brace Jovanovich, 1974); to the Reverend Walter Hooper's admirable bibliography of the writings of C. S. Lewis, as revised and printed in *C. S. Lewis at the Breakfast Table*, edited by James T. Como (Macmillan, 1979); to the bibliography by Joe R. Christopher and Joan K. Ostling entitled *C. S. Lewis: An Annotated Checklist of Writings About Him and His Works* (Kent State University Press); and to the bibliography *Farther Up and Farther In: C. S. Lewis as Reflected in Recent Secondary Sources*, by Lois Larson and D. W. Krummel.

No words of mine can express adequately my gratitude to Professor Clyde S. Kilby and my debt to the magnificent collection of "Lewisiana" he has built up in the Wade Collection at Wheaton College. I am grateful to Walter Hooper for much kindness and for being the first to suggest that I might write something about C. S. Lewis. Nothing could have exceeded the generosity of Stephen Schofield, editor of *The Canadian C. S. Lewis Journal*, except his energy in showering me with information and articles of all sorts about C. S. Lewis. I am grateful to Humphrey

Carpenter for advice and for giving me a copy of the then unpublished series of letters written by C. S. Lewis to his brother between 1930 and 1941. I have also derived much help from his splendid volume *The Inklings* (Allen and Unwin, 1978). I have received valuable help from Paul Ford, author of the encyclopedic *Companion to Narnia* (Harper & Row, 1980); Neville Randall; Jane Gaskell; Mary Neylan; Dr. R. E. Havard; Professor Lyle W. Dorsett, author of *And God Came In: An Extraordinary Love Story; Joy Davidman, Her Life and Marriage to C. S. Lewis* (Crossway, 1991); and especially Lady Dunbar of Hempriggs and Leonard Blake. I have often felt that the friends of C. S. Lewis cannot help being friends of each other.

PREFACE:

Our First Meeting

Mr. Lewis, sir?" said Kirby, the omniscient head porter of Magdalen College, Oxford. "New Buildings, third staircase, third set of rooms."

I slipped on the sleeveless and buttonless black cloth gown that ordinary undergraduates wore in 1934 on formal occasions (and still do), and walked diagonally across the front quad past the open-air pulpit where sermons have been preached since 1480, through dim cloisters scarcely altered since the fifteenth century, and emerged at the edge of the great lawn in front of the stately Palladian block of twenty-two bays still called "New Buildings," though built in 1733.

I inhaled the rich scent of the wisteria that grew on the vast arcaded south portico. Up and down the arcade I walked until I found an archway with the figure 3 above it. As I looked at the list of occupants of the rooms, someone walked briskly past me and up the stairs. Yes, here it was, MR. C. S. LEWIS, the third name from the bottom. I found the name again, painted in white over a doorway on the first floor. Standing outside was a neat, gray-haired man with a pipe in his mouth and a puckish face. "Are you a pupil come for a tutorial?" he asked.

"No. But Mr. Lewis is going to be my tutor next term. I've come to find out what he wants me to read during vacation."

"You're lucky in having him as your tutor," he said.

Just then the door opened. A young man in a scholar's gown came out and went rapidly down the stairs. The puck-faced man asked if he could slip in before me. "I only want to retrieve a manuscript," he said. He left the door open. Through it I could hear a strong, rich voice.

"Splendid, Tollers. Just the man I wanted most of all to see. I've read what you gave me with great pleasure. When can we talk about it? Can you stay now and have some lunch in college? Give me five minutes with a new pupil. Then I can be with you." The puck-faced man said he would sit in the sun until Lewis was ready. I went in and sat next to the fireplace opposite Lewis.

He was a heavily built man who looked about forty, with a fleshy oval face and a ruddy complexion. His black hair had retreated from his forehead, which made him especially imposing. I knew nothing about him, except that he was the college English tutor. I did not know that he was the best lecturer in the department, nor had I read the only book that he had published under his own name (hardly anyone had). Even after I had been taught by him for three years, it never entered my mind that he could one day become an author whose books would sell at the rate of about two million copies a year. Since he never spoke of religion while I was his pupil, or until we had become friends fifteen years later, it would have seemed incredible that he would become the means of bringing many back to the Christian faith. Astonishing, too, that this almost unknown academic should become a popular broadcaster whose talks would play a valuable part in sustaining British morale during the darkest hours of the war.

"Tell me, Sayer, why do you want to read English?" he asked.

"I suppose it's mainly because I enjoy reading, especially poetry."

"Well, that's a good answer. What poetry do you like?"

"Oh, lots. Wordsworth, Shelley, Keats, and, of course, Shakespeare."

"Have you read any long poems, such as *The Prelude*?"

"No, I haven't read that," I said. (In fact, I did not know who had written it.) "But I've read some of *The Revolt of Islam* and the whole of *The Ballad of the White Horse*."

"Good. What can you quote from that?"

I quoted the one verse that had stuck in my memory:

> "*The great Gaels of Ireland*
> *Are the men that God made mad.*"

I got no further on my own, for with gusto and a glowing face he declaimed the next lines with me:

> "*For all their wars are merry,*
> *And all their songs are sad.*"[1]

"Marvelous stuff, isn't it? Don't you like the way Chesterton takes hold of you in that poem, shakes you, and makes you want to cry? I think I like best of all the last part. What's it called? 'Ethandune.' Here and there it achieves the heroic, the rarest quality in modern literature." His face glowed with delight as he declaimed:

> "'*The high tide!*' *King Alfred cries,*
> '*The high tide and the turn!*
> *As a tide turns on the tall grey seas,*
> *See how they waver in the trees,*
> *How stray their spears, how knock their knees,*
> *How wild their watchfires burn!*'"[2]

"Let's get down to business," he said after a pause. He dictated a list of books for me to read in the weeks ahead. It included the study of an Anglo-Saxon primer and the reading of most of Chaucer's *Canterbury Tales*.

As I walked away from New Buildings, I found the man that Lewis had called "Tollers" sitting on one of the stone steps in front of the arcade.

"How did you get on?" he asked.

"I think rather well. I think he will be a most interesting tutor to have."

"Interesting? Yes, he's certainly that. You'll never get to the bottom of him."

The following term, when I went to one of his lectures, I learned that the man with whom I had been talking was actually J. R. R. Tolkien. But who was he? We undergraduates came to know him only as a lecturer in Old English. Nothing could have seemed more improbable than that he should become world famous as the author of *The Lord of the Rings*, the heroic romance selling millions of copies all over the world.

Tolkien was right. Although I became a friend of Lewis, I never got to the bottom of him. My object in this book is to present the factual background to the motivation and character of a remarkable man who has had, and is having, a profound effect on the modern world.

1

Very Different Strains

"Two very different strains had gone to our making."

C. S. LEWIS,
SURPRISED BY JOY

Although he regarded Ulster as his homeland, Clive Staples Lewis denied being Irish. "I'm more Welsh than anything," he once said to me, "and for more than anything else in my ancestry I'm grateful that on my father's side I'm descended from a practical Welsh farmer. To that link with the soil I owe whatever measure of physical energy and stability I have. Without it I should have turned into a hopeless neurotic." During the disappointments and emotional difficulties of his twenties, this link with the land gave him self-confidence. It was a quality he badly needed, for it was then his conviction that, as he wrote to his friend Arthur Greeves, "we hold our mental health by a thread."[1]

But, in fact, the last Lewis ancestor to till the soil as his main occupation was his great-great-grandfather Richard, who was born about 1775. He was also the last to live in Wales or to be entirely Welsh. His farming was done at Caergwrle in Flintshire, not far from the English border. There was one unusual thing about him. In a country in which most small farmers were "chapel," he and his wife were "church." This gave to his children the advantage of being able to learn to read and write at the little church school in the village, and a faith to which the family for the next one hundred years remained unswervingly loyal.

Joseph, his fourth son and Clive Lewis's great-grandfather, moved across the English border to a small holding at Saltney, then a separate village, now a suburb of Chester on the river Dee, southwest of the city. He seems soon to have quarreled with the vicar of the parish because he felt he was not given sufficient prominence in the church services. He left, joined the Methodist church, and became its minister. He kept on the small holding to supplement the necessarily small amount of money he was given by his flock, but his heart was in the ministry and especially in preaching, which, in the highly emotional style then common, was powerful. It made such an impression that even now it is possible to find elderly men and women who have heard of him from grandparents. From him Clive inherited three qualities far more important than Welshness: religious enthusiasm, a fine resonant voice, and real rhetorical ability.

Joseph was the father of eight children. His fourth son, Richard, was Clive's grandfather. The ablest and most ambitious of the children, Richard worked hard to educate himself. He attended night school while a workman on Merseyside and acquired some elementary knowledge of ship's engineering. In 1853 he married a woman named Martha Gee, probably a Liverpudlian and English. Soon afterward he moved to Cork, where he worked as a boilermaker in a ship repair yard. All of Richard's six children—Martha, Sarah Jane, Joseph, William, Richard, and Albert—were born there within eleven years. Albert, Clive's father, was born in 1863. A year later, the family moved to Dublin when Richard took a better job as foreman, or "outside manager," for the shipbuilding firm of Walpole, Webb, and Bewly. Here he met and impressed John H. MacIlwaine, a rather older ship repairer who had saved a little money. In 1868 they moved to Belfast, the great bustling shipbuilding metropolis of the country, and went into partnership as "MacIlwaine and Lewis: Boiler Makers, Engineers, and Iron Ship Builders."

The business prospered, with a bad effect on Richard's character. He soon came to love wealth and became arrogant and snobbish. He moved from the rather humble Mount Pottinger area of Belfast to the higher-class Lower Sydenham, where, with the help of a mortgage, he bought a house called Ty-issa. His prosperity did not last long. From about 1884, there was disagreement between the partners. The causes are obscure. MacIlwaine is said to have been harsh and Lewis a little unscrupulous in a dispute about responsibility for a defective boiler. The result was that Richard left the firm in 1886 and soon afterward got a job with the Belfast harbor board at a salary of £150 a year, about £4,000 or £5,000 of current English money. During the last years of his life—he died at age 76 in 1908, a year that turned out to be calamitous for Clive—he was helped with money by his sons, especially by Albert. He was a difficult man to live with, his moods alternating violently between the heights of optimism and the extremes of depression, a characteristic inherited by three of his sons, including Albert. Although a snob, Richard's table manners were appalling. He insisted on being served first at meals, even if there were visitors, and ate rapidly and greedily.

Of his four sons, the eldest, Joseph, born in 1856, was the uncle that Clive and his brother, Warren, liked best. Described in *The Lewis Papers* as "lacking the spasmodic generosity of Albert, the irascibility and prodigality of Richard, and William's morose ostentation, he was the best balanced and most uniformly kindly of the four brothers."² Joseph, a marine engineer, had a strong sense of family and the ties of blood. He took an interest in Clive and Warren, but unfortunately died in the same year as his father and their mother, before he could know them well.

The second son, William (1858—1946), "was the least amiable of the three brothers—the most easily depressed and the most rarely elated. . . . His mind was heavy, commonplace, and self-centred. With him sententiousness took the place of sentiment." He married a woman of higher social class, "in whom few but himself could detect any attractions . . . enjoyed the pleasures of the table, and, though not intemperate, was fond of the bottle." We are told that "he succeeded in making his house so uncomfortable to his children that they successively revolted."³

In one respect he had an influence on Clive's father. His desire to enhance his social self-esteem caused him to be the first member of the family to send his sons to somewhere thought more gentlemanly than an Irish school. He sent them to public schools in England. The example was followed by his younger brothers, including Albert. It had the common result of producing boys who despised their own parents.

William had a business in Glasgow that sold rope and felt, and he was joined in it by Richard. Born in about 1861, Richard was of mercurial character, given to outbursts of sudden anger, but often happy, thanks to a simple sense of humor that included an appreciation of the fantastic and a liking for practical jokes, especially if they were at Albert's expense.

Albert James was born in 1861. He was "dogmatic, loquacious, and sensitive on the point of dignity," and therefore particularly vulnerable to teasing. He has recorded that it was Richard's teasing and temper ("We can't stand this fellow James any longer")⁴ that caused his father to send him to a boarding school instead of to the national school where the other children had gone, as a matter of course. He had the good luck to have in W. T. Kirkpatrick a headmaster with whom he got on exceptionally well. As soon as he left school, he was apprenticed to a solicitor, qualified with distinction, and, after a brief partnership, set up in practice on his own in Belfast. He was a success, thanks to an excellent memory, great industry, a quickness of mind that included a gift for telling repartee, and a fine resonant voice, all gifts that Clive inherited. He was an attorney of complete integrity, finding it hard to represent a cause or client he did not believe in. His managing clerk, and, following him, both sons, liked to tell the story of his way of dismissing clients of doubtful integrity. They told me he would almost shout, "In fact then you want me to use my legal knowledge to help you to commit a swindle. Get out of this office." The effect was that of a kick from a boot.

He often appeared for the prosecution in the Belfast police court, and, although he was fair, he had the reputation of being severe in cross-examination. A cartoon published in a local paper shows Albert as a man of commanding presence, formally dressed, good-looking, but with a disapproving and slightly sulky air.

He was a kind man all the same, generous to the poor and unfortunate, both in gifts and money and in legal work, which he would often undertake without payment. Clive had the same generosity and perhaps learned it from him. Both father and son practiced it in spite of a fear of being bankrupt. Both were inept in the investment of money and both, as we shall see, could be miserly.

Albert had ambitions outside the law. He was a member of Belfast literary societies and quite a practiced political speaker. His purely literary work, nearly all unpublished, consists of poems and short stories. The poems are a little like those of

Charles Lamb, mildly romantic or whimsically humorous. The short stories are much better and reveal his dramatic sense, humor, and gift for dialogue. It is quite possible that, if he had persevered, he would have become a successful novelist.

In the opinion of his sons, he might also have become a successful politician, but he was handicapped by a lack of private means and a "fine" sense of honor. His speeches show a real rhetorical gift. He spoke in admirably rhythmic sentences, was shrewd in his attack on his opponents, convincing in his show of moderation and, above all, had the gift of presenting a complex argument in convincingly simple terms. Both his sons inherited the gift of simple exposition. They owed far more to him than either realized and, in fact, shared most of his good and bad qualities.

The boys tended to despise their father's family, but were proud of their mother's. Flora Hamilton had on her father's side "many generations of clergymen, lawyers, sailors, and the like behind her."[5] On her mother's side she was a Warren, descended from a Norman knight who was buried at Battle Abbey in Sussex.

Flora's father, Thomas Hamilton, was vicar of Saint Mark's, Albert Lewis's local church in the Belfast suburb of Dundela. Clive usually referred to the family as southern Irish, but this needs qualification. The Hamiltons were not in race Irish at all, but descended from a titled Scottish family that was planted— that is, allowed to take over land—in County Down in the reign of James I. In the eighteenth century, Thomas's grandfather was a fellow of Trinity College, Dublin, and then an Irish bishop. Thomas himself, born in 1826, graduated at the top of his theology class at Trinity College, Dublin. In his subsequent career, he showed himself both exceptionally brave and exceptionally foolish with a stubborn devotion to principle characteristic also of his grandson. His health was poor, yet he volunteered to serve as a naval chaplain during the whole of the Crimean War and in addition volunteered for duty in camps where deaths from cholera took place every day. Because of his belief that swearing was a deadly sin, he was most unsuited to life in the navy. He went so far as to publicly reprimand officers who swore at their men, and it is not surprising that he did not last long. He was an extremely emotional man who preached with so much feeling at Saint Mark's that he often wept in the pulpit, to the amusement of some children and the intense embarrassment of others, including the children in his own family. One of the themes of his sermons is still current in Belfast today: that is, his extraordinarily violent attacks on Roman Catholics, whom he regarded as literally possessed by the devil. He does not seem at all to fit the description of the Hamiltons in Clive's autobiographical *Surprised by Joy*: They "were a cooler race. Their minds were critical and ironic, and they had the talent for happiness in a high degree."[6] Nor is this comment true of Clive's mother or of any other members of the family.

Thomas's wife, Mary Warren, was a far more intelligent woman, yet, especially by northern Irish standards, an incompetent and disorganized housewife. In the eyes of Clive and Warren, she was aristocratic. She came from an Anglo-Norman family that had been planted in Ireland in the reign of Henry II and had been landowners ever since. She introduced into Saint Mark's rectory the free and easy, disorganized way of living common among the Anglo-Irish gentry of southern Ireland. The house was untidy and dirty, but had some very good old furniture and plate, much of it in dilapidated condition. Animals were everywhere except in the master's study: "The house was typical of the woman: infested with cats (which were however rigorously excluded from the study); their presence was immediately apparent to the nose of the visitor when the slatternly servant opened the front door. . . . The hand which his hostess extended to him would gleam with valuable rings, but would bear too evident traces of her enthusiasm as a poultry keeper."[7]

There are many descriptions of such rooms in Anglo-Irish literature, for instance, in Somerville and Ross or in Flora Shaw's delightful novel, *Castle Blair*. All his life, Clive Lewis preferred them to rooms that he called "uncomfortably tidy"; indeed he did not mind if the wallpaper hung loose from the walls or if it had been stripped off so that the bare plaster showed. His own house, the Kilns, was for years in this state, but his study, the room in which he worked, was always clean and tidy.

Mary Warren Hamilton's main interest and subject of conversation was politics. She was a Liberal and a supporter of home rule for Ireland, a proposal that would give the whole of Ireland (not just the southern part) a parliament of its own, so that it would be self-governing without, however, ceasing to be part of the British Empire. This and her habit of employing southern Irish servants caused her to be unpopular with many Belfast people.

The Hamiltons were bad parents with no talent for making their children happy. They openly and obviously favored two of their children, Lilian and Cecil, and almost ignored Flora and the younger boy, Augustus. The members of these pairs had nothing in common with each other except the determination to oppose the other pair. Lilian and Cecil were "at perpetual and sarcastic discord." Cecil was insolent. Indeed, he would have to have been to hold his own against Lilian, a clever, eccentric, handsome girl of "extremely quarrelsome disposition" who enjoyed being at war with as many members of the family as possible. (She once said of Albert, in his presence, and in regard to a legal matter, "for poor Allie is so ignorant.") After the death of her husband, who spent most of his short life in a mental hospital, a cook sorely tried by her vegetarianism and other dietetic theories retorted after a sharp verbal exchange, "Sure, didn't your husband, poor man, get himself put into a lunatic asylum to get away from you?"[8] Perhaps when he came to write *The Voyage of the Dawn Treader*,* Clive took her as his model for Alberta Scrubb, Eustace's unpleasant feminist and vegetarian mother.

After her husband's death, Lilian devoted herself to feminism, the suffragette movement, eccentric theories about food, and her collection of cats. She also wrote long pseudophilosophical letters to Clive and, worse still, sometimes visited him at Oxford.

Augustus, or "Gussie," as he was always called, was as a boy academically backward and almost illiterate. Because his father, who disliked him, refused to spend money on his education, it was not discovered until he was middle-aged that he had great mathematical ability. He left school early and, after an apprenticeship with MacIlwaine, Lewis and Company, went to sea as an engineer. After some years of this (Albert was horrified at the way in which he would set off for, say, Calcutta, without saying goodbye to his equally unconcerned mother), he left the sea, settled in Belfast, and founded the marine engineering firm of Hamilton and McMaster. He is described in *The Lewis Papers* as "thoroughly selfish and mean,"[9] yet with a sense of humor and an original mind that made him an interesting person to know. He sponged on Albert Lewis, yet somehow managed also to be one of his closest friends.

The youngest child, Flora, was a slim girl with fair hair and pale blue eyes. She had nearly as much mathematical ability as Gussie, enjoyed reading, was good at English, and therefore managed to secure a college education. She read mathematics and logic at Queen's University, Belfast, at a time when its reputation

---

*For a list of works by C. S. Lewis, see the bibliography at the end of this book.

for these subjects was extremely high. In her first public exam in 1880 she got a first in geometry and algebra, and in her finals in 1881, a first in logic and a second-class honors degree in mathematics.

She did not really make any use of her academic ability, perhaps because a teaching job would have required her wildly inefficient mother to employ an extra maid. Nor did having a degree make her happier; it meant that she was dubbed a bluestocking and teased a good deal. One would think that she would have leaped at any opportunity, including marriage, to leave so unhappy a home. It says much for her high principles and for the coolness of her disposition that for years she refused to marry a man she did not love deeply.

She was courted first by Albert's eldest brother, William, but soon told him that she could never love him. He was a dull man whose conversation she must have found even more boring than her father's harangues against the Roman Catholic church and her mother's endless talk of the necessity of home rule. She regarded Albert's later courtship differently. While she did not love him enough to marry him, she wanted to keep him on the hook.

He therefore charged her with being cold and heartless, an accusation she strongly denied. She wrote in a letter that she knew she was not demonstrative, but when she thought of the many nights she had cried herself to sleep and the way every day since their parting "had been saddened by the memory of what is past," she felt that she did not "deserve to be thought of as heartless." This is the most emotional sentence to be found in what we have of her correspondence. It was surely prompted by her fear of losing his friendship. She knew that she often said "sharp, unkind things." She hoped that this fault, which had left her with very few friends, would not come between them, and that in a few years "when you have forgotten your love for me, a friendship such as I feel for you will always remain."[10] And so it went on for a few years, with Flora concerned with maintaining a rather cool friendship and Albert going as far as he dared without provoking rejection.

She was not Albert's first love. From the time he was sixteen until he was twenty-two, he carried on a most affectionate correspondence with a girl called Edie Macown. His letters, carefully written, usually with the aid of a preliminary draft, are suspiciously flowery. Thus on one occasion he assures her that until he returns "that little lock of golden hair and that little bunch of forget-me-nots," he will be "the truest and most loving friend" she has on earth. He thanks her a thousand times for her last letter which he would cherish until it dropped "to pieces with continual reading."[11] About this passage Warren Lewis wryly commented that "the letter in question is as fresh and unfrayed as the day the paper was first folded."[12]

All Albert's letters tended to have a literary quality. He seemed to regard them more as compositions that might one day be published than as spontaneous expressions of his thoughts and feelings. His relationship with Edie lasted nearly five years. At the end of it, each accused the other of flirting with someone else.

It is not surprising that the correspondence on Albert's side contains much sentiment that does not ring true. What is surprising is that he kept Edie's letters and his own draft replies for the rest of his life, entirely unaware of their frequent falsity and absurdity. "He saw life in terms of a stage play—sometimes a melodrama—in which it behooved him to give of his best in whatever role chance or his own inclinations had temporarily cast him. . . ."[13] His feelings about the role he should play in relation to particular people crystallized early and then hardly ever altered.

Albert's role in his relationship with Flora was that of the devout lover who would wait forever. Her offers of only friendship rebuffed him not at all. He managed to keep in close contact with the family by making himself useful to Flora's parents and later to Flora herself.

Flora's mother eagerly took up Albert as a listener apparently interested in her political views. It was an exciting period. Not only was there fierce opposition to Irish home rule from the House of Lords (home rule was abhorred by the English upper classes), but there was also a split in the Liberal party that resulted in the balance of power being held by the Irish members of Parliament. The sensational adultery of their leader, Charles Stewart Parnell, added to the ferment. Since the members of her own family were uninterested in her endless political conversation, Flora's mother frequently invited Albert to the house so that she could air her views.

Flora's father also found a way to make use of Albert's love for his daughter. He had Albert arrange and pay for a series of short holidays that he felt he needed, probably as a change from the unhappy and untidy life at the vicarage. As for Flora, she used her admirer to praise and criticize the articles and short stories she wrote for two or three years from 1889. In spite of Albert's help, not one was published.

Her feelings for him did not change, but after seven years she came to believe that it was unfair to make use of his friendship without agreeing to be his wife. Perhaps, too, the fact that she was now in her thirties may have had some influence. Albert, who was—or thought he was—rather short of money at the time, suggested that it might be as well to postpone their marriage for a year or so. She agreed with an enthusiasm that suggests no strong desire to marry him at all and in addition prudently asked for the engagement to be kept secret for a few months. There was nothing to prevent them changing their minds if they saw any reason for doing so.[14]

She is touchingly honest about herself and her own lack of feeling. She wishes she had more to give in return for his devotion. He won't be getting much from marrying someone who has neither beauty nor money "nor anything else." But she is sure that she is very fond of him and hates the prospect of ceasing to see him, which she would have to do if she refused to marry him. It would be unfair to let the relationship drift on for any longer. She fears that love has blinded him to her faults. It will be "rather a pity" if he discovers that she is no better than other people.[15]

Nearly all her letters show anxieties of some sort. She wants to live simply and thinks luxuries little more than social display. She fears she may be inadequate as a housewife, for she knows nothing about cooking and little about household management—certainly she could not have learned this art from her mother. She is a little worried about her health—she is already suffering from the headaches that were to pain her for the rest of her short life. She is self-conscious at being two years older than Albert and looking it. She addresses him as "my old bear" or "my poor boy."

On August 29, 1894, Albert and Flora were married. He gave her as a present a piece of diamond jewelry that cost him between £70 and £80, the equivalent of $4,000 modern currency, a large sum in those days for anyone in his position but an expense indicative of his character, for all his life he vacillated between great generosity and almost equally great meanness. The ceremony was performed by the bride's father at his church, Saint Mark's, Dundela.

Their honeymoon tempted Albert to do something most uncharacteristic. He very nearly neglected an important client, the duke of Abercorn. The matter is worth recording for the light it throws on the political state of Northern Ireland.

The duke of Abercorn had represented Donegal in Parliament from 1860 to 1880 and was now involved in political sessions aimed at revising the list of those qualified to vote in elections. In fact, it was a fight between paid partisan lawyers, who would do their best to get as many as possible of the voters who "were not of the right way of thinking" struck off the list. Albert was a supporter of the Unionist party, led by Lord Salisbury, and an opponent of the Gladstonian party, now led by Lord Roseberry, which was in favor of home rule for Ireland and (how modern!) the abolition of the House of Lords. The duke of Abercorn, desperate for Albert's support, sent three insistent telegrams reminding him that he had promised to appear at the revision sessions. Albert seems in the end to have given way to this pressure and cut short his honeymoon. He used to tell a story about one of the revision courts in which the presiding officer, after listening to arguments by the solicitors about whether or not a particular voter was qualified, cut the proceedings short by remarking, "Ah, well, he's a nasty fellow anyway; we'll strike him out."[16] Such gerrymandering seems to have been taken for granted in the north of Ireland, and there is no reason to suppose that Albert or his sons ever felt indignant about it.

2

Good Parents, Good Food, and a Garden

Flora started housekeeping in Dundela Villas with the two servants common in middle-class families of those days, a cook and a housemaid. That both were Roman Catholics from southern Ireland irritated certain neighbors and local Protestants. Disparaging messages were occasionally chalked on the walls of the house or scrawled on notes pushed through the mail slot; Warren told me one read, "Send the dirty papists back to the Devil where they belong." The cook was paid £15 a year, the housemaid £12, generous wages for those days.

With two servants and a small house, it might appear that Flora had little to do. Her tasks, however, were many. To quote from the copy of Mrs. Beeton's *Household Management* that she received as a wedding present, her role resembled that "of the general of an army or the manager of a great business concern." It was her responsibility to "see that all runs smoothly, that meals are to time, and well cooked, the house kept clean and tidy, and the general well-being of each member of the family considered."[1] It was her task to engage the servants, to organize their work, and to pay them. She would plan the meals, keeping detailed accounts of every item of food and drink prepared. Once or twice a week, she would walk to the shops and order food from the butcher and the greengrocer, telling them what to send and on which days—middle-class women in those days did not carry shopping baskets. Each month she would settle the accounts with the shops.

In raising her sons, Flora undoubtedly followed the customs of the period. Both boys would have been born at home; breast-fed every four hours during the day, but not at night, even if they cried; and carefully protected from exposure to drafts and bright light indoors and out. By the time Clive was one month old, Flora had engaged three more servants—a gardener, a governess, and a nursemaid, the latter named Lizzie Endicott from County Down, "in whom even the exacting memory of childhood can discover no flaw—nothing but kindness, gaiety, and good sense."[2] Though her household had grown—she now had five servants to supervise—Flora probably had more spare time after Clive's birth than before. She spent it engaged in the only leisure activity that she and Albert shared—voracious reading. After dinner the couple would settle down in armchairs and read for a few hours. This is a custom that Clive would later follow. It is no exaggeration to say that the general structure of his Oxford life was formed during his years in Belfast.

An entirely artificial city, Belfast was formed early in the seventeenth century by the deliberately planned colonies of English and Scottish settlers after the defeat of Hugh O'Neill and the Ulster chieftains who fought under him. There were important differences of race, language, and religion between the two groups of settlers. The English worshiped in the manner of the denomination that would later be called Church of England; the Scottish were usually Presbyterians. Both groups were aware of living in a foreign country among people of different race and religion. They thought of the Irish rather as they thought of the

Indians native to America and considered ruling them an attractive challenge. Sir Arthur Chichester, to whom Belfast was first granted, declared that he would "rather labour with my hands in the plantation of Ulster than dance or play in that of Virginia." The words *dance* and *play* suggest that he thought "that rude and irreligious corner of the North," by which he meant Northern Ireland, the tougher proposition of the two.

King James I gave Belfast a charter in 1613, but his motive was purely political. To be sure of a Protestant majority in the parliament that he intended to call in Ireland, he decided to create forty new boroughs, each with the right of returning two members to that parliament. There were many protests against some of the "poorest villages in the poorest country in Christendom" being given charters, but the move was of great economic benefit to Belfast, making it a free port, exempt from paying customs and tolls. It prospered to such an extent that by the end of the century it had become the fourth port in the kingdom. Trade was mainly agricultural, but exports of textiles, especially linen, had already begun. Many more Scottish settlers arrived during the later years of the century, so that, by the end of it, Presbyterians outnumbered Episcopalians, and feeling between the two groups became rather sharp. There were few Roman Catholics; a return made in 1708 stated that there were not above seven papists in the town and not above 150 in the whole barony. At this time, an enormous impetus was given to the linen industry by French Huguenot refugees settling in Ulster. Irish exports of linen rose from less than two hundred thousand yards in 1701 to seventeen million in 1773. Two-thirds of these exports went through Belfast, often in the ships of Belfast merchants.

In the nineteenth century, the growth of the city accelerated. Because of a shortage of hand-weavers, power looms were introduced in the linen industry. The harbor was extended, the port improved by the digging of new channels. In the 1850s, the great firm of Harland and Wolff was founded, which created a need for labor. Irishmen, often from the southern part of the country, were imported for heavy manual work. As a result, the Roman Catholic population increased rapidly, and a bitter hostility between Catholics and Presbyterians came into being. The population doubled between 1835 and 1850, and then increased fourfold to 350,000 by the end of the century.

Until the end of the First World War, Belfast enjoyed stable prosperity. The city was given its character by the enterprise and energy of its citizens, who were clannish, conservative, rather intolerant, abrasive in speech, and proud of their city and its surroundings. At times Belfast people were too enterprising, an example of this being the Garden City scheme in which Albert Lewis invested and lost money. Houses were to be sold at cost, from £240 each for the cheapest, in a complex that would have included gardens, a cricket field, playgrounds, a teahouse, and a bandstand. Ten thousand shrubs were to be planted, and the tree-lined streets were to have garden names such as Hollyhock, Daffodil, and Aster. Sadly, but not surprisingly, it was uneconomical, and the plan failed.

Belfast was a city of strongly held political views. Because all the raw materials for the great shipyards were imported, usually from England, a close relationship with England was economically essential. It is not surprising, therefore, that the wealthier Belfast men were Unionists opposed to home rule. Belfast was also a city of churches and churchgoers. Nearly everyone went to church on Sunday, but never to each other's churches. For protection and mutual support in the frequent riots, working-class Catholics and Protestants tended to live near their own churches. To this day, there are entirely Catholic and entirely Protestant parts of the city, and the hostility between the two groups is still intensely bitter.

For a boy with an interest in the sea and ships, a house with a view of Belfast Lough was the most fascinating place in the British Isles. There were ships of all sorts, liners and warships alike, and surrounding them a forest of cranes and gantries. The view, Clive records, was "a delight to both us boys, but most of all to my brother."[3]

The surroundings were beautiful. The city was ringed by green hills, and to the northwest there were "interminable summer sunsets behind the blue ridges."[4] Such surroundings formed Clive's passion for fine scenery.

In spite of these many advantages, Belfast was not a healthy city. There was serious overcrowding in the center, an inadequate sewer system, and a shortage of good water. Outbreaks of such diseases as cholera, typhus, and typhoid had reduced the average life expectancy in 1851 to only nine years. In 1897, the year before Clive was born, an outbreak of typhoid fever affected 27,000 people. The prevalence of typhoid was enough to make any Belfast parent cautious and apprehensive, but to understand the nervousness of Clive's parents, the modern reader must also remember that many diseases that have mysteriously become mild or rare today were then common and real killers. The medicine then available could treat only the symptoms of such diseases as diphtheria, scarlet fever, and tuberculosis, and the infant mortality rate was alarmingly high.

Fear of these diseases caused middle-class Belfast parents to move from the center of the city into the higher, and far healthier, suburbs. Far more attention than now was paid to the coughs and colds from which children inevitably suffer.

There is no evidence that Clive had more coughs and colds than other children, but Flora and Albert, both anxious parents, very quickly jumped to the conclusion that he had "a weak chest." The fear had important consequences. He was kept indoors when it was cold and damp outside. As Warren put it:

> To be caught out in a shower without an overcoat was a minor disaster which entailed changing all your clothes the minute you got back to the house; on threatening days you were allowed to use the garden, but only on the strict understanding that you came indoors at the first spot of rain; and on wet days it was forbidden to leave the house on any pretext whatever. The prospect of being thus penned in until bedtime became almost unendurable; literally penned in, for on wet days the nursery door was left open and a sort of half gate was inserted in the door jambs and bolted on the outside, at a height to which we could not reach.[5]

These long wet days, however, were to pay a handsome dividend in the years to come. The indoor pursuits that Clive was forced to follow hastened his intellectual development. It could even be argued that the precautions taken against exposure to the elements and to the unsanitary conditions of Belfast provided the impetus for his literary career. They also had much to do with his passion for the sea.

Because fevers such as typhoid are more common in warm weather, it was usual for middle-class mothers to take their children away to the seaside for up to three months of the year. Flora, accompanied by a nursemaid and one or two other servants, took the boys to a furnished house at Castlerock, a small north coast bathing resort in County Derry. She wrote long letters to Albert, expressing anxiety at being away from him while he was in London (she lay awake at night "hearing noises and imagining things"), sharing worries about her own ill health (she suffered from headaches and asthma), and telling him of the children's health and growth (atop a piano stool, Clive played and sang "in the most approved style," revealing his precociousness and an early talent for mimicry).[6]

For the boys, the seaside holiday was the great delight of the year from the moment the packing began. The first thrill was the ride to the station in a real horse-drawn cab. This was a most special event because in those frugal days no one except the very extravagant ever took a cab in Belfast if it were possible to walk or go by tram. To sit behind the horse was a luxurious novelty as well as a delight in itself. It was followed by "the glorious excitement of the train journey and, supreme bliss, the first sight of the sea."[7]

Trains and the sea would remain great pleasures for the brothers. The first toy that Clive asked for was a little wooden railway engine, price one penny. To the end of his life he enjoyed traveling by train, the slower the better, and, if possible, in the front carriage.

However, he took the greatest delight in the sea. At the age of two he enjoyed watching the waves and wanted to go into the water. But Flora, worried by his cough, did not allow it. The minor diseases of childhood—coughs, colds, cut knees, and skin rashes—were far more of a concern to her than to them. That summer and every summer for years after, they were completely happy playing in the sand, looking for crabs and small fish in the rock pools, paddling, and watching the waves and boats. Clive was quite fearless, dashing into the water when allowed to paddle, and filled with delight when after a month he was allowed to bathe. It was some years before he was able to swim, but this mattered little. It was the immersion in the water, bathing rather than swimming, that was his lifelong pleasure. As a man he delighted in physical contact with water and would plunge boisterously into whatever body of water happened to be near.

His love for Castlerock and the little rocky bays of the north Irish coast was lifelong, too. Probably the seeds of his romantic love of "northernness," one of the most important of his feelings, were sown during these seaside holidays.

While on holiday Flora wrote frequently to Albert. It is of social interest that she thought her sister Lily would go bankrupt for paying a servant as much as £24 a year and that she objected to having to share a pew in church on Sundays. Their pew was full of "those horrid boys." She was sorry she had not stayed at home. They really must do something about getting a pew to themselves.[8] She chastised Albert for his fits of depression. They were not good for him. He excited himself far too much and then let himself get miserable too easily. She was worried about her own health as well as that of the children, and even about money, although their expenses were extremely modest by modern standards. While on holiday she could just make do on Albert's quarterly allowance. In two months she used £20, of which £5 went on the wages of Martha and two other servants. There was actually a little left over.[9] This shows that Flora was a frugal housekeeper, but suggests that she did not get a fair share of Albert's income, which, judging from a financial statement that he drew up, entitling it rather grandly as his "map of life," must have been about £800 a year, the equivalent today of at least $80,000.

As a baby Clive was a dainty feeder, but by the age of four, he seems to have acquired the hearty appetite he maintained most of his life. "Babs takes a fine dinner now, vegetables, soup and everything, and comes up from it with a satisfied air of repletion that is very funny."[10]

At about this time he suddenly announced that his name was "Jacksie" and refused to answer to any other. Shortened to Jack, this was the name by which he was always known to his close friends.

It is surprising that Flora does not seem to have read to her children, taught them nursery rhymes, or told them bedtime stories. Her closest contact with Jack (as I shall now call him) was when she took him into her bed at night if he was unwell, frightened by thunder, having a nightmare, or could not get to sleep. The reading and storytelling was done by Lizzie Endicott. When he was two and a half, we are told that she read "The Three Bears" to him. She read many more fairy tales and also told him the stories she had heard in her own childhood in County Down—stories of leprechauns and crocks of gold hidden at the foot of the rainbow; of Becuma of the White Skin; or of Fionn, Morgan, and Cuchulain.

The Irish country notion that a crock of gold is buried at the foot of each rainbow once got the boys, especially Jack, into serious trouble with their father. The story illustrates a permanent trait of his character—the tendency not just to think an idea, but to act it out. While out on a walk away from the house, they imagined that the rainbow ended in the front garden, in the middle of the path from the gate to the front door. Jack persuaded Warren that they must dig there.

It was late afternoon, but by the time it was dark they had made quite a big hole. Their father, on his way home from the office and wearing his best office clothes, fell into it. After he had collected his hat and gathered up the scattered legal papers, he accused the two boys of making a booby trap for his discomfiture or even injury while he was out earning a living for them. Not for one moment could he accept Jack's explanation that they really were searching for a crock of gold. He was convinced that they were only making the crime worse by lying, and lying very badly at that.

It is hardly fair of Jack to quote this as an example of his father's unreasonableness. One can't blame a man for getting angry if, after a tiring day at the office, he falls into a hole dug by his sons in his garden path. It seems odd that no one in the house noticed what they were doing. Miss Harper, the governess, had given them lessons only in the morning. Flora might have been deep in a novel by Meredith; the cook and the housemaid would not have thought it part of their job. As for Lizzie—it must have been her afternoon off.

There is no doubt that the brothers were left on their own on most afternoons. As they did not go to school, they met few other children. Fortunately, they got on very well together. Jack tells us that Warren was not only his brother, but his best friend. By the standards of present-day England and America, they spent "an extraordinary amount of time indoors."[11] This is according to Warren, who gives too much credit for the confinement to the Belfast weather (after all, Belfast is on the average not as wet as Bristol and has only two inches more rain a year than Torquay) and too little to Flora's anxieties, but describes brilliantly the results:

> We would gaze out of our nursery window at the slanting rain and the grey skies, and there, beyond a mile or so of sodden meadow, we would see the dim high line of the Castlereagh Hills—our world's limit, a distant land, strange and unattainable. But we always had pencils, paper, chalk and paint boxes, and this recurring imprisonment gave us occasion and stimulus to develop the habit of creative imagination. We learnt to draw: my brother made his first attempts at writing; together we devised the imaginary country of "Boxen" which proliferated hugely and became our solace and joy for many years to come. And so, in circumstances that might have been merely dull and depressing, my brother's gifts began to develop; and it may not be fanciful to see, in that childhood staring out to unattainable hills, some first beginnings of a vision and viewpoint that run through the work of his maturity.[12]

The ships in Belfast Lough became for Warren a lifelong passion, and Jack, too, loved to visit the docks. Sometimes their father would carry one of them there on his back. All three drew many pictures of ships. Jack, who in his early years fancied himself quite as much an artist as an author, drew a large diagram showing one in minute detail from topmast to keel.

This picture of Albert sharing the activities of his sons and drawing pictures with them will come as a surprise to those who have read only the account of him that Jack presents in *Surprised by Joy*. Albert always took an interest in what Jack wrote and tried to help him. Indeed, if any one person besides Warren encouraged Jack to write stories, it was Albert.

But in other ways he was remote. He never went away with the boys on their summer holiday. He was happily wedded to his office routine and hated change of any kind. He was miserable if he had to spend a single night away from his own house. On a holiday or away from home, he had not the slightest idea what to do or how to amuse himself. "I can still see him," wrote Warren in 1965, "on his occasional flying visits to the seaside, walking moodily up and down the beach, and every now and then giving a heartrending yawn and pulling out his watch."[13] The really remarkable thing was that Flora, who did not think Dundela Villas good enough for a family in their social position, got him to move to another house in 1905. It must have taken years of tactful diplomacy.

Sometime then the boys began to call Albert the "pudaita" or the "pudaitabird" or just "P," nicknames that arose from their father's Irish way of pronouncing "potato." Many of their father's friends, who tended to be staid, correct, conventional, and obsessed by a sense of duty, spoke with the same Irish accent that the boys had been taught to despise; they were also dubbed "pudaitas." The boys, on the other hand, who went their own

way and lived for pleasure, called themselves "pigiebothams."
Warren was the "Archpigiebotham" or "APB," Jack the
"Smallpigiebotham" or "SPB." The names arose from Lizzie
Endicott drying, and later on threatening to smack, their little
"piggiebottoms" when they were young. Jack used these nicknames to the end of his life, and after Jack's death Warren sometimes referred to him as his "beloved SPB."

Their new house was called Little Lea. It was built on a plot
of land that Albert bought about two miles away from Dundela
Villas on the outskirts of the city off Holywood Road, near what
is now the Craigavon Hospital, and not far from open farmland.
It was a large house, three stories high, built of brick, with
dressed-stone bay windows and porch. Part of the upper part was
faced with stucco, and there were impressive chimney stacks,
vaguely Tudor in style. The large bay windows (which made
some of the ground-floor rooms exceptionally bright and sunny)
were at the front of the house, the side nearest to the street. The
front door and entrance porch were at the back, so that visitors
had to walk around the house to get to them. There was plenty
of room for parents, children, the cook Martha, the maid Lizzie,
and the governess Miss Harper. Later on Albert's father came to
live in a room on the first floor. As at Dundela Villas, there were
animals: a Yorkshire terrier called Tim, perhaps a cat, certainly
a black-and-white mouse called Tommy, and a canary called
Peter. The family had always had animals, and Jack (and, to a
lesser extent, Warren) acquired a lifelong love of them.

Warren describes the house as atrociously uneconomical in
design, but, for romantic boys, this was an advantage. There was,
for instance, an attic running underneath much of the roof, and,
higher still, just under the ridge tiles on the roof, there were
tunnel-like passages through which they could crawl. There was
room for great quantities of books, many in handsome leather

bindings: works of the great poets, essayists, and novelists; works of history, philosophy, art, and music. There was also a His Master's Voice gramophone with a large horn, and the boys soon became keen collectors of records.

The brothers were their own best friends, but they had interesting neighbors, too, including their cousin Joseph Taggart Lewis, who eventually became one of the leading blood specialists in the north of Ireland. Few girls their age lived near them, and in later years Warren suggested that this was possibly the main reason why they had remained single, Warren for life and Jack until near the end of his life. (However, as we shall see, there are more probable explanations.)

Among their neighbors were the Ewarts, cousins of Flora and wealthy Belfast linen manufacturers. The boys loved to go to their big house, Glenmachen, and the well-wooded glen in which it was situated. They were always made welcome. When the boys were young, the Ewart girls—Hope, Gundreda, and Kels—who were older, would come and take them out in a donkey trap pulled by a recalcitrant animal named Grisella. Jack, even then sensitive to feminine beauty, said that Gundreda was the most beautiful woman he had ever seen, with "a radiant and infectious, almost childlike gaiety which was always bubbling over into delighted and delightful laughter."[14] She could mimic very well the broad County Down accent, an accomplishment Jack admired and set out to imitate, with considerable success.

Both boys had bicycles and, in good weather, were allowed off on their own. Endless bliss seemed ahead of them, but, alas, this joint exploration of the countryside could only take place during school holidays for, within a month of their move to Little Lea, Warren, then aged ten, was sent off to endure four years of utter misery at Wynyard School, Watford, Hertfordshire, as bad a school as could have existed in England during any period.

They had time, however, in those few weeks to discover "the secret dark hole upstairs" and to claim it for their own. It was a large attic below the ridge tiles, with little, very low rooms separated from each other by small cupboardlike doors. Here they had "glorious privacy, never invaded by officious tidying maids."[15] An unfinished story written later by Jack suggests what the "hole" looked like after a year or two. It was a narrow room where trunks and suitcases were stored, where spiders hibernated or spread their webs and dead flies littered the windowsills. Another little room contained a wobbly three-legged table, and still another room, a pile of torn canvas and stacks of old newspapers. But the real treasure of the place, according to Jack's story, was a knee-high "miniature mountain" of poems, plays, stories, and songs that the hero of Jack's story had written, and, with them, dusty pictures that he had drawn long before, "only because he did not know how to write."

"This pile of rubbish," the story goes on, "was my treasure, my religion, for it was my past, and the past was all I had yet made my own." But there was another treasure, a dark corner where, if one knelt down, particularly on a lonely day, he would hear, not only the gurgling, hissing, and splashing of the cisterns, but also the wind going through the "inwards" of the house, between walls and through ceiling and rafters; and he would feel an emptiness occupied by the terrible Lar, Roman god of houses. Kneeling there, one could easily believe that the soul of the house was in the imprisoned wind.

Warren warns us not to take the story as strict autobiography, but it is difficult not to think it so when, in the same narrative, we read of the two lives that Jack describes elsewhere—one of strange and delectable longings, and the other of hatred of schoolmasters and the daily round; also of a bossy father who insists that his son should leave the cold and dirty attic and sit

with him downstairs in a long and desperate session at the dining table and on through the evening. Further, the hero of the
story has a weak chest, and Jack's father had written in a letter
of November 15, 1910, that Jack had a weak chest, "weaker than
any other that I have known."

The attic became at once the center of life for the boys. Here
they were not just brothers, but friends exploring a common and
lively world, a world largely enunciated by Jack while Warren
looked on with admiration as his little brother wrote story after
story and drew picture after picture. Sometimes the pictures came
first and the stories later. Sometimes there were pictures without
stories. Imagination even crudely at work is interesting, but the
imagination of a boy as lively and poetic as Jack, a boy who
launched upon whole histories of peoples, was something of a
spectacle. Warren constructed maps of his own play world, India,
and acted as a critic of his brother's teeming outflow. The pastime
of drawing ships continued at the new house, big and little ships,
ships in black and white, ships in color.

Jack had begun to make up stories before he could write,
with his father acting as amanuensis. (Note that it was the father
whom he disparaged who encouraged him in literature and art,
not the mother whom he loved and admired. But it is hard for
any man to be fair to his own father.) As soon as he could write,
he turned out accounts in his big round childish hand of such
characters as Sir Peter Mouse, "knight"-in-waiting to King
Bunny of Animal-land who reigned in the fourteenth century; of
Tom and Bob Mouse, sons of Ic-this-oress; and particularly of Sir
Ben, a frog who was to become, in due time, a great hero.[16]

Warren's letters home from Wynyard do nothing to explain
to his parents and younger brother what a cruel and inefficient
school it was. Perhaps he knew that letters home were censored,
a common practice in prep schools in the twenties and thirties,

and one that sometimes still continues. The letters to his parents are normal and boyish. He wants a play-box to be sent, filled with "biscuits and drinks etc.," especially Swiss milk chocolate. He loses things and asks for replacements. They have played a cricket match and been beaten, an embarrassing event, since it was against girls. "I am cept in pretty often, but most of the others are cept in too," he writes.[17] And always he is concerned about the number of days to the beginning of the holidays.

His letters to Jack are as much concerned with the latter's writing as anything else. In one of his replies, Jack gives Warren what must have been a very satisfying report of his recent writing about Boxen. He wrote that Boxen was "SLIGHTLY CONVULSED." King Bunny was a prisoner. The colonists, who were the war party, were in such a bad way that they hardly dared "leave their houses because of the mobs." The Prussians and the Boxonians were "at fearful odds against each other." However General Quicksteppe was "making plans for the rescue of King Bunny." Jack was about eight when he wrote this letter. As it shows clearly, the subject matter of Boxen was military and political, aspects of life in which the adult Lewis showed no interest whatever.

After finishing a play, Jack started a history of Mouse-land, whose Stone Age ran from 55 B.C. to A.D. 1212, when Bublich I started to reign. His son, Bublich II, discovered "indai," was much concerned with the Lantern Act, and died in 1377. Clearly Jack was now learning history from Miss Harper!

A diary written by Jack during the Christmas holidays of 1907 contains some pleasant banter about the maids and what may be an accurate picture of his parents. "Papy of course is the master of the house, and a man in whom you can see strong Lewis features, bad temper, very sensible, nice wen not in a temper." Mamy is "like most middle-aged ladys, stout, brown hair, spectaciles, knitting her cheif industry." Then himself: "I am like most boys of nine and I am like Papy, bad temper, thick lips, thin, and generaly wearing ajersy." Grandfather has his own little room upstairs, but, although he is "a nice old man in some ways," he pities himself too much, "however all old people do that." The worst thing about him was that he was dirty— "allways spitting and smoking ugh!"[19]

Warren's banishment to an English prep school brought Jack closer to his mother. She gave him lessons every morning in French, Latin, and math, and occasionally went for walks with him in the afternoon. More often she rested and left him free to do whatever he wanted. He was very soon reading as voraciously as she, and more widely.

The house contained many books because both his parents bought and kept the books that they wanted to read. Jack was always given unrestricted access to their books; he was well-read by the age of eight. He read all the books about animals, including such stories as *Black Beauty*. He read *Strand Magazine* from cover to cover, especially enjoying the magic stories of E. Nesbit: "The Phoenix and the Carpet," "The Story of the Amulet," and, a little later on, "The Magic City." These formed his idea of what children's stories should be like.

A complete list of books that he had read by the age of nine would be very long. Some were advanced even by the standards of Macaulay's schoolboy; some reveal lifelong tastes acquired at an early age. Take, for instance, his diary entry of March 5, 1908: "I read *Paradise Lost*, reflections thereon."[20] In the last year of his life, he was still reading *Paradise Lost* and reflecting thereon.

By the age of ten, he had acquired the habit of writing. He spent some time every day and most of his time on rainy days in the attic writing and illustrating books. He produced a bibliography, a "list of my books," seven items, including a novel, "Man

Against Man," a history called "The Relief of Murry," and "My Life" (a journal).[21]

But the most important experiences of his childhood, indeed, of his whole life, were not literary. They were mystical experiences of the presence of God, rather like those described by Wordsworth, Traherne, and Ruskin. They arose from seemingly incongruous events, incongruous, that is, until one remembers that the Spirit "blows where it listeth." He chose the word *joy* to describe these experiences. It is the best possible word, the shortest and fullest. Joy is the ever-present, central quality in all forms of religious experience. The first time it came to him from the memory of a small garden that his brother had made for him out of a biscuit tin filled with moss, stones, twigs, and tiny flowers. It came again while he was reading a book by Beatrix Potter, his favorite, *Squirrel Nutkin.* He valued these experiences of joy more than anything else he had known, and he desired, as all who have experienced them desire, to have them again and again. It was this mystical quality that set him apart from other boys. He was surprised by joy. He spent the rest of his life searching for more of it.

With the idea of improving their French, Flora took the boys in the summer of 1907 for a holiday to a seaside village called Beneval, near Dieppe. They stopped in London, where Jack enjoyed a visit to the zoo. Flora and Warren both record that they found it hard to get him away from a cage of white mice.

They liked the French pension, but were rather disappointed to find that almost all the people there were English. Even on holiday Jack wrote. Warren reports that he started a new book, *Living Races of Mouse-Land,* which would be very good when it was finished.[22]

Flora still worried, mostly about money. "I do hope we shall not have so heavy a year for a long time," she wrote.[23] On the way home, they spent two nights in London. When asked what he most wanted to see, Jack said, "The Tower." Forty years later, he still remembered how much he enjoyed the visit.

The first recorded example of Jack's gift for repartee dates back to his return from the French holiday. "Entering the study where his father was poring over his account books, Jack flung himself into a chair and observed, 'I have a prejudice against the French.' His father, interrupted in a long addition run, said irritably, 'Why?' Jack, crossing his legs and putting his finger tips together, replied, 'If I knew why, it would not be a prejudice.'"[24]

Flora's tiredness, headaches, and lack of appetite became worse during the autumn and winter. Early in 1908, there were consultations with specialists. Abdominal cancer was diagnosed and an operation advised. It took place on February 15, in the house, as was usual in middle-class families of those days, with the aid of three doctors and two nurses. There was a temporary recovery, so that she was able to go away to the seaside with Jack in May, but she had to go back to bed in June. Albert recorded her death and last words in one of his notebooks. In the middle of the night of August 21 he spoke to her of the goodness of God. Like a flash she said, "What have we done for Him?" Words that he prayed he would never forget.

She died on his birthday, at 6:30 in the morning of August 23. "As good a woman, wife and mother as God has ever given to man."[25]

It was a terrible year for Albert. His father had died earlier in the year, and his brother Joseph was to die ten days after his wife. The immediate problem was what to do with Jack. Albert felt that, without Flora, he could not provide a home for him by the time school began. It is not surprising that he sent him back with Warren to Wynyard School, for Warren, who had probably already formed the view that parents can never understand a child's miseries, had said nothing to convince him that Wynyard was a remarkably brutal and inefficient school.

It tears the heart to think what Jack suffered. The operation and the whole period of his mother's illness had been a nightmare, for he had become very close to her since Warren had been sent away to school. Now she had just died, and the sensitive little boy who had never been away from home before, except with his mother, was taken away from his governess and the happy attic he had made his own, to live under the eye of a certainly brutal and probably insane tyrant of a headmaster. Within a very short time, both boys were writing pathetic letters home, begging to be taken away.

3

Into Bondage

J ack was quite unsuited to the stifling atmosphere of his boarding schools. His interests were literary and artistic, but he found it difficult to live in the bright, clean world of his imaginary Narnia at school. Although he spent less time away at school than his brother Warren, he was obsessed throughout his life by dark memories of his schools, memories that forced squalid images and lurid pictures into his mind and often tempted him to sadistic or prurient thoughts. To liberate himself, he wrote the autobiographical *Surprised by Joy*, in which he devotes seven astonishingly vivid chapters to his memories of these schools.

He was sent with Warren in 1908 to Wynyard School because of the disorganization of his home life, but he no doubt would have gone sooner or later even if his mother had not died. Albert would have thought it unfair to deprive him of the educational and social advantages that he supposed Warren was enjoying. Albert sought the advice of his old Lurgan College headmaster, W. T. Kirkpatrick, on the value of preparatory and public school education. (In England, prep schools prepare boys for the public school entrance examination, and public schools are actually private, or independent, schools that accept boys between the ages of thirteen and eighteen, mainly as boarders, rather than as day students.)

Kirkpatrick had made sure that Albert had no illusions about the educational advantages of boarding schools. "I sent my son to a Preparatory School," Kirkpatrick wrote, "Temple Grove ... for two years, then to Charterhouse for five. The money expense was not under £200 a year, and when he left, he knew nothing. Since I came here, I have had boys from Public Schools, whose parents asked me to prepare them for the Army or something. Not one of them had been taught."[1]

He is vague on the advantages of public school education, saying that "it will be good for the boy himself to be away, and look to his home as a holiday haven."[2] This argument must have seemed strong in the case of Warren, who was big for his age and turning out to be difficult for Miss Harper to manage. Then and throughout his school career, he was the sort of boy whose main object when faced with academic work was to avoid doing it. As Albert indicated in various letters to headmasters, "he needed discipline." Albert also had the feeling that it was bad for the boys to be taught too long by women. They must be made more manly, "able to stand on their own feet."

Jack writes in *Surprised by Joy* that his father's intention "was, of course, to turn us into Public School boys."[3] But Albert's motive was not just snobbery or class-consciousness. He knew that a public school education would be a great advantage, even in some cases indispensable, if his sons wanted to go into the civil service or to become officers in the army or navy. In fact, as it turned out, it helped both in this way. Warren became a professional soldier, and Jack was an officer in World War I. Albert supposed that such an education would help his sons if they later wanted to go on to Oxford or Cambridge, universities that recruited their students largely from the public schools. And he was right. The fact that Jack had studied at Malvern, the school to which he went after leaving Wynyard, quite likely helped him to get a scholarship at University College, Oxford. Though he had spent only a year at Malvern, he stated on the entrance form that it was his place of education.

But Albert's main motive was social, the desire for his sons to attain and preserve the status of gentlemen, to sound and look right, to talk without an accent, to wear the right sort of clothes, and to have good manners (that is, manners acceptable to older men of the same class). There is evidence that Flora had valued these social advantages more highly than Albert did. Kirkpatrick wrote that she "would not be satisfied with Campbell College"; and of Irish schools in general, he wrote, "However good the teaching may be in some cases the drawbacks are severe." It is pretty certain that he meant that the students were not "gentlemen," but "vulgar" boys who spoke with strong accents. His advice was, therefore, to "send your boy to a good prep school in England and run him for a scholarship. . . . [I]t is your only chance to secure him attention at the Public Schools. Their reputation depends on the success of their scholars. The others are of no account."[4]

At Kirkpatrick's suggestion, Albert wrote to Messrs. Gabbitas and Thring, the well-known London scholastic agents, for suggestions, and then to individual prep schools for prospectuses. It never occurred to him that there was more to be done. He never visited a single school, nor did he ask a friend or relative in England to visit one on his behalf.

Although he was to blame for an unfortunate choice, the process by which he selected a school was not unlike that used by many British parents, even to this day. It was common then for parents not to visit the schools under consideration. They would rarely bother to talk with housemasters, department heads, or the parents of other students; they would commonly ignore the school's nutritional program and sanitary conditions.

Nevertheless, it is hard to understand how he managed to choose a school quite as bad as Wynyard School, Watford. Kirkpatrick had recommended a well-known school at Rhyl in Wales, which would have meant a much shorter and easier journey from Belfast. But Wynyard's cost must have been in its favor. Albert did not want to pay more than £70 a year, and he regarded a school that charged £90, no matter how good, as quite beyond his means. He must have been depressed at the time by his recurring fear of going bankrupt.

It is sometimes suggested that Jack exaggerated the evils of Wynyard. But this does not seem to be the case. Jack's apparently highly colored account agrees with the slightly more sober one of his brother in *The Lewis Papers* and with the opinions of other former pupils.

Even as a building, Wynyard was a terrible place. It was a semidetached house of "hideous yellow brick." There were only one schoolroom, one very low-roofed dormitory, and one washbasin. One bathroom served everyone, and each boy was allowed a weekly bath. The sick room was actually an attic junk room. The playground outside was a patch of gravel strewn with flints. Beyond this there was an open-fronted corrugated iron shed where boys kept their lunch boxes and where the primitive lavatories were also housed. "Even in 1905," wrote Warren, "any Sanitary Inspector would unhesitatingly have condemned these places; their stench in summer is one of my own most abiding memories." No parent of a boarder visited the school while Warren was there. There were no playing fields, workshops, or library at all. "I cannot better describe the deadly monotony of the life than by telling you of its official diversions; to be selected to carry a parcel of foul linen to Mrs. Norris, the laundress, before morning school was a high privilege. . . ."[5]

The headmaster was the Reverend Robert Capron, a clergyman of the Church of England. Aged about sixty, he was still a physically powerful man. Warren continues, "I have seen him lift a boy of twelve or so from the floor by the back of his collar, and holding him at arm's length, as one might a dog . . . apply his cane to his calves." There is some evidence that Capron suffered from mental illness. His rage could not be contained. "He was the most complete domestic tyrant I have ever met with or even read of."[6]

At meals, which were times of terror, only his son Wyn (Wynyard Capron, an old Etonian, as his father boasted) dared to start a conversation, and then only with his father. Mrs. Capron was a "little, timid, faded woman" who ventured no original remark. The three daughters ate in complete silence and had food inferior to that of the two men; for high tea they had the ordinary school fare of "thick bread and thin butter."[7] In their younger days, the girls had often been caned as if they were schoolboys. They now lived a life of complete domestic drudgery. Wyn, nicknamed "Wee-Wee" by the boys, had as a boy at the school been flogged during the school term and holidays. He was now a broken-spirited young man, invariably deferential to his father.

Capron, nicknamed "Oldie," had no friends in Watford because he had quarreled with everyone there. He ate the often nauseating school food at a wolfish pace; a boy who could not keep up or eat everything on his plate might be severely punished. Perhaps it was this that caused poor Jack for the rest of his life to gobble his food.

As for the teaching, Warren reports that it "was at once brutalising and intellectually stupefying. It consisted of learning by heart. His class stood in front of him while reciting their lessons, and as some trembling boy blundered through his task, he would say to his head boy in a tone of anticipatory relish, 'Give me my

cane. I see I shall soon need it.' Armed with this, he would further terrify the unfortunate child by violently flogging the lid of
his desk until rising, he would exclaim, 'Come out, Come out,'
and execution would be done on the spot."[8]

When they were not reciting lessons, boys spent all their
classroom time working out sums on slates. There was no idea
of progress or advance in this. Warren remembers that he spent
the best part of one year doing just four sums over and over again
in rotation. Jack thought it possible that the inhibitions produced
by this were the reason for his inability to understand simple
math in later life. Geography was a meaningless list of rivers,
towns, imports, and exports; history a list of kings, battles, and
dates. "I cannot remember," wrote Warren, "one single piece of
instruction that was imparted to me at Wynyard, and yet when
I first went there, I was neither an idle nor a stupid boy."[9]

The effect on romantic, supersensitive Jack was devastating.
He wrote letter after letter home pleading to be taken away at
once. After a few weeks, Albert realized that something was
wrong and persuaded his sister-in-law, Annie Hamilton, to inves-
tigate on his behalf. A formidable woman, she got the better of
Capron, and, for a time, conditions in the school were better. But
the following term, in January, Warren wrote: ". . . [W]e both
think we would like to go to Campbell College. Of course, as you
say, the boys may not be gentlemen, but no big school is entirely
composed of gentlemen, and I think English boys are not so honest or so gentlemanly as most Irish ones. After all there is no need
to mix with the nasty boys."

Albert's reply has not survived, but we know that he began
to negotiate with the headmasters of Shrewsbury and Malvern
about a place for Warren. Although the correspondence suggests
that Shrewsbury, under Cyril Alington, was a more efficient
school than Malvern, under S. R. James, Albert chose the latter,

and Warren went to School House, one of the college's ten boarding houses, in September 1909. Jack had to stay at Wynyard for another two terms. He was taught nothing there. "[I]f I had been left for two years more," he wrote, "it would probably have sealed my fate as a scholar for good."[10]

There were some consolations. Since the school was small, there were no organized games, which Jack thought at the time a great blessing, because he had never been taught and had no wish to play games (although in his early years at Oxford, he would play tennis, Ping-Pong, and badminton). Rather than playing games, the boys were sent on walks. They did more talking than walking, and their talk was not confined to the narrow interests of most public school boys. During one walk, Jack engaged in the first metaphysical argument that he can remember. It concerned the nature of the future: Is it like a line that you can't see or a line that is not yet drawn? He would delight in such arguments for the rest of his life.

A good result of Wynyard, he often said, was that it taught him to join forces with the few remaining boys against the tyrant Oldie (numbers were so miserably depleted that, after Warren's departure, only five boarders remained). In conversation with me, he once defended the school by saying, "It taught all of us at least one good thing. It taught us to stick together, to support each other in resistance to tyranny."

There was a time at Wynyard, too, when Jack became a believer in Christianity. Although he had often been taken to church by his parents, the Sunday services to which he went held little meaning for him. He had come away with no knowledge or understanding of Christianity. Neither did he remember being taught to pray at home, although it is likely that he was taught to say prayers, set prayers that meant nothing to him. (In later life he was, of course, almost allergic to set prayers.) At Wynyard he was taken twice every Sunday to Saint John's, the Watford Anglo-Catholic church. His initial, extremely unfavorable reactions were typical of the northern Irish Protestant. It was, he wrote, a church that "wanted to be Roman Catholic, but was afraid to say so," an abominable place of Romish hypocrites, where people cross themselves [and] bow to what they have the vanity to call an altar."[11] But the influence of the church on his intellect soon became far more important than its influence on his feelings. For the first time, he heard in sermons not "general uplift" but the essential doctrines of Christianity taught by men who really believed in them. He began to pray seriously, to feel for and to follow his conscience, and to read the Bible. He also talked about religion with other boys "in an entirely healthy and profitable way."[12]

These conversations on religion and metaphysics show what sort of a boy Jack was becoming, an intellectual whose mind and decisions would be influenced by rational thought as well as by intuition, a boy whose eventual conversion to Christianity would be, in part, philosophical. But the candles and incense of Saint John's almost certainly increased the anti-Catholic bias he had inevitably acquired in Belfast. Sectarian feeling there was nearly as strong as it is today, even if it was not often so bitterly expressed.

Jack left Wynyard not because his father came to realize that it was far too bad a school for him, but because it had to close down for lack of pupils. Oldie retired to become vicar of the little parish of Radstock in north Hertfordshire. His end was sad indeed. Old, poor, stripped of his tyrannical power, saddened and weakened by the desertion of "the last of his slaves, his daughters, he shivered for a time in the cold wind of reality . . . and then did the only thing that was left him to do—he died."[13]

That was in 1911. For the next fifty years, Jack felt anger and resentment toward Oldie. Once he had become a Christian, he tried hard to forgive, to heal the memory, and free himself from an almost obsessive resentment. But he did not succeed until he was lying ill in Oxford's Acland Nursing Home in the last July of his life.[14]

Despite the damage caused by Oldie's cruelty, Jack maintained that the school had done him more good than harm. He learned there to get along with other boys in the face of oppression, to discuss serious subjects and to argue, to read the Bible and to pray, and to have a sense of the reality of sin.

He has suggested that his reading deteriorated while he was at Wynyard, although it was there that he came to prefer the novels of Rider Haggard to the animal stories of Beatrix Potter and there that he began avidly to read historical novels of the ancient world. In *Surprised by Joy*, he condemns his taste for novels of ancient Greece and Rome as morbidly erotic. He seems to have read such books as *Ben Hur* and *The Last Days of Pompeii* for the scenes of cruelty, the beatings of slaves, and the gruesome performances of gladiators in the arena. Such scenes aroused in him what he later recognized as sexual emotion. Here, perhaps, as in the feelings aroused in him by Oldie's beatings of his schoolmates (he himself was never beaten), lies the origin of the sadistic fantasies that plagued his adolescence. It is significant that the most vivid scenes by far in his descriptions of Wynyard and Malvern College are scenes of cruelty.

Jack's taste for novels of the ancient world remained with him past his adolescence. Many years later, he enjoyed the novels of Rex Warner and Mary Renault, especially *The Last of the Wine*. His novel *Till We Have Faces* evolved from this taste.

Still another literary passion that he acquired at Wynyard had a permanent influence on him: his avid reading of the science fiction novels of H. G. Wells and any other space-travel books that he could find. It was an intense passion that made him feel almost drunk, a passion he describes as a coarse, heady attraction to be exorcised, more a lust than a genuine imaginative experience, and an affair for the psychoanalysts to explain. Perhaps. But from this passion, there arose the three magnificent space-travel novels, *Out of the Silent Planet, Perelandra*, and *That Hideous Strength*, that he wrote thirty or forty years later.

After he left Wynyard in July 1910, Jack went for half a term to Campbell College in Belfast, a school organized along the lines of an English public school. Although he was there as a boarder and he disliked the lack of privacy and the noisy common rooms in which the boys spent much of their free time, Campbell was bliss after Wynyard. It was located only a mile from Little Lea, and he was allowed to go home every Sunday. Had he been given time to settle down at Campbell, he might have been happy there.

Even so, during the half term that he spent there he had an important experience: He heard a fine reading by his English teacher, J. A. McNeill, of a great Matthew Arnold poem, *Sohrab and Rustum*. He loved the poem as soon as he heard McNeill read it and never ceased to love it or to hear McNeill render it in his deep, resonant voice. Perhaps it was because of his early exposure to *Sohrab*, which is the most like Homer of all English poems, that he came to love the *Iliad* as soon as he read it, and after that nearly all heroic poetry. He was lucky at age eleven to have had a teacher like McNeill. Teachers today are likely to find *Sohrab and Rustum* too difficult for children of that age, and many children may go through all their school years without exposure to any great heroic poem.

He was taken away from Campbell College on November 15, 1910, because he had come home that morning with a bad cough. In his diary Albert records that he is uneasy about Jack's "poor chest—the poorest I think I ever saw in a boy of his years."[15]

No doubt Albert sent Jack to Malvern because the town had a great reputation as a health resort, especially for diseases of the lungs. According to a guidebook of the period, the air was "of almost Alpine dryness. Statistics show that ordinary forms of acute inflammation of the lungs and air-passages . . . are but rarely found in Malvern. . . . The earlier stages of phthisis [tuberculosis] are perhaps most benefited."[16] The famous Malvern water, which even then was bottled and exported, might also have attracted a resident of Belfast, where the water supply was still suspect.

Warren and Jack remembered that a boy from Wynyard had gone to a Malvern prep school called Cherbourg. It seemed just the place for Jack. It was a small school in a regency-style house on the slopes of the steep hill just above School House, where Warren was. How convenient! The boys could travel together and Warren would look after Jack. Albert did not visit the school, but he did ask Warren to make local inquiries. This time he was less unfortunate, for Cherbourg turned out to be a school with some merit, where Jack was well taught and, on the whole, happy. But it had serious faults, too, as we shall see.

Jack's first impressions of Malvern were favorable. He wrote home that "Malvern is one of the nicest English towns I have seen yet. The hills are beautiful but of course not so nice as ours."[17] When he went to Cherbourg, he was still a small boy with a plump oval face and bright eyes. He was unathletic and rather poorly developed muscularly, although he enjoyed swimming. Even then he was an extremely amusing storyteller, which made him quite popular with other boys. Perhaps he acted the clown. Certainly he tended to be rebellious, to play the fool, and to enjoy teasing his schoolmasters whenever he had an opportunity.

Probably the company of his sophisticated elder brother encouraged him to be "a naughty boy." Albert supposed that on their journeys to and from school they went directly to Malvern and that Warren kept his brother out of mischief. But Warren had already learned most of the tricks of schoolboy travel. They would stop at the Lime Street Hotel in Liverpool and sit there smoking, until they could board a train that would arrive at the last possible moment allowed by the school. Jack started his life-long habit of smoking at the age of twelve.

At Cherbourg he was soon in trouble, having to do (according to his diary) "hundreds of impots," that is, impositions, tasks assigned to him for breaking school rules, misbehaving in the classroom, and not preparing his work. This diary, like all the other diaries he began, was kept for only a short time. It contains the thoughts of a typical schoolboy: Masters are "rotten" when they punish one for misbehaving; it is great fun to rag them, and so on.

Cherbourg was generously staffed. The headmaster, A. C. Allen, was a good teacher of Latin and English, and there were three other masters for the seventeen boys. Nevertheless, it was quite a feat on their part to have brought Jack in two years up to the Malvern College entrance standard, considering how little he must have learned at Wynyard.

But to be a good headmaster, a man must be more than a good teacher. He must also be able to identify students who might need help with emotional problems. Allen quite lacked this ability. He showed no understanding of the ordinary boy, let alone one as sensitive as Jack. He was also harsh and intolerant in his dealings with the staff, a characteristic revealed in his treatment of the woman who became Jack's first surrogate mother.

Her name was Miss Cowie, and she was the school's exceptionally kind and efficient matron. She recognized at once that

Jack was almost an orphan and mothered him with a special degree of love and care to which he responded gratefully. "They all love her," he wrote, "I, an orphan, especially." He did not tell his father that she was dismissed from her post largely because of her relationship with him. According to Sir Alexander Clutterbuck, who was a contemporary of Jack at both Cherbourg and Malvern, she was dismissed for two reasons: The headmaster found her holding Jack in her arms (she did this with other boys, and her embraces were thought in the school to be innocently motherly), and she took his part when he complained that he was not allowed to send letters to his father without having them first censored by a master. He regarded this censorship as disgracefully tyrannical. Even at Wynyard, correspondence had never been censored.

Miss Cowie's dismissal came at an unfortunate time for Jack. He was now an overgrown boy of thirteen in the highly emotional stage of puberty. An extraordinarily sensitive boy, he regarded *Charicles*, a book written by a staid German professor that he had been given as a prize, as pornographic, and he felt he had been corrupted by having read it. He writes that it was "a tale illustrative of private life in the time of the Ancient Greeks." On one occasion he tells us he felt an electric thrill of lust for a teacher of dancing. "It was not her fault: she lifted a flag, pressed it to her face, remarked, 'I love the smell of bunting,'" and he was undone.[18] This susceptibility and sensitivity to beauty lasted much of his life. When he was a tutor at Magdalen College, Oxford, twenty years later, he had to give up teaching a female pupil because he found her so beautiful that in her presence he was rendered speechless.

Now at Cherbourg, he "underwent a violent and wholly successful assault of sexual temptation."[19] He began to masturbate. One can only imagine the sense of guilt he felt. In those days, clergymen and schoolmasters often spoke of masturbation as the sin against the Holy Ghost; some doctors said it could lead to insanity as well as to various bodily diseases. The habit caused him more misery than anything else in his early life.

Of course, he struggled against it, but the agony of the struggle intensified the sense of guilt. He resolved fiercely never to do it again, and then suffered over and over again the humiliation of failing to keep his resolution. His state, he tells us, was that described by Saint Paul in Romans 7:19–24: ". . . for the good that I would do, I do not: but the evil that I would not, that I do. . . . I delight in the law of God . . . but I see another law in my members, warring against the law of my mind. . . . O wretched man that I am, who shall deliver me from the body of this death?"

He prayed, too, and, because his prayers were not answered, he soon lost his faith. But it had already been weakened by conversations with Miss Cowie, who seems to have been a devotee of oriental religious thought and was perhaps a theosophist. Ironically, when he regained his faith eighteen years later, it was through the vice that had originally caused him to lose it.

To attain psychological balance, he had to suppress his strong feelings of guilt, a feat he accomplished by rejecting Christianity and its morality. He went in for bravado, blasphemy, and smut, startling and even shocking the boys who knew him best.

His state was not improved by his "crush" on a foolish young schoolmaster whom he called "Pogo," a "bit of a lad," and "a man about town." Although there was nothing physically sexual about the relationship, it corrupted him and vulgarized his taste. "I began to labour very hard to make myself into a fop, a cad and a snob," he wrote.[20] Like his brother, he also began to ask for money for hair oil, to discuss who was and was not a gentleman, and to show an interest in musical comedy actresses. Although his state should have been obvious to any good schoolmaster, nothing whatever was done to help him. He was astonished when he found out thirty years later that the good schoolmaster thinks it part of his job to counsel such boys in their moral, spiritual, and emotional difficulties. "What a difference that would have made!" he exclaimed. "What a difference!"

Nevertheless, his taste for the arts developed rapidly at Cherbourg. He went to a performance of Handel's *Messiah*, which he described as "simply lovely," and to Shakespearean plays performed by Sir Frank Benson's touring company, which he also enjoyed.

His writing developed precociously. He produced a stream of stories, as well as essays on many different subjects. Some, such as those on "Party Government" and "Richard Wagner" show a wide vocabulary and astonishing maturity—he already thought Wagner the greatest composer of all time. His essay "Are Athletes better than Scholars?" shows his development as a philologist, or even as a philosopher, for he devoted most of it to considering the meanings of the word *better*. He might have taken exactly the same line ten or twenty years later.[21]

Jack also wrote at home during the school holidays, but often at a more childish level. He continued the stories of talking animals that he had begun in Dundela Villas at the age of six. During the Easter holiday of 1912, he wrote a complete novel in two volumes—that is, in two school exercise books. Entitled "Boxen, or Scenes from Boxonian City Life," it was generously illustrated with colored drawings, over which Jack took at least as much trouble as with the text. It is an odd work for a sophisticated and well-read boy of thirteen. His desire to recover a lost paradise and to live in a simple and innocent child-world suggests insecurity, dissatisfaction with the present, and the need to escape.[22]

The political and military events of the Boxen stories may

seem unlike paradise to us, but, at the age of six, Jack probably thought that war and politics were the main occupation of grown-ups, because they were the main things he heard talked about in his father's house. In the family papers there is an interesting passage by Warren relevant to this:

> Neighbours would from time to time drop in of an evening for a chat with our father, and in those days—perhaps indeed today—amongst the upper middle class in Belfast, politics and money were almost the sole topics of conversation, with politics as the main dish. At the best of times political conversation is of all conversation the dullest, and only bearable when two friends hold opposing political views. But such was not the case in any Belfast house I ever visited. The religious, political and social cleavage between the Protestant Unionist and the Roman Catholic Nationalist was as deep and rigid as that which separates the Moslem from the Hindu. I for instance had never in my life spoken to a Roman Catholic with my own social background until I entered Sandhurst in 1914. No man came to my father's house who did not hold exactly the same political views as he did himself; from which it followed that there was nothing which could be properly described as discussion between host and guest at all, but rather a contest as to which could say the most insulting things about "this rotten Liberal Government."
>
> Any ordinary parent would have sent us boys off to amuse ourselves elsewhere when one of these symposiums took place, but not my father; he would have thought it uncivil to the guest. Consequently we had to sit in silence whilst the torrent of vituperation flowed over our heads. The result in Jack's case was to convince him firstly that "grown-up" conversation and politics were one and the same thing, and that therefore he must give everything he wrote a politi-

cal framework; and secondly to disgust him with the very word politics before he was out of his "teens."[23]

Jack and Warren spent as little time at home as possible on weekends and weekday evenings. Jack was led by his elder brother, even more than by Pogo, to affect sophistication. An undated letter written to Warren from Cherbourg conveys his attitude: "Thus in the holidays, rows after tea and penitential strolls in the garden are pleasant, but a soft bed, a nice Abdullah, a lazy walk with Tim, and occasional Hippodrome or Opera House have their consolations." (Abdullah was a make of Turkish or Egyptian cigarette. Tim was their dog. The Hippodrome and the Opera House were Belfast theaters, the former hosting music or variety shows, the latter, pantomime or musical comedy.)

By this point, what he calls "vulgarity" had entered his life. In *Surprised by Joy*, Pogo gets most of the blame for this, but surely Warren should share it. He was not doing well at Malvern College; a couple of extracts from his diary will make it obvious why. "Coll. [class] was rotten. Was put on to translate and didn't know it. . . . Coll. in the afternoon was awfully slack. Read 'Enoch Arden.' After supper ragged with Cullen and Blode." And: "Made a bet with Pritchard that I should be bottom for the week. Won. . . . Did not want to play house games in the afternoon so got gated for the Fish. . . . Put down Hebblethwaite and Crosland for being late."[24]

There he was, a prefect, punishing junior boys for a slackness of which he himself was guilty!

Warren delighted in breaking rules. In the summer of 1912, he tried to persuade his father to send him the money to buy a motorcycle. He gave Albert the impression that he would keep it at Malvern until the end of term and use it to come home for the holidays, but, of course, his real object was to ride it during the term, which was forbidden by school rules. Although Albert did not perceive his son's motive, he was not persuaded to buy the bike because he thought it too expensive.

In spite of what happened in the classrooms, Warren enjoyed Malvern. In 1953 he wrote for *The Beacon*, one of the college magazines, a delightfully nostalgic account of his days there. It was written with the object of counterbalancing his brother's lurid account in *Surprised by Joy*, to which he always objected, and it reveals his love for fancy dress, good food and wine, and general revelry.

Work was never a serious problem in S. H. [School House] for the House had discovered the value of specialization long before my day. In a House over fifty strong, we argued there must be one man who can do some one thing better than the average; so why have fifty men wasting their time trying to do half a dozen things? Let the Grecian do Greek, the Latinish Latin, and so on, all *pro bono publico*. This suited me down to the ground; the only thing that I was interested in was writing English essays, and as time went on and my clientele expanded, I was able to make this almost a whole time job; for of course the bulk of my other work was traded off against the essays.

I have just been reading of modern "privileges" in *The Beacon*. In this respect things are made easier for the present generation than they were for us; in my time brilliantine, a gold tie pin, brightly coloured socks, and a flower in one's buttonhole marked the man who had "arrived." But you yourself were the judge of when you should sport any of these distinctions; it needed the most critical self-examination to decide whether you could risk, say, a loud pair of socks, and woe betide you if your seniors' opinion of your standing turned out to differ from your own. For the happy few, the athletes, these nice points did not arise; the athlete . . . could do what he pleased, when he pleased and where he pleased, irrespective of his seniority. . . . He was in fact at least unofficially a person of vastly greater importance than an undistinguished Coll. Pre. [College Prefect].

I have forgotten the time of lights-out, but I do remember the admirable punctuality with which our Housemaster went round his cubicles, and his still more admirable habit of never doing so a second time, thus enabling one to return to one's study at a comparatively early hour for that well-earned glass of port which ushered in the sweet of the night.[25]

This article is interesting not only for what it tells us about Malvern College, but for the light it throws on the character of the brother who was also Jack's best friend. It shows Warren as unwilling to face the realities of school life, just as later on he was unwilling to face the realities of life in the army. His escape was to indulge in the fantasy of being "a bit of a lad," a cynical character addicted to drinking, rule-breaking, and so on. Later on it took the form of living the life of an officer and gentleman, and being a snob and in fantasy an aristocrat of the grand era of Louis XIV.

It is not surprising that Warren's reports from Malvern College were bad. In one midterm report, his formmaster wrote of him: "He is the most helpless boy at Greek and Latin that I have ever come across. . . ." This caused Albert to write in some distress to the headmaster, the Reverend S. R. James, and the result was that Warren was transferred to the science form. In his *Beacon* article, Warren tells this story rather differently. He suggests that the transfer was his choice and calls the science courses "a nonstop Fun Fair." "Provided that we did not actually blow the roof off the building," he writes, ". . . we could do much as we pleased. How my fellow scientists fared . . . I don't know; my only contribution to research was the discovery that if, on a hot summer afternoon, you put a lump of ice in a beaker of water, and add sulphuric acid to taste, you get a tolerable substitute for lemonade."

The change to science did not help to keep him at Malvern. He was once too often caught smoking and asked to leave at the end of the spring term in 1913. Albert, feeling hurt, angry, and depressed, asked the advice of W. T. Kirkpatrick, who suggested the army as a career, on the grounds that neither brains nor industry were necessary. Kirkpatrick successfully coached Warren for the entrance examination at Sandhurst.

Albert had great ambitions for his sons. His misery over Warren's failure at Malvern was compensated for by Jack's success at Cherbourg. "Your successes are a tonic to me," he wrote to Jack. "I hope you are beginning to gather the first fruits of a great scholastic career." Boys at Cherbourg were awarded stars for unusually good work, and, in his long and frequent letters, Albert would urge Jack to "make some more astral captures soon." When he sent Jack his usual pocket money of a shilling a week, he sometimes included "a bit more to pay for some stars that decorate my study when I want brightening up."[26]

Albert always tried hard to be a companion as well as a father to his sons. When he found out that the boys enjoyed vaudeville and music shows, he developed an interest in such entertainment and sometimes went to shows with them. There is a letter in which he describes a visit to the Belfast Hippodrome to hear Sir Harry Lauder. He reports that Lauder did not sound as good as he had on the gramophone. "Still he was very funny, a desperately ugly little man."[27] Alas, his sharing of what he supposed to be his sons' interests was unappreciated. Letters that Jack wrote about this time show that he already despised his father for what he regarded as Albert's lack of culture. But, in fact, Albert was remarkably well-read for a busy, hard-working attorney. He had read Euripedes and Aristophanes in translation, for instance, and had discussed them with Jack. In one letter, he drew an interesting comparison of his and Jack's style of writing and Warren's style. Warren, he said, would be classically severe, with one adjective too few rather than one too many. On the other hand, his and Jack's style "strives for that witchery of words which can be to the human ear the ripple of the sea beneath the sea, or the roar of the ocean as the hurricane drives it."[25] The judgment is acute, and, though made when the boys were very young, it is, to a large extent, true. Compare the style of Warren's *Splendid Century* with that of Jack's *Perelandra* or *Till We Have Faces*.

Jack stayed an extra year at Cherbourg in order to take the entrance scholarship examination. His success would mean lower tuition fees, greater prestige, and, so Kirkpatrick assured Albert, the certainty of far more careful teaching. Unfortunately, Jack was taken ill with a virus a few days before the exam. He nevertheless got up from bed in order to take the test, and, although he surely could not have done himself justice, he managed to win a second-rank scholarship. His English essay was better than that of any other candidate, but he was decidedly weak in math, and there were boys who got higher overall marks in Greek and Latin. Yet the examiner recognized Jack's potential. His note reads: "Prose translation not above Exhibition standard—careless mistakes, even of English spelling. Came into his own in the verse. Some of his rendering truly alpha, with a poetic feeling rare in any boy. I believe he is just the sort to develop to gain a Classics award at Oxford."[29]

Culturally, the most important event of his two years at Cherbourg was the discovery of Wagner. It began with a visual experience. Someone had left lying about in the big schoolroom a periodical that contained a review of Margaret Armour's recently published translation of *Siegfried and the Twilight of the*

Gods. Best of all, the article included an Arthur Rackham illustration of Siegfried, sunlit against a background of dim and distant mountains, gazing in wonder and astonishment at the sleeping Brunhilde. He has cut off her breastplate and is gazing at her naked breasts.

The text that goes with the picture in the original book is unlikely to have been quoted in the review, but it describes very well what must have been Jack's feelings on seeing it:

> *Magical rapture*
> *Pierces my heart;*
> *Burning with terror;*
> *I reel, my heart faints and fails.*[30]

The picture brought to him a sense of joy, the same great spiritual feeling that had been triggered by two other objects—his brother's miniature garden and the book *Squirrel Nutkin*—when he was a younger boy. His next insight into joy came as a result of reading Longfellow's translation of Tegner's *Drapa:*

> *I heard a voice that cried,*
> *Balder the beautiful*
> *Is dead, is dead—*

This too uplifted him "into huge regions of northern sky," into a world that was "cold, spacious, severe, pale, and remote."

Since his earlier experiences with joy, he had loved "northernness." This was one of the most important loves of his life; it became a description of a particular imaginative world. Perhaps the passion for northernness predates his first acquaintance with Norse mythology. Its basis may have been geographical, connected with the stories Lizzie Endicott told him, some of which were set in the wild, northern county that was her home, or it may have been ancestral though neither Warren nor his parents shared the taste. As a result, Jack thought Down, Antrim, and, when he came to know it, Donegal, as far more beautiful than any place in France or England, simply because they were more northern. He even went so far as to use northernness as a criterion by which to judge his schoolmates, writing that at Wynyard northern boys were "more decent" than southern boys.

During the next school holiday, he came across synopses of Wagner's *Ring* in a gramophone magazine to which he and Warren subscribed, *The Soundbox*. In intense excitement, he immediately began a heroic poem based on them. Written in couplets in the style of Pope's translations of Homer, the poem is a remarkable achievement for a boy of thirteen or fourteen.

On the next holiday, he discovered in a Belfast music shop a gramophone record of *The Ride of the Valkyrie*. From then on listening to Wagner's *Ring* became a passion, an ecstasy, "a conflict of sensations without name." This passion was given further impetus when, at a cousin's house, he found a complete copy of *Siegfried and the Twilight of the Gods*. In the review he had seen earlier, one of Arthur Rackham's illustrations had inspired joy in him. Now, on his cousin's drawing-room table, there was the book itself—a limited edition, numbered and signed by the artist, bound in vellum—and he longed for a copy of his own. "I have seldom coveted anything as I have coveted that book," he wrote.[31] The limited edition was far beyond his means, but with Warren's help he soon managed to buy a cheaper edition. For weeks and weeks, living in the world of Richard Wagner was more important to him than anything else.

We shall not understand Jack unless we can appreciate his gift for being utterly absorbed in the imaginative world of a great writer, artist, or musician. It is not easy to think of other British writers of similar sensibility. Perhaps Keats and Shelley were as sensitive as Jack was, not merely to words, but to the whole world of the human imagination and to nature. But Jack never nurtured his sensibility as Keats sometimes did. He had no need to. It came to him unbidden when he was young and was at times so strong that he was frightened of madness. But usually it was a source of delight.

Love of Wagner and northernness led him to read everything he could find on Norse mythology; he became quite learned on the subject. When walking or cycling in the country, he found himself looking for places such as caves and woods and waterfalls that might fit in with scenes in the Wagnerian world. He appreciated scenery not only for itself, but also for its romantic suggestions. It became and remained a lifelong joy and the inspiration of some of his finest writing.

He hid his imaginative life from others, not by choice, but because, until he met Arthur Greeves, he had no friend with whom to share it. Indeed, he knew no one who could even understand. He feared ridicule and perhaps even the accusation of madness. The self he showed to his contemporaries was that of the witty, blasphemous, sex-obsessed schoolboy. This double life is the key to understanding "Bloodery" and "Light and Shade," the chapters in *Surprised by Joy* that describe the year (September 1913 to July 1914) he spent at Malvern College.

4

Malvern College

Jack wrote lengthy, lurid accounts of his experiences at Malvern College during the year he spent there, September 1913 to July 1914. His struggle to control his sexual and sadistic fantasies intensified and caused him great psychic pain. For many years, he blamed the school for his suffering and as a result rarely missed an opportunity to attack public schools. Only near the end of his life, when he was confronted with arranging the education of his stepsons, did he recognize that his impressions as a fourteen-year-old boy may have been unbalanced.

A primary source of strife for Jack was his obsession with sex. From his first night at Malvern, when glances from older boys aroused his suspicions, he supposed that homosexuality was a common practice there. But his notion of what went on at Malvern was based more on fantasy than on fact. According to Warren, his knowledge of other boys' relationships came from "such scandalmongering and rumour as filters down to him. To him an association between a big and a small boy is an open admission of immorality, and Jack seems to have been quite unaware of the fact that many of these associations—as any senior boy knew—were purely platonic."[1]

Warren notes that Jack later admitted his error in supposing that homosexuality was a topic of widespread interest at

Malvern. "When I first read *Surprised by Joy,* I called Jack's attention to his absurd statement that 'there was only one topic of conversation' in the House. I said that without stopping to think I could remember . . . musical comedy actresses, music hall stars, horse-racing, clothes, holidays past and to come, and of course hot disputes about who should be given the vacant place in the First Eleven. . . . When I had done speaking, he admitted that his picture of Malvern was overcharged."[2]

Another cause of the frustration Jack felt at Malvern was the cultural differences he perceived between himself and other boys. In *Surprised by Joy,* he states that Malvern corrupted him, not by introducing him to "a very furnace of impure loves," but by making him a prig. "When I went there," he writes, "nothing was further from my mind than the idea that my private taste for fairly good books, for Wagner . . . gave me any sort of superiority to those who read nothing but magazines and listened to nothing but the then fashionable ragtime." Although he protests that, if he truly reflected on his tastes, he probably would have actually felt inferior to other boys, it is clear from the essay on Wagner, written at Cherbourg when he was thirteen, that he felt superior and was something of a prig a year before his arrival at Malvern.[3]

Shortly after coming to Malvern, he wrote of "a companion—one Waley of School House, who talked an amazing amount of agreeable nonsense. I pretended to be interested in, and understand, his explanation of how an aeroplane engine works, and said 'Yes' and 'I see' and 'really!' at suitable intervals. . . . I am very pleased that he has gone . . . as I prefer Tennyson to lectures, however learned, on aeronautics. . . ."[4] Warren commented to me about this, "I cannot remember Waley, but unless he was a very stupid boy indeed, I doubt if he was deceived by Jack's simulated interest in aeroplanes; for Jack, throughout his life and especially his earlier years, was a very poor hand at feigning interest in anything that bored him. Indeed the necessity of constantly having to make the attempt was one of his chief grievances against Malvern and one of the reasons for his early departure from the College."

Coming to Malvern with high expectations, Jack was disappointed to find that most of the students were Philistines who neither appreciated the music he liked most nor cared to read his sort of books. In the only letter he wrote to Arthur Greeves from Malvern, he comments on the dreariness of the place. What irked and irritated him most of all was not the work, the school food, and the discomfort. It was "the absolute lack of appreciation of anything like music or books" which he found among his companions. He detested having to live for twelve weeks among boys whose thoughts "never rise above the dull daily round of cricket and work and eating."[5]

Few would regard Jack's priggishness as a serious fault. Indeed, it would have been difficult for such a precocious and clever boy not to feel superior. Jack's charge against his school has been uttered throughout the years by many bookish and unathletic boys who do not fit into the collective-minded and standardizing public school system. By his temperament, he was bound to be a misfit. There was much work, strenuous play, and little leisure.

Work began with a class period before breakfast and continued after breakfast with four more classes and compulsory chapel service. On whole school days—Mondays, Wednesdays, and Fridays—there were more classes in the afternoon. Up to about two hours of study might have to be done each evening. Jack would share a study with several other boys. On most afternoons, junior boys would be expected to exercise, usually by playing cricket or football, though there were also facilities for gymnastics, squash, racquetball, tennis, boxing, fencing, and other games. Fagging, that is, acting as a servant to an older boy, was an important part of his life. Cleaning shoes and running errands for senior boys would cut into what little free time there was. Except on Sundays and perhaps on rainy afternoons, Jack would not have had the long periods of time that he desired for reading and literary composition. Perhaps his brother was right in thinking that he should never have been sent to a public school at all. His literary and artistic interests made him at the age of fourteen an object of suspicion. In Warren's opinion, he was lucky to leave Malvern before the system had done him any lasting damage.

Jack tells us that he went to Malvern prepared to worship senior boys. It is not easy to believe this, if one considers the kind of inside information he had been given by his cynical elder brother. But, indeed, he must have been bitterly disappointed if he really expected to find School House seniors interested in Wagner and Norse mythology. His disillusionment colors his description of the most influential senior boys, called "Bloods," and of the prefects. He describes the latter as mainly interested in games and the preservation and extension of their own privileges, which included exercising power over junior boys, whose lives they often made miserable by the system of fagging. He spoke of them in the same scornful tone that he used to describe them in *Surprised by Joy*. According to Judy Porch, who was then the tutor at School House, he enjoyed "inventing scurrilous gossip about masters, prefects, and senior boys." He was also constantly inventing satirical nicknames—the Count, the Parrot, Stopfish, Yards-of-Face, and so on—that shocked and amused his contemporaries and made him unpopular with older boys. If a prefect were named Surridge, for instance, Jack might mumble something about Borage or Porridge or Burrage in such a way that Surridge half overheard him. When challenged, he would then say, "You misheard me. I never mentioned your name at all." *Surprised by Joy* contains some satirically described characters who are based on boys Jack knew at Malvern.

Warren, who had himself been a prefect, strongly objected to Jack's account of them, as he objected to almost everything his brother wrote about Malvern. In his preface to *The Letters of C. S. Lewis*, he writes: "I had been on more or less close terms with all the brutes of prefects whom he describes, and I found them (with one exception) very pleasant fellows. How did they come to change their characters entirely during the summer holidays of that year?"[6]

Jack's bitterness toward the older schoolboys may have resulted from his feeling that they had betrayed him. Because many of the prefects were Warren's friends, he had expected that they would also be his friends. He felt shocked and hurt to discover that the social conventions of the school dictated that none of the older boys could give more than cursory attention to a "first year nip," particularly one who was more interested in music than in sports.

His deeper objections to the Bloods were, however, fundamentally moral. They lived by selfish abuse of power, according to base pleasures and low ideals. They were tyrants who manipulated junior boys and hoodwinked housemasters. He came to believe that by their very existence these elite circles of callous bullies formed a standard of evil to which most public school boys aspired. Seeing the same system at work at Magdalen College, he would later satirize it in *That Hideous Strength*. He was inclined to believe that elitism, what he called "the inner ring," was common in British life, and that it derived directly from the public schools. "Spiritually speaking," he wrote, "the deadly thing was that school life was a life almost entirely dominated by the social struggle . . . and from it, at school as in the world, all sorts of meanness flow. . . ."[7]

To understand Jack's exaggerated account of Malvern, one must consider the miserable state he was in. He had apparently lost his religious faith and had certainly lost his innocence. Prayer had not helped him cope with the intense guilt he felt about his practice of masturbating. He therefore despaired of divine aid and regarded himself as an atheist. Furthermore, he had lost his strength; he found the work difficult and frequently felt exhausted.

Ten days after his arrival he wrote to his father complaining that the work was hard and that it was difficult to find time for it in a way of life that was "a perpetual rush at high pressure. . . ."[8] In November he was ill with what seems to have been bronchitis and was sent to the school sanatorium for two weeks—a respite he rather enjoyed.

We have an objective account of what he was like at Malvern from two letters written to me by his contemporary and study companion, Donald Hardman (later Air Chief Marshall Sir Donald Hardman, C.B.E., K.C.B., D.F.C.). The first was written before he had read *Surprised by Joy:*

> He was a bit of a rebel; he had a wonderful sense of humour and was a past-master of mimicry. I think he took his work seriously, but nothing else; never took any interest in games and never played any so far as I can remember unless he had to. The quite extraordinary thing about Lewis is the complete transformation of character that took place after he left Malvern. I met him in Oxford after the war and noticed he had changed, but was staggered to find him the author of *The Screwtape Letters*. When I knew him I can only describe him as a riotously amusing atheist. He really was pretty foul mouthed about it.[9]

In another letter to me, Sir Donald Hardman comments on Jack's account of Malvern in *Surprised by Joy*. It is, he writes:

unbalanced and exaggerated. This is not to say that some of the practices and customs he complains of did not exist; they did, but Lewis has blown them up out of all proportion. . . . "Tarting" [homosexuality] did exist, but I'm sure to nothing like the extent he makes out. He has a good deal to say about fagging: it could at times be very irritating, but we took it as all in the day's work and I have never known it [to] leave those scars on anyone else. Every House must have its good and lean years in House Prefects, and we were not particularly blessed with ours in Lewis's day. We were worked pretty hard; my memory is in no doubt about this and I can well understand that a rather overgrown gangling boy might be overtired. . . . Indeed I had the same experience as Lewis—'over moved up' in form and wheeled up before the Headmaster for slacking when I was getting up regularly at 6 o'clock to get in an hour's work before chapel or early morning school. Lewis blames one of his prep. schools for the fact that he was no good at games. I blame both for a good deal more than that. I think that they, coupled with an inadequate home life (no mother and a curious father to say the least), made him the abnormal boy he was when he went to Malvern. Even so, I am sure he was not unhappy all the time. I can remember going [on] long walks with him on Sundays when he was in the gayest of moods . . . storytelling and mimicking people—one of his chief butts being the worthy master in charge of the O.T.C. . . . It is surprising that he should forget the happy times and remember only the unhappy ones.[10]

In Jack's letter to Arthur Greeves, there is no mention of homosexuality, bullying, or even physical tiredness. He praises the school's library, the Grundy, as the best stocked one that he knew. There he discovered W. B. Yeats, "an author exactly after my own heart," in a fine set of volumes printed by the Shakespeare Head Press and bound in white vellum. Yeats's works, he comments, "have all got that strange eerie feeling" that he and Arthur much enjoyed.[11]

The Grundy also had the two-volume set of the *Corpus Poeticum Boreale,* which not only opened to him the world of Norse poetry, but also inspired him to write *Loki Bound,* an opera libretto based on Norse mythology but written in classical form.[12] The theme is interesting in relation to the development of Jack's thoughts and feelings. Loki, with whom the author clearly sympathizes, has quarreled with the gods because he foresaw that the creation of man would produce injustice and has tried to prevent it. Thor hates Loki because he is wise and unorthodox (Jack said that the clash here was between the games-playing Blood of Malvern College and the intellectual) and persuades Odin to bind him to a rock. But Odin, who is not wholly evil, dislikes the prospect of losing Loki's friendship and also being left with a world of slaves. He therefore offers to let Loki off if he will toe the line. Loki rejects the offer. He refuses to compromise and accept a position of privilege in an unjust world.

When, later on in life, he reviewed what he had written about Malvern, he exclaimed, "Lies, lies!" and then went on to explain that he was really telling the story of two lives, the life of an over-tired rebel and an imaginative life consisting of moments "when you were too happy to speak."[13]

Many of these "moments" must have taken place during the fourteen hours a week that he was taught by Harry Wakelyn Smith. A great schoolmaster, Smith was eccentric in almost every respect. He was a thin, scraggy man who wore oversized clothes and a great billowing gown in which he would drift along the corridor, waving it from side to side. Though he was only fifty-four when he taught Lewis, he looked much older with his gray hair and white mustache, and very odd and old-fashioned in his turned-up collar and bootlace tie. "Smugy" (this was his nickname) was a joke to the rest of the school, but every boy in the upper fifth felt proud and honored to have his name on the printed form-list, which bore at the top the form's motto, *Virtus Tentamine Gaudet* (virtue glories in competition).

Smugy's method of marking was quite peculiar. He gave plus points and minus points according to whatever was positively good or bad in a piece of work, and at the end of the term he added all the plus and minus marks together. The leading student, who might easily end with about two thousand points, would be rewarded with a chit so that he could go to a local florist and buy himself a flower on Smugy's account. Although ordinarily a junior would not be allowed such an eccentricity of dress as a flower in his buttonhole, the boy who had won the flower from Smugy met no opposition from masters or prefects as he proudly wore it, keeping it alive as long as he could.

Such proud honors fell to few, but every boy would delight in and look forward to the occasions when Smugy would move around the classroom, sit next to each in turn, and carry on with him two or three minutes of half-whispered conversation. "These were the highspots of all my years at Malvern," a former student wrote. "He seemed to understand me better than anyone else has ever done, and could pack into those few minutes a great deal of advice and encouragement."

Smugy's charm came partly from his manners and partly from the way in which he read poetry. In the words of C. B. Lace, the leading student in his class in 1918, to whom I am indebted for much of this information:

He called us gentlemen, treated us like gentlemen, and we behaved like gentlemen. No one ever tried to tease or rag him, and even the dolts worked hard. If one did particularly good work, one might be given a little present. I regarded him not so much as a schoolmaster but as a friend and, in company with other boys, was often asked to tea in his house.

The work he set us was unlike that set by other masters. ... [Once] we had to design a tombstone with an eagle at the top, bearing an epitaph in English verse and ending with a suitable Latin quotation. I think that, of all poets, Horace was his favorite. Because he read his poems with love, he made us love them too.

He passed two qualities on to Jack. The first was the power to analyze the grammar and syntax of a poem in such a way as to increase its aesthetic appeal; the second was to read poetry with so much attention to its rhythm and music that the result was almost a song. Jack often said that his own style of reading poetry was based primarily on his memory of Smugy's reading. Although he did not have Smugy's lovely musical voice and could not read romantic poetry with Smugy's power to enchant, Jack excelled in reading heroic verse and such poetry as Milton's that required a grand style. Even in his mature literary criticism, he was indebted to Smugy. More than any other modern critic, he was sensitive to the music of poetry, the sound of the verse, and, although he was intensely concerned with grammar and scansion, his technical analysis of a verse would always enhance one's appreciation of its beauty.

Jack was usually in the lower half of his class. At this time, he showed little sign of great academic ability in Greek and Latin, and he was weak in mathematics, but according to A. F. Lace, a contemporary of Jack's at Malvern, Smugy realized that Jack had a deeper feeling for poetry than anyone else in the class: "Smugy was always ready to leave Latin and Greek to launch out on a vast variety of topics—to our great benefit and delight. . . . [Once he] was talking about English Literature, and started to read a poem by Tennyson, I am almost sure, *Enoch Arden*. At the end of the reading, Smugy turned to Lewis and made a remark about the poem that indicated to me that when it came to that sort of thing he and Lewis were able to appreciate it at a level far beyond the rest of us. . . ."[14]

Smugy was a close friend of Sir Edward Elgar when the composer lived in Malvern. He introduced Jack to Elgar's music and on one occasion took Jack and two other boys for a drive into the lovely hills and valleys of Birchwood, where they viewed "Elgar's summer residence," the house in which he had written *Dream of Gerontius*.

On October 19 of his first term, Jack was sent to the headmaster in recognition of a distinguished poem that he had written, *CARPE DIEM? After Horace.*

His father sent it to Kirkpatrick, who commented, "It is an amazing performance for a boy of his age—indeed for a boy of any age."[15] A. F. Lace adds: "I think there is no doubt that it was being taught by Smugy that made life bearable for Lewis, and it was inevitable that he would have wanted to leave at the end of his year with him."

Jack never ceased to be grateful to Smugy. Once we went together to visit Smugy's old classroom. Jack stood for a long time in silence gazing at the large framed photograph and the commemorative plaque. When I spoke to him, he did not reply. Later he commented, "There are some experiences that paralyze you. You feel so much that you can't speak." Despite Jack's closeness to Smugy and the "periods of ecstasy" he experienced, he was deeply unhappy at Malvern. He wrote several letters asking to be removed, but it was not until he threatened to shoot himself that his father took his misery seriously. Warren, now training at the Royal Military College, Sandhurst, was distressed that his brother should not get on at the school where he had been so happy and recommended sending him to Kirkpatrick, who ran a small cramming school in Surrey. There he could let off "his little stock of intellectual fireworks under old Kirk's nose."[16] Albert regretted the need to take him away, for he had hoped that a public school education would help to break down the "morbid desire for isolation and seclusion" that Jack had inherited from him, but agreed that the risk made it necessary.[17]

Albert's comment may seem odd to many who knew the brothers in later life. Jack tended to suffer from loneliness and long for congenial company, whereas Warren developed in the opposite way, tending to withdraw from all social occasions or meetings with people whom he did not already know.

Kirkpatrick wrote accepting Jack in a letter that sounds almost like an advertisement for his tutoring: "We all know the Public Schools . . . turn out boys so completely moulded in the same pattern that they suggest productions from an automatic machine. Individuality is discouraged or rather finds it impossible to take root in such a soul. Yet the genius[18] of the younger Pitt was nursed in solitude."

On September 9, 1914, Jack went to study with Kirkpatrick at what was then the pleasant village of Great Bookham in Surrey.

5

Great Bookham

The two and a half years that Jack spent with Kirkpatrick were the most peaceful years of his entire life. His freedom at this time from emotional, academic, literary, and monetary pressures enabled him to discover his own tastes, the daily routine he liked to follow, the sort of friends he wanted, and the books he most enjoyed reading.

At Great Bookham, he was introduced to a routine that he would follow for the rest of his life. He arose at half past seven every day and spent a few minutes walking in the garden before breakfast. A substantial meal served at eight, breakfast consisted of porridge and a cooked dish, such as fried eggs and bacon, kippers, finnan haddock, or sausage, bacon, and tomato. To his delight, he found that Mrs. Kirkpatrick's "good Irish soda bread" was always served at breakfast. Work with Kirkpatrick began at a quarter after nine and continued until a cup of tea was served at eleven (Jack preferred strong India tea to coffee). Work would continue until lunch was served punctually at one. Then he was free for the afternoon "to read, write or moon about in the golden-tinted woods and vallies of this county."[1]

Afternoon tea, served at a quarter past four, was a social meal to which Mrs. Kirkpatrick might invite her neighbors. Jack enjoyed the tea but not the gossip. Sometimes, to avoid joining the conversation, he would claim to have important reading to do. Thinking it would have been "a kind of blasphemy" to read while other people were talking, he would excuse himself to read Lamb's essays perhaps or Boswell's *Life of Johnson* or *Tristram Shandy*. Mrs. Kirkpatrick might have thought Jack unsociable, but she was accustomed to similar behavior from her husband, an eccentric man who had no use for frivolous conversation. Like his tutor, Jack was disdainful of small talk; he made a lifelong practice of avoiding parties. Work resumed between five and seven and continued after dinner with a course of reading in English literature (although Jack needed no guidance in this). After nine he was free to write. The Narnia stories, the space-travel novels, and many of the religious books were written during evening hours when he was too tired for what he would have called serious work. In later life, he often spent an evening or two each week visiting with friends.

William T. Kirkpatrick (1848–1921) is almost the only person in *Surprised by Joy* whose physical appearance is described in detail. He was very tall, thin, and muscular. Much of his long, shrewd face was covered with gray hair, but his chin was clean shaven. He spent much of his time vegetable gardening and, perhaps because of this, usually wore very shabby and sometimes dirty clothes. His hands were, like MacPhee's in *That Hideous Strength*, "very large and coarse in texture,"[2] and, according to Warren, his fingernails were rarely clean. He smelled of tobacco, for he smoked a pipe, and he had the vile habit of resmoking remnants of tobacco that he had knocked out from previous pipefuls. He was proud of this and of many other economies.

His conversation, like his aroma, would not have suited everyone. He prided himself on being a rationalist and a logician; thus, the most ordinary or casual remark would be taken "as a summons to disputation."[3] Mrs. Kirkpatrick, a gentle woman of musical tastes, must have sometimes found him infuriating. He might walk in during one of her bridge parties and, no matter what the subject, ask the women to "clarify their terms."[4] As Warren once commented, "You could not say something about the weather without being pounced on." Jack discovered this upon his arrival at Great Bookham Station. When he remarked that the scenery of Surrey seemed wilder than he had expected, Kirkpatrick demanded to be told what he meant by wildness and on what he had based his expectations. Jack was soon obliged to agree that his remark was meaningless and that he had no right "to have any opinion whatever on the subject."

At first Jack was startled by Kirkpatrick's method—he had expected "dear old Knock," as his father often called him, to be sentimental and cuddly—but he soon revelled in such tests of logic, because he found that he could quite easily give as good as he got. His delight in Kirkpatrick's technique was such that he made it his own, and, after a couple of months of practice, he wrote to his father that "he really must expose the logical weakness of his position."[5] Although the sharp, priggish tone of his letters soon became less marked, he delighted in logical argument all his life. He even enjoyed setting technical traps for his opponents, some of whom enjoyed it. According to Bede Griffiths, one of Jack's first pupils at Magdalen College, Oxford, Jack and his good friend Owen Barfield went at it almost nonstop whenever they were together during the twenties and thirties. But, to some of his pupils, the method made him so formidable as to be inhibiting. Likewise not all seniors at Magdalen enjoyed his presence when he was in the mood to tear a casual remark to pieces.

Jack progressed rapidly in his studies. Kirkpatrick did not make the common mistake of doing too much of the work for his pupil, and his method of teaching suited Jack admirably. With his strongly guttural Ulster accent, Kirkpatrick would read about twenty lines of the *Iliad* or whatever work they were studying, translate about a hundred lines quickly and roughly, and then tell his pupil to go through it in detail with a grammar book and a dictionary, while he went back into the garden. At first Jack found it difficult in the time allotted to work through more than about twenty of the lines that the "grinder" had translated, but before long he was able to work through even more than had been read aloud. He found that he could think in Greek. (Years later in the 1950s he used the same method to help me brush up on my Italian. I learned a lot, but not, alas, to think in Italian.)

Of course, he studied much besides Homer. There was Virgil, whom he did not enjoy (does anyone before the age of thirty?); Lucretius, Catullus, Tacitus, and Herodotus; Cicero and Demosthenes (whom he calls "the Two Great Bores");[6] and the dramatists. He was taught French by Mrs. Kirkpatrick in much the same way as her husband taught Greek and, it seems, with as much success. He read in French works by Voltaire, Stendhal, Anatole France, Balzac, and many others. Toward the end of his time at Great Bookham, he learned Italian, beginning with Dante's *Inferno*. One of his regrets was that he did not stay long enough to master his German better. He took for granted his gift for languages. Once he said to me, "Ability in foreign languages is no criterion of intellectual ability. Think of the hotel porters and cook's men you have come across who can speak French and German really well."

Jack needed only enough guidance to teach himself, and he thrived under Kirkpatrick's tutelage. Whereas other boys might have found the dictionary and grammatical work tedious, Jack found it stimulating. When at work on, say, Homer, he let the heroic poetry shine through the language. "I can't resist telling you," he wrote to Arthur Greeves, "how stirring it is. Those fine, simple, euphonious lines, as they roll on with a roar like that of the ocean, strike a chord in one's mind that no modern literature approaches."[7]

Kirkpatrick did not share Jack's literary temperament. In fact, there is no evidence that he liked poetry at all. But, as his first report to Albert shows, he was quick to recognize Jack's talents:

> I do not think there can be much doubt as to the genuine and lasting quality of Clive's individual abilities. He was born with the literary temperament, and we have to face that fact with all that it implies. . . . [I]t is the maturity and originality of his literary judgements which is so unusual and surprising. By an unerring instinct he detects first rate quality in literary workmanship, and the second rate does not interest him in any way. Now you will observe that these endowments, in themselves remarkable, do not facilitate the work of the teacher. . . . The ideal pupil for University Scholarship purposes is a boy gifted with memory, receptiveness, patience, and strict attention to grammatical accuracy. . . . The fact is that a critical and original faculty, whatever may be its promise for the future, is as much a hindrance as a help in the drudgery of early classical training. Clive has ideas of his own, and is not at all the sort of boy to be made a mere receptive machine. . . . [8]

At Great Bookham, as at Malvern, Jack led a double life. With one faculty of his mind, he was logical and rational, thanks to Kirkpatrick's training. With another faculty, he was as intensely romantic as a young nineteenth-century poet, so romantic, in fact, that at times he feared his feelings would lead him into madness. Both faculties were of great importance, not only to his development, but also, when he eventually brought them into harmony, to his achievement as a creative writer and literary critic. We have an excellent account of the romantic Lewis in the letters that he wrote to Arthur Greeves between the summer of 1914, his last term at Malvern, and 1963, the year of his death.

Arthur Greeves grew up in a house called Bernagh almost opposite Little Lea on North Circular Road in the Strandtown area of Belfast. His father, Joseph Malcomson Greeves (1858—1925), who managed a prosperous linen firm, was tall and good-looking, but severe and humorless in expression. He bullied his five children unmercifully and treated his wife so harshly that she was often in tears. We are told in *The Lewis Papers* that Joseph Greeves "was timid, prim, sour, at once oppressed and oppressive." An uncompromising Plymouth Brother, he conducted frequent family prayer sessions, reading the same passages from the Bible and expounding the same explanations over and over again. Not surprisingly, he died unmourned. Albert Lewis described his funeral as the most cheerful he had ever attended.

Arthur's mother, Mary Gribbon (1861—1949), of Brooklyn, New York, was simple and warmhearted, but naive to the point of foolishness. "Sillier she was and sillier she became" after her husband's death. Though her conversation consisted largely of the attempt to tell stories and riddles, she never "reach[ed] the end of her anecdote without either missing the point or frankly breaking down. If stories ceased for a moment, she would talk about the Kaiser."[9] Indeed, she is an extreme example of the sort of conversationalist that Jack and Warren found especially unbearable.

Mary Gribbon was also inconsistent. She forbade her sons to drink whiskey (except Arthur, on whom she doted), but she herself usually drank a glass or two of wine every night at dinner.

All five children "had all been subjected to a baptism by total immersion *en masse* when the youngest was about twelve. It had been carried out in the bathroom where the young men, the young women, and the boys, in their bathing suits, had been plunged one by one in a bath of tepid water." We are told that the children abandoned their parents' religion. "[A]ll, except Willie, bore the ugly marks of ex-Puritanism—of those who are brought up in a crude antithesis of Grace and Nature, and who therefore, when they abandon the Grace straightway become startlingly natural. All revealed each passing sensation of greed, jealousy, anger, pleasure or disappointment in an almost savage nakedness."[10]

Of Arthur's sister Mary Elizabeth, or "Lily" (1888—1976), *The Lewis Papers* record that "she was beautiful in body but not in fact," and that although "she was the most selfish and unreasonable of the family . . . it was hard to dislike her." Of Arthur himself, Warren wrote: "He bears a remarkable resemblance to his sister Lily, even physically." Until he was overtaken by premature baldness, he was

a very good-looking man with the same golden hair and roses-and-cream complexion as Lily, and something of the same gestures and movements. . . . [L]ike Lily Arthur is as devoid of self-control as a child. "I want" is to him the ultimate and unanswerable justification of every line of conduct. The pains and frustrations of life present themselves to him in terms of the "nasty table hit me and hurt me." . . . [H]e has never been compelled to face the issues of life . . . has never had to earn his living. . . . [H]is character is the result of an accident of his youth—while he was still a boy, a Doctor diagnosed him as suffering from a weak heart, and by the time the diagnosis was disproved, he was already a confirmed valetudinarian. . . . [H]e was exempted from the discipline of school and preoccupations of a career, made into an invalid by his mother, whose favourite he is, and encouraged to float rudderless and motiveless down the years. . . . [He is] a talented fellow, a very fair musician, and a painter of more than usual amateur distinction; but he has never learnt—probably

never conceived—that even pleasure is not obtainable without drudgery. By pleasure I mean . . . that satisfaction which
is derived from the accomplishment of self-imposed task. . . .
[He is] much preoccupied with his health, and is constantly
discovering a new doctor who "really understands the case."
. . . [B]ut when the worst has been said of him, and when the
atmosphere of his home and the nature of his upbringing are
considered, the remarkable thing about Arthur is not that he
has faults, but that he has virtues . . . a genuine appreciation
for what is good in music and literature . . . a sense of beauty,
a love of the country and country things, a kindliness, and a
generosity which makes him an attractive person.[11]

The Lewis Papers record many examples of Arthur's bad and
childish manners (once he put his feet on the dining table while
others were still eating). Jack wrote in his diary, after discovering
that Arthur had borrowed his bicycle and was riding it "with his
knees coming up to his chin at every stroke of the pedal," that
"Arthur is an incorrigible baby after all." There were occasions,
too, when he "positively lost his temper" with Arthur. Arthur
was not clever—he was certainly incapable of the intellectual discussions that delighted Jack—and he took no pleasure in poetry.
Why then were Jack and Arthur intimate friends for nearly fifty
years?

What first brought the boys together was their discovery that
they shared something they thought of as a rare taste. Not long
before Jack left for his last term at Malvern, a message came
across the road from Bernagh that Arthur was in bed and would
like to see him. He hardly knew Arthur except by sight, partly
because Arthur was three years older, but mainly because he disliked and was bored by other members of the Greeves family. He
was astonished to find Arthur sitting up in bed with a copy of H.
A. Grueber's *Myths of the Norsemen*. They talked about it and

found that they both liked the same thing "and even the same parts of it and in the same way." For both, the arrow of joy was "shot from the North."[12]

Grueber's book has been neglected by students of Lewis. It is a large collection of Norse myths, well-printed and illustrated with, as the blurb puts it, "sixty-five exquisite full-page illustrations from important works of great artists."[13] (No one would rank the illustrations with those that Arthur Rackham had done for the story of Siegfried, but Jack was moved by some of them, such as those of Aslaug and The Ride of the Valkyrie.) The style is pedestrian, but it is brightened by quotations from translations of the Sagas, Eddas, and Lays, and from the Nordic work of English poets. There are few pages without generous quotations, and it is this characteristic that distinguishes the book from others.

Here Jack was introduced to William Morris and reintroduced to Matthew Arnold, both favorites for life. Some of the quotations became quite important to him—this passage, for instance, from Carlyle's *Heroes and Hero-Worship*: "To know the old Faith brings us into closer and clearer relation with the Past—with our own possessions in the Past. For the whole Past is the possession of the Present; the Past had always something true, and is a precious possession." He was thrilled by this passage from William Morris: "This is the great story of the North which should be to all our race what the Tale of Troy was to the Greeks—to all our race first, and afterwards, when the change of the world has made our race nothing more than a name of what has been—a story too—then should it be to those who come after us no less than the Tale of Troy has been to us."

"Northern mythology," Grueber tells on the first page, "is grand and tragical. Its principal theme is the perpetual struggle of the beneficial forces of Nature against the injurious, and hence it is not graceful and idyllic in character, like the religions of the sunny South. . . ."

Enthusiasm for Grueber caused Jack to buy another book in the same series, T. W. Rolleston's *Myths and Legends of the Celtic Race.* He never liked Celtic mythology as much as Norse, but he was influenced by it. Within a very short time he wrote to tell Arthur that he was planning a tragedy about Queen Maeve, and an allegorical story about the conflict between the light and beautiful Shee and their oppressors, the hideous and monstrous Formans. "The Formans could be taken as typical of the stern, ugly, money grubbing spirit, finally conquered by that of art and beauty, as exemplified by the lovely folk of the Shee."[14] Subsequent letters instruct Arthur about the life lived by the Shee in their fairy forts or underground dwellings. He writes, too, of the difficulty in finding a theme that is not too long for his Celtic narrative poem.

Jack was sensitive all his life to every sort of beauty, and he was attracted by Arthur's charm and striking good looks—his fair hair, fresh complexion, and blue eyes. I have been tempted to suppress this obvious fact, because I know it may encourage some people to speculate that they may have had a sexual relationship. However, I feel confident that they were not lovers. Although they confided to each other the sexual fantasies from which they both suffered, these fantasies did not involve each other. And while it is known that Arthur's older brother, John, among others, teased him for his delicacy (caused, no doubt, by his "weak heart"), there is no evidence that he was effeminate, except to the extent that all sensitive men have a feminine side.

They influenced each other in many different ways. Both enjoyed listening to the exposition of visions different from their own and despised the ordinary anecdotal conversation of others. They were both romantics, but while Jack's taste was for the strange, the remarkable, and the distant, Arthur was more interested in everyday sights. On their walks, Arthur appreciated things that Jack would hardly have regarded when alone. Whereas Jack might be absorbed in a cloud formation spiraling to heaven, Arthur would be concerned with the arrangement of plants in a nearby garden.

Jack guided Arthur in his reading, although he never succeeded in getting him to like poetry, and encouraged him in his composing and painting. It was because of Jack's influence that, from autumn 1921 to June 1923, Arthur studied at the Slade School of Fine Art in London.

Because of Arthur's enthusiasm, Jack read many of the classical English novels in his father's library that he had never thought of reading before. Many of these, such as the Waverley novels of Sir Walter Scott, were books he would enjoy for the rest of his life. He tells us that Arthur taught him to enjoy the domestic parts of *The Antiquary*, particularly the description of how Jonathan Oldbuck lived and what he ate. He, in turn, would teach many of his pupils to enjoy such things. He read the Jane Austen novels and in later life often reread them. His favorite was the quietest one, *Persuasion*. Arthur loved the Bronte novels, and by his influence so did Jack. He read them all at once and read them again in later life. Perhaps *Villette* was his favorite. He acquired, too, something of Arthur's habit of gloating over a single sentence, often the first in a novel. He once surprised me by his delight in the very domestic opening of Charlotte Yonge's *The Trial.* "Richard? That's right! Here's a tea-cup waiting for you."[15] He also came to enjoy other Victorian writers, such as Elizabeth Gaskell and Anthony Trollope.

Indeed, during the Great Bookham period, Jack was more open and responsive to Arthur's guidance than he was to anyone at all in later life, except his wife and Charles Williams. He wrote in October 1916 that he wanted to settle down to "some more books of the 'Cranford' type: your description has made me quite enthusiastic." In the same letter he reports that he has finished *The Antiquary* and asks which of Scott's novels he "should try next." Through following Arthur's advice, Jack became a far more complete reader and attained a far greater wholeness as a person than would otherwise have been likely.

Both boys were desperate for a friend. Each had family difficulties, Arthur living in a Philistine family that despised the things he thought most important in life, Jack having a father who, without meaning to be, was so dominant that he stifled Jack's individuality. Both benefited immensely from sharing their difficulties. Each needed and gave the other encouragement and the confidence to oppose Pudaitas and Forsytes (those who, like the characters in *The Forsyte Saga* by John Galsworthy, were mainly interested in wealth and social position) and to follow their own glimpses of truth.

They also confided to each other the personal problems of adolescence. Jack told Arthur about his sexual fantasies and his habit of masturbation (called "IT" or "THAT" in his letters to Arthur). Although Jack went through a period when he was rather sorry he had confided so much, he wrote in 1931 that he was inclined to agree with Arthur in not regretting it. Nevertheless, after Arthur had sent the letters to him so that Warren could use them in *The Lewis Papers*, Jack withdrew some of them, his reason being that they gave away some of Arthur's secrets as well as his own, and he did not want Warren to recall "such things." What things? Warren did not share the sado-masochistic tendencies of Jack's late teens, but he surely must have known of them. Whatever Jack's secrets, Arthur was an utterly safe confidant. He needed to be, for there was a period when Albert Lewis might search Arthur's room at Bernagh for letters from his son.

Both Jack and Arthur believed that loyalty is vital to friendship. They realized that their relationship was precious, and both were determined not to let it be permanently damaged by disagreements. They were, in fact, nearly always happy when together. Jack, who rarely spoke about his friend, told me before one of his last visits to Ireland, I think in 1956, that he was anxious about whether he would still be able to get along with Arthur. When I asked the reason, he said, "theological disagreements." Later he told me that after the first day they had gotten along splendidly, that it had been "just like old times."

In spite of suffering from some of the common troubles of adolescence, Jack was idyllically happy most of the time. He was beside himself with delight in some of the books that he discovered. The very first ones he mentions in letters to Arthur are the poems and Celtic plays of W. B. Yeats. Presumably the Kirkpatricks had copies, but that was never enough for Jack. "I must try to get it next time I am at home," he wrote.[16] Book buying was for him a lifelong habit. He knew that if he really liked a book, he would want to read it again and would find new delights in it when he did. He would, therefore, have to own it.

He felt that life without a copy of Malory's *Morte d'Arthur*, for instance, would be quite unbearable, and he wrote to Dents for their Everyman's Library edition. His critical comments on Malory reveal his maturity. Although the book opened a new world to him, he felt that Malory was not a great author; rather, the book was great because it was based on genuine folklore. "Malory has the gift of lively narrative and," he wrote to Arthur, "the power of getting you to know characters by gradual association." Although Malory never sits down to describe a man's character, by the end of the first volume, Lancelot, Tristan, Belin, and Pellinore are "real life people." Even the names of the chapters, such as "How Launcelot in the Chapel Perilous got a cloth from a dead corpse," bear with them a fresh sweet breath from the old-time faerie world wherein the author moves.[17]

After the Easter holidays of 1915, Jack began his letters to Arthur with the address "Dear Galahad," or "My Dear Galahad," and once, "My Furious Galahad." He used the form of address until the summer of 1918. Why did he start? In spite of the expurgations of the letters, it is not difficult to know the reason, thanks to the resourceful way in which Walter Hooper has restored the sentences that have been crossed out.

The answer is found in Jack's letter of June 1, 1915. He is discussing a letter in which Arthur had mentioned attacks of sensuality. It becomes clear that Jack had previously told Arthur of a period of extreme sensuality, and that Arthur had not understood, presumably because he did not at that time masturbate or fantasize. Jack, therefore, nicknamed him Galahad, "whose strength is as the strength of ten, because your heart is pure."[18] Jack is surprised at Arthur's sensuality, thinking that, since he is three years older than Jack, he ought to be past it. Of course, it does not enter his mind that his own conversations may have been the impetus of Arthur's sensuality.

It took Arthur some time to understand what Jack meant by "the sensuality of cruelty," which was a subject of his fantasies for years. In a letter of January 1917, he compares himself to William Morris, remarking that he often thinks Morris must have been "a special devotee of the rod." To support this thought, he points to an idea from *The Well at the World's End* that it is better to possess slave-girls than wives "so long as the twigs smart and the ships sting." Later in the same letter, he writes of the enjoyment he could get from punishing a female member of the Greeves family, probably Arthur's sister Lily. By

February 1917, he was writing quite explicit letters. Not surprisingly, Arthur did not share his love of the rod.

Jack makes it clear that his "physical feelings" are raised by the thought of the whip. One of his letters is signed "J. Philom.," an abbreviation for *philomastix*, the Greek for "lover of the whip." He records his pleasure in reading the flagellant passages in Rousseau's *Confessions* and notes, "His taste is altogether for suffering rather than inflicting: which I can feel too, but it is a feeling more proper to the other sex."[19] The objects of Jack's flagellant fancies seem always to be beautiful women, but in June 1917, while up at Keble College, Oxford, he became drunk for the first time in his life and went around imploring the other men there to let him whip them for a shilling a lash.

There is no sign that he felt guilt or shame in making these confessions to Arthur, whom he accuses of being a prude. In later life, when he discussed the sins of his youth, he stressed that he felt no guilt at all. Yet, as a mature critic, when he noticed sadomasochism in other authors—and he was, as one would expect, quick to do so—he regarded it as reprehensible. He leveled such a charge at E. R. Eddison and at Naomi Mitchison, who he told me was "a sophisticated and highly self-conscious woman perfectly aware of the nature of what she is feeling."

It is easy to identify elements that contributed to the development of Jack's sadomasochistic tendencies, most notably that he was forced to witness countless beatings at Wynyard. He has left us with an all too vivid description of the punishment of "poor P.,"[20] and we know that at a very early age he was aroused by scenes of cruelty in his reading. The loss of his mother when he was still quite young may also have contributed. Perhaps her death caused him to feel betrayed and led to a subconscious desire to humiliate women. But such theories are a matter for psychologists to argue. Jack's extraordinary sensibility put him at the mercy of good as well as evil experiences. At Malvern, by his own admission, and one suspects even earlier, at Cherbourg, he had managed to live a double life of squalor and ecstasy. The dichotomy continued at Great Bookham and for years afterward. His fantasies of self-indulgent cruelty did not prevent him from being open to the highest influences. Though he could not have put a name to it, he was aware of holiness.

In his copy of Yeats's *Poems*, there is an interesting passage underlined: "There can be no language more worthy of poetry and of the meditation of the soul than that which has been made, or can be made, out of a subtlety of desire, an emotion of sacrifice, a delight in order, that are perhaps Christian, and myths and images that mirror the energies of woods and streams, and their wild creatures."[21] In later life, Jack was an indefatigable underliner of passages of which he approved, but he did not often do it during the Great Bookham period. His underlining this passage suggests that he was, to some degree, open to Christianity.

The writer who most influenced Jack in his journey toward Christianity was the Aberdeenshire minister George MacDonald (1824–1905). Jack found his book *Phantastes* at the book shop in Great Bookham Station and paid one shilling and one penny for it. He read it with intense delight and wrote at once to Arthur, describing it as "a great literary experience."[22] He had no idea then that it was also a spiritual experience. Not until years later did he call it "Holiness."[23]

MacDonald sees divinity in most things. His story is dream-like and otherworldly, and his descriptions shimmer with insight. While Jack appreciated the beauty of MacDonald's writing, he was most influenced, at a subconscious level, by the symbolism. A list of the themes of *Phantastes* would read like chapter headings to a book by Carl Jung. Indeed, one often wonders if Jung knew the book and was influenced by it. Thus Anodos, the hero of *Phantastes*, is pursued by a shadow, a baleful influence that is both outside him and in his mind.

> Everything, henceforward, existed for me in its relation to my attendant. . . . I lay down to rest in a most delightful part of the forest, carpeted with wild flowers.
>
> I lay for half an hour in a dull repose, and then got up to pursue my way. The flowers on the spot where I had lain were crushed to the earth: but I saw that they would soon lift their heads and rejoice again in the sun and air. Not so those on which my shadow had lain. The very outline of it could be traced in the withered lifeless grass, and the scorched and shrivelled flowers which stood there, dead and hopeless of any resurrection.[24]

Anodos's quest is for the feminine, as would be that of Dymer, the hero of the major poem Lewis was to write. He meets several women, good and evil. He finds one in a cave, another in a block of marble, the outer parts of which he has patiently chipped away. He embraces another who turns out to be an evil destroyer. One story made a deep impression on Jack: Cosmo, a highly imaginative student, buys from an antique dealer an ancient mirror in which he sees the image of a beautiful lady. He is obsessed by her with a love that "withered into a passion." Jack read this story, which ends in death, at least three times. In fact, there was a period when he read MacDonald almost as often as Cosmo gazed into the mirror. But though the main subject of *Phantastes* is death, the book had a life-enhancing effect on him. He linked the experience with his memory of the two holy people he had known as a child: "For the first time the song of the sirens sounded like the voice of my mother or my nurse."[25]

The influence of *Phantastes* on Jack lasted for many years, perhaps all his life. Because it was greatest at psychic depths of which he was only partly aware, he was at a loss to give a clear account of it. He was aware that it purified his imagination, making all his erotic and magical perversions of joy appear sordid and unworthy. More surprisingly, it had a transforming influence on his attitude toward the ordinary, common things around him, imbuing them with its own spiritual quality.

Strangely, the only other work by MacDonald that he read at Great Bookham was his wonderful children's story, "The Golden Key." It was "absolute heaven from the moment Tangle ran into the wood. . . ."[26] Several years were to pass before he read *A Diary of An Old Soul*, *Lilith*, and *Unspoken Sermons*, and was influenced by them as profoundly as a man can be influenced by his reading.

During this period, Jack read many books that became favorites for life. He enjoyed the romanticism of the early nineteenth century, and he loved the wild, the strange, and the unearthly. He liked *The Crock of Gold*, by James Stephens, so much that, after he had finished it, he found it difficult to decide whether it or *Phantastes* was the finer book. A faerie extravaganza containing whimsical humor shot through with wisdom and flashes of beauty, it "ends in an ecstasy that has about it a touch of Borrow and a note from the very flute of Pan." As soon as he could afford them, he bought copies of Stephens's other books, *The Demi-Gods* and *The Charwoman's Daughter*. He read much Swinburne and mapped out a course of reading in Swinburne for Arthur. To this unfashionable taste he remained loyal. In later life, he sometimes said that Swinburne's fault was not that he was deficient in meaning, the usual criticism, but that he was too rich, almost overwhelmingly rich in meaning.

He read at Great Bookham two of the subjects of his finest mature literary criticism: Spenser's *Faerie Queene*, which he read in one sitting, regretting that it was not longer; and Sidney's

Arcadia, "a glorious feast."[27] When he had become a tutor, there was no book he rated more highly or recommended more often to his pupils than *Arcadia*.

The works of William Morris, especially *The Well at the World's End* and *The Life and Death of Jason*, were also favorites. In those days, he was rather concerned with the physical format of his books, a taste that he had perhaps acquired from Arthur, and he took pleasure in collecting Morris in the neat little dark green cloth edition published by Longmans Green in its Pocket Library. Later he bought Morris's complete works in a sumptuous library edition, but even though shelf space was extremely short, he never parted with those little dark green volumes.

He read Milton's *Comus* with great enjoyment, loved Keats, especially his *Endymion*, and Shelley, whose *Prometheus Unbound* he found more "wild and out of the world than any poem I have read," although it was spoiled, he thought, by carelessness in meter, rhyme, and choice of words. He read *The Pilgrim's Progress* twice at Great Bookham and was "awfully bucked" by it (of course, he read it as a story and probably had no interest in its doctrine).[28] The earlier literature he enjoyed included *Sir Gawain and the Green Knight* and *The Canterbury Tales*. He complained to Arthur of Chaucer's garrulity and coarseness, although he liked the two tales that he would rate most highly twenty or thirty years later, the Knight's and the Franklin's. He read Milton's *Paradise Lost* with keen appreciation. By and large, he formed his literary tastes in his teens and hardly altered them. Even then he had an astonishing gift for distinguishing the best from the second-rate.

Jack did all he could to encourage and help Arthur in developing his interests in painting, composing, and writing. He suggested that Arthur should compose the music for the opera libretto he had written, *Loki Bound*. He also encouraged Arthur in his desire to provide illustrations by suggesting suitable subjects.

Loki Bound was a tribute both to Jack's love of Norse mythology and to his study of the Greek dramatists. The Norse story came from his reading of Grueber; and such characters as Odin, Thor, Freya, and the giant Fasold were familiar to him from Wagnerian opera. But the form was strictly Aristotelian, with a *prologos*, a *parodos*, three *episodes*, and an *exodos*. The plot is given in detail in a letter he wrote to Arthur in October 1914 (probably the letter of October 6, but one is often unsure of the dates of Jack's letters): Loki is a clever and cunning boy who is enslaved to Odin. The opera traces his rebellion against the injustice of Odin and other gods.

Jack realized later that his motive in writing *Loki Bound* was probably his loathing of the School House prefects, and that he, or part of him, was Loki. The characterization is therefore interesting. Loki is proud, defiant, scornful, self-righteous, cunning, and resourceful, in fact, very like Jack's view of Milton's Satan. He covers up his real character and motives with a mask of hypocrisy. When alone, he sometimes shows his real feelings in outbursts of angry cursing. Unfortunately, little of the work survives. The theme haunted Jack until the publication of *Dymer* in 1926.

Jack also wrote part of a prose romance called "Bleheris," the story of a young knight in armor who sets out to prove himself by a quest in the evil and bitter north for a person called Striver. Accompanied by a dwarf and a squire called Nut, he comes, after a fearful visit to the Sunken Wood, to the Hostel of the Crossways. Here they meet three men: Gerce, a tall, strong man who can see things that others cannot; Wan Jadis, a handsome young man with half-closed eyes who seems to dream of some old, sad memory; Hyperetes, a mighty man with a golden beard who regards Bleheris with joy and offers him fellowship.

Gerce explains that he seeks for tomorrow, Wan Jadis that he seeks for yesterday. When accused of being a sorcerer, Hyperetes answers, "I am but the servant of him they call the Striver, to do his will and call men unto him." Though he is sure that, deep in his heart, Bleheris desires "him who strives," Hyperetes allows him to go off with Wan Jadis in the direction of Mothlight. Led by Wan Jadis, Bleheris comes to Things Passed, a land of "soft mists and trees that ever shed their leaves in the drowsy winds." There they meet three great literary heroines, Helen, Isolde, and Guenevere, "deathless forever in their sorrows and loveliness as the ancient singers made them." They travel westward until they find moored to a rose bush in an autumnal place a little boat (called a "shallop") that will take them to Yesterday. Just after they have embarked, terrifying shadows appear from across the water, the shallop sinks, Wan Jadis dies, and Bleheris is left sinking in mud or quicksand. But the Rose Bush put its arms around him and drew him back, in the process burying some thorns in his arms. He still feels that he is really journeying toward the Striver, but, when he buries his face in the rose petals, "his old childish love" returns to him, the bush vanishes, and in its place stands a beautiful woman whose manacled arms are stretched toward him. Then this vision vanishes.

A good deal later on, Gerce and Hyperetes come back into the story. Gerce suggests that it is the Rose, not Striver, who is drawing Bleheris on. All the same, argues Hyperetes, "many come to him by way of the Rose, or rather they so used ere she was led captive." When they get to the "city of the King," a great white city, Gerce quarrels with Bleheris by sneering at his God. Swords are drawn, but they are reconciled by Hyperetes, who helps them to realize that they both love Striver and his servants.

In the city there is a Christian cathedral with a temple to Odin by its side. There Christians and heathens live in peace together, "being too thoroughly busy in their daily life to waste their strength in shadowy things."[29]

Though unfinished, the story is easy to interpret. Its allegory and symbolism seem to relate to almost every event in Jack's life, but it is most obviously a quest for the deity and for the feminine, the two not necessarily at variance with each other. However, Jack may have been unaware of this. In a letter to Arthur, he wrote that the inner meaning would, if discovered, not please Arthur as a Christian. It was not Christianity itself that he was sneering at, but "Christianity as taught by a formal old priest like Ulfin [Bleheris's tutor, or spiritual director], and accepted by a rather priggish young man like Bleheris."[30]

This attack on the formal, legalistic religion that the churches have often made of Christianity has been enlivened by many young Christians who would also attack the strife between different Christian sects and state that the heathen and Christian religions serve the same God (to mention two other obvious themes of "Bleheris"). What is surprising about the play is that it is, in some respects, Christian. For instance, it is not difficult to regard the golden-bearded Hyperetes as a Christ figure. Jack uses phrases that occur in some translations of Saint Matthew's gospel to describe him: He is "the servant of him they call the Striver to do his will and draw men unto him." Yet at about the time that Jack was writing "Bleheris," he was describing himself as an atheist.

Arthur sometimes asked Jack about his religion. In response, Jack wrote two letters in which he attacked Christianity and all other religions on conventionally rational and anthropological grounds—he had read *The Golden Bough* and Lang's *Myth, Ritual, and Religion* and had no doubt discussed them with his atheist tutor. He writes that he believes in no religion because there is no proof of any and that religions should be called mythologies. They are human inventions, Christ as much as Loki. He describes, entirely conventionally, how man deified natural forces such as the sun and the wind. Great men, too, are regarded as gods. "Thus after the death of the Hebrew philosopher Yeshua (whose name we have corrupted into Jesus) he became regarded as a God," and a cult grew up. In every age thinking people have been emancipated from superstitious beliefs such as this, "though usually outwardly conceding it for convenience."[31] Perhaps in this phrase he is thinking of the way he went to church with his father when he was at home and of how he had traveled from Surrey to Belfast just to be confirmed when he was a nonbeliever. In later life, he was ashamed of this insincerity.

Of course, religious ideas don't "make any difference to morals"; we owe it to our manhood to be "honest, chaste, truthful, etc." Something may exist outside the material world—"any thing MAY exist." The universe is an absolute mystery that he wants to understand, but, until he has, he will not go "back to the bondage of believing in any old . . . superstition." He is quite prepared to live without belief in a "bogey who is going to torture me forever," if he should fail in living up to "an almost impossible ideal." The Christian God is "a spirit more cruel and barbarous than any man."[32]

The contrast between these rationalistic views and those implicit in the imaginative world of "Bleheris" is striking. Jack was still very much a divided person. The logical method that he had learned from Kirkpatrick served to protect him from an excess of romantic sensibility. Without it, he might have become too wayward and undisciplined to gain an Oxford scholarship in classics. The books he read and his own writing were far more real and important to him than the ordinary events of life. He was often carried away by music, painting, and pictures in his own mind. He had so many and such wild interests that there was a real risk of dissipating his talents; he even feared madness. To all this, Kirkpatrick was a valuable antidote. The strong feeling for academic logic that Jack had inherited from his mother made it easy for him to enjoy his methods.

The "grinder" had no doubt of Jack's ability to get an Oxford award, in spite of a weakness in history and an almost total ignorance of science. "I do not look on Clive as a schoolboy," he wrote to Albert on April 7, 1916. "The very idea of urging or stimulating him to increased exertion makes me smile. Rather have I had to act in the contrary direction, and to remind him that I find it inadvisable for him to read after 11 p.m. If he were not blessed with such a store of physical health and strength, he would surely grow weary now and then. But he never does. . . . [H]e has read more classics . . . than any I ever heard of, unless it be an Addison, or Landor, or Macaulay."[33]

A month later he writes that Jack will probably gain an award in classics in any of the Oxford colleges, although he "knows nothing of science and loathes it and all its works."[34] Unfortunately, he would become liable for military service a month after entering Oxford. The only way out of this would be to go, not to Oxford, but to a university in Ireland, where there was no conscription. However, as Albert wrote, "Clive has decided to serve in the War, but he also wishes to try his fortunes at Oxford."[35] Albert feared and hated the prospect of having a second son at the western front.

A possible alternative would have been for Jack to work in an English munitions factory, but, as Kirkpatrick wrote, this would hardly have done, for "handling tools of any kind is so utterly alien to his temperament that I cannot conceive him at such a job."[36] (All his life, Jack was incapable of doing simple household repairs, and, in spite of his many attempts, he never succeeded in learning to drive a car.)

On December 4, 1916, Jack went to Oxford to take an entrance scholarship exam in classics. On the entrance form, he named Malvern College as his place of education, probably because he thought it would have gone against him if he had stated that, for two years, he had been staying in the house of a crammer. When Warren later asked him how this came about, Jack claimed responsibility and asked his brother not to tell their father. He feared that it might get back to Kirkpatrick, who might even denounce it as a lie. He added, "I have now got to that stage when I am beginning to sentimentalize about the Coll[ege]."[37]

His first taste of Oxford is described in amusing detail in *Surprised by Joy*. After a day there, he wrote enthusiastically to his father: "The place has surpassed my wildest dreams. I never saw anything so beautiful."[38] However, diffidence and inexperience gave him the impression he was doing badly in his exam. Kirkpatrick thought so, too, and wrote to Albert that "Clive could hardly have been more unfortunate in the papers. He was not assigned to write about any of the Greek or Latin authors he knew best, and, Kirkpatrick said, "the German was quite impossible . . . a poem of Goethe which I could hardly make into any sense myself."[39] His father's sympathy and kindness when he went home and said that he thought he had failed was touching.

But, as often, his characteristic pessimism misled him. On December 19, Albert received a letter from R. W. Macan, master of University College, Oxford, to say that, although New College, his college of first choice, had passed him over, his second choice, University College, had awarded him the second of their three open scholarships for classics. By coincidence, the two men who were to become his closest Oxford friends, Owen

Barfield at Wadham and A. C. Harwood at Christ Church, were elected to scholarships at the same time.

Like much else at Oxford, the entrance procedure is odd. Although Jack's scholarship, a much coveted distinction, entitled him to free rooms in his college and a grant of money toward his expenses there, it did not give him entrance to the university itself (his college was a semi-independent unit of Oxford). To gain admission to Oxford, he would have to pass a separate exam called "Responsions." So after a holiday at Little Lea, during which he read Hawthorne (whom he much admired), Aeschylus, Arnold Bennett, Edward Fitzgerald, Robert Bridges, Newman's *Apologia*, Catullus, Herrick, Apollonius, Maeterlinck, Sir Thomas More, Tennyson, Mangan, and several other writers, he returned toward the end of January to Kirkpatrick to prepare for the exam. For most boys of scholarship standard, Responsions was little more than a formality, an exam for which it was not necessary to work. But this was not true in Jack's case. The exam included mathematics, the subject at which he was abysmally weak. Nor was Kirkpatrick much good at teaching it to him. He had little insight into Jack's difficulties with math, and, rather than sitting by his pupil's side and working through his problems, he allowed Jack to do too many other things.

Jack enjoyed learning Italian, for him a far easier language than German, and, almost as soon as he took it up, he began to read Dante with intense delight. His love for *The Divine Comedy* was lifelong. Of all poets, he thought Dante the most sublime and considered the *Paradiso* the summit of European literary achievement.

Though the Kirkpatricks taught him to read French and Italian fluently, they paid little attention to the way he read it. All his life, he read and spoke these languages with a strong English accent, and, in this respect, he never attempted to improve.

Except during the First World War and on the occasion of his visit to Greece many years later with Joy Davidman and Roger Green, he never traveled abroad at all. Warren was equally insular; he wrote a succession of brilliant books about the France of Louis XIV without ever having visited Versailles.

Jack's main motive for studying Italian was, however, to provide a career should his weakness in math prevent him from getting into Oxford. If his plan of entering Oxford fell through and he was reduced to "something desperate like trying for the Foreign Office, he would have three modern languages in his pocket."[40]

After about a week in Great Bookham, on January 28, he was summoned to the master of University College for an interview. "He was a clean shaven, white haired, jolly old man, and was very nice indeed," Jack wrote. "He treated me to about half an hour's Oxford manner." He was told that if he passed Responsions in March, he could come up for the summer term and join the Officer's Training Corps. This plan would give him the best chance of getting a commission.[41]

He took Responsions on March 20 and 21 and afterward spent a month in Belfast. There his main literary activity was his work on *Metrical Meditations*, a collection that grew to fifty-two short poems that he had begun writing on Easter 1915. He copied them into an old Malvern College divinity exercise book, a relic of his days under Smugy. According to Warren, he now "added no fewer than ten pieces; of these, four were published as then written, two were published in an altered form, and four remained unpublished."[42]

He also worked on a prose version of the poem that was eventually published as *Dymer*, and on one entitled *The Childhood of Medea*. The latter was going to leave off shortly after Medea's meeting with Jason, where most poems about her began. It would depict her as a lonely frightened girl living "in a castle with the terrible old king, her father, and how she is gradually made to learn magic against her will."[43] He felt the subject was well suited to the form of a poem or even a prose romance. It is written in the same meter as that of *The Life and Death of Jason*, although he was trying not to imitate Morris.

Jack had not expected to be allowed to go into residence at Oxford before the start of the academic year in October 1917. He was therefore delighted to receive a letter from his college informing him that he could come up on April 26 for the start of the summer term. His father wrote to Warren: "We have received a list of the things he is required to take with him to furnish his rooms."[44] Naturally, they assumed that he had passed Responsions. But it was not so. He had failed the math paper. Kirkpatrick suggested that the examiners "have taken a sort of malicious pleasure in teaching a University Scholar the lesson that he must not consider himself above accuracy in doing elementary maths." Jack "looks on it all with contempt," he said. "It is a way with literary men. . . ." He forecasted that Jack would "get thro' easily next time."[45] But he was wrong. Jack failed the exam when he took it again in June and, in fact, never passed it. He was allowed to attend Oxford after the war only because the passing of Responsions was waived for men who had been in the service. If it had not been for this piece of academic generosity, Jack would probably never have passed and never been able to make a career at Oxford or any other British university.

Nevertheless, the college allowed him to come up to study for the exam and to enter the O.T.C. His notebook entry of April 28 reads: "Matriculated. College Library. Entered name in Coll. books."[46] His Oxford career had begun.

6

Into Battle

Jack's letters from Great Bookham to Arthur Greeves and to his father show almost as little awareness of the Great War of 1914–18 as Jane Austen's novels show of the Napoleonic Wars of a hundred years earlier. One reason was certainly that, for people who lived in Ireland, especially Northern Ireland, the Irish political and military situation seemed much more critical than the campaign on the continent of Europe. In 1914 Ireland was on the verge of civil war. Structurally, the country still consisted mainly of a native Irish population dominated by an artificially planted, and basically English, landowning hierarchy. In the north of the country, especially in County Antrim and County Down, there were also many immigrants, both landowners and tenantry, from the Scottish lowlands. In both north and south (there was then no political division between the two), the native Irish population was Roman Catholic, economically poor, and, to some extent, still dependent on the potato crop.

The Irish have notoriously long memories, and they did not forget that in the 1840s when the potatoes rotted in the ground because of a blight that had just crossed the Atlantic, many thousands died of starvation or were forced to emigrate. Memory of the famine and of other misfortunes intensified the demand of the impoverished majority for a greater share in the economic wealth of the country and for home rule. The group of Irish M.P.s (members of Parliament) in the British House of Commons had tended at times to hold the balance of power between the Liberal and Conservative parties. This eventually led to the conversion of Gladstone to home rule and the introduction in 1886 of a home rule bill, which was, however, defeated by a combination of the Orangemen in the north of Ireland and the Conservative party in the rest of Britain. When another home rule bill was introduced in 1912, the Irish Republican Brotherhood planned a revolutionary uprising. On Easter Monday 1916, they established a provisional republican government in Dublin, which was subsequently suppressed in about a week.

The danger of insurrection and civil war continued and forced the British government to keep an army in Ireland. Unlike the rest of Britain, Ireland was never at war with Germany, nor was there ever compulsory military service there.

Jack could have avoided military service if he had gone to an Irish university, but no Irish university had the glamour of Oxford, and worse, going to one might mean he would have to live at home. Perhaps, too, Warren's patriotism had some influence on him.

After a term of cramming under Kirkpatrick, Warren had won one of the twenty-five prize cadetships awarded each year at the Royal Military College at Sandhurst and was before long made a second lieutenant in the Royal Army Service Corps. He was not as happy at Sandhurst as at Malvern College and wrote to his father comparing it unfavorably. He found the chapel services "very shoddy." and the intellectual atmosphere appallingly shallow. "Here the only subjects of conversation are Women—cards—theatres—athletics—racing AND the service. . . ." Soon after the outbreak of war, he wrote of his eagerness "to kill some Germans," so that, should he become a casualty, he might have his name enrolled in "the gleam of yonder brass" in Malvern College chapel.[1]

By November 1914, he was with the British Expeditionary Force in Le Havre, wishing he had worked harder at French while at Malvern College. He moved toward the front and settled down in the mud and drizzling rain of a French winter. He made a friend, a brother officer called Collins, with whom he could talk about some of the essential things of life. With "whiskey on the table, the kettle on the hob, and our pipes drawing evenly," their talk would range over the whole field of English literature, the conversation "gradually widening into a reconstruction of the post-war heaven" that would be built after they had won the war.

But the whole winter was not as cozy as this. Life in the army was neither easy nor safe. It was not long before a twelve-inch shell burst thirty yards away from Warren, cutting trees through as cleanly as if it had been a circular saw and knocking everybody down into the mud. Perhaps it was at this point that he began to drink too much whiskey, drifting into the alcoholism that was his bane for the rest of his life.

On April 26, 1917, nearly all those who would normally have been students were in the army when Jack, loaded with pillowcases, sheets, towels, tablecloths, dusters, knives, forks, and all else that he had been told to bring, arrived at University College, Oxford. He described his reception and first impressions in a vivid letter to Arthur. The sandy-haired porter shouted for the underporter, "Jo," who took his bags and led him up "three very bare noisy flights of stairs, between stone walls, dark with tiny windows"; and stopped before the "oak," the traditional massive outer door of an Oxford set of rooms, which could be "sported" or shut when the occupant did not want to be disturbed. He was amazed by the suite. The sitting room was larger than his father's study at home; the furniture was dark and richly carved and seemed to him probably very valuable; there was a carpet and a "profusion of rugs."[2]

These turned out to be the wrong rooms. They were those of "a tremendous blood" who was at the front. But his rooms (the fifth set of rooms on staircase number twelve of the front quad of University College) were also delightful. The furniture included a grand piano ("Couldn't we have great times, ami?" he remarked to Arthur). He liked sitting in his rooms in the evening when the fire was burning brightly and he could boil a kettle ("How I love kettles!") to make the tea that was for him already a habit.[3] Dinner was served in a small lecture room, and other meals, except afternoon tea, which he had to make himself, were carried to his room by the staircase servant, called the "scout" at Oxford.

One whole quad of the college was occupied by wounded soldiers, with a staff of nurses to care for them. The atmosphere of the place was more military than academic. Thus the dean of the college declined to map out a course of studies for him because he would very soon be in the O.T.C. (Officer's Training Corps) and have no time for anything else. However, the bursar of his college found him a math coach, "a very pleasant Scotsman," J. E. Campbell of Hertford College.[4] Campbell had Belfast associations and knew Jane McNeil, a friend of the Lewis family.

Of the twelve undergraduates in the college, only two others were freshmen. One of them, Edgell, seemed to spend a good deal of time in Jack's room, in spite of the fact that they did not get along very well. Jack found Edgell's ignorance of books and his limitless piety hard to endure. Edgell lectured Jack on his "weakness of character" and was "economical and methodical to the verge of insanity."[5]

In spite of Edgell's harangues and the O.T.C. training that often made him very tired, Jack was soon writing that he had never been so happy in his life. He enthusiastically described an early-morning swim. It was a lovely morning with a deep blue sky, "all the towers and pinnacles gleaming in the sun and bells ringing everywhere." They set out on borrowed bicycles for the swimming hole called "Parson's Pleasure" and swam "without the tiresome convention of bathing things," surrounded by "those level daisied and buttercupped fields and overhung by those short, fluffy trees—name, I don't know."[6] This passage introduces us to two more of Jack's characteristics. Throughout his life, he loved to go skinny-dipping, and, although he loved nature, he was forever ignorant of the names of plants and trees.

Jack joined the Union, Oxford University's debating society and club, and particularly enjoyed the library, not merely because of its books, but because of the paintings high up on the walls done by William Morris, Arthur Hughes, Sir Edward Burne Jones, and Dante Gabriel Rossetti. He would already have known and liked the work of Arthur Hughes, the illustrator of George MacDonald's books.

He wrote at some length about his friends, including a man called Edwards, who had "rather an unpleasant accent," but who interested him because he had, until recently, been an atheist but was "now engaged in becoming a Catholic or is very near it." He keenly enjoyed late-night talks ("How I like talking!") about every subject under the sun, mainly serious ones, that are typical of Oxford and perhaps of all university life.

Even when he was in the O.T.C., his days were still pleasant. He was called by his scout at seven so that he could tramp down to the parks for an early parade before a bath and breakfast at a quarter till nine. He worked until one, but had to march in the afternoon from two until four. Then he was free for the rest of the day. He usually went to the river for a swim, read until dinner at seven, and after dinner worked "mildly" or talked, or played cards, or sometimes went for a bicycle ride.

He wrote to his father that "the Corps proves very much more agreeable than the Malvern one—everyone is so friendly and reasonable." Although "a huge mass of military" were encamped in Oxford, the Oxford University O.T.C. was quite small. Most of the others were cadets from other O.T.C.s sent to train for commissions. Jack writes scornfully of them, as most Oxford freshmen straight from public school would: "They are rather a bad lot, and certainly an ill-bred lot, especially the Flying Corps."[7]

His presence in the O.T.C. worried Albert: "It is the beginning of his military career and the prospect covers me like a pall." He had wanted Jack to apply to join the Army Service Corps where Warren was and which Albert, in his ignorance, supposed to be safe. He was distressed that Jack wanted, for "some fanciful reason of his own," to serve in a still more dangerous branch of the army. "Consequently it is almost certain that he will be rushed into the Infantry, either with a commission or in the ranks. I wonder how long 'IT' [Jack] would last as a ranker in the trenches."[8] But Jack was also doing some things of which his father wholeheartedly approved. He was learning to row, and "that is the very best exercise for putting a chest on a man."[9]

Jack's letters to his father suggest that he was living the life of a good practicing Christian, going to church or college chapel every Sunday. But there is no mention of this in the description of a typical Sunday that he sent to Arthur on May 13. He began work at seven, read until half past eight, took hot and cold baths, had a leisurely breakfast with his new friends at the invitation of T. R. F. Butler, a "very senior man" whose company he liked, went for a swim at Parson's Pleasure and then to the Union for the rest of the morning. Of course, these activities left no time for college chapel. He must already have been deceiving his father about this.

In spite of the military service before him, he wrote blissful letters from the university: "Oh, Galahad, you simply must come up after the war. This at present is only a shadow of the real Oxford, yet even so I never was happier in my life. Do make an effort!"[10] He wrote happily to Arthur of the Thames Valley scenery, with its two rivers and tall poplars, "all beautifully fresh and green and sleepy."[11]

He was not able to stay very long in his delightful rooms at University College. "Jack's career as an undergraduate has come to an end," Albert wrote to Warren, "in my view very harshly and unjustly. He has not been at the University eight weeks. . . . Yet after four weeks and with only a few drills in the O.T.C. he has to leave his College and join a cadet Battalion in training with a view to obtaining a Commission."[12]

He was put into "a carpetless little cell" at Keble College, Oxford, with little furniture, apart from two beds on which he and his roommate had to sleep without sheets or pillows. Still, there were several "gentlemen" in the cadet battalion, and he was lucky in having one as his roommate. Considering that he had spent only one year at a public school (Malvern) and, as he had not yet passed Responsions in mathematics, was not yet a member of the university, his letter about his fellow cadets is snobbish and condescending. He divided them into three groups. The largest group, "rankers," were men who had been at the front and had come back to England to get commissions. They were, for the most part, "jolly good chaps, clean, honest, infinitely good natured," but their "naive conceptions of how gentlemen behave among themselves [would] lead them into an impossible politeness that is really very pathetic." The next group consisted of "cads and fools," some vicious, some doltish, "all vulgar and uninteresting." "They drop their h's, spit on the stairs." His own set consisted of "public school and varsity men," and his "chief friend" was a scholar of Eton and King's College, Cambridge, who, though very quiet, was "very booky and interesting."[13]

This letter contains the first mention of "Paddy" Moore (Edward Francis Courtenay Moore, 1898–1918), his roommate, who, with his mother and sister, was to have a great influence on him. He is described as a "good fellow," but at this stage "a little too childish for real companionship." A letter written a few days later shows that Jack had already revised his opinion of his roommate: "Moore is a very decent sort of man." For the first time he mentions Moore's mother, "an Irish lady" (Mrs. Janie King Askins Moore, 1872–1951), who was temporarily staying in Oxford in order to see as much as possible of her son before he went to France (like everyone in England, she knew that the casualty rate on the western front was very high). Mrs. Moore was accompanied by her daughter, Maureen, then a girl of eleven, who would later become Lady Dunbar of Hempriggs, a baronetess in her own right. In the same letter, Jack invited his father to come to Oxford for his four-day leave, perhaps with the thought that he might not get to see much more of Albert.

In speaking of Mrs. Moore to me in later life, Jack once said, "One of her great virtues was hospitality. It was she who taught me to be hospitable." She showed this quality at once by inviting, not only her son's roommate, but several other of his fellow cadets to the furnished rooms she had taken.

There is plenty of evidence that Jack was at the time rather homesick for Ireland. He wrote to Arthur of one conversation with the Moores: "Like all Irish people who meet in England we ended by criticisms on the invincible flippancy and dullness of the Anglo-Saxon race." He had no doubt "that the Irish are the only people."[14] This feeling must have increased the pleasure he took in the company of the Moores, particularly Mrs. Moore, whom he regarded almost as a mother. A month later, after staying with her, he wrote to his father: "I like her immensely and thoroughly enjoyed myself."[15]

This letter also contains an amusing description of a military exercise in Warwick. Six of them were billeted in the house of an undertaker, with three beds between them, "of course no bath, and execrable food." They found the "little backyard full of tombstones" more comfortable than the "tiny dining room with its horsehair sofa and family photos." On the other hand, he spent an enjoyable night in the open on the Cumnor Hills outside Oxford: "There was plenty of bracken to make a soft bed, and I slept excellently" and later awoke "in a flash without any drowsiness, feeling wonderfully fresh."[16] The precocious and rather priggish intellectual was adapting astonishingly well to army life. He seemed to like, or at least be able to get on with, quite a number of ordinary people, enjoyed many simple pleasures, and was at times positively happy. He even had a warm and cordial relationship with his father—just for the time being, however, for they were on the brink of a quarrel from which their relationship never recovered.

After passing a simple exam, he was made second lieutenant and attached to the Third Battalion of the Somerset Light Infantry. Before being posted for active service, he was given a month's leave from September 28. He did not go directly to his father's house in Belfast, but accepted an invitation from Paddy Moore to stay at his mother's house on 56 Ravenswood Road in Bristol. On October 12, he traveled to Ireland, spending only half of his leave at home. Albert was deeply hurt. The result was an estrangement of father and son.

Why did Jack do it? We would know the answer if we had all the letters that he wrote to Arthur between August 4 and

October 28. But we have none. They were certainly destroyed by either Jack or Arthur. Nevertheless, the letters that are left make it quite clear that he loved Mrs. Moore. He must have discussed his love or infatuation for her with Arthur in Belfast, but no doubt wrote to Arthur as soon as he got back, telling him to forget that it had ever been mentioned. It was something that must, at all costs, be kept from his father. One result of his relationship with Mrs. Moore was that he wrote more often to her than to Arthur and sometimes sent her messages. There is a change in the handwriting of the letters that he wrote after his leave with her. It is larger and seems less disciplined, more relaxed, more flowing.

After his month's leave, he was sent to a camp at Crown Hill near Plymouth. The letter he wrote to his father shows the class-conscious attitude common in his letters of the period. Most of the men were "hardly after my style," but they were also mostly "well bred and quite nice." Life was quite bearable, "even pleasant." All he had to do was lead his party in a parade and hand them over to an instructor; then he could "walk about doing nothing for several hours a day." He added that it was "a little tiring to the legs and I think will finally result in atrophy of the brain."[17]

Albert wrote a polite letter to Mrs. Moore to thank her for her kindness to Jack in often inviting him to her house and in looking after him when he was unwell. She replied:

Dear Mr. Lewis,

Thank you for your letter about the small kindnesses I have done to Jack. . . . One is only too pleased to do anything one can for these boys at present. . . . Your boy, of course, being Paddy's roommate, we knew much better than the others, and he was quite the most popular boy of the party; he is very charming and most likeable and won golden opinions from everyone he met here. Paddy is so very much disappointed that they are not both in the Somersets; he would so very much rather have Jack with him than anyone else. . . . I am sure you, like myself, would rather be in the trenches than have them there.

Yours sincerely
Janie K. Moore.[18]

Mrs. Moore was at that time forty-five. She had a maternal attitude toward Jack, who was then eighteen, and for the rest of their relationship would call him and Warren "the boys." For Jack, who had lost his mother when he was a child and was, in addition, rather homesick for Ireland, it must have been a great pleasure to meet an Irish woman who was kind enough to "mother" him.

On November 15, Jack sent a telegram to his father to say that he had arrived at Bristol on forty-eight hours' leave: "Report Southampton Saturday. Can you come Bristol. If so meet at Station. Reply Mrs. Moore's address." His intention was to tell Albert that, after his leave at Bristol, he would be shipped from Southampton to France.

Not surprisingly, Albert failed to understand. He did not expect Jack to be sent to the front for months. He wired back: "Don't understand telegram. Please write." Jack sent a second, soothing telegram: "I have just got your wire; it is perfectly wretched giving me such short leave. Please don't worry. I shall probably be a long time at the base as I have had so little training in England."[19]

Albert has been severely blamed for not rushing to see Jack before he went to France. But Jack's first telegram really was incomprehensible. Furthermore, the European war seemed remote to people living in Ireland, and not long before Jack had written to say that he thought that his regiment would be sent to Ireland. Apart from this, Albert, who was without a partner and had much police court work, would not want to travel to England unless it was absolutely necessary. The letter he wrote to Warren eleven days later on November 26 suggests that he had only just discovered what had happened to Jack. It seemed to him "brutally unjust" that a boy of eighteen should be sent to France after no more than four weeks training.

The reality was even worse. Jack was actually in the front line trenches on his nineteenth birthday, but he did not mention this to his father. Instead, he wrote a letter saying that he was just beginning to know the men and understand the work, and praising his commanding officer, a Lieutenant Colonel Majendie, as "a splendid fellow."[20] He always concealed from his father the fact that he had been rushed to the front just twelve days after his arrival in France. The same thing had happened to Paddy Moore, who was a far stronger and more physically mature boy.

He first mentioned being in the trenches in a rather cheerful letter written home on January 4, 1918. His pay was sufficient, he wrote, for "all my needs and comforts. . . . I have been up in the trenches for a few days . . . attached to a company for instruction, and the number of shells that went singing over our heads to fall on the batteries far behind did not . . . weaken my affection for the infantry." He said that he was now on a bombing course and that the bombing officer was "a very nice fellow of literary tastes." The dugouts were surprisingly comfortable, very deep, and with bunks and braziers for warmth and cooking. In fact, they tended to get too hot and "of course the bad air makes one rather headachy."[21] He indicated that he was having quite a pleasant time. He had gone on with his reading and had found the *Mill on the Floss* even better than *Adam Bede*.

But a month later, Albert received a letter from the war office announcing that Jack was now in the hospital at the coastal resort of Le Treport, suffering from "pyrexia," or fever. In fact, he had trench fever, "a mild but unpleasant disease transmitted by body lice." Nevertheless, Jack wrote about "having a comfortable rest from the line" and asked his father to send, of all things, Burton's *Anatomy of Melancholy*.[22] After twenty-seven days in the hospital, he was sent back for what he calls "a four days tour of the front." On March 4, he wrote that he had had "a fairly rough time" and had lost one or two of his best friends, including an old Malvernian.[23] Nine days later, he wrote that he was in the hospital in Etaples. The only wound he mentioned was one in his left arm.

When Warren heard the news, he borrowed a bicycle and rode the fifty miles to Etaples, where he found Jack "only slightly wounded and in great form, expecting to be sent home. Thank God he is out of it for a bit."[24] To cycle one hundred miles in one day was a great achievement for Warren, who was neither athletic nor energetic. This incident marks the end of his estrangement from Jack (caused by their differing opinions of Malvern College). From this point, they resumed the close friendship of their boyhood, a friendship marred only by Warren's bouts of heavy drinking, or "binges," as his friends called them.

In his diary, then called "April Notes," Warren wrote: "It will be a very long time before I forget that ride to Etaples and waiting in the Hospital Hall to see him. But the mental and physical pain was more than counterbalanced by the joy and thankfulness of seeing him sitting up in bed. It's funny how relief from fear turns to irritation. I was really angry to have had to go through such hours for nothing."[25]

It soon became clear that Jack had not one wound, but three, all caused by pieces of shrapnel. Warren wrote to their father:

"[A] shell burst close to where he was standing, killing a Sergeant, and luckily for 'IT' he only stopped three bits; one in the chest and two in the hands; he then crawled back and was picked up by a stretcher bearer."[26] More details came from Jack in letters sent on May 4 and June 14. He was hit in the back of the left hand, on the left leg just above the knee, and on the left side just under the armpit. In the earlier letter, he wrote that he had only flesh wounds, but in the later one he admitted he had been wrong and that the piece of metal that went in under his arm was now "high up under my pigeon chest." Because it was near his heart and difficult to remove, it was left there, but it would never cause him discomfort. It was the wound in his left hand that thereafter bothered him most. He joked that he would have to be sent home as a stretcher case because he had no clothes. People at the dressing stations had a mania "for cutting off a wounded man's clothes whether there is any need for it or not. . . . I mourn the undeserved fate of my breeches."[27]

He also wrote for the first time of the death of his friend and roommate, Paddy Moore. His "friend Mrs. Moore" was in great trouble, because Paddy had been missing for over a month and was almost certainly dead. He had been the first to go of Jack's particular set at Keble. It was "pathetic to remember that he at least was always certain that he would come through."[28] According to Mrs. Moore's daughter, the long delay before his mother heard of his death was caused by the fact that the war office communication was sent to his father in County Wicklow, Ireland, who failed to write to his wife about it.

When Jack was transferred to Endsleigh Palace Hospital in London, he suffered intensely from the loneliness and depression to which he was liable all his life. He telegraphed his father, asking him to visit, and also wrote: "You will be able to come over, will you not, if only for a few days? We must get Kirk up to meet you and have a famous crack."[29] Why did he now want to see Albert rather than Mrs. Moore? He knew it would not work to see them both at once, and perhaps he wanted to free himself from his emotional attachment to her. Albert replied in a few days that he had bronchitis and would be unable to visit. Nevertheless, he continued to go to his office every day.

On June 20, Jack wrote a long, lyrical, and nostalgic letter to his father, describing a visit with Kirkpatrick at Great Bookham. His letter contains a deeply felt appeal to his father to visit him in his convalescence, although he did not yet know to which convalescent home he would be sent. "But wherever I am," he wrote, "I know that you will come and see me." He blamed the English schools for the difficulty he and many of his generation had in understanding their parents, and he assured his father that he was "never before so eager to cling to every bit of our old home life and to see you." He admitted that he had "often been far from what I should" in his relationship with his father. "But please God, I shall do better in the future. Come and see me. I am homesick, that is the long and the short of it."[30]

It is difficult to understand how Albert could have resisted the appeal of this, the warmest and most pathetic of all the letters that Jack wrote to him. But after Albert's failure to visit, which must have hurt Jack bitterly, it is not surprising that Jack was especially glad to see Mrs. Moore when she came to London to visit her sister, who worked at the war office. ". . . [W]e have seen a good deal of each other," he wrote. "[S]he has certainly been a very, very good friend to me."[31]

Jack craved love and affection and wanted very much to be transferred to a convalescent home in Ireland. When he was told that was impossible, he chose one in Bristol, "where I could have the society of Mrs. Moore and also of Perrott of the Somersets." On June 25, he was transferred to a hospital at Clifton, Bristol, with other officers and men in the Somerset Light Infantry. He was going to be allowed two months of convalescence, until August 24, after which he might have to return to France. Asking his father to visit once again, he wrote, "we could have a delightful little holiday together." He was surprised by the extent of the confinement of the "gilded youth" at the hospital. He and his fellow patients were "close prisoners" there. He wanted only to be left alone in some quiet place where he could read, but found that the building "echoes to the crack of their billiard balls and their loud tuneless whistling." Until he found "a little disused writing room at the end of the house" where he could sit "in comparative safety and read Burton's *Anatomy [of Melancholy]*," he was miserable. He referred obscurely in one letter to some infectious disease: "If I should happen to get the disease, all my bits of things will be burned. I could sit down and cry over the whole business." He was particularly depressed that his friend Johnson, who had been a scholar at Queen's College, Oxford, was dead. "Indeed nearly all my friends in the Battalion are gone."[32]

He was terribly lonely, and, as he sometimes would in later life, he turned to animals for comfort. The house was "a 13th century castle often rebuilt," which had a deer park. Wandering in the bracken, he would occasionally "come upon the solemn face and branching antlers of a stag, within a few feet of me. He examines me for a few moments, snorts, then kicks up his heels and is gone."[33]

The next letter to his father, written on October 3, indicates a deep estrangement because of Albert's failure to visit. "It is four months now since I returned from France, and my friends laughingly suggest that 'my father in Ireland' of whom they hear is a mythical creation like 'Mrs. Harris.'"[34] He mentions that there is a possibility that he may be sent back to France, although the wound in his leg is still painful.

Deprived of his father's affection, Jack sought the company of Mrs. Moore, who opened her home in Bristol to him. His convalescence at the hospital was made bearable by frequent visits to her. He must have wanted to do everything in his power for her when the news of Paddy's death finally came through.

Albert wrote a letter of condolence, to which she replied:

> . . . [I]t is very hard to go on now. . . . [T]hey are buried with so many others in that wretched Somme. . . . Of the five boys who came out to us so often at Oxford, Jack is the only one left. His and Paddy's chief friend "died of wounds" the other day in Palestine, a very clever boy and a scholar like Jack. This was SO wicked and cruel—I feel that I can never do enough for those that are left. Jack has been so good to me. My poor son asked him to look after me if he did not come back. He possesses for a boy of his age such a wonderful power of understanding and sympathy. He is not all fit yet, and we can only hope will remain so for a long time.[35]

This letter is vital to the understanding of Jack's relationship with Mrs. Moore. His attachment to her was compounded of gratitude for her motherly kindness and generous hospitality, of pity for her as the mother of his closest wartime friend, and of the undertaking he may have been given to look after her if Paddy was killed. All his life Jack took the duties and delights of friendship seriously. He had already shown this in his relationship with Arthur Greeves. Even if he had never fallen in love with her or regarded her as a second mother, it would have been astonishing if he had not felt both real affection and an obligation to do all he could for her.

Jane King Moore (born Askins) had had a difficult life. The family was clerical; her father was the Vicar of Dunamy in County Armagh, and a brother became the Dean of Kilmore in

Cavan. After the death of her mother, when she was only eighteen, and of her father a few years later, she, as the eldest child,
had the task of bringing up the four younger children. This made
her autocratic. Her marriage at the age of twenty-six was
unhappy. She and her husband separated, but there was no
divorce. Surprisingly, he turned out some years after her death to
be heir to the Baronetcy of Dunbar of Hempriggs in Caithness,
Scotland. In order to give her son Paddy the advantages of a public school education at Clifton College, she moved with him and
her daughter Maureen to Bristol, where one of her brothers, Dr.
John Askins, was a government medical officer. Hospitable in the
Irish manner, she naturally invited her son's friends to her house
when she moved to Oxford to be near him. She, too, was brought
up in a tradition according to which friendship is a deep and lasting relationship.

Although she had little formal education, she was quite well-
read, and in the early years of their relationship she and Jack
would often lend each other books and discuss them. She always
regarded Jack as a boy and affectionately called him "Boysie."
His name for her was "Mother" or "Minto." Her main virtue
was kindness, especially to those in any sort of need. Her main
fault, that of being too autocratic and controlling, was the almost
inevitable result of having to take charge at an early age of a large
house and family.

Jack's melancholy did not lead him to be inactive in reading
and writing. His letters to Arthur Greeves were longer than ever,
and he soon made it clear that he was compiling a little collection of lyrics, some of which he had written at Great Bookham,
others in France or in England after being wounded. On about
September 12, 1918 (his letters to Arthur were usually undated,
a reaction against the business methods of his father), he wrote
to convey "the best of news! After keeping my MS for ages,

Heinemann has actually accepted it." He added that it might be well to reconsider the inclusion of some of the pieces "which are perhaps not on a level with my best works." Arthur was instructed on no account to tell Albert about the acceptance, "as he might be hurt at not being taken into my confidence"; "I will let him know when I next write."[36] This emphasis on what might or might not be passed on to Albert was already an established feature of Jack's letters to Arthur and continued to be one until his death.

Heinemann's interest in Jack's little book of poems actually produced a temporary reconciliation with his father. Jack initially thought of the title "Spirits in Prison" by a pseudonym, Clive Staples. Albert pointed out helpfully that there was a novel by Robert Hichens with the same title. Jack wrote back, thanking him for his "cheering and encouraging letter" and explaining that the book consisted of "the working out, loosely of course and with digressions, of a general idea," in form a little like *In Memoriam*, but with the poems in different meters. He therefore wanted to use "A Cycle of Lyrics" as a subtitle (*cycle* was an objectionable word, but *series* and *sequence* seemed even worse).

He went on to discuss the pseudonym. His reasons for wanting to have one may seem strange to those who knew him in later life when he had a sturdy contempt for what other people thought of him: "My only reason for choosing a pseudonym . . . was a natural feeling that I should not care to have this bit of my life known in the regiment. One doesn't want either officers or men to talk about 'our b[lood]y lyrical poet again' whenever I make a mistake."[37] However, he is not sure how much importance he ought to attach to this. He considered turning Lewis into "Wiles" or "Welis," but seemed at that time rather inclined to drop the disguise altogether. He wondered if "Clive" might be too famous a surname to adopt, and then on November 18 he thought of "Clive Hamilton" as a pseudonym, "a name which we have the best of reasons to love and honour."[38]

Ten days before Heinemann had written suggesting omissions, complaining of the too frequent use of the word *universe* and of some poor rhymes. Warren had indicated that Jack should recast the poems in accordance with all of his publisher's criticisms.

Jack had by this time been moved to a "Command Depot" on Perham Down near Andover in Hampshire. He was glad to be out of a hospital ward at last and to have a room to himself, even though the place was in some respects a "glorified hospital." Another letter written from Perham Down explains that wounded men were now being kept in convalescent homes rather than sent home to recuperate, probably because the end of the war was plainly near and the first thing most of them did when they got home was to indulge in the "only two interests of the average uniformed bounder—alcohol and women—" activities that would "make them more unfit for return to the army."[39]

A vivid description of the ending of the war is given in Warren's diary for November 10, 1918:

> Things were about as usual in the morning and in the afternoon. I was in the office at about 9 p.m., and suddenly there was an outburst of sirens, rockets, Very lights, hooters, searchlights and all sorts of things. Hurried back to the mess and found everyone dancing round the room. . . . Australians were firing Very pistols in the square. . . . [And there were] six bonfires going with Belgians dancing and shouting round them with our lads. Cathedral and Church bells pealed most of the night. Got home and to bed about 2:30 a.m. . . . A very great day indeed. So ends the war.[40]

The entry for the next day includes the sentence: "Thank God Jacks has come through it safely, and that nightmare is now lifted from my mind." He uses the word *nightmare* quite literally. Since Jack had crossed over to France, Warren had tended to wake up in the middle of the night wondering if he was still alive. This was characteristic of the close attachment of the brothers, an attachment that never ceased. Unfortunately, the nightmares had the effect of increasing his intake of alcohol. His practice was to take what he called "a good dose of whisky" to get to sleep again.[41]

Before the end of the month, Jack was moved again, this time to the officers' command depot at Eastbourne in Sussex. He wrote to his father in disapproval of the jubilation reported in Warren's diary: "The man who can give way to mafficking at such a time is more than indecent—he is mad. I remember five of us at Keble, and I am the only survivor: I think of Mr. Sutton, a widower with five sons, all of whom have gone." Like Warren and innumerable other men who had been at the front, he was for years troubled by nightmares, "or rather the same nightmare over and over again."[42]

He was now, of course, eager to get back to Oxford and thought he was well enough. "I can now do everything except hold my left arm straight above my head. . . . The effects on general health are very small; I have had one or two stoppages of breath which I am told are not unusual after a chest wound and which will disappear." He asked his father to send him his Greek lexicon and some of Sophocles' plays, so that he could start studying for the classics exam that he would have to take after four terms at Oxford.

He liked Eastbourne and was preserved from homesickness by the company of Mrs. Moore, who had come at his suggestion "and is staying in rooms near the camp, where I hope she will remain until I go on leave."[43] The frank and open way in which he wrote to his father about her shows a clear conscience in his relationship with her. He needed the warmth of her friendship and was genuinely grateful for the way in which she was willing to move to be near him when he was transferred from one camp to another. He seemed to have forgiven his father for not coming to cheer him up in England, perhaps preferring the company of Mrs. Moore and Maureen.

Jack failed to get Christmas leave to go to Ireland, but, to the surprise of his father and Warren, who was already there, he turned up on December 27. "We had lunch and then all three went for a walk. It was as if the evil dream of four years had passed away and we were still in the year 1913. In the evening there was bubbly for dinner in honour of the event. The first time I ever had champagne at home. Had the usual long conversation with Jacks after going to bed." The following day "passed quietly and pleasantly in reading and chatting, with gramophone interludes. . . ."[44]

So the war for Jack ended in this remarkably happy reunion at Little Lea in Belfast. The following month he went to Oxford for the start of the first postwar Lent term and, a still more important event for a boy who had always wanted to be an author, to await the publication of his first book.

7

Spirits in Bondage

The authorities of Oxford University, that is, the fellows of the colleges, feared the arrival of the soldiers. It was widely thought that they would be licentious, unruly, drunken, and certain to demand radical changes in university structure and discipline. Some colleges went so far as to recruit officers from the Brigade of Guards, disguising them as academics or perhaps as bursars or deans, under the supposition that they would be experts in maintaining discipline. Their presence turned out to be quite unnecessary and actually had the effect of lowering the university's academic standards. The men who had come back from the front were essentially conservative. They wanted to rediscover the Oxford they had known before, resented whatever changes they did find, and were anxious to get down to hard work as soon as possible.

Jack's first letter home to his father is indicative of such feelings: "The porter knew me at once and ushered me into the same old room. . . . It was a great return and something to be thankful for." He was delighted to find an old friend there named Edwards, who had never been called up for service, and he found the postwar college far preferable to the ghost he had known before: "True, we are only twenty-eight in College, but we DO dine in hall again, the Junior Common Room is no longer swathed in dust sheets, and the old round of lectures, debates, games and what-not is getting under weigh [sic]."[1]

Much of the rest of the letter is about work. As a soldier who had served for over six months, he was excused from Responsions. He had the choice of either going straight on to the Honours School of Literae Humaniores, popularly called "Greats" and basically a course of study in classical philosophy, or to take "Honour Mods," mainly a course of study in Greek and Latin texts. His tutor, Arthur Poynton, to whom he confided his ambition of obtaining a fellowship, advised him to take Mods first. Here, "except for the disadvantage of starting 18 books of Homer to the bad I find myself fairly alright," he wrote. The work was "pretty stiff," but he thought Poynton "a quite exceptionally good tutor" and he was keeping his head "above water."[2] The best lectures were those by Gilbert Murray; he always felt much better for going to them.

He was happy in college ("our little body gets on very well together and most of us work") but sorry that the "cosy custom" of serving breakfast in the men's own rooms had been abolished—it was now served in the dining hall. Once again he was struck by Oxford's extraordinary beauty: "The place is looking more beautiful than ever in the wintry frost: one gets splendid cold colouring at the expense of tingling fingers and red noses."[3] He was elected secretary of the Martlets, a 300-year-old college club of twelve undergraduate members that held meetings to listen to and discuss literary papers and to hold discussions: "Someone will read a paper on Yeats at our next meeting; we are also going to have one on Masefield, and we hope to get Masefield himself . . . to come up and listen to it."[4]

The letter ends: "Smugy is dead." This information seems to have come to Jack from Warren, who had written: "Smugy died of influenza during the last epidemic. . . . He was a scholar and a gentleman and a good friend to me." Warren contributed to a memorial to Smugy but thought that Jack would not want to: "Owing to his deep dislike of the Coll. he might greatly dislike his name giving countenance to a Malvern Memorial." He went on to write a sentence that showed a lack of understanding of his brother's thoughts and feelings: "Besides the 'New Thought' may regard memorials to 'the loved and honoured dead' as an exploded superstition ranking with witchcraft and Divine right of Kings!"[5] In fact, of course, Jack was never such a radical. For an intellectual undergraduate, he was decidedly conservative, even reactionary, in his views. He was, for instance, old fashioned in his appreciation of Gilbert Murray, whose romantic approach to Greek drama was already being derided by the smarter and more up-to-date undergraduates.

The most important event of his first year at Oxford must have been the publication of his first book, *Spirits in Bondage*. This extremely rare and valuable book is a slim, blue octavo that was published by William Heinemann in March 1919. It is sub-titled *A Cycle of Lyrics* and is written in three parts: "The Prison House," "Hesitation," and "Escape." From the publisher's advertisements at the back of the book, we learn that Jack was one of Heinemann's "Soldier Poets," the others being Siegfried Sassoon, R. S. Vernecle, Robert Graves, and Geoffrey Dearmer. Oddly, Jack is named as "George Lewis" and as "Lieut. G. S. Lewis." He did not know how this mistake had occurred.

The poems were written from 1915 onward, many of them when he was sixteen or seventeen. After rejecting the title "Spirits in Prison" because it was used on an already published work, he thought of several other titles for the collection. "Metrical Meditations of a Cod" ("cod" is a Belfast slang term meaning an eccentric) and "Spirits in Bonds," suggested by Albert, were rejected because they might prompt jokes about whiskey. Finally, he settled on "Spirits in Bondage."

The poems had been sent first to Macmillan, which declined them, and then to Heinemann's, where C. S. Evans took a special interest in them. John Drinkwater, the well-known poet, playwright, and literary critic, had seen the manuscript in Heinemann's office and had asked if he could publish one of the poems, "Death in Battle," in a literary magazine called *Reveille*. It appeared in the February issue, together with poems by Robert Bridges (the poet laureate), Hilaire Belloc, and Siegfried Sassoon. The last poem printed in *Spirits in Bondage* (in the "Escape" section), it conveys the delight that will come after death and contrasts the beauty of the afterlife with the corruption of war. It is a musical poem, full of imagery, and deserving of inclusion in any anthology of Great War poems. Albert, proud father, thought Jack's poem the best poem in *Reveille*.

The theme of *Spirits in Bondage*, according to the author, is that nature is malevolent and that any God that exists is outside the cosmic system. He wrote a letter to Arthur Greeves that gave a clear account of his philosophy of life. He did not believe in any God, least of all in one that would punish him "for the lusts of the flesh"; but he did believe that he had in him a spirit; and "since all joyful things are spiritual and non-material," he must take care "not to let matter (= nature = Satan, remember) get too great a hold on me, and dull the one spark I have."[6] In the poem "Satan Speaks," Satan announces himself as the maker of material things, as nature, the "Mighty Mother" and the law to which there is no alternative.[7] He issues a solemn warning to those who hate his world, who dream vain, romantic dreams of "good their kind shall not attain," and who suffer from a "loathing for the life that I have given." Yet this poem, like the others in the collection, is not the work of an atheist, but of a Manichee, a dualist, who is torn between two Gods, one good and one evil.

The theme of the distant, uncaring God and the poet's struggle against Satan is presented powerfully in the poem entitled "De Profoundis." In spite of the apparent hopelessness of this struggle, the poet will not give in. He will continue to resist the "relentless might" of the dark lord. He will go on thirsting for the right and, in spite of every calamity, resist evil. Satan may laugh, slay, and destroy everything of value, "heap torment still on torment for thy mirth." He still will not have attained a complete conquest "while there are men on earth."[8]

"Satan Speaks" also introduces the primary difficulty Jack was having at this time in his life in the conflict between the rationalism that he had perhaps acquired from Kirkpatrick and his romantic imagination. His problem was how to integrate the two in order to become a whole person. In the meantime Satan can present himself as "the fact and the crushing reason to thwart your fantasy's newborn treason."[9]

The same antithesis occurs in a later poem, "The Philosopher." He considers what sort of seer we need to lead us to "... the real things that lie / Beyond this turmoil. . . ." It will not be ". . . an elder, bent and hoar," because, through age and too much study, he will himself have become insensitive to the joys we seek. The leader we need will have to be "young and kind" and not schooled in reason, but open to the intuitions and perceptions of his "fancy" (or imagination—Jack never made much of the Coleridgean distinction). Such a man "may live a perfect whole."[10] The romantic rejection of rationalism makes this poem particularly interesting. Kirkpatrick encouraged Jack to be excessively argumentative, but as a philosopher, he seems to have had little influence on Jack's thought.

The theme of "Victory" is the triumph of the human spirit

and its renewal out of the ashes of destroyed ideals. It opens with a fine lament for the dead heroes and heroines of romantic myth and poetry, and ends in a triumphant verse that introduces an unexpected idea: that the effect of a long succession of setbacks can be to raise and exalt the human spirit to an even greater height, "till the beast becomes a god."[11] The whole poem has a force and power rare in Jack's early verse.

"Irish Nocturne" is remarkable not so much for its satanism and sense of frustration as for one or two beautiful descriptive phrases. "Spooks" illustrates Jack's taste for the eerie. "Apology" and "Ode for New Year's Day" display a Swinburnian hatred and a satanism that is no more convincing than it is in Swinburne. However the long lines and the stanzaic form are skillfully managed.[12]

"To Sleep" shows the influence of Yeats but still more of Keats. The poet asks to have his pain quenched in "draughts of cool oblivion" and to enjoy "sweet half-wakeful moments in the night in which to hear the falling rain." It is a charming, musical, romantic poem that has little to do with "The Prison House," the section of the book to which it belongs.[13]

The fetters of "In Prison" are made up of the pain of man and "the hopeless life that ran for ever in a circling path." But the poem is interesting not so much for this as for a beautiful central space-travel section. He loses his way "in the pale starlight" and has a far-off vision of our planet "with leagues on Leagues of stars above and powdered dust of stars below."[14]

No matter how intense the misery of his prison house, the poet never quite gives way to despair. He is saved by the mystical experience of beauty that in his letters to Arthur and his autobiography he calls joy. "Dungeon Grates" contains one of the finest of all his descriptions of it and tributes to its value. The beauty is "unsought" and comes in "some casual hour," (which is a way of saying that it is a "grace," or gift of God). It enables us to see "all things aright . . . seven times more true than . . . in vulgar hours." For a moment "we are one with the eternal stream of loveliness." The experience is momentary, but it is sufficient to alter our lives permanently. It will have taught us that we are "not made of mortal stuff." It will make it possible for us to bear severe trials and persecutions, "For we have seen the Glory—we have seen."[15]

The theme of "Song of the Pilgrims," which could be influenced by Flecker, is spiritual search. The pilgrims have turned their backs on the world "and all her fruitless pain" and, though their fellowship has been thinned by many deaths, they are still seeking the red-rose gardens that blow "somewhere, somewhere past the Northern snow." It speaks of God as creator, "ere God sat down to make the Milky Way." At one point the pilgrims waver in faith, as all believers sometimes do, but the poem ends with a reaffirmation of faith.

"Our Daily Bread" is another religious poem. Its theme is that we are never far away from spiritual experience. To invoke it we do not need "barbarous words" or solemn ceremony. "It lies before our feet."[16] For some people, including the poet, it is an almost everyday event, part of the daily bread, which, in the Christian communion service, symbolizes spiritual nourishment. The poet, when in "many a vulgar or habitual place," may hear the call of "the Living voices." Following "a strange God," he will "leave both friends and home" and live a life of spiritual pilgrimage, searching for "that gulf of light"

> *Wherein, before my narrowing Self had birth,*
> *Part of me lived aright.*[17]

There is an interesting similarity between the concept of pre-existence in this poem and that in Wordsworth's "Ode on Intimations of Immortality":

> *Our birth is but a sleep and a forgetting:*
> *The Soul that rises with us, our life's Star,*
> *Hath had elsewhere its setting,*
> *And cometh from afar.*

"Our Daily Bread" may be pantheistic or it may be Christian; it is certainly not atheistic.

The thirty-third poem of the collection, "How He Saw Angus the God," is full of lovely imagery. It tells of a young man creeping down the stairs of a house and out onto the wet grass, "at that pure hour when yet no sound of man, / Stirs in the whiteness of the wakening earth." He comes into the cool, wet wood that he always enjoyed and rests in the sweet heather:

> *When suddenly, from out the shining air*
> *A god came flashing by.*

In the last verse, there is a surprise when the glorious horse-god of Irish mythology is found changed into "a solemn bull." The poem illustrates the sudden changes from the "real" to the imaginative world, or from one imaginative world to another, that Jack experienced all his life and loved to write about.

"Tu Ne Quaesieris" is another poem of longing. It marks a development toward what can only be called the Christian position. He realizes that, as long as he is confined to his "narrow self," there will be a conflict between his will and God's will:

> *Yet what were endless lives to me*
> *If still my narrow self I be*

And hope and fail and struggle still,
And break my will against God's will.[19]

Because he is imprisoned in the self, he is "as through a dark glass scarce can see / A warped and masked reality." The way out is for his "searching thought" to be mingled in the large divine.

Spirits in Bondage was reviewed in good papers, such as the London *Times* and *The Scotsman*, and described as "graceful and polished," "strongly imagined and never unhealthy, trifling or affected." These epithets are accurate enough, but they were quite insufficient to sell the book, and after a few years most copies were destroyed.

Even if the youth of the author is not taken into account, the poems seem better than most others published at the same time, better for instance than those by R. E. Vernede and Geoffrey Dearmer advertised in Heinemann's list, and more interesting than many by Siegfried Sassoon. Nevertheless, Jack was disappointed by their reception, and he abandoned the thought of becoming a lyric poet.

Warren expressed disapproval of the book in a smug letter to their father:

> While I am in complete agreement with you as to the excellence of part of IT's book, I am of opinion it would have been better if it had never been published. Even at 23 [Warren's age] one realises that the opinions of 20 are transient things. Jack's Atheism is I am sure purely academic, but, even so, no useful purpose is served by endeavouring to advertise oneself as an Atheist. Setting aside the higher problems involved, it is obvious that a profession of a Christian belief is as necessary a part of a man's mental make-up as a belief in the King, the Regular Army, and the Public Schools."[20]

Jack himself was surprised that Warren or anyone else should think the poems blasphemous. Here and there, a few pieces might shock, but only if they were read out of the context of the book as a whole. He defended the right, indeed the duty, of a writer to be honest: "You know who the God I blaspheme is and that it is not the God that you or I worship, or any other Christian."[21] He soothed his father by reporting that he was regularly reading lessons in chapel and saying grace before meals in the dining hall. It is unlikely that his father ever realized that this was one of the routine duties of a scholar of the college.

Jack, like almost everyone else discharged from the army at that time, expected to be made a member of the permanent army reserve and to be kept on half pay. He was surprised to find that this was not the case and that he would receive no army pay from December 25, 1919. With the help of his father, he applied for a wound gratuity and, after the usual official delay, obtained a single payment of £145, about the equivalent of $3,000, and a great help to him in his first two years at Oxford. The wound in his wrist bothered him for the rest of his life, tending to interfere with his writing.

Why did he write almost nothing about the war? I can offer only two suggestions: One is that he felt it too strongly, so strongly that he could not bear to recall it. The other is that he was preoccupied with his life as an undergraduate and with his dependence on a father who was jealous and suspicious of his relationship with Mrs. Moore.

8

Mrs. Moore

Jack returned to Oxford in time for the Lent term of 1919. When the term ended eight weeks later, he did not immediately go back home to Belfast, but spent the first part of his vacation helping Mrs. Moore move from Eastbourne. She moved, not to Oxford, but to Bristol, which may suggest that they were not so close as before Jack's drafting to the western front, or perhaps the infatuation was, and had always been, on his side rather than on hers. We can only guess. At any rate, it was perfectly reasonable that, whether or not he had given a promise to Paddy Moore, he should help her move house.

Nevertheless, Albert and Warren began to show strong disapproval of the relationship. On May 10 Warren wrote to his father:

> The Mrs. Moore business is certainly a mystery but I think perhaps you are making too much of it. Have you any idea of the footing on which he is with her? Is she an intellectual? It seems to me preposterous that there can be anything in it. But the whole thing irritates me by its freakishness: there is really no knowing what a fellow like our IT is going to do under any given set of circumstances. If the woman were . . . a loose 'un by nature the thing would be of no importance

whatsoever: but by all accounts she's a lady. . . . Probably the whole dread mystery is a product of our own imaginations.[1]

Albert's reply showed that he was greatly depressed and worried. All he knew about Mrs. Moore was that she was separated from her husband, was old enough to be Jack's mother, and was "in poor circumstances." Jack had frequently given her cheques for sums up to £10 at a time. He would not be so worried "if Jacks were not an impetuous kindhearted creature who could be cajoled by any woman who has been through the mill." He feared too that the husband, who he had heard was a scoundrel, "might try a little blackmailing."[2]

The correspondence is interesting. Albert recognized that it was improbable that Jack could be having an ordinary love affair with Mrs. Moore, but he did not realize how significant it was that she was old enough to be his mother. Because Jack, an unusually sensitive person, had lost his mother at a vulnerable age, and this had been followed at once by banishment to an exceptionally brutal boarding school, he felt the lack of mother love as psychological insecurity. Mrs. Moore, a homely woman, and like his mother from southern Ireland, seemed fit to act as another mother and to provide the love and security that he wanted. She would have been of no interest to him if she had been nearer his own age. Albert may have felt this subconsciously and would have considered it an act of disloyalty to Jack's real mother and to himself, for he had consciously tried to take Flora's place. Mrs. Moore had stolen a son from him, just as Warren, another insecure person, felt that she had stolen a brother.

As soon as the summer term was over, Jack helped Mrs. Moore to move again, to 28 Warneford Road in Headington, a village just outside Oxford. From this time onward he lived, as far as possible considering his position in the university, with Mrs. Moore and Maureen. He was not then, or at any time in his life, sufficiently secure to be able to live alone. For eleven years they lived in rented houses. They occupied at least nine addresses in the Oxford area until they bought the Kilns in 1930.

In the beginning, he combined the life of an undergraduate with that (to use his own expression) of a "country house-holder." At first he slept in the free rooms to which he was entitled as a scholar of University College and ate his meals there, but spent his afternoons with Mrs. Moore and her daughter. As a second-year student, he was allowed to live off campus. He also spent his nights in the houses that Mrs. Moore rented, returning each morning to the college to work at his books.

To avoid a violent quarrel with his father, Jack concealed the amount of time he was spending with the Moores. He wrote less frequently and went to Belfast less often and for shorter periods. Albert was suspicious, jealous, and often angry: "It is sometimes difficult to keep one's temper with Jacks. . . . I am afraid I understand the situation all too well. . . . Always Mrs. Moore first. On one occasion he had six weeks leave and spent five of them with her. . . ."[3]

Jack tried to justify his delay in traveling to Ireland during the long vacation of 1919 by lying, saying, for instance, that the "summer term really continues for a fortnight or three weeks after its official decease." He eventually went to Belfast on July 28 and soon after had his first really serious argument with his father. It was about money. Albert asked him how much he had in the bank. When he said about £15, Albert read to him a letter from the bank that he had found in Jack's room that made it clear that Jack was, in fact, overdrawn. "Instead of defending himself," to quote Warren's diary, "he weighed in with a few home truths about P."[4]

That August was one of the unhappiest months of Albert's life. He could not understand why Jack should have lied and then "said terrible, insulting and despising things" to him. The only wrong he could think of was his failure to visit Jack in the hospital. In all other respects he had a clear conscience. He had worked hard and sacrificed himself for his sons. He longed and prayed for a return of the old loving relationship, which was the thing in his life that he valued most.

As for Mrs. Moore, it was entirely in character that she should devote herself to looking after this poor young man who had lost his mother. She would have done it even if he had not been her son's friend. She was generous and hospitable to a fault and made a lifelong habit of caring for anyone in need. No doubt Jack responded with love, even adoration. That they wrote to each other every day in 1919 shows the closeness of their relationship.

Were they lovers? Owen Barfield, who knew Jack well in the 1920s, once said that he thought the likelihood was "fifty-fifty." Although she was twenty-six years older than Jack, she was still a handsome woman, and he was certainly infatuated with her. But it seems very odd, if they were lovers, that he would call her "mother." We know, too, that they did not share the same bedroom. It seems most likely that he was bound to her by the promise he had given to Paddy and that his promise was reinforced by his love for her as his second mother.

Some of those who have written about C. S. Lewis regard his living with Mrs. Moore and Maureen as odd, even sinister. This was not the view of those of us who visited the Kilns in the thirties. There she was, a rather stately woman, sitting at the tea table. "Mother, may I introduce Mr. Sayer, a pupil of mine?" is what he would say. Like his other pupils, I thought it completely normal in those days that a woman, probably a widow, would make a home for a young bachelor. We had no difficulty accepting her even when we came to realize that she was not his mother.

But if the relationship were innocent, why was Jack so secretive about it? Certainly, he did not want to worry Albert and various other people in Belfast who would have disapproved. Probably, too, Mrs. Moore had asked him not to tell anyone, and he had given his word. If Mr. Moore found out about Jack and thought that Jack and his wife were living together in adultery, he would have had grounds to divorce her and would not have owed her a cent. (In fact, she wanted a divorce, but he would not agree. This made it impossible for her to have a fair share of his income and obliged her to live in near poverty.)

Of the people who knew Mrs. Moore, Warren seems to be the only one who disliked her. Nevertheless, writers on C. S. Lewis tend to follow Warren in supposing that she had a bad influence on Jack's literary and academic career. There is no evidence of this. In fact, considering the magnitude of his achievements in scholarship and literature, it is unlikely. He said in conversation with me that she did him a great deal of good. "She was generous and taught me to be generous, too," he once said. "If it were not for her, I should know little or nothing about ordinary domestic life as lived by most people" and, "I was brought down to earth and made to work with my hands." His worry about taking his first public exam at Oxford was caused, not by her preventing him from doing enough work, but by the self-distrust and pessimism characteristic of most members of the Lewis family. This lack of self-confidence was unwarranted. He wrote to Albert in March 1920 that he had been placed first in Honour Mods.

In the same letter, he refers to a walking companion, "a man who has been asking me for some time to go and 'walk' with him. . . . We are quite alone and live an idyllic life on eggs, bully beef and—divine treasure—an excellent ham which Aunt Lily very opportunely sent."[5] Who was this mysterious man? One is tempted to think that he was actually Mrs. Moore or Maureen. In the pre-Christian stage of his life, Jack did not hesitate to write whatever he thought necessary to keep his father happy.

His real feelings toward his father were expressed in letters to his brother. Albert "is fast becoming unbearable. . . . I needn't describe the continual fussing, the sulks, the demand to know all one's affairs. . . . I wish to the Lord we had a small income of our own to fall back on in case of emergencies." Plainly he thought there was a risk of Albert's stopping his allowance. But, in fact, Albert agreed to give him £30 (about $1,000) at the beginning of each term and some more money from time to time "for extra expenses."[6] For placing first in Honour Mods, his college gave him a prize of £5 to be spent on books.

His letters to his father are notably conservative, particularly regarding politics, but they also include some lighter subjects. In one letter, he writes about a visit to Belfast: "I am still debating whether I can sufficiently brace my nerves for such an ordeal."[7] He was referring, not to the difficulties of deceiving his father, nor, of course, to the danger of bombs, as would nowadays be assumed, but to the risk of traveling in the sidecar of the motorcycle that Warren had just acquired. He was already fearful of the internal-combustion engine and remained so all his life. Later on he tried to learn to drive a car, but never a motorcycle.

His conservatism in poetic taste was already well established. Where he differed from hundreds of other conservative undergraduates was in wanting to do something about it. He and a few others were putting together an anthology as "a kind of counterblast to the ruling literary fashion here, which consists in the tendencies called 'Vorticist,'" that is, free verse poems that are sometimes clever, often affected, and "a good few, especially among the French ones, indecent: not a sensuous indecency, but one meant to nauseate, the whole genus arising from a 'sick of everything' mood." He was planning with a few others to do something to oppose the new fashion for free verse by producing an annual collection of poems in the hope that it might convince some of his contemporaries that it was still possible to write poetry that rhymed and scanned and was on "sane subjects."[8]

Although Jack's political and literary views were quite close to those of his father, his visit to Belfast in the summer of 1920 was unhappy. Albert complained of the absence of "the old loving intimacy" and wondered to what extent Warren was responsible for the change.[9] He much disliked what the English educational system that he had chosen for his sons had done to them, turning one into an extravagant and class-conscious officer and gentleman, and the other into a clever, conceited Oxford undergraduate. Both sons found staying in Albert's house almost unbearable. He would never leave them alone. He always wanted to know what they were doing and never hesitated to read their private letters if he found them lying about. Sometimes he would even go into the Greeves' house to see if he could get any information about Jack from Arthur.

To quote from Warren's diary: "P. has got on my nerves badly today. Somehow he has the knack of saying the one thing on any subject which is sure to infuriate me."[10] Warren records an occasion when early in the morning his father "sneaked downstairs to see if there was any letter for me . . . Careful as I had been, there was the P. bird waiting for me with that most irritating 'Well?'"[11]

Toward the end of March 1921, Jack saw the announcement of W. T. Kirkpatrick's death in the London *Times*. "Poor old Kirk," he wrote. "I owe him in the intellectual sphere as much as one human being can owe another. That he enabled me to win a scholarship is the least he did for me. It was an atmosphere of unrelenting clearness and rigid honesty of thought that one breathed from living with him."[12]

Early in 1921, he had begun to work on his entry for the vice-chancellor's essay prize on the assigned topic "Optimism." He had felt almost inspired while writing it: "I have almost lived with my pen to the paper. It has been one of those rare periods . . . when everything becomes clear and we see the way before us." Winning the prize was one of his most important academic achievements. Coincidentally, the runner-up, Brundrit, had been with him in Smugy's class at Malvern College. As winner of the prize, Jack was required to read his essay at Encaenia. He described the event amusingly in a letter to his father: "Although the ceremony was at noon, people wore full evening dress and caps and gowns. The procession of heads of colleges, doctors and others made a very strange show, half splendid and half grotesque, for few dons' faces are fit to bear up against the scarlet and blue and silver of their robes."[14] The men who were to receive honorary degrees included Clemenceau, the French statesman. But the one who impressed Jack most was a priest and well-known theologian, Louis Batiffol, Canon of Notre Dame. Jack's strong attraction to a man whom he felt to be a great priest is odd, considering that in his essay he had declined to admit the existence of God. The state of his belief is summed up in the remark he made at about that time to his friend, L. K. Baker: "The trouble about God is that he is like a person who never acknowledges your letters and so in time you come to the conclusion either that he does not exist or that you have got his address wrong."[15]

In July Jack received a letter from his father, announcing that he was going to take one of his rare holidays. He would travel to England by car, and, much to Jack's alarm, he intended to visit Oxford. Jack tried to put him off again by inventing an imagi-

nary man: "I have been moved out of College and you will prob-
ably find me sharing with a man who is up to his eyes in work.
This means we can't spend much time on my own hearth. . . .
What do you say to a few weeks later on somewhere in
Westmoreland or N. Wales? We might do a bit of country by
walks rather than a big bit by motor."[16] The object of this sug-
gestion was, of course, to prevent his father from meeting Mrs.
Moore. (It also shows Jack's lifelong preference for walking in a
small area rather than for driving.) The suggestion worked.
According to Warren's record: "On the 20th of July Albert left
Belfast on one of his rare holidays—the last he was ever to have—
and the most enterprising which he had taken since his visit to
Paris in 1912. In company with his brother and sister-in-law,
Augustus and Annie Hamilton, and travelling in their car, he tra-
versed Wales and then proceeded via Oxford to the West of
England and Land's End."[17]

To Jack's relief, the party stayed in Oxford only long enough
to have lunch. In a letter to Warren, he wrote satirically of his
father: "The first and by far the funniest piece of scenery I saw
was my first glimpse of the Old Air Balloon himself outside the
Clarendon in Cornmarket . . . almost a bit shrunk: pacing along
with that expression peculiar to him on a holiday—the eyebrows
halfway up his forehead." Jack was warmly welcomed, but he
adds, "I was in a great flutter for fear of meeting some fool who
might out with any irrelevance." Most fortunately, his father
"seemed dazed by his surroundings and showed no disposition
to go and see my rooms."[18]

They went to Wells Cathedral, of which he wrote: "The pleasure one gets is like that from rhyme, a need and the answer to it
following so quickly that they make a single sensation." They
traveled through the part of Somerset that he and Mrs. Moore
had once explored together and eventually to Cornwall. "At first

I was disappointed, for, to be candid, it is so like County Down or parts of Antrim that it felt uncanny. The same absence of bright colours, the same cottages, the same sloping, somewhat bare hills, grey rather than green. . . ."

At Tintagel he recorded that, although there was no evidence to connect the place with King Arthur, "some wretch had built a hotel there called King Arthur's Hotel." In the hotel lounge, he found a set of Lubbock's Best Books, a well-known Victorian series that included Dante's *Divine Comedy*, Virgil's *Aeneid,* and Aristotle's *Ethics.* Of them he commented priggishly: "How I abominate such culture for the many, such tastes ready made, such standardization of the brain." (How different would his tastes be in twenty or thirty years time! I remember his commending the series when he found two or three volumes in my library.) "The whole place infuriated me," was how he summed it up. "But the coast was like the Antrim coast, only better."[19]

Jack often began a diary, but never kept one going for very long. The one he began in the spring of 1922 is particularly interesting for what it tells us about his life with the Moores. It is surprisingly normal and like that of many other householders. He shows an interest in domestic tasks such as the orange marmalade that Mrs. Moore was making. He often helps himself and enjoys the work. Thus he "had fun shovelling to get the roof clear" of snow. But it was only if there was a household crisis that he seems to have had a great deal to do. Thus on one April day when Mrs. Moore was ill, he got up early, cleaned the grate, lit the fire, made breakfast, and put a piece of ham on to cook for lunch. For the first time we hear a good deal about Mrs. Moore's daughter, Maureen, then a high-spirited schoolgirl of sixteen. He enjoys helping her with her woodwork. He draws a great sea serpent "with tail in mouth" as part of the design for a wooden box that she wants to paint and draws a dwarf blowing bubbles as a design for a wooden teapot stand. He even makes designs for Mrs. Moore's needlework, for a curtain she is making out of an old army blanket and on which she is embroidering a tree, "storks and lilies and a moon with stars." Like many other households, they are short of money and worry about how they are going to pay their bills. Mrs. Moore's husband, nicknamed "the Beast," sometimes fails to pay the money for her support. At times it seems that they have hardly enough "for bare rent and food." Perhaps they will be unable to afford Maureen's school fees.

Yet in spite of poverty, he is happy. They enjoy their friends. There is Mrs. Moore's brother, Dr. Askins (usually called "the Doc"), who visits them almost every day, and many others by no means all academics. Some of their meals are riotous: "Sheila Gonnere came to tea; Jenkin arrived rather later. We all sat down to tea and were, as Bozzy says, in extraordinary spirits when Miss Wibelin arrived—a fat, plain, shy, giggling woman. A most insane meal—what the stranger thought of us I cannot imagine. . . ."[20]

Surely, life with the Moores provided the future novelist, writer of children's stories, and popular Christian apologist with a better preparation for his career than life in college with only academic friends would have done.

Of course, like every other undergraduate, he had long conversations with fellow students, but he also talked at length with more worldly men and women, such as the Doc, about morals, philosophies of life and, especially, immortality. The breadth of knowledge he thereby acquired is fully reflected in almost all of his books. Through living with the Moores, he learned to care about other people. He was concerned about Mrs. Moore's physical and mental comforts and about Maureen's difficulties as a student and later on as a violinist and music teacher. He also came to know how ordinary people thought and felt and was therefore able, when the time came, to stir their thoughts and feelings. And he learned to express himself in direct and simple English. Perhaps his life with the Moores made it more difficult for him to excel academically, but, far more important, it enabled him to become a great popular writer.

Family life did not stop him from reading extensively. He spent two months before taking Greats in June 1922 reading widely. His list included Seneca, Thucydides, Jonson's *Volpone*, Croce, Aristotle, Solon and the early Attic writers, Bosanquet, Freud, Havelock Ellis, Spenser, Kant's *Metaphysics of Morality*, Strindberg, William James's *Varieties of Religious Experience*, Myers's *Dawn of History*, Bradley's *Ethical Studies*, the *Antigone*, Hume's *Of Morals*, Gosse's *History of Modern English Literature*, and Raleigh's *Wordsworth*.

The exam for Greats lasted six days, and on each day students wrote two three-hour papers. The subjects were as follows: Roman history, Greek unseen translation, philosophical books, translation from Roman historical texts, translation from Greek texts, translation from Plato and Aristotle, logic, general ancient history, Latin prose, moral and political philosophy, and Greek prose.

After taking the exam, Jack thought immediately about getting a post, presumably as a schoolmaster. However, his lack of athletic ability would go against him in that pursuit. Furthermore, his tutors advised him not to take such a job in a hurry, as a university teaching appointment was sure to turn up. Another year of university study was suggested. If he placed first or second in Greats and first the following year in English literature, he would be in a very strong position.

Normally, one of the periods of greatest strain for an undergraduate is the long interval between taking final exams and learning how the college has ranked his degree. Jack passed the time rather unhappily in job hunting, but very happily in social life.

He was offered a one-year fellowship at Cornell University, but refused it because, although the salary was good, there was no allowance for the cost of travel between Britain and the United States. Although he liked the look of the undergraduates "of both sexes," he was rather glad to be unsuccessful in his application for a lectureship at Reading University because it would have meant either his living there alone or moving Maureen to another school for a year. He turned down a position as junior dean at Wadham College because of the stipulation that he must eventually become the Law Tutor, a job that he knew would never have suited him. He failed to obtain work as a reviewer for the *Manchester Guardian* and was reduced to offering to tutor a student at Lynam's, an Oxford school for boys aged eight to thirteen.

In spite of these difficulties he celebrated riotously the end of the last year of his degree course. The sudden arrival of Arthur Greeves, much improved and with much luggage, added greatly to his happiness. Other members of the house party were his friends Baker and Owen Barfield and Mary Wibelin, who was giving Maureen violin lessons in exchange for Latin lessons given her by Jack. The entertainment included a burlesque poem in *terza rima*, wonderfully unself-conscious dancing by Barfield, Schubert and Mendelssohn from Mary Wibelin, and high spirits and "plenty of ragging" from everyone else.

Mrs. Moore's house was always full of characters. There was, for instance, a wonderful seventy-eight-year-old woman who, in order to come for lunch at Headington, bicycled all the way from London, a distance of about sixty miles. There were girls, friends of Maureen and young women whom Mrs. Moore had befriended. Jack undoubtedly took pleasure in the company of some of them. There was Veronica with whom he went canoeing on the River Cherwell. They landed at a meadow near Parson's Pleasure (the male nudist bathing place), sat in the hay, and drank ginger beer through straws. Jack recorded one good remark of hers: "An educational career is a school of hypocrisy in which you spend your life teaching others observances which you have rejected yourself." There was Maisie, a big nineteen-year-old "with a most beautiful figure," who danced for them one evening. There was Maureen herself and her friend Helen with whom he played bridge, croquet, and Ping-Pong. Very often there was Mary Wibelin, whose nickname (they delighted in giving each other nicknames) was Smudge.[21]

Poor Smudge! She fell in love with Jack, and "one lovely dark night" after a game of hide and seek in the garden, while he was walking part of the way home with her, she broke down and showed her feelings. Poor Jack! He liked her, was sorry for her, and admired her courage—her father had died in debt, and she was trying through teaching to help the younger children, but, of course, he was in no position to marry her. When he discussed the incident with Mrs. Moore, she told him that he had gone too far in repulsing Smudge—which she would never have said had she been Jack's mistress.

A discordant note was struck by Warren, now "grown enormously fat," who booked in at an Oxford hotel. He stood his brother a bottle of champagne, but declined to stay with them in Headington. The following day he even refused to meet the family at tea. This behavior is unlikely to surprise those who knew Warren in later life. He was always reluctant to meet people, especially women, whom he did not already know. Perhaps, too, he was already drinking heavily and was wondering if he could get sufficient supplies while staying with Mrs. Moore.

But Jack persisted and in the end persuaded Warnie to stay for about ten days. The visit was not entirely happy. They depressed each other by a visit to Wynyard School, which aroused "vindictive memories and . . . dreams of hate," and by the discussion of their unhappy relationship with their father. They agreed that Albert did not make the slightest effort to break down the barriers that separated them. There were occasions when Warren joined in the games and the ragging, but at other times he sulked and described himself as bored. It is quite likely that he had already come to feel unhappy in any house where he could not easily get a drink.

In his diary and in the introduction to *The Letters of C. S. Lewis*, Warren presents a most gloomy picture of Jack's relationship with Mrs. Moore. He sums it up as "restricting and distracting servitude."[22] In the diary he dwells obsessively on her egotism and "intense selfishness." Although this account is very different from Jack's own, as presented in his letters and diaries, it has been followed by most of those who have written on Jack's life. In *C. S. Lewis: A Biography*, Green and Hooper describe the relationship as "a curious state of bondage" and give an unbalanced view of her character, describing her as "highly possessive and selfish—or thoughtless—to an astonishing degree."[23] They have little to say about her good qualities, nor of the happiness and good fellowship enjoyed by most of those who stayed in the house during the early years of Jack's relationship with her. Similarly Humphrey Carpenter writes in *The Inklings* of the "innumerable domestic chores that Mrs. Moore was in the habit of devising for him."[24] This is going too far. In fact, the diary Jack kept at this time indicates that he sometimes did housework simply because he wanted to. Quite often he complains because Mrs. Moore did not let him do as much as he wanted.[25] Of course, if you love a woman as Jack loved Mrs. Moore at this period, you want to do all you can to help her, but, apart from this, the brothers had quite different attitudes to housework. While Jack was always anxious to do his share, his indolent brother detested all work of the sort and did his best to avoid it. I cannot think of anything at all that he did to help in the house or garden on the many occasions he stayed with us.

It is also untrue that Jack had to confine his reading for his second degree in English language and literature to "the moments he could spare from domestic life." Many of the books that he used in preparation for the exam survive. They show careful scholarly annotation that certainly required far more time than he would have had available if he had done much housework.

Mrs. Moore possessed to a high degree the virtue of hospitality. Her house was always open to her daughter's friends and their friends too. Everything Jack said to me on the subject of her hospitality convinces me that he approved and learned much from it. Leonard Blake, who became Maureen's husband, found that visitors to the Kilns were "usually having a very jolly time." On the two occasions when I was invited to go and have tea on the lawn with Mrs. Moore, I found the atmosphere pleasant and cheerful.

She was a most generous person who gave shelter to many, usually, but not always, young men and women who needed help and kindness. Impulsive, enthusiastic, and perhaps rather scatterbrained, she tended to be emotionally involved with all of them, which made her exaggerate their virtues when she first knew them and then become disillusioned and even dislike them later. Some took advantage of her impulsive kindness. A girlhood that had obliged her to act the role of housekeeper for her widowed father and mother for the younger children had made her bossy and self-opinionated. Age and infirmity, such as the nagging discomfort of varicose veins, unfortunately increased these defects.

On the strength of his ranking in Honour Mods and in Greats Jack competed unsuccessfully for a fellowship by examination at Magdalen College, Oxford. It was a fortunate failure because it caused him to take a degree in English Language and Literature in one year. This and his revision of *Dymer* were his most important activities during 1923. If he had succeeded in obtaining his fellowship in Greats, it is most unlikely that he would have produced *The Allegory of Love* and his other great works of English literary criticism.

9

Into Poverty

In Jack's day the syllabus of the Oxford Honours School of English Language and Literature was far more concerned with language study than that of most other universities. Students were required to study Anglo-Saxon or Old English, from learning the grammar to making a detailed study of *Beowulf* in the original, textual difficulties and all. There followed the study of the development of the language through Middle English into modern English. Students had to read many important texts, including much of Chaucer, some of Gower and *Piers Plowman*, all of *Gawain and the Green Knight*, almost the whole of Milton's poetry and some of his prose, much Shakespeare, and most of Spenser. Exams included passages known as "gobbets" that were marked for detailed comment and translation. The idea was to give the study of English status as an intellectual discipline, to prevent it from being a "soft option," the ideal subject for the lazy undergraduate. In fact, it was a difficult syllabus to cover in a year, as Jack had to.

Once again he was lucky to have good tutors. For literature (except Old English) he had Frank P. Wilson, later to become Merton Professor of English literature, but then a fellow of Exeter College and only about ten years older than Jack. He was an excellent tutor and remained a friend until 1963, the year in which they both died. Jack described him to me as "the man responsible for most of my better literary ideas"; he certainly gave Jack the idea for his first great work of literary criticism, *The Allegory of Love*.

His tutor in Old English was Edith Wardale of St. Hugh's College. He found her an efficient tutor with real enthusiasm, which she quickly conveyed to him. Almost at once he wrote that he was happy to be "thus realising a dream of learning Anglo-Saxon which dates from my Bookham days."[1] He liked even the unpopular parts of the subject. Though most students found phonetics very dull, Jack soon became reconciled even to "trying to reproduce the various clucking, growling and grunted noises which are apparently an essential to the pure accent of Alfred."[2]

Despite his close relationship with his tutors, his intense delight in great literature, and his wide tastes, Jack was not gloriously happy in his studies. He was disappointed with many of the "old men" who lectured and taught in the school and with the standard of most of his fellow students. The only lecturers he really liked were George Gordon, the Merton Professor, who later became president of Magdalen College, and C. T. Onions, the lexicographer, already famous for his work on the *New English Dictionary* (or the *Oxford Dictionary*). Of most of the others he was contemptuous. They seemed to him pedantic and ill-bred (he remarked of one "that it is nice to see an English don behaving like a gentleman").

He made only one friend of his own age in the English school, and that not until the second term when he met Nevill Coghill of Castle Townshend in County Cork, Ireland—a tall handsome, aristocratic man with an original mind and great charm. Coghill had previously studied modern history and now, like Jack, planned to complete the English course in one year. He also was a pupil of F. P. Wilson, who kept the two men very much in step in their work, though they never seem to have shared tutorials. They met first in the discussion group run by George Gordon during the Michaelmas or fall term. Jack's paper on *The Faerie Queene* attracted Coghill's attention because of the way Jack championed Spenser's ethical values and conveyed so intensely his enjoyment of the story that its knights, dwarf, and ladies seemed real.

They don't, however, seem to have spoken until the following term, after Coghill had read a paper on the subject of realism. A week later they went for the first of many walks over the Cumnor Hills, walking almost as fast as they talked of the books they were reading under Wilson and having "thunderous disagreements and agreements." They agreed in liking the same passages in Milton's *Samson Agonistes*, usually the ones in which the emotions are on an epic scale and the verse is strongly rhythmic. They revelled in reciting to each other lines such as

> *O dark, dark, dark, amid the blaze of noon,*
> *Irrevocably dark, total eclipse*
> *Without all hope of day!*

and

> *While their hearts were jocund and sublime,*
> *Drunk with idolatry, drunk with wine*
> *And fat regorged of bulls and goats . . .*[3]

They disagreed violently about Restoration drama, which Coghill had just discovered, but which Jack thought heartless, cynical, even disgusting. In his diary of the period he described Dryden as "an intolerable worm." Though in later life he came to see the merits of Dryden as a poet, he thought him in almost every way inferior to Pope. After his conversion to Christianity his dislike of Restoration drama became even stronger. Coghill attributed it to Northern Irish Puritanism and noted that he seemed generally disinterested in the theater. I don't think this was true. The real reason why Jack was not a frequent theater-goer was that he was usually far too busy, even if only with reading, writing, and talking. It is easy to think of occasions when visits to the theater gave him immense pleasure. Coghill's production of *The Winter's Tale* entirely transformed his conception of the play. He could enjoy even modest amateur productions. At a performance of *Twelfth Night* in the gardens of Lady Margaret Hall, he was delighted by the way in which the verse was spoken, by the beauty of the Viola, and by the lovely voice of the girl who played Olivia. I can vouch for the fact that at a performance of Shaw's *The Apple Cart* in Malvern, he laughed more loudly than anyone else in the auditorium, that he regarded *Murder in the Cathedral* as a great play, and that, when he saw *Comus* on the stage, he declared at once that it was better than *Comus* on the printed page, even in an edition illustrated by Arthur Rackham.

When he left the army, Jack was a slim young man, but by now, five years later, he had put on so much weight that he was nicknamed "heavy Lewis" by other members of his college. Coghill described him as "a largish unathletic-looking man, heavy but not tall, with a roundish, florid face that perspired easily. . . . [He] had a dark flop of hair and rather heavily pouched eyes; these gave life to the face, they were large and brown and unusually expressive. . . . [There] was a sense of simple masculinity, of a virility absorbed into intellectual life." Coghill goes on to state that, unlike most men of his age, "he seemed to have no sexual problems or preoccupations, or need to talk about them if he had them. . . ."[4]

Among the other subjects they discussed was what action

they would take in the event of another war. Both thought they would be pacifists, though both doubted if they would have the courage. Coghill surprised Jack by saying that the only answer to war was Christianity. Coeducation was one of the subjects on which they disagreed. Coghill was violently opposed, but Jack thought that the presence of girls in a school would much improve the manners and morals of the boys. (He never ceased to think schoolgirls far nicer beings than schoolboys!) Jack mused on the unpredictability of life. Looking back, he found many things that had mysteriously influenced or failed to influence him, often in ways that no one else could understand. One could calculate nothing.

The spring of 1923 was a difficult time for Jack. He and the Moores had to move to another rented house, the tenth such move since 1919. The new house, Hillsborough, was in such a bad state of repair that he and Maureen were obliged to do a great deal of painting and wallpapering. The weeks thereafter were, he wrote, "so busy and so miserable that I had neither time nor heart to continue my diary, nor poetry, nor pleasant effort of any sort." Because they had been let down by a friend, they had had to camp in the house for a fortnight before their furniture arrived. Mrs. Moore was unwell, suffering from indigestion, varicose veins, and the damage done when during the move a wardrobe fell on her.

All his life, even when affluent, he was subject to periods of depression. Now poverty intensified the mood. "Like most poor families," he wrote, "we usually eat margarine with jam." Mrs. Moore was sent little or no money by her husband, and Jack's allowance from Albert, and the scholarship money, which University College generously continued to pay him on condition he took another degree, though quite sufficient for his personal support, were certainly not enough for three people, one a girl at a school where fees had to be paid. He tried to borrow money from Warren, but discovered to his amazement that his brother had spent during the first year of peace nearly all the money that he had saved during the war, and could do no more than lend Jack a five-pound note now and again.

Another misery of that spring was the mental illness of Mrs. Moore's brother, the Doc. In a vivid letter to Arthur he called it "war neurasthenia." The Doc, who was then living with them, endured "awful mental tortures. . . . had horrible maniacal fits. . . . had to be held down." They were up for the whole of two nights at the start of the attack and then for two, three, or four times a night thereafter. The poor man suffered from the delusion that he was going to Hell. The psychiatrist who treated the Doc told Jack that "every neurotic case went back to childish fears of the father." This prompted Jack to write to Arthur ". . . whatever you do, never allow yourself to get a neurosis. You and I are both qualified for it, because we were both afraid of our fathers as children." He passed on to Arthur the psychiatrist's advice: "Keep clear of introspection and brooding. Keep to work and sanity and open air. . . . We hold our mental health by a thread, and nothing is worth risking for it. Above all, beware of excessive daydreaming, in seeing yourself in the center of a .drama. . . ."[5] After three weeks of misery, the Doc was sent to a hospital in Richmond, where on April 23 he died suddenly of heart failure. This terrible mental illness of a man whom he respected and regarded as a friend made a permanent impression on Jack. He was always deeply moved when he heard of anyone suffering from mental illness. He gradually cured himself of the habit of introspection and did his best to correct the habit in his friends and pupils.

He did not think he had done well in the exam that he had taken that summer. It began on June 14 with Old English, of which he wrote, "I could make no serious attempt at the Grammar in spite of all the hard work that I have done." In the afternoon, he wrote a paper on the history of language, which was "even worse; and even when I got a question on Milton which I knew, my memory deserted me and I could do nothing." But if this is an accurate account, he must have done brilliantly in the other papers, because the oral exam (called in Oxford a "Viva") on July 10 was purely formal and he was subsequently awarded a first-class honors degree.

Though he had now obtained three first-class degrees, in Honour Mods (Greek and Latin texts), Greats (classical philosophy) and English Language and Literature, he was still living in acute poverty and did not seem much nearer to a suitable job. To save money, he gave up smoking and they began to manage without a maid, a severe economy for a middle-class family in the days before the general use of labor-saving domestic appliances. He began to suffer from headaches and indigestion, both probably the result of nervous strain. He found it hard to sleep and had one or two dreadful nights of real panic. He suffered from the feeling that his best creative years were slipping past him, without giving him a chance to write the great poem or prose work that he had always wanted to write and believed he could write.

He was depressed even by the thought of what might happen to him if he did succeed in getting one of the fellowships for which he was applying. Thus he wrote of a Trinity College fellowship in philosophy, worth about £500 (perhaps about $12,000) a year: "The possibility of getting it and all that would follow if I did came before my mind with unusual vividness. I saw that it would involve living in, and what a breakup of our present life that would mean; and also how the extra money would lift terrible loads off us all. . . ." He feared that he might become "submerged and the poetry crushed out." But although the cost would be high, he was, if forced to choose, prepared to give up poetry for stability. He had an image of himself in the future, looking back on the years since the war "as the happiest or the only really valuable part of my life, in spite of all their disappointments and fears." But stronger than this feeling was "the longing for an income that would free us from anxiety."[6]

Jack regarded friendship as a lifelong relationship. He was always made acutely unhappy by serious disagreements with his friends or by their foolishness or moral deterioration. He was most depressed by the ways in which Arthur Greeves seemed to have changed when he visited him in July 1923. "Someone has put into his head the ideal of 'being himself' and 'following nature.' . . . He has taken over from psychoanalysis the doctrine that repression is bad and cannot be brought to see that repression is quite different from self-control."[7] (This was a view that he held all his life. The only teachings of Freud that he thought true and of practical value were those dealing with the relationship of parents and children. Carl Jung was the only philosopher of the Viennese School for whose work he had much respect. Arthur is described in the diary as "very rude and objectionable." He went so far in following nature that he came down to lunch still dressed in his pajamas and sat there with his feet on the dining room table.[8]

Jack was now in real poverty. He had ceased to receive any money from University College and had only the £85 a year (about $1,700) that his father continued to pay him, and the small amounts he earned from grading school examination papers and from tutoring one student at University College. Then in May 1924, almost a year after he had completed his English studies, he was offered a full-time job at Oxford.

E. F. Carritt, the philosophy tutor at University College, was going to America in the fall of 1924 to spend a year at the

University of Michigan. Jack was invited to undertake his tutoring during his absence and also to give lectures. Although the pay
did not seem generous, a minimum of £200 for the year (about
$4000) and the job was only temporary, he unhesitatingly
accepted the offer.

For his course of lectures he chose the subject "The Moral
Good—its place among the values." Preparing them he regarded
as his "best job" so far in life. He wanted to avoid the main fault
of most other lectures, which seemed to him to contain little
material padded out to a great length. When a fellow of the college gave him the advice, "Of course, your first lecture will be
INTRODUCTORY," he wanted to reply, "Of course, that's why
I always skipped your lectures!"⁹ He wrote to his father, "I am
to lecture twice a week next term, which comes to fourteen hours
talking in all. . . . I rather fancy I could tell the world everything
I know about everything in five hours—and Lord, you hear
curates grumbling because they have to preach for twenty minutes a week . . . must learn that slow deliberate method dear to
the true lecturer." Fortunately he never learned that method. If
he had, he would not have become the only Oxford lecturer of
the thirties and forties to attract and hold large audiences.

Soon after beginning to work on his lectures, Jack recorded
his first quarrel with Mrs. Moore. Her good temper had been
undermined by their poverty and, as there was now no servant,
she had come to expect domestic help from Jack during the
period of his unemployment. "She was very tired and cross
today," he wrote. He had done some shopping for her "and was
immediately sent back into Headington with another message."
When he got home, she turned on him "rather savagely for having forgotten to take Pat [the dog] out with me." He found self-
control very difficult and did not reply because he feared that he
might say "regrettable things." The episode is of the sort com-

mon in the experience of almost every family, but Jack reacted excessively: "After lunch the nervous irritation bottled up inside me reached such a pitch and my thoughts became so irresponsible and foolish and so out of control that for a moment I was really afraid that I was going into hysteria."[10] Later on he came to regard domestic life as a school of virtue. He found it quite hard to acquire the necessary cheerfulness and self-control and did it only gradually.

Although in later life, when discussing Mrs. Moore, Jack strongly defended her generosity and hospitality, her habit of inviting to the house friends, relatives, and especially almost anyone who was in need must have added a great deal to the strain of family life, particularly when they were short of money and neither of them felt well. There were so many visitors! To give an example, on the day after the quarrel, Mrs. Moore's cousin Norah Murray came to visit. In the afternoon Jack took her and Maureen to watch the college eights racing on the River Isis, but up to the last he "had great hopes it would rain." Two days after that, children from the Holmes family arrived. Mrs. Moore announced that their mother was dying and that the children would stay for the night "and until further notice." "Jack never felt at ease with children and must have wished very much that they were not there, but later the same day there arrived a visitor whose company he always enjoyed, his old friend, Cecil Harwood, happy, solid, imperturbable. He talked about the Rudolf Steiner school in which he was teaching, "such a breath from the comfortable, easy outside world." That evening they sat in the dining room and "Harwood and I had a good talk of books and of friends and every sentence brought me back to sanity." But even so, when left alone that evening he suffered from depression and nervous indigestion. "My pains were pretty bad." And he thought about Mrs. Holmes, who died the next day.

Harwood was very good at entertaining the Holmes children—Jack in his diary notes that he would at their age have resented grown-up interference with his "endless drawings and soliloquies." As in later life the presence of a close friend meant much to him. But not all their talk was cheerful. Out walking, after seeing "hordes of drowned and drowning insects" under a river bridge, they talked of "the horrors that occurred in one square mile of the insect world every month. Harwood thought that their consciousness might be so rudimentary that their death struggles might mean no more than a confused malaise."[12] The subject was one that interested and disturbed Jack all his life. After he had become a Christian, he usually thought of animal suffering as a consequence of the Fall.

But Harwood, like Barfield, was a poet, and there was "blessed peace" in the evening when they read and criticized each other's poems. Jack admired the precision, elegance, and humor of Harwood's poems, but still thought his own best. For his part, Harwood approved of the sixth canto of *Dymer*, but was unhappy about the eighth. The following day Jack did something that he always found spiritually therapeutic; he went for a "wonderful" country walk with Harwood and Pat, the dog.

He was far happier during the remaining months of the summer, sustained by contact with nature, the company of friends, and now and again by the experience of great music. On June 5, sitting in his favorite fir grove near Horspath on the southern slopes of Shotover Hill, he "had the 'joy'"—or rather came just within the sight of it. He went to concerts with Maureen, whom he regarded very much as a sister, and sometimes felt uplifted "even to rapture" by the second movement of Beethoven's Mass in D. He visited Harwood in London and went with him and Owen Barfield to a performance at Covent Garden of *Die Walkyrie*. It raised him "to the heavens" and brought back all his old enthusiasm for Wagner. It is interesting that the singer who really gave him "the feeling of divinity" was the English mezzo-soprano, Edna Thornton, as Fricka, goddess of wedded love and domesticity. Thirty years later he was still talking about the experience, and how after the opera the three of them had walked home through the London streets with their heads "striking the stars."[13]

Once again he earned money by grading English Literature papers for the Oxford and Cambridge Schools Examination Board. Since in those days the finest works in the language were chosen, he enjoyed the reading he had to do: Lamb, Wordsworth, *Hamlet, Macbeth, Richard II, Lear, Twelfth Night, Eothen, David Copperfield.*

The work itself he found "cruelly dull," because hardly any of the papers contained anything interesting, original, or amusing. Personal experience was rare; all too often the boys and girls aimed at nothing more than the repetition of whatever their teachers had taught them.

He took pains in reading up the books for his tutorials before the start of the autumn term. He reported to his father that his pupils included some quite good men. "I have seen only one real dud so far—a man who celebrated his first hour by telling me as many obvious lies as I have heard in a short space. . . ." One of his students was captain of the football team. Jack studied even "THAT subject . . . in order to be able to talk to him."[14] It is hard to imagine him doing such a thing ten years later when he was securely installed at Magdalen.

In preparing his course of fourteen lectures he read widely in philosophy and ethics, enjoying especially Hobbes, Bergson, and Hume. He decided not to write the lectures out in full because "read lectures send people to sleep and I think I must make the plunge from the very beginning and learn to talk not to recite. I practice continually, expounding my notes to imaginary audiences."[15] In spite of this admirable resolution and his careful preparation, his first lecture in October was a fiasco. He was billed to speak at the same time as a far better-known man. And through a misprint in the notices, he was put down to lecture at Pembroke rather than at University College. It was a wonder that anyone turned up at all, but four people did. By February his audience had dwindled to two, including an elderly parson. With the object of being less formal, he invited them to his rooms and told them to interrupt him whenever they felt like it. It was a great mistake. The elderly parson interrupted so often that Jack "could hardly get a word in."[16] Fortunately as time went on, a larger number of people came to his lectures but the most persevering continued to be the old parson who took very full notes and compensated for talking less by glaring at Jack now and again.

During his year at University College, Jack slept at Hillsborough, Mrs. Moore's house, on weekends and during the vacations. On week days in term time, he usually gave tutorials in the morning, went to Hillsborough for lunch, did a few odd jobs there, took a walk, returned to the college in the later afternoon, did some more tutoring, and dined in college. Dinner was a formal occasion. Fellows of the college and their guests sat on a dais at one end of a large and magnificent hall. Everyone, professor to undergraduate, was required to wear a gown. Before the meal started, a Latin grace was said, and during it, a member of the college staff would mark off the names of those present. Conversations, begun at the High Table, often continued in the candle-lit senior common room, accompanied by glasses of wine, usually port. After this enjoyable ceremony Jack retired to his rooms, where in the morning he would be served breakfast.

This schedule did not vary much, but sometimes he would go to a play or concert in the evening, as on February 10, 1925,

when he saw the Oxford University Dramatic Society's production of *Peer Gynt:* "I was very disappointed in the play," he
wrote. "The general idea of a history of a soul is alright, but
Peer's soul hasn't enough in it to last for four hours: most of it is
mere Nordic windbagism. No good making a story of Peer: you
only want to kick his bottom and get on."[17]

He recovered the interest in Maureen's girlfriends that he had
shown a year or two earlier. His remarks about Valerie Evans,
whom Maureen had invited to stay for a few days, show that he
found her attractive, and reveal immaturity as well as insight:
"She is prettier than ever: but the knowledge of this fact is rapidly
spoiling her. Her main interest is now dress and she has
adopted—perhaps innocently and unconsciously—all those
provocative little mannerisms which underline the fact that blind
nature made her for one purpose. If only pretty women would
realize with how many and with WHAT people they share the
power of attracting in this way!"[18] Surely this is far too severe. It
shows no understanding of the temptations to which a pretty girl
is subject and no appreciation of the fundamental part played in
her life by what we would probably now call "her genes."
Incidentally the phrasing in this diary entry suggests that she may
be the girl of the poem "Infatuation," who is "a blind tool, when
nature bids her, labouring as she must," and to whom "friendship is a tittering hour of girl's caresses." He wrote approvingly
of Maureen's school friends Helen Rowell and Dorothy
Vaughan, the latter a lonely girl that Maureen, who shared her
mother's warmth of heart, had befriended. "Dorothea (Dotty or
Toddy or Totty, for D. has not yet settled her name) seems to have
many good qualities. She believes herself to be plain, always has
holes in her stockings and seldom has clean hands, has girlish
views on power and over interest in clothes." He described her
as "absolutely unaffected—a loud floundering, untidy, excitable

person." He even approved of her intellectually, commenting she "has read fairly widely and is full of extreme views on all imaginable subjects—just as one ought to be at her age."[19] He noted that she was also anxious to help in the house and had brought Mrs. Moore a present of oranges, which were at that time hard to find in the shops. Jack hoped that her father, who was impoverished, would allow her to stay at school for another year "and board with us at cost price. . . ." Mrs. Moore had already passed on to him her characteristic virtue of hospitality to the needy.

During this year of teaching at University College Jack applied for all fellowships in philosophy and English that were offered by Oxford colleges. The very last one he applied for was to teach English at Magdalen College. He had no serious hope of success because many senior men, including his old tutor, had put in for it. The telegram announcing that he had been elected reached his father on May 20: "Elected fellow Magdalen. Jack." Albert wrote in his diary: "I went to his room and burst into tears of joy. I knelt down and thanked God with a full heart. My prayers have been heard and answered."[20]

The appointment was initially for five years from June 25, 1925. Jack wrote to his father, thanking him wholeheartedly for his generous support over the last six years, which had enabled him to hang on for so long. He attributed his success to his being probably the only candidate who could teach both English and philosophy, the combination the college wanted because it was thought that few undergraduates would want to read English, a comparatively new subject. Jack unhesitatingly agreed. "I need hardly say that I would have agreed to coach a troupe of performing blackbirds in the quadrangle."[21] The pay was good, as fellowships went, starting at £500 a year, with provision made for rooms in college, a pension, and a dining allowance.

Jack's period of poverty ended with the Magdalen fellowship, but it marked him for life. From that time on, he found it difficult to spend more than the minimum amount on himself or more than a necessary amount on anyone or anything. His only personal luxuries were beer, whiskey, and tobacco, the first and last of which he regarded almost as necessities. He seems never to have owned a watch or a good fountain pen. What he gained from those years was a complete freedom from the snobbery based on possessions, and sympathy with and understanding of poor people. The many thousands of pounds he was to give away in the years ahead were nearly always bestowed on those short of money.

Mrs. Moore, Maureen, and Jack celebrated his success by taking a two-week holiday in Somerset. They seem to have traveled by train to Minehead and then by charabanc, "a long open vehicle with seats extending across and facing the front." He felt scared "on the nightmare hill from Porlock." On the day of their arrival in their Exmoor village Jack and Pat took a marvelous walk. When they came to a river, he took off his shoes to walk across it. The fording of that river with its cold water and smooth stepping stones realized his "best dreams."[22]

10

Fellow and Tutor

Jack spent thirty-five years of his life living, learning, and teaching in a town quite unlike all other university towns except Cambridge. There is no central campus, no obvious administrative center, at first sight no university. Instead, sited at various places throughout the town, there are about thirty colleges, many medieval in appearance and so independent that, not long before Jack's day, they could almost have been regarded as separate universities.

Of all Oxford's colleges, Magdalen is probably the loveliest. Jack found it "beautiful beyond compare."[1] Located just outside the old city walls on the banks of the Cherwell River, it is one of only three Oxford colleges that have water on their property (the others are the modern Saint Catherine's and the Victorian Saint Hilda's). It is not as closed in by buildings as the other medieval colleges. Behind it to the north, there is an extensive deer park, the only one in Oxford. In Jack's day, a fine herd of fallow deer enjoyed the shade of magnificent elms (which, unfortunately, have since fallen to Dutch elm disease). Across the river to the east are water meadows that are especially beautiful in early summer when masses of wild snake's-head fritillaries are hanging their heads in full flower. Around the meadow runs the famous Addison's Walk, and on its northern side there is the charming, secluded Fellow's Garden. The buildings of Magdalen cover more space than those of other colleges and form attractive clusters. The center of the college looks today much as it did at the time of its construction in the second half of the fifteenth century. There is a lovely, authentically medieval cloister enclosing a square of perfect grass, on which the college fellows have for hundreds of years played bowls; an exuberantly decorated chapel; and a dining hall with linen panelling that is said to have been brought from Reading Abbey at the time of the dissolution of the monasteries. More beautiful still is the elegant and slender tower, perfectly placed on High Street. Even the kitchens deserve careful study, for they date back to the thirteenth century.

Jack's rooms were not located in the medieval section of the College, but on the third staircase of New Buildings, a magnificent, austere structure of 1733, perfect in its proportions, with a portico twenty-seven bays long. Separated from the cloister by a fine lawn, it had the deer park on one side and at its back, so that undergraduates with ground-floor rooms could feed the deer from their windows. In spite of this attraction, fellows at the college preferred rooms on the first floor. Jack was delighted with the view. His big sitting room looked north. From it he could see no town buildings at all, "not even a gable or a spire." Below him there was a stretch of level grass, and beyond it a grove of "immemorial forest trees," which were at that time of year "coloured autumn red." The deer strayed over the grass. His other rooms faced south. From them there was a view "across a broad lawn" of the main buildings of Magdalen College including its famous tower.[2]

But it was a "crushing blow" to discover that his rooms were unfurnished, or almost so. He had to buy in haste enough furniture for two spacious sitting rooms and a bedroom: "carpets, tables, curtains, chairs, fenders, fire irons, coal boxes, everything." Although some things were bought secondhand, it cost him over £90 (equivalent perhaps to $6000 of modern money).[3] He was helped by a gift from his father and by the loan of some furniture, including two large mahogany bookcases that Mrs. Moore had brought over from Ireland and had kept in storage.

At Magdalen he was looked after by a scout, a manservant whose duties included waking him up in the morning; bringing hot water for washing and shaving, for the rooms in New Buildings were without modern conveniences; clearing out the grates and lighting fires in one or both sitting rooms (there was no central heating); making the bed; and cleaning and tidying the rooms.

In many other colleges, the scout would have also brought breakfast and lunch, but this was not the custom at Magdalen. Meals here were not normally served in rooms unless their owner ordered food specially, as for a party. On all ordinary occasions, the fellows of the college ate in the dining room of the Senior Common Room or, for dinner, in hall. Breakfast was eaten (one can hardly write served, as fellows served themselves) at a very large, round table, beginning at eight o'clock. During the first fifteen years of Jack's career, there was conflict between those who wanted to talk and those who wanted to eat breakfast in silence. To quote Lord Wolfenden, who preferred silence: "The oldest were the first to arrive; and not all of them had learnt in their long lives, that the breakfast table is no place for conversation. There were newspapers, and the more civilised of us took refuge behind them. But that did not provide complete escape from booming reminiscence or vituperative University politics."

Jack liked to eat breakfast early, because he would then have more time to complete his daily work. He arrived at eight or, when he had become a Christian, at a quarter past eight, after the fifteen-minute service in the college chapel, and usually found himself sitting with three others, Paul Benecke, J. A. Smith, and Adam Fox, all of whom liked to talk. This suited him perfectly; there were very few occasions when he did not enjoy good conversation.

Paul Victor Mendelssohn Benecke was the senior fellow of the college, a man thirty years older than Jack. He had been a "demy," the Magdalen term for a scholar entitled to free tuition and rooms, and had been awarded first-class degrees, as had Jack, in Honour Mods and Greats. He had also received top ranking in theology. The grandson of the composer Mendelssohn, he was himself a magnificent pianist, but, though he had a magnificent grand piano in his rooms, which were, like Jack's, in New Buildings, he never played it during term for fear of disturbing men who might be working. Another fellow with rooms in New Buildings, Dr. Hugh Sinclair, described Benecke to me as "the nearest approach to a saint" that he had ever known. In 1926 or 1927 Jack wrote a character sketch of him that shows Benecke's deep love of animals, the subject on which he spoke with most confidence, and an unusual insight into holiness. Benecke's holiness was revealed especially in his understanding of animals. He once told Jack that he understood why Indians perceived the deity in the elephant, and that the sadness in a dog's eyes arose from "its pity for men."[4]

He was an extraordinarily handsome man, who lived the life of an ascetic. Indeed, except for the fact that he drank nothing alcoholic, a description of his habits resembles Jack's own ten or twenty years later. He got up early in the morning, never missed a chapel service, and fasted on Fridays. He wore very old and ragged clothes, and during the Second World War, a time of fuel rationing, never had a fire in his rooms, so that in winter his pupils had to wear overcoats and several sweaters when they went to be taught by him. During the period of food rationing, which lasted until well after the end of the war, he tried to live without eating any rationed food at all, until a serious shortage of Vitamin A made him quite ill. He spent his leisure in charitable work, volunteering to do the dullest administrative tasks, just the ones that most people would try to avoid.

Jack always sprang to Benecke's defense when younger fellows made fun of him. He was deeply influenced by Benecke and thought of him as the model of a sanctity that he could never attain.

Another man Jack ate breakfast with was J. A. Smith, the Waynflete Professor of moral and metaphysical philosophy. Smith was a learned Scotsman who had the habit of coming into the breakfast room and discussing the odd little problems on which he had been speculating before going to sleep or when awake during the night. Adam Fox records that one morning he said that he had been thinking how terrible it would be for a learned Chinese to go blind. The reason, it seemed, was that the ideograms that compose Chinese writing convey meaning to the eye, but have no sounds attached to them. Reading, therefore, was like looking at a picture book.

Jack always enjoyed acquiring such strange pieces of information, but he was most influenced by J. A. (as he was always called) in his role as philologist. In his old age, J. A. specialized in combating accepted notions of what words really meant. Thus he once surprised Adam Fox by stating that *cheir*, the usual Greek word for "hand," really meant "forearm." This interest in words also became a habit for Jack. (The habit was further encouraged by frequent conversations with Professor C. T. Onions, one of the editors of the great *New English Dictionary* and a man of vast learning, who unfortunately did not often appear at breakfast although he often dined in hall.) Some of the meanings in Jack's book *Studies in Words* are certainly indebted to J. A. As Jack once wrote, living on the same staircase with him was in itself a "liberal education." Like J. A., he must have educated hundreds of pupils in the true meaning of that phrase. I remember him saying, "You've got it wrong. *Liberal* comes of course from the Latin, *liber*, and means free. A liberal education is then the sort of education suitable for a free man, as distinct from a servile or mechanical education, one suited for a slave or an artisan."[5]

Another breakfast companion was Adam Fox, the devout and gentle dean of the Divinity School, who helped Jack along the road to Christianity by his example and wise advice. Fox was also a lover of poetry, although not as an academic. His election to the professorship of poetry in 1938 was a complete surprise and the result of an impulsive remark that Fox had made at the Senior Common Room breakfast table. Senior members of the university with masters' degrees would make the appointment by nomination and election. Fox heard at breakfast that some members had nominated E. K. Chambers, an elderly, learned, but reputedly dry-as-dust scholar. He was horrified and said, "This is simply shocking. They might as well make me Professor of Poetry."

Jack said at once, "Right, we will." And he set to work, lobbying and gaining the support of an influential group of dons, including Lord David Cecil, J. R. R. Tolkien, and Hugo Dyson. Other members of the English faculty thought Fox an unsuitable candidate because he was entirely unacademic and had published nothing except a "long and rather childlike poem" called *Old King Coel* in 1937. They therefore made the mistake of putting up a second academic candidate whom they thought stronger than Chambers. The result was that the academic votes were divided, and Adam Fox was elected.

In asking us to vote for Adam Fox, Jack said that he believed Fox would say "a great many things about poetry that are true and are rarely, if ever, said." In fact, his lectures were a disappointment. In a letter to Warren after he had listened to the first one, "given in what must surely be the most beautiful room in Oxford, the old Divinity School," Jack described it as "very good but not capital."[6] In later years, he usually admitted that his advocacy of Adam Fox as a professor was a mistake. It was one that many members of the faculty found hard to forgive.

Although Jack normally felt at his best early in the morning and enjoyed the conversational breakfasts of the days before majority opinion enforced silence, he did not linger long over them. He had far too much work to do. His first pupil was due for a tutorial at nine, and Jack, always an extremely conscientious tutor, never saw a pupil without preparing the subject of his essay, even if only by a few minutes of reading or rereading.

He enjoyed dinner in the evening even more than breakfast. The meal was very much part of a fellow's life in those days, the terms of his appointment including a free dinner at hall. And what a dinner it was at Magdalen! In one way, it was less formal than at most other Oxford colleges because the dons did not always dress for it. Black dinner jacket, black tie, and starched shirt were required dress only on Sundays when the president dined there. (Otherwise, the president dined at home with his family, the women of his household being the only women living on college grounds, the families of other dons living in private houses, perhaps in north Oxfordshire a few miles away.) The president would give advance notice of his intention of dining at hall, and a note would be sent to all the fellows to warn them to dress.

The hall at Magdalen has at one end an early seventeenth-century screen richly carved with scenes from the life of Saint Mary Magdalen and above it a minstrel's or choir's gallery. At the other end of the hall, a low dais runs across the entire width of the room and supports the high table, which, like all the tables in the hall, is made of English oak. Before dinner fellows might meet in the Senior Common Room to sip glasses of sherry while undergraduates and other members of the college would take their places at the hall and remain standing. Demies and senior members wore billowy, black gowns, and undergraduates wore odd little gowns cut like sleeveless jackets but without buttons. Fellows, also wearing gowns, would enter in procession, led by the president or vice-president, the rest in order of seniority. Their places at the high table would depend on seniority, too. The president, vice-president, or senior fellow would say a grace in Latin, after which everyone would be seated.

College servants carried large trays of food to the high table. Five courses were usually served: soup; an entree or fish course; meat, game, or poultry; a pudding; and a savory. Luxuries, such as oysters, smoked salmon, or caviar, would sometimes be served. The food was carried around on large silver dishes from which fellows would help themselves. French or German wine was the most usual drink, but a fellow could order what he liked for himself and his guest, if he had one. The meal was leisurely and the diners talkative. Long before it was over, the inferior beings at the other tables would have gone to drink coffee in the Junior Common Room or each other's rooms and then to their evening pursuits. The slow pace caused some difficulty for Jack, who had been a very quick eater ever since Wynyard. When he became vice-president, he altered the serving routine so that he would be served last, rather than first. Even so he managed to clear the plates in front of him before most others at the high table. The vice-president who succeeded him was quick to reinstate the old routine.

Dinner at hall, especially in winter, was a lovely sight. The great room was lit entirely by table lamps screened with silk shades. There was sufficient light to dimly illuminate the low-pitched oak roof and on the walls at the far end the portraits of past members of the college, including that dashing seventeenth-century cavalry officer, Prince Rupert.

After the savory had been eaten, the dons who were going to take wine would hang their gowns up in the vestibule of the Senior Common Room and then move to the dining room where many of them had eaten breakfast. Now it would be lit only by candles. Silver dishes of fruit and nuts gleamed softly, and decanters of wine were at the ready. The president, if he were present, would no longer preside—his status there was that of a guest. The place of honor would be taken by the vice-president or, in his absence, the senior fellow. Guests were usually seated with fellows other than their hosts. The vice-president would help himself to a glass of wine, vintage port, Madeira, claret, or brown sherry, the latter being Jack's favorite after-dinner wine. The decanters would be passed around slowly in a clockwise direction, the way of the sun. Only a limited amount of wine would be put out on the tables, perhaps enough for each fellow to have two glasses, but through a device called a "buzz" an extra decanter could be demanded. This occurred when a decanter was emptied by turning it upside down into a glass, so making that glass about half full. Then a clean glass and another full decanter of the same wine would be brought, and the receiver of the "buzz" would have the option of not drinking the partly filled glass. The theory behind this practice was that mixing wine from two different bottles in the same glass might destroy the distinctive character of each. While wine was being passed, nuts would be cracked and fruit eaten with silver fruit knives and forks. For many older dons, wine in the Common Room was the happiest time of the day. Conversation was far-reaching, and it was not thought correct to talk about one's own professional subject of study. After the wine had been drunk, there came a pinch of snuff and coffee. Then the dons would return to their rooms or houses.

The fellows of the college in Jack's day formed a largely bachelor community, and "wines" were extremely popular and well attended. (Today they are rarely held.) Magdalen and other Oxford colleges were proud of their cellars. Wine was carefully bought by a select wine committee and left to mature in the college's cellars for up to twenty years. The fine wine, lovely surroundings, and brilliant conversation were immensely enjoyable. Jack talked with many brilliant men in the Common Room. There was Lord Adrian, a doctor who won the Nobel Prize in 1932 for his work on pain and nerve cells; John Austin, a most gifted philosopher; Gilbert Ryle, whose linguistic thinking revolutionized Oxford philosophy; and A. J. P. Taylor, a witty and controversial historian. Besides the fellows, there were the guests, among them the brightest and wittiest men in Oxford.

Much as Jack enjoyed drinking wine after dinner, he did not have time to go to the Common Room more than twice a week. During the term, his evenings were full. On one evening, he usually had a class in Anglo-Saxon with his pupils; on another (usually a Monday), he would read a play with a group of undergraduates; on still another, he would join J. R. R. Tolkien and a few others in a meeting of the Coalbiters, an Icelandic society (later succeeded by the Inklings), the object of which was to read the Sagas and Eddas in Old Norse. He was also busy preparing lectures, reading for tutorials and for pleasure, and writing letters and the drafts of his first great academic work, *The Allegory of Love*. We do not know much more about his life during his early years as a tutor. Even his correspondence with Arthur Greeves lapsed for a time, and he wrote far less often to his father and brother.

The tutorial system, the distinguishing characteristic of

Oxford education, is not an old tradition, but a product of the nineteenth century. Nevertheless, to understand how the system developed, it is helpful to know some of the history of the university. This was a subject that Jack liked to explain.

In medieval Oxford, the university hardly existed. The colleges, which, by royal charter, were independent, self-governing bodies, provided free board and education to a particular number of scholars, usually with special qualifications or from a specified part of the country. Thus, the purpose of Exeter College was to educate scholars from the diocese of Exeter. These scholars governed the college, but most of the business would be done by the senior scholars who had earned masters' degrees and who in the course of time came to be known as fellows. Quite early on, these scholars allowed other students, then known as commoners, now as undergraduates, to live with them at their own expense. In the middle of the nineteenth century, most colleges still restricted fellowships to unmarried men born locally or to men with special educational qualifications.

Each college had its own income, endowed by gifts of land and buildings. In addition, the university also received endowments, often for professorships in classics, mathematics, and the small range of subjects that were then studied. These professors lectured to all members of the university. On the other hand, the fellows, or senior members of colleges, lectured only to members of their colleges. The standard of teaching varied greatly from college to college, and the standard of degrees awarded by the university was low compared with those of other countries and of the new civic universities in London, Manchester, and Birmingham.

During the latter part of the eighteenth century and before the reforms of 1803–1807, it was possible for undergraduates to choose, not only the books on which they were to be examined, but also, by paying a modest fee to the proctors, their examiners. The exams would be mainly or entirely oral reviews and the questions, if the student knew his examiner, quite predictable.

The first reforms came at the end of a century during which university professors and college fellows did very little teaching. Most professors did not lecture at all. Even by 1800, when standards were rising, only one in three gave lectures. The usual excuse was either that no one turned up to hear the lectures or that too few turned up to form a quorum. If a lecturer arrived and found only two or three present, he was at liberty to simply repeat a Latin formula, say "*Valete*" (Latin for "farewell"), and leave.

A man could probably get university teaching (even lecturing) if he could collect a quorum of serious students among his friends and then boldly approach a professor who had not made other arrangements. However, very few undergraduates in those days were suited to this method of teaching; they were too young. Many came to Oxford, as did Edward Gibbon (author of the great *Decline and Fall of the Roman Empire*), at the age of fifteen. Only with the development of England's grammar schools did the age of college entrance rise.

Yet the eighteenth-century curriculum was, in its way, a broad one. It was a seven-year course, starting with one year of studying grammar and rhetoric and another year of studying Aristotle's ethics and politics, logic, and economics. The third and fourth years were devoted to logic, moral philosophy, geometry, and Greek; and the three years between the bachelor's and master's degrees to geometry, astronomy, metaphysics, natural philosophy, ancient history, Greek, and Hebrew. This was a splendidly comprehensive course on paper, but an impractical one unless backed by a demanding examination system.

To supply this need and to reform the university, a succession of royal commissions was set up by Parliament. Early commissions strengthened the structure of the university and introduced a higher level of evaluation in which students were ranked according to first-, second-, third-, or fourth-class honors. This had the effect of forcing the colleges to take more seriously the task of teaching undergraduates.

In 1854 the territorial link between colleges and particular parts of the country was abolished, and professors opened their lectures to men in other colleges. The standard was still often deplorably low, but because colleges were in competition with each other, it tended to rise, although slowly. (For a long time—indeed, until the beginning of the Second World War—admission to Oxford depended far more on being able to pay the fees or on having been to the right schools than on possession of academic ability.) Thus, political writer William Cobbett commented in his *Rural Rides* in 1821: "Upon beholding the mass of buildings at Oxford, devoted to what they call 'Learning,' I could not help reflecting on the drones that they contain and the wasps they send forth! However, malignant as some are, the great and prevalent characteristic is *folly*; emptiness of head; want of talent; and one half of the fellows who are *educated* here are unfit to be clerks in a grocer's or mercer's shop."

The frequency with which commoners failed exams led the colleges to appoint fellows to tutor them. Thereafter, fellows were often appointed because it was thought that they might make good lecturers or tutors. As more and more academic books were published, undergraduates tended to rely more and more on the teaching of their tutors rather than on learning through lectures. Thus, the tutoring system evolved.

In Jack's day, there still existed notoriously lazy tutors who did not always bother to show up. But for a conscientious man like Jack, tutoring was hard work, especially if one considers that he had lectures to give, classes to take, college business to attend to, and his own academic writing to get on with.

The tutorial was a formal occasion. Wearing a gown, a pupil would stand outside the tutor's door and wait until the clock struck before knocking. Jack's door, like all the doors in New Buildings, was thick, but through it one could easily hear the strong, booming voice say, "Come in." The room was adequately, but rather shabbily, furnished. On one side of the lovely eighteenth-century fireplace, in which a coal fire would be burning during cold weather, was a sofa upon which Jack sat; on the other side was an armchair for the student.

The tutorial always began the same way. The pupil would read the essay that he had been told to write the week before. Jack, who would have spent some time that week reading the books with which the essay was concerned, would sit listening, very often lighting, smoking, and relighting his pipe, and perhaps making a few notes. Afterward, he would make wide-ranging criticisms, some of them semantic or philological, for he always hated the inexact use of words.

"What exactly do you mean by the word *sentimental,* Mr. Sayer?" he might begin. Then he would present a summary of the ways in which the word had been used in the past, perhaps adding, "Well, Mr. Sayer, if you are not sure what the word means or what you mean by it, wouldn't it be very much better if you ceased to use it at all?" Some of the words that he discussed in tutorials are among those he later included in *Studies in Words.*

He never used fashionable literary jargon and was severe on those who did. He would often affect Socratic ignorance: "I am not quite sure what you mean by this term. Perhaps you would be so good as to translate it for me into plain English." This process taught the pupil to be careful about the language he used.

Years later he and I discussed why there was an increasing tendency to use technical, pseudoscientific language in literary criticism. We decided that it was because those who read and taught English literature were all too aware that their subject of study was regarded by other people as simple recreation. To be their equals, indeed, to justify their existence, English tutors cultivated a jargon that gave their work a pseudoscientific character.

Of course, Jack expected his pupils' essays to be entirely their own work, and he was properly unmerciful with those who used unacknowledged quotations. Thus he wrote in his diary of one student, John Betjeman (who later became Poet Laureate of England), that he soon discovered that the apparently excellent essay Betjeman had read to him was "a pure fake," for the subsequent discussion showed that his pupil knew nothing about the subject. Jack wished he "could get rid of the idle prig."[7]

This illustrates another point about the tutorial. In the discussion that followed the reading of the essay, the student was expected to defend and enlarge on the opinions and statements he had made in the essay. If he had been told the week before to read novels or poems in addition to those covered in the essay, he would be asked fairly searching questions about them, too.

When he first began tutoring, Jack was severe, harsh, and argumentative. One of his very first pupils Bede Griffiths had taken his first degree in Greek and Latin texts and was already searching for the emotional and intellectual wholeness that is part of the theme of his books *The Golden String* and *Return to the Centre*. He explained to Jack that he wanted to read English literature because it would involve, not just his intellect, but his whole personality. Jack argued quite violently with him, much to his astonishment. The desire for emotional involvement, Jack said, was the wrong motive entirely. The romantic sensibility was something to be restrained. Griffiths should study English for linguistic reasons, because of an interest in the development of language and in the authors' ideas. Fortunately, Griffiths did not take this advice. He felt that Jack was running away from his own excessive romantic sensibility and that what might be true for Jack (and he doubted if it were true) need not be true for him.

Jack's attitude toward his pupils became far gentler and more sympathetic within a few years, when he learned how to conceal his diffidence and sensitivity under a hearty and frequently humorous manner. His early harshness resulted in part from his expecting too much of his students. He had been appointed a fellow to teach English, but he had few pupils to teach because the Honours School of English Language and Literature had just been formed. Furthermore, the students he had, for the most part, were not clever, and some were lazy. He also shared with Harry Weldon the responsibility of teaching some philosophy pupils, and he complained that Weldon took the best: "He regards [them] as his if they turn out well and mine if they turn out ill—and I am now heartily sick of the whole business."[8]

He found Magdalen College undergraduates less civilized than those he had known at University College, and he was astonished to find no literary society, a lack that would be "laughable" in any other College. The reason was that in the time of the last president of Magdalen, all college societies had been forbidden in order to protect the position of the exclusive clubs of rich, hard-drinking undergraduates who dominated the whole life of the place. This prohibition stifled all intellectual life to such an extent that the undergraduates who were interested in things higher than "rowing, drinking, motoring and fornication" made friends outside the college and rarely discovered those fellow members who had similar tastes.

With the help of one or two other fellows, Jack set out to start a literary society. This had to be done with tact and delicacy, which meant "endless waste of time." They had to persuade other fellows to agree to the relaxation of the rule against societies. Then they had to be very careful in the choice of undergraduates as members. It was important that the scheme should not seem obviously to be run by dons. He worried that the whole show might be a dismal failure because of the low calibre of the students.

Jack felt that the college would never be more than a club for "the idiot bloods of Eton and Charterhouse" while undergraduates thought it "bad form" to discuss among themselves the subjects of their academic essays. Magdalen undergraduates were both "absolute babies and terrific men of the world," he wrote. They had, as Henry James put it, both "the cynicism of forty and the mental crudeness and confusion of fourteen." Would England, he wondered, "kill the public schools before the public schools kill it?" The most scholarly and the best-mannered men seemed to come from the great day schools, often with the aid of scholarships. Except in the case of a few students of classics at Winchester, the public schools gave to their pupils nothing of value "beyond the surface of good manners," "unless contempt of the things of the intellect, extravagance, insolence, self-sufficiency, and sexual perversion are to be called gifts."[9]

The play readings were not always pleasant for him. Thus, after a reading of Webster's play *The White Devil*, he recorded that all but one of his pupils turned out "rather vulgar and strident" with "guffaws at obscenity." Though he was willing to socialize with his pupils outside the college, he did not always find their company congenial. He records in his diary an afternoon tea party with John Betjeman. He did not want to go when Betjeman rang up the same morning, but felt obliged to accept. He entered a very beautiful panelled room looking across to Christ Church and found himself "pitchforked into a galaxy of super-undergraduates." Among those he remembered were "an absolutely silent and astonishingly ugly person called McNeice, of whom Betjeman said afterwards, 'He doesn't say much but he's a great poet . . .'" Jack found that the conversation was mainly about architecture, "the strange habits of hearties," and such things as china ornaments, lace curtains, and the advantages of silver versus earthenware teapots. What interested him most was Betjeman's "very curious collection of books." After the party he walked back to Magdalen with his host "in order to pull him through Wulfstan till dinner time." He concluded that "in spite of all his rattle," Betjeman was just as "ignorant and stupid" as his other undergraduate pupil, Valentin.[10]

The word *hearties* deserves comment. During the period between the wars, undergraduates who had come from socially prestigious boarding schools tended to split into two groups. Those who played football, cricket, and the other games that had been compulsory at their public schools were called "hearties"; those who despised the emphasis of school culture on sports and who showed their disdain by decorating their rooms oddly, perhaps with surrealist pictures, and by reading authors such as Gide and Oscar Wilde were called "aesthetes." Members of the two groups wore different clothes: conventional gray flannel trousers with tweed jackets and school or club ties for the hearties; corduroy trousers, brightly colored silk shirts, and velvet ties for the aesthetes. The two groups despised each other. Most undergraduates at the time did not have mistresses or lovers of the same sex, but it was often rumored of certain aesthetes that they were homosexual. Once, in looking across the lawn from their New Buildings window, Jack and Warren noticed two brightly dressed aesthetes walking arm in arm together. Warren remarked that in spite of all their plumage, he thought them quite an ugly pair. Jack replied, "Well, buggers can't be choosers!"

Both Jack and Warren dressed like hearties, only more untidily, but neither took the slightest interest in games or sports, except for croquet, badminton, and table tennis. Jack was also unlike an aesthete in the practical and businesslike way in which he conducted tutorials and in the anti-romantic views he often expressed.

Professor John Lawlor, who had expected Jack to be something of an aesthete, records his surprise: "My first tap on the door drew a bellowed 'Come in!'—and there was my mentor for the next three years—red-faced, bald . . . dressed in baggy jacket and trousers (alas! no pastel tie) and obviously in no mood to waste time—a permanent characteristic, I found." He mentions, too, "Lewis's determined impersonality towards all except his very closest friends." Like many other people, Lawlor had the impression that Jack hated teaching. He must have been frustrated by his students' poor work. Lawlor writes that "he tended to accept them with ironic resignation."[11] He also regretted that tutoring took time away from his work on *The Allegory of Love* and the space trilogy (*Out of the Silent Planet*, *Perelandra*, and *That Hideous Strength*).

But if he did at times dislike tutorial work, he never showed it to his students. To them he was unfailingly courteous, genial, and cheerful. He made efforts, too, to put his pupils at ease, sometimes offering them cigarettes and beer. If one made a good joke in his essay, he would laugh heartily. In fact, he was probably at his best with shy and diffident pupils, to whom he would try to give confidence and encouragement. He had nothing of the bully about him and would never use his great learning and powers of argument to crush a defenseless opponent. On the other hand, the clever, conceited undergraduate would arouse in him

JACK: A LIFE OF C. S. LEWIS

the desire to go into battle. Thus he once said to me of Kenneth Tynan: "He is a very clever man and knows it. I am tempted to do all I can to prevent him getting a First, but I don't think I should succeed even if I tried my hardest. All I can do is to try to knock some of the conceit out of him."

Jack tried to help his pupils get the best degrees possible, for he knew how important first-class honors were for a student who wanted a university teaching job. In his own mind, he rather sharply categorized students as first- or second-class and thought it a great triumph if a man who was, in his opinion, second-class got a first. He changed his views about this after ten years of tutoring, believing then that if he had helped a second to get a first, he had been involved in an almost dishonest act. On the other hand, he came to think that it never mattered very much if a first-class man got a second. It might help to preserve him from the sin of pride. In general, the diffident but intelligent students thought him an excellent tutor, whereas the conceited were often unhappy with him.

Everyone recognized the breadth of his knowledge. He was widely read and had a remarkable memory that enabled him to quote at length from any author who interested him and even from some who did not. No pupil of his will ever forget the way he quoted the poetry he enjoyed. The voice was rich, the delivery rhythmical with full attention to the meter of the lines. There would be a light in his eyes and a look of intense joy on his face. His delight was infectious.

Until very late in his career, he took no interest at all in free verse, and even then perhaps only in a little poetry by Edith Sitwell and T. S. Eliot. He tended to regard the new poetry with its formlessness and lack of poetic diction as a revolutionary movement deliberately directed against the traditions of English poetry. The part played in it by Ezra Pound and T. S. Eliot had much to do with his anti-American bias. He was, in fact, ignorant of much modern writing, especially if it was fashionable.

Most of his views were privately held. A student who asked him a direct question would get a direct answer, but generally students were kept so busy that there was no time for such questions. It would have been easy to have been taught by him for three years without realizing that he was a Christian. Likewise, a student would probably not be aware of his literary tastes, except perhaps the dislikes he could not keep to himself— Restoration dramatists and the then-fashionable Jonson, Middleton, and Marston. When I was his student, he ceased to regard me impersonally only when I told him that I had come across a remarkable book by an author whom I had never heard of before, a book that I thought he might enjoy reading, George MacDonald's *Lilith*. He remarked at once, "Holy Writ apart, I know of no book that is in a spiritual sense more deeply moving." From that moment on, his attitude toward me completely changed. A few weeks later, he shared with me one of his discoveries, *The Place of the Lion* by Charles Williams, a book that I think he had heard about from Nevill Coghill.

Although the real man was hidden behind the mask of the self-assured, hearty, argumentative tutor, all of his students shared certain impressions. He was known as a man of exceptional intellectual and even physical vitality, a quality that grew over the years. His flow of wit, humor, and vivid stories told in his deep, rich voice was inexhaustible. He was a good listener as well, and one knew that he would never disclose a confidence entrusted to him. He was a man of his word, a man of integrity, a man of honor.

11

Dymer

Jack began work at Magdalen College in October 1925. The following year, his long poem *Dymer* was published. Although it was the least successful commercially of all his works, it took the longest to write, was the most personal, and changed him most deeply.

In one way or another, he spent nine or ten years on it. In the preface to the 1950 reprint, he tells us that he was aware of the basic myth when he was about seventeen. He neither dreamed it nor consciously invented it—it just came into his mind, "the story of a man who, on some mysterious beast, begets a monster, which monster, as soon as it has killed its father, becomes a god." The first version does not survive. We know that it was written in prose in 1916 and that an early title was "The Redemption of Ask" (even during his atheist period, he was concerned with redemption). The first four cantos of the poem were written in 1922 in what seemed a rush of inspiration; the other five cantos were written in 1924 and 1925.

Dymer is about the relationship of fantasy to reality. All through the years that Jack spent writing it, he was worried by the intensity of his imagination and alarmed by his tendency to withdraw from life and to luxuriate in self-flattering fantasies of love, cruelty, lust, or heroism. In his diary, he wrote of the dangers of such daydreams, calling them "Christina dreams," a term inspired by Christina Pontifex, the heroine of Samuel Butler's *The Way of All Flesh*. He wrote in his entry of May 24, 1922, that Owen Barfield and he "walked to Wadham gardens and sat under the trees. We began with Christina Dreams: I condemned them—the love dream made a man incapable of real love, the hero dream made him a coward. He took the opposite view and a stubborn argument followed." Years later he would still argue the same point. In a letter he wrote in 1956 to a Mr. Masson, he states that the real evil of masturbation is that it "sends the man back into the person of himself, there to keep a harem of imaginary brides. And this harem, once admitted, works against his *ever* getting out and really uniting with a real woman. . . . Among those shadowy brides he is always adored, always the perfect lover; no demand is made on his unselfishness, no mortification ever imposed on his vanity. In the end they become merely the medium through which he increasingly adores himself."

His objection to indulgence in Christina dreams—that they weaken and corrupt the dreamer's personality—is the point assumed in *Dymer*. In writing the poem, Jack worked through his obsessions and did much to cure himself of his excessive fantasizing.

The poem begins, rather in the manner of Byron's *Don Juan*, with several brilliant stanzas of satire on the Platonic, or totalitarian, state. Jack put into them, as he tells us, both his hatred of Malvern College and army life and his disapproval of Plato's perfect city, which is like that of *Brave New World*, of *R. U. R.*, of genetic engineering, and of the extremes of communism.

In this perfect city "no hour was left uncharted . . . love was in a schedule," and the state chose who would mate with whom. The hero, Dymer, was brought up in the public creche, and "twenty separate Boards of Education closed round him." He passed every test, and for "nineteen years he bore it meekly."[1]

Nature is the enemy of the Perfect City. Dymer is stirred by nature to rebel against authoritarianism. He is in a room being lectured when he feels a little breeze and sees a brown bird perched on the windowsill, and, suddenly feeling that there is something ludicrous about his lecturer, he bursts into laughter. When told to be silent, ". . . he struck the lecturer's head, The old man tittered, lurched and dropt down dead."[2] The curt, semicomic language conveys Dymer's lack of guilt at this moment. Later in the poem, he develops a conscience or a sense of guilt, and this is one of the poem's themes, but first he wants to revel in his new freedom. He strips off his clothes and runs around wildly. Soon, however, he begins to feel the purposelessness of his actions.

By evening he is hungry and cold and finds the darkness menacing. Nature is not evil; perhaps it is both good and evil. But without some sort of faith or the strength that comes from wholeness of personality, he is unable to endure contact with nature and therefore takes refuge in fantasy. Music draws him into a palace where he finds a large mirror in which he sees himself naked. Near the mirror hang clothes of all kinds. In spite of scruples, possibly because he is stealing, but more likely because in dressing up he will be surrendering to a variety of make-believe fantasies, he helps himself to them. He feels himself to be a fine-looking fellow and dreams the hero dreams. First he dreams that he will lead a rebellion in the Perfect City, but this fantasy does not satisfy him. Dreaming more deeply, he imagines himself as a destructive tyrant who will lead a mob to destroy the City.

The next phase is gluttony. After eating and drinking well, he desires richer and more intoxicating fare. He is drawn through curtains into a dark, womblike place that is not wholly evil and perhaps not evil at all. It has "a cool smell that was holy and unholy" (in Lewis's work, coolness usually goes with goodness). Air "Sharp like the very spring and roughly sweet / Blew towards him."[3] He finds himself knee-deep in pillows on the ground. What follows, intercourse with "the mysterious bride," is also "holy and unholy." It seems that he is not spiritually ready for union with her, although she represents both the deity and the feminine principle for which he is unconsciously searching and which he needs for his completion. His union with her is both destructive and procreative, like nature: Night both "swelled the mushroom in earth's lap" and "sent the young wolves howling after blood."[4] The mysterious bride is gone when he wakes in the morning. He longs more than anything else to be with her again, and the rest of the poem is the story of his search for her.

When he tries to reenter the palace, he finds the way barred by a monster in the likeness of an old woman with "pale hands of wrinkled flesh, / Puckered and gnarled with vast antiquity." She is "the old matriarchal dreadfulness, immovable, intolerable."[5] Some critics have erroneously seen her as a representation of Mrs. Moore. But Jack could never have depicted an intimate friend in this way. It would have been incompatible with his conception of loyalty and good manners. Others take her to be Lust. But this is also unlikely. For one thing, Jack knew perfectly well that Lust must be, in part, attractive. For another, the union that she is barring is partly unholy, and it is inconceivable that Lust would object to unholiness.

Dymer is not ready for the mysterious bride as long as he is "the weak, the passionate, the fool of dreams." He must first grow up, overcome his fault, and accept his destiny. In the next canto, he feels guilty. He learns that the rebellion, which had been kindled by his attack on the lecturer and escape from the Perfect City, has ended in the misery of a civil war savagely waged by rebels and suppressed by soldiers. Dymer's daydreaming is to blame, not only for his personal defeat, but also for a political rebellion that has done terrible damage to others. From now on he is driven by guilt and shame: "Little thoughts like bees . . . pricked him on and left no ease."[6]

Obsessed by his own worthlessness, he wishes for death. Now that his search for self-fulfillment and individuation have failed, he falls into a state of neurotic self-pity. He slips and nearly falls down a cliff to his death, but cares about life just enough to hang on. He is rescued from this agony of despair by something like a miracle, an experience of joy: "a pure voice of a lark . . . that bird sang out of heaven."[7]

Humility makes it possible for him to glimpse the world as it really is, undistorted by his daydreaming. However, the quest for truth is so arduous that he is still tempted to dream. This temptation is strongest in the sixth and seventh cantos, after he has gone into the house of a master magician for a meal. Dymer distrusts him at once because he shot the lark, but a good meal makes him drowsy and easily influenced. The magician talks

> till he had quite stolen away
> Dymer's dull wits and softly drawn apart
> The ivory gates of hope that change the heart.

The magician induces Dymer to tell his story and then sets out to tempt Dymer to dream again and more deeply. He must close his eyes to the real world and live as far as possible in the world of fantasy, where he will forget his guilt. The magician suggests that Dymer's moral standpoint is itself a fantasy, and eventually persuades him to share a drink from a magic cup. While the elixir makes the host wildly sick, it stimulates Dymer, who has an erotic dream, beautiful but without any of the warm love he seeks:

It is a world of sad, cold, heartless stuff,
Like a bought smile, no joy in it. . . .[8]

He meets a fantasy woman and is very nearly seduced. But he rejects her, and then he is offered only "King Lust with his black, sudden, serious stare."

There follows one of the most vivid orgies of sexual temptation in the whole of English poetry. There are preying fingertips, warm mouths, rolling breasts; shaggy satyrs, devil dancers, and the incessant beating of a drum. Dymer escapes the orgy because he asks about the moral consequences of giving way: "How close to the soft laughter comes the scream?"[9] The magician turns him out of his house and, as he runs away, wounds him with a rifle shot. In great pain, Dymer again meets the mysterious bride. She explains her nature to him, and he then realizes that what he had really loved was spirit. Before she vanishes, she warns him that he is still dreaming and that his obsession with death is in itself a harmful fantasy.

Dymer reviews his life, thinks of the several Dymers he has been that have died, and suspects that there is another manifestation of himself yet to die. He is surprised to find himself struggling toward "the old superstition," a place with a belfry and a graveyard. Here he has the remarkable experience of spiritual ascent. The last supports of everyday life fell away from him. The "one spark of soul" to which he was reduced "swam in unbroken void. He was the whole."[10]

He meets a sentry whose duty it is to protect mankind from strange monsters that roam at night. He is advised to leave but refuses. Then he hears an objective account of himself and of the conception of the monster who is his son. How he, ignorant of himself, "swollen with youth" and "blind from new-broken prison," mated with he did not know whom, "he mortal, she immortal, and begot this monster of the night."[11]

Dymer knows at once that it is his duty to face and fight the monster. Whatever the outcome, he will redeem himself by facing himself and the results of his own actions. He will attain full manhood and in the process do something to redeem the earth. Although he is quickly crushed and killed, his courage in facing the truth sets off a process of cosmic rebirth: Plants blossom; the country is clothed with dancing flowers. He himself shares in the general purification and becomes a god.

Dymer is a genuine myth. One critic, Marjorie Mack, has interpreted it as being essentially about Lewis's search for his poetic muse. According to Mack, Dymer is Lewis seeking his true literary vocation. He fails to find it where he first seeks it, in the palace of romantic tradition set in nature. Only through disillusionment and suffering can he obtain an accurate view of his literary vocation, a perception that will involve a correct relationship with both tradition and the cosmos. Only the death of Lewis-the-romantic-dreamer can make possible the birth of his new literary vision, one based, not on self-centered fantasy, but ultimately on God, the great and true romantic.[12]

The manuscript of *Dymer* was offered to Heinemann under the terms of the *Spirits in Bondage* contract. After Heinemann had refused it, it was sent to and accepted by J. M. Dent and Sons and was published under the pseudonym of Clive Hamilton on September 20, 1926. It is a well-printed octavo of 104 pages, bound in cloth.

The reviewers received it remarkably well. Hugh d'A Fausset, who reviewed it for *The Times Literary Supplement*, wrote privately to Jack: "I have not read any poem recently which has so impressed me by its inevitability of expression and by the profundity of its metaphysics. . . . [I]t is by its metaphysical reach that your poem stands head and shoulders above most modern verse. But it is a metaphysic which is wholly . . . translated into terms of image and symbolism, and this seems to me the final test of greatness in poetry." *The Spectator*'s reviewer described it as "a little epic burnt out of vital experience and given us through a poet's eye." *The Poetry Review* was "wholly delighted by the lyrical quality of many of the lines." *The Times* compared it to John Masefield's *Dauber*. Dilys Powell in *The Sunday Times* admired its "consistent craftsmanship" and "unusual sureness" but thought that the idea was not suitable for treatment in verse ("as a prose tale how splendidly it would have flowed!").

After such reviews, it is remarkable that the book failed so completely. So few copies of the first edition were sold that it is now an even rarer book than *Spirits in Bondage*. Not more than a dozen copies are known to exist. But everything except its intrinsic merit went against it. It was a long poem at a time when long poems, unless written by such well-known poets as Masefield and Bridges, had ceased to be read. It was unfashionable in that it rhymed and scanned and had complex stanzas at a time when free verse was the "in" thing. Its imagery was traditionally poetic, as Tennyson and Swinburne would have understood the term, at a time when these poets were both despised. It was grammatical and made sense at a time when poetry was expected to be obscure. It was written to be read aloud at a time when the reading of poetry aloud was out of fashion and perhaps beginning to be a lost art.

The tide of fashion has not yet turned. Even the best of Swinburne is unappreciated today, but it is far too early to form a just estimate of *Dymer*. Certainly the poem has great merits. It is an original myth, one that very different people feel to be profound, even if they cannot comprehend it intellectually. It uses traditional folklore elements, such as the enchanted palace and the mysterious bride, with fresh symbolic power. Its main subject, the dangers of fantasy or excessive daydreaming, is of lasting importance. The story is well told and at times even exciting. It contains splendid poetry, diverse in kind. The satirical stanzas at the beginning are as good as any in *Don Juan*, the scenes of horror as convincing as any in modern literature. Throughout there are lovely passages of natural description. Occasionally, there are lines that surprise us with their power and originality of thought. Eventually perhaps *Dymer* may come to be accepted as one of few long poems of real excellence written in this century.

12

The Pilgrim's Regress

Jack's conversion to Christianity occurred over a period of several years—from 1926, the year *Dymer* was published, when he began to believe in a nebulous power outside himself, to 1931, when he became a believer in Christ. As Warren wrote, his conversion "was no sudden plunge into a new life but rather a slow steady convalescence from a deep-seated spiritual illness of long standing."[1] This diagnosis is correct. Jack was very much a beginner in the Christian faith, and it was his recovery from spiritual sickness that made him a mature Christian. We cannot regret the lapse. Without it he would never have had the imaginative sympathy and understanding displayed in, say, *Till We Have Faces* and *The Screwtape Letters*.

His negative attitudes toward Christianity had begun to be formed in his childhood. At Saint Mark's in Dundela, where his grandfather Hamilton was rector, he was offered only "the dry husks of Christianity." He and Warren went regularly to church on Sundays, but both boys were perfectly aware that churchgoing was not so much a religious as a political rite, the weekly demonstration of the fact that they were not Roman Catholics. "Our butcher and our grocer attended," Warren wrote, ". . . primarily to draw customers' attention to the fact that at their shops could be bought decent Protestant food untainted by the damnable heresies of Rome."[2] Although the acoustics of Saint Mark's were bad and much of the service inaudible, the boys were forced to sit so close to the pulpit that they could not avoid hearing most of their grandfather's sermons, in which he frequently attacked the Roman Catholic church and broke into fits of weeping. The tirades and the tears made the boys giggle, largely from embarrassment, and they were subsequently reprimanded by their parents. It is not surprising that Jack acquired a dislike of church services and a low opinion of what he knew as Christianity. Of course, he saw no connection between these dull, loveless rituals and his personal religious experience of joy.

Services in the Malvern College chapel meant nothing to him, "no more than two hours of blessed inactivity in which to dream his dreams secure from interruption."[3] At Great Bookham, he did not usually go to church at all. This period was the nadir of his unbelief, but he hid it from his father and even allowed himself to be confirmed in Belfast, a piece of hypocrisy of which he was deeply ashamed in later life.

Though his return to spiritual health had perhaps begun in his adolescence by the influence of George MacDonald's *Phantastes*, he did not think of the book as Christian. Rather he responded to MacDonald's holiness without recognizing it as holiness and at the same time indulged in sadomasochistic fantasies and blasphemous rationalizations. This lack of integration continued for many years.

The compulsory church parades that he had to attend in the army did nothing to make Christianity attractive. Warren has given us a vivid description of them: "The officers sat in apathetic rows, frequently consulting their wristwatches; occasionally one would remark to his neighbour in a voice which he took little trouble to lower, 'Hope the old basket makes it snappy this morning, I want to catch the 1:42.' Behind him sat the troops whose only contribution consisted in giving their own version of the better known hymns."[4] The terrible experiences of the western front affected him so much that until late in life he never wrote and rarely talked about them. He came back wounded, lonely, and more introspective than before. The easiest escape from his misery was to live in the world of his fantasies. But he avoided becoming a complete introvert, largely due to the friendship of Mrs. Moore.

Many men who read Greats (classical philosophy) at Oxford read it as a subject of academic study, not as something that might affect their conduct. Jack, on the other hand, wanted the study of philosophy to be a road to belief. He never merely thought ideas; he also felt them. Two philosophical trends dominated Oxford at the time: the rival groups led by F. H. Bradley and J. Cook Wilson. Though their ideas derived from Hegel, both men were critical of Hegel's idealism and even more critical of each other. Bradley believed in an absolute and thought that the knowledge toward which humans should strive was a participation in the absolute's knowledge of itself. Wilson, on the other hand, insisted that knowledge is a distinct experience: "A person knows that he knows, and he knows too that the experience of believing is a different experience. When he does know he cannot be in error."[5]

What a system for the introspective undergraduate—what hours he could spend considering which things he believed and which he knew! But whichever side he leaned toward, respect for the other school would probably have prevented him from being a firm adherent. Most tutors encouraged their pupils above all to doubt.

It was consistent with Jack's character, given his practicality and sense of purpose, that philosophy did not remain for him a purely speculative occupation. Although all philosophers derived a tenet from Hegel that one could not contact the absolute, Jack set about trying to. He began to meditate on the supreme spirit. He tried to still the incessant chatter of the mind and to peel away layers of thought so that he might be in the presence of pure spirit. He was following the prayer process of contemplatives of all races and religions, oddly, without realizing it, without recognizing that the supreme spirit could also be called God. Why didn't he see this? "I suspect there was some willful blindness," he writes in *Surprised by Joy*. But he tells us, too, that the experience of the absolute "is more religious than many experiences that have been called Christian."[6] It could have been nothing else than an experience of the immensity and the glory of God. He was praying without knowing it.

Another influence on Jack's thinking was the philosophy of Australian-born Samuel Alexander. The study of Alexander's only important work, *Space, Time, and Deity*, increased his distrust of introspection and modified his attitudes toward joy and the idealist philosophy. Alexander makes a distinction between enjoyment, which means experiencing something, and contemplation, which means thinking about it. Thus, one can enjoy a pain and later contemplate one's enjoyment of the pain. Likewise, a man can love a woman when he is with her, but not when he is merely thinking about her or his love for her. In Alexander's concept of contemplation, one has contact, not with the object, but merely with the idea of it. Jack applied this notion to joy. "I saw that all my waitings and watchings for Joy, all my vain hopes to find some mental content on which I could . . . lay my finger and say, 'This is it,' had been a futile attempt to contemplate the enjoyed."[7] Yet he thought that joy must be the desiring of something outside the self, and he began to concentrate on that something. He became a follower more of Berkeley than of Hegel.

At the time of the publication of *Dymer*, he was aware of and worried by his skepticism and mental confusion. There is an interesting description in his diary of the "unholy muddle" he was in about imagination and intellect. "Undigested scraps" of psychoanalysis and of the Anthroposophy, which he had got from Barfield, were conflicting in his mind with orthodox idealism and "good old Kirkian rationalism." In addition, he was aware all the time of the danger of "falling back into most childish superstitions," or in order to escape, of fleeing into "dogmatic materialism." He hoped that the poem he was working on, *The King of Drum* (later published in *Narrative Poems* as *The Queen of Drum*), would "write itself so as to clear things up" in the way that his earlier poem *Dymer* had "cleared up the Christina Dream business."[8]

He was concerned with anthroposophy because two of his closest friends, Owen Barfield and A. C. Harwood, became anthroposophists. "I was hideously shocked. . . . For here . . . were all the abominations . . . gods, spirits, after-life and pre-existence, initiates, occult knowledge, meditation."[9] Thus began his long argument with Barfield that both called "The Great War." Barfield convinced him that it was impossible for him to be a realist and cured him of the idea that his philosophy of life should be a contemporary one.

Like many other men at Oxford in the 1920s, Jack was interested in the new psychology of Freud and the Viennese School. Barfield tells us that at one time Jack was eager to analyze himself and his friends in terms of the "latest perversions." The subject, like the occult, had for him a fascination that he later regarded as morbid. He was cured of this interest by many things, most notably the terrible fate of Mrs. Moore's brother, Dr. Askins, who suffered from agonizing bouts of what was then called "war neurasthenia." A passage in Shelley's *Cenci* expresses his view on the subject. He often drew his pupils' attention to it.

> *. . . 'tis a trick of this same family*
> *To analyse their own and other minds.*
> *Such self-anatomy shall teach the mind*
> *Dangerous secrets: for it tempts our powers,*
> *Knowing what must be thought and may be done,*
> *Into the depth of darkest purposes. . . .*[10]

This dislike and distrust of psychology, occultism, and introspection made him desire a religion with an objective, traditional morality. It was clear that Christianity, if only he could accept it, would suit him admirably.

By 1926 he was a practicing theist who had no belief in the gospel story or in the doctrine that Jesus Christ is the Son of God. He had read *The Everlasting Man* by G. K. Chesterton and had come to feel "that Christianity was very sensible apart from its Christianity."[11] Soon after, he had an experience that made him take the gospel story seriously. It came from a most unlikely source, a man whom Jack disliked.

T. D. ("Harry") Weldon was the tutor and college lecturer in the Greats at Magdalen College. He was a cynic who scoffed at all creeds and almost all positive assertions, a man, Jack once wrote, who "believes that he has seen through everything and lives at rock bottom."[12] One day they were talking in Jack's rooms about the odd events of history when Weldon remarked that there was good evidence supporting the historicity of the Gospels. "Rum thing, that stuff of Fraser's about the Dying God," Weldon said. "It almost looks as if it really happened once."[13] Jack could hardly believe his ears. His guest was drinking whiskey but showed no sign of being drunk. When Jack pressed him for more information, he seemed anxious to change the subject.

The effect on Jack was shattering. He examined the evidence on his own and had to agree that it was surprisingly good. From this time onward, he felt under pressure to believe. He could not get out of his head such arguments as Chesterton's that, in claiming to be the Son of God, Jesus Christ was either a lunatic or a dishonest fraud or He was speaking the truth. Jack reread the Gospels and became more and more aware that they were not myths or made-up stories at all, because the authors were simply too artless and unimaginative.

Although he still disliked church services, especially the hymns, in 1929 he began regularly to attend Sunday services at his parish church or the college chapel. It was a strange thing to do. His own explanation is that he wanted to show the world that he believed in God. I suspect that his opposition to a group of atheist dons in his college may also have had something to do with it.

It took him two years from this time to become a full, practicing member of the Church of England. The final part of his conversion took place while he was sitting in the sidecar of Warren's motorcycle. In *Surprised by Joy* he also mentions a few intermediate influences, notably a midnight conversation with Hugo Dyson and J. R. R. Tolkien. We may add to these the death of his father.

Albert retired from all legal work in May 1928. He was unhappy in his retirement. He had no idea what to do with himself, and he felt lonely and depressed. His health was poor, although no one seems to have supposed that he was seriously ill. While Jack still found it difficult to be happy in his father's company, he went to stay with Albert for some part of nearly every vacation. With Warren stationed in Shanghai, Albert became rather dependent on Jack.

By August 1929, it became clear that Albert was seriously ill. Jack did everything possible for him during that month, running errands, helping him to eat and shave, and reading to him. Early in September, he had an operation that the doctors deemed successful, although it revealed cancer, because they thought that "he might live a few years."[14] Jack, therefore, went back to Oxford on September 22 to prepare for the Michaelmas term. He was called back to Belfast two days later, and when he arrived on September 25, he learned that Albert had died during the previous afternoon.

He wired the news of Albert's death to Warren on September 26, but Warren did not sail from Hong Kong until February. Even then he traveled by cargo ship via Japan and the United States, thus further delaying his visit to Little Lea. Jack was bitterly disappointed by Warren's absence. He felt that Warren would be a better executor than he, more of a businessman, better able to answer the letters written by J. W. A. Condlin, the lawyer who was handling the estate. Furthermore, dealing with the contents of the house was something he could not do alone. With Mrs. Moore's help, he made some decisions about which books and furniture to send to Oxford, postponing other such matters until Warren's arrival.

Albert's death affected Jack profoundly. He could no longer rebel against the political churchgoing that was part of his father's way of life. He felt bitterly ashamed of the way he had deceived and denigrated his father in the past, and he determined to eradicate these weaknesses in his character. Most importantly, he had a strong feeling that Albert was somehow still alive and helping him. He spoke about this to me and wrote about it to an American correspondent named Vera Matthews. His feeling of Albert's presence created or reinforced in him a belief in personal immortality and also influenced his conduct in times of temptation. These extrasensory experiences helped persuade him to join a Christian church.

He was also influenced by his brother, who arrived in

England in April 1930 and stayed until December 1931. Warren, he learned, had also been thinking of becoming a Christian and had been going to church quite often, although he had not yet begun to receive communion. In 1931 the two regularly attended church services together. They each disliked some things about Christianity, but they were also rather reluctantly coming to the conclusion that the gospel story was true. Each thought the acceptance of such a faith would help the other. Warren might be cured of his indolence and alcoholism, and Jack might attain the secure foundation he felt essential to realizing his potential as a writer and a tutor.

But it was difficult for Jack to see the point of becoming a full, communicating member of a church. Although he accepted God, the historicity of the Gospels, and probably Jesus as the Son of God, he felt uneasy about other Christian concepts. He had no understanding of the sacramental system and could not see the relevance of concepts similar to those found in pagan mytholo- gies—for instance, the ideas of sacrifice, propitiation, the shed- ding of blood, communion, and redemption.

What changed his thinking more than anything else was a conversation he had on September 19, 1931, with J. R. R. Tolkien and Hugo Dyson, his guests at dinner that evening at Magdalen College. After the port had been drunk, they strolled around Addison's Walk and talked about myths. Jack said that he loved reading and thinking about myths, but that he could not regard them as being at all true. Tolkien's view was radically dif- ferent. He said that myths originate in God, that they preserve something of God's truth, although often in a distorted form. Furthermore, he said that, in presenting a myth, in writing sto- ries full of mythical creatures, one may be doing God's work. As Tolkien talked, a mysterious rush of wind came through the trees that Jack felt to be a message from the deity, although his reason told him not to be carried away. Tolkien went on to explain that the Christian story was a myth invented by a God who was real, a God whose dying could transform those who believed in him. If Jack wanted to find the relevance of His story to his own life, he must plunge in. He must appreciate the myth in the same spirit of imaginative understanding that he would bring to, say, a Wagnerian opera.

It was not until three o'clock in the morning that Tolkien went home to his wife. Dyson continued talking with Jack, striding up and down the arcades of New Buildings. His main point was that Christianity works for the believer. The believer is put at peace and freed from his sins. He receives help in overcoming his faults and can become a new person.

Soon after this evening, Jack wrote to Arthur Greeves: ". . . I have just passed on from believing in God to definitely believing in Christ. . . . My long night talk with Dyson and Tolkien had a great deal to do with it."[15]

The conversion took place on September 22, 1931, while Jack was sitting in the sidecar of Warren's motorcycle en route to Whipsnade, the safari zoo. "When we set out I did not believe that Jesus Christ is the Son of God," Jack wrote, "and when we reached the zoo I did." It was not an emotional conversion, nor was he aware of his reasoning. "It was more like when a man, after long sleep, still lying motionless in bed, becomes aware that he is now awake."[16]

But it was not quite as simple as that. He still had doubts and still found the Gospels and most church services unappealing. There is no evidence that he ever seriously considered becoming a Roman Catholic. He bought a Roman missal and skimmed through it, but he could not see that it contained much of value that was not part of the Anglican services. Early in December, he told the vicar of his parish church in Headington Quarry and

Adam Fox, Magdalen's Dean of Divinity, that he wanted to become a practicing Christian. He received communion for the first time since boyhood on Christmas Day at the church in Headington, where he would be buried thirty-two years later. By strange coincidence, Warren, who was in Shanghai at the time, also received communion on Christmas Day 1931.

At first Jack followed his childhood practice of receiving communion only on great holidays, such as Christmas and Easter, but before long he wrote to Warren that receiving communion once a month was a good compromise between being Laodicean and enthusiastic. This still seemed to be his practice when he stayed with me at Malvern in the early 1950s, but in the last fifteen or so years of his life, I think he normally received communion every week.

Having discovered the therapeutic value of writing through his work on *Dymer*, Jack was encouraged to write another book. He began a prose account of his conversion to theism, but soon gave it up, probably because he found that he was moving toward a Christian position. When he became a practicing Christian, he found that his life had a new center and what he hoped would be a new stability. To define it, he began in the early part of 1932 a verse account of his conversion, but he soon gave that up, too. His third attempt resulted in a complete book.

The Pilgrim's Regress was written in a fortnight while he was staying with Arthur Greeves at Bernagh in August 1932. In this witty allegory based on the work of Bunyan, he traces the journey of John back to Mother Kirk via the experiences, temptations, and false philosophies that had confronted him in his own life. He originally called the work "The Pilgrim's Regress, or Pseudo-Bunyan's Periplus: An Allegorical Apology for Christianity, Reason, and Romanticism," which tells something about the work. His own route had been one of regress, and the book really is an apology. By "romanticism" he meant the desire for joy, or what is spiritually highest, ultimately the deity. The book describes the false joys and idols the pilgrim meets on his journey and contrasts them with the true joy. The sole merit that Jack claimed for it was that it was "written by one who has proved them all wrong" by experience, "such experience as would not have come my way if my youth had been wiser, more virtuous, and less self-centred than it was."[17]

Although it is a serious book—primarily an attack on spurious satisfactions, false philosophies, and physical and spiritual temptations—it has a captivating freshness. No other book of his is written with such a light touch, and few are so often witty and profound.

It is astonishing how much sharp thought is packed into some of the very short chapters—he already had the tutor's gift for presenting complex ideas in simple form. There is a shrewd summary of idealism and a miniature examination of the origins of moral values and logical categories. He brilliantly satirizes Freud's psychology and attacks free verse and the whole modernist movement.

John's object in *The Pilgrim's Regress* is to tread the fine line of virtue across the Brook of Death to Mother Kirk. He is sustained by her food, but before he can get to her, he must avoid being entrapped by thought and feeling. Thought is represented by the northerners, who include men with dogmatic systems— the Marxists, the humanists, the Anglo-Catholics. Emotion is represented by the southerners, who include D. H. Lawrence, occultists, and broad churchmen. All are shown to be wrong, not because they are opposed to orthodox Christianity, but because they are irrational or deny the romantic. The polemic has a sharpness often present in Jack's conversation but rarely in his later writings. His views hardly changed, but he usually softened their expression.

Most of the book is written with wit and precision, but in the last sections it rises to mystical heights. Guided by the very bright figure of Contemplation, John has a vision of true heavenly joy. Here the prose rises to the greatness of the theme:

> I saw where they came down to the white beaches of a bay of the sea, the western end of the world, a place very ancient, folded many miles deep in the silence of forests; a place, in some sort, lying rather at the world's beginning, as though men were born travelling away from it. It was early in the morning when they came there and heard the sound of the waves; and looking across the sea—at that hour almost colourless—all those thousands became still. And what the others saw I do not know: but John saw the Island. And the morning wind, blowing offshore from it, brought the sweet smell of its orchards to them, but rarified and made faint with the thinness and purity of early air, and mixed with a little sharpness of the sea. But for John, because so many thousands looked at it with him, the pain and the longing were changed and all unlike what they had been of old; for humility was mixed with their wildness, and the sweetness came not with pride and with the lonely dreams of poets nor with the glamour of a secret, but with the homespun truth of folktales, and with the sadness of graves and freshness as of earth in the morning.[18]

("Because so many thousands looked at it with him"—here is the effect on Jack of becoming a communicating member of the Church and part of the mystical body of Christ.)

The final section makes clear the significance of the title. Now that he has become a Christian, John is told to retrace his steps. He passes once again through all the countries of the mind that he had traversed before his conversion. He now sees them quite clearly as the unpleasant or irrational delusions they really are. In the end, he comes to his parents' cottage in the land of his childhood, Puritania, where he finds his final resting place and his deep joy.

In its latter pages, the book contains several religious lyrics, among them two of his finest: "He whom I bow to only knows to whom I bow" and "My heart is empty."[19] It is not unlikely that he spent more time on them than on all the prose in the book.

The manuscript was sent to J. M. Dent and Sons in December 1932 and published in May 1933. It was bound in brown cloth and had attractive maps on its endpapers that Jack had "had great fun drawing the sketch for." The reviews, though few in number, were mostly favorable. Nevertheless, only about 650 of the first printing of 1,000 copies were sold. Jack was far less upset by this failure than by that of *Dymer*, probably because he had spent so little time on the book and because he had cared more for success as a poet than as a writer of prose. Although he was disappointed, he could also regard the cauterization of his literary ambitions as a blessing. He wrote to Arthur Greeves as early as 1930 that a man cannot enter the kingdom of Heaven until he has reached the stage "of not caring two straws about his own status."[20]

The later history of the book is quite interesting. Two or three of the reviewers assumed that the author was a Roman Catholic, probably because of the introduction of Mother Kirk (Mother Church) and the rational defense of Christianity. This brought the book to the notice of Frank Sheed, of Sheed and Ward, the Roman Catholic publishing house. Dent printed an additional 1,500 copies for them, and Sheed issued this second edition in

1935. Jack's letter to Arthur describing this event reveals that he was still very much a Belfast man:

He did not like having a book of his handled by a "Papist publisher," but he submitted since they thought they could sell it, and Dent couldn't. For doing this he was "well punished," for without his authority Sheed printed on the inside of the dust jacket this blurb, "This story begins in Puritania (Mr. Lewis was brought up in Ulster)." This implied that the book attacked his own country and his own religion. He asked Arthur to tell anyone interested that he was not consulted and the blurb was "a damnable lie told to try to make the Dublin riffraff buy the book."[21]

Yet he allowed Sheed and Ward to reissue the book in 1944. The splendid preface to this edition is valuable for its definitions of the romantic and romanticism and for a note on the "dialectic of desire" and other terms that may puzzle the reader. He also apologizes in this preface for what he considered the book's chief faults—needless obscurity and an uncharitable temper. To remedy the former, he supplied running heads for the pages, which unfortunately make the allegory seem cruder than it is and also make it more difficult to read the book as just a story. This third edition has since been reprinted. Although to the lay reader the book may seem dated, to the scholar with a knowledge of the philosophical and literary movements of the 1920s, it remains a delight.

Jack's conversion to Christianity made him a different person. His search for belief was over; he now had a strong platform on which to stand. No longer an introspective young man, he became far more confident in his work as a tutor. He devoted himself to developing and strengthening his belief, and almost from the year of his conversion, he wanted to become an evangelist for the Christian faith. The way had become clear for his great career as a Christian novelist and popular theologian. But first of all, highbrow and intellectual as he was, he would have to learn to write simply, to make things easy for his readers.

13

The Kilns

When Warren returned to England in April 1930, he and Jack went through their father's belongings and papers at Little Lea. It was an emotional event for both of them. After a visit to the house, Warren wrote in his diary: "Had not Jack been with me . . . I would have had one of my worst fits of depression."[1] They moved everything they wanted to have with them in England into one room, set aside other things to be sold at auction, and threw out still other items, among them, the box of animal figurines that had been the basis of the Boxen stories. "And this, I thought, was to be the end of Boxen," Warren wrote, "but I was never more mistaken in my life. . . . Almost to the very end, 'Boxonian' remained for Jack a treasured tongue in which he could communicate with me, and with me only. The Harley Street specialist of that world had been a small china salmon, by name Arrabudda; and Jack, during the closing weeks of his life, on the days when the specialist was due to visit him, would say to me with a smile, 'I'll be seeing that fellow Arrabudda this morning.'"[2] Without this ability to recall and live imaginatively in the world of childhood, Jack could never have become a great writer of stories for children. On their last visit to Little Lea together, Jack and Warren each wrote for the other a little epitaph. The theme of Jack's was that there is always a memory further back.

Albert had kept a massive number of papers connected with the family, including many letters written to him by his sons. Encouraged by his brother, Warren conceived the idea of editing and typing them as a family history. They were arranged chronologically in eleven bulky volumes named *The Lewis Papers* and bound under the "imprint" of Leeborough Press.

Jack and Warren agreed to use the money they would receive from the sale of Little Lea to buy a house, which they planned to share with Mrs. Moore and Maureen. (Warren was now stationed in Bulford, a village on Salisbury Plain, and hoped to retire from the army within a year or two.) Albert's estate, however, was worth far less than either of them had supposed. It seemed that they would be very lucky to get £3,000 (about $90,000) for the house and that Albert's investments would not provide an income of much more than £100 ($3,000) a year. He was, in fact, a poorer man than they had thought; he had been living mainly on his retirement pension of £500 ($15,000) a year. To buy a house they would pool their resources with those of Mrs. Moore.

Early in July they found the Kilns, a house in Headington Quarry that excited them tremendously. The place was lovely and secluded, but only about three miles from the center of Oxford. Half of it was a wooded segment of Shotover Hill, and the rest was level ground covered with grass, garden, orchard, tennis court, and the house itself. Between the upper and lower parts of the lot was a large pond, formerly a pit from which clay had been dug for brick making. The kilns in which they were fired still stood in ruinous condition, but were delightfully covered with ivy and weeds. Between the kilns and the house, there was a greenhouse, and beyond the kilns, a wooden hut. Water was supplied by a spring at the top of the woods where there was a rocky section that the brothers sometimes called "the cliff." A long driveway full of potholes led to the house from Kiln Lane, a little-used road in bad condition. Between the lane and the house, there was a large garage and a shed. A farmhouse the other side of Kiln Lane was the only nearby dwelling at the time the Kilns was bought. It really was possible to live there and feel completely secluded, as if in the country. Headington Quarry, only half a mile away, retained some of the atmosphere of an English village, and the church where they worshiped had the feeling of the country.

But, as J. R. R. Tolkien sometimes observed, they hadn't enough money to remain secluded. They paid £3,300 for the house and about eight acres. For an additional £300, they could have bought a large field adjoining the house, but they thought they could not afford it. Before long it was sold to a speculative builder who put up a row of houses that detracted from their sense of privacy and remoteness.

The Kilns had plenty of rooms. On the ground floor were two reception rooms, one on each side of the front door, and two bedrooms. The second floor had three bedrooms, but you had to go through one bedroom to get to another, an inconvenient arrangement. There was also a kitchen, a scullery with a back door, and a very small maid's bedroom opening out of the kitchen.

Except for the water supplied by the spring, the house was lacking in conveniences. The gas-driven generator that provided electricity for lighting had such an unreliable engine that it was necessary to have on the estate someone who could put it right. Open fires and paraffin stoves were the only source of heat, and, unless good fires were lit in the main rooms, the house tended to be cold in winter. Bathroom water was heated by an inefficient stove in the kitchen. These inconveniences seemed less bothersome during the summer months. In good weather, Mrs. Moore and Jack and sometimes Warren would sit outside by the rose arbor, drink tea, and talk. Jack and Warren would swim in the pond, sometimes twice a day. Maureen would have tennis parties, followed by tea on the lawn.

The property was bought in Mrs. Moore's name and was legally hers. Warren and Jack put up £1,500, and the same amount was provided by the trustees of her brother Dr. Askins's estate. No interest was paid or expected to be paid on these loans. To secure Jack and Warren's position, Mrs. Moore made a will in which she left the house to them for their lifetime. After the death of whichever brother lived longer, it would become Maureen's absolute property.

Considerable improvements were made almost at once. Two ground-floor rooms were added, one as a workroom for Jack and another, opening out of it, for Warren. Jack's room was not large, but it had space for a massive bookcase, two upholstered armchairs, and the fine large writing desk that had belonged to his father. In winter it was pleasantly snug.

For much of the time until 1939, the household consisted of Mrs. Moore, Maureen, Jack, Warren, Fred Paxford, one or two maids, and some dogs and cats. Paxford was a great character, an unkempt, burly Oxfordshire countryman of the same age as Jack, "earthy" in the best sense of the word and unspoiled by book learning. He had a deep, intuitive understanding of plants, animals, and people, was unswervingly loyal to his employers, yet an independent thinker with great integrity. A remarkably frugal man, he had all the skills of the traditional handyman and would make do in every way possible, never buying something new if he could patch up something that he already had.

He raised fruits and vegetables, and I remember he was often disappointed that few people in the house took much interest in his produce. He would frequently argue with whoever was cooking about which vegetables should be harvested, taking the view that the cook should prepare whatever he chose to give her. If the cook asked for, say, two heads of cauliflower, he would say, "Them's nawt ready," or make another excuse for not being able to produce them. After Mrs. Moore's death, he was inclined to bemoan the brothers' lack of taste for vegetables and fruit. "If the Major'd eat more of 'em," he would say, "the drink wudn't take 'im so bad."

He seemed to welcome my visits to the Kilns, partly so that he could unload vegetables on me, but mainly so that he could talk about gardening. "Come to th'ouse," he would say, meaning the ancient, ramshackle greenhouse that he almost regarded as his property. Although it looked almost past repair, it remained dry and cozy, and Paxford spent some of his leisure time sitting there in his shirt sleeves.

Paxford was naturally economical, all the more so when his employers told him that they wanted to save money. One of his tasks was to do the daily shopping for the household. He refused to buy provisions until he had searched the larder and kitchen and made sure that the last packet of tea, flour, or sugar really had been used up. Then he would buy whatever was asked for in the smallest quantity.

Although he was well aware that Jack paid the bills, he regarded Mrs. Moore as his employer. The two had a high opinion of each other. She took his advice about most things and often infuriated Warren by quoting him as an authority, even on such subjects as which was the largest house in England. "I thought we were over the period of Paxolatry," Warren wrote, "but I fear me not."[3]

Paxford always described Mrs. Moore and Maureen as "all right," which from him was quite high praise. Although Mrs. Moore became "a bit difficult" in her later years, he maintained that "all people, when they get on, get a bit more irritable." Mrs. Moore was very good to him he said, "a good cook, and a good nurse, and kindness itself." She was kind also to Jack, who was susceptible to "flu and suchlike germs floating about." He would always go to the Kilns when he was ill, and she would put him to bed and look after him. As soon as he or anyone else got a cold, "out came the thermometer." Paxford gave me many other examples of Mrs. Moore's kindness. She bought a bungalow in sections and had it put up on the grounds to provide a home for an old woman who was poor and miserable after the death of her daughter. Luncheon guests at the Kilns often included the poor and hungry.

Until early in the Second World War, Jack owned a second-hand car that he had bought on Paxford's advice. Paxford tried to teach him, but Jack never succeeded in learning to drive. He was therefore chauffeured by Paxford or Maureen. Both brothers enjoyed being driven.

With Paxford's help and under his direction, they set about improving the property. Paxford planted the flat ground between the house and the road as an orchard. Four varieties of plums and a dozen different sorts of apples and pears were planted. Paxford filled in the ditch that divided the grounds from Green Lane, the road on the Oxford side of the property, and put up a wooden fence. Meanwhile, Warren and Jack set to work on the pond. They bought a punt, which they used to clear away the weeds that covered much of the water's surface, and cleared the banks and made a landing dock of brick. The lake was home to many fish, including roach, perch, and pike, which were fed upon by two swans that had been given to Jack by the provost of Worcester College.

All over the property, especially on the higher ground, a great deal of clearing was done, mainly of bramble and elder. Jack and

Warren then planted trees, mainly chestnut, mountain ash, oak, and fir. By March 1931, forty-three trees had been planted, and most of them prospered, except for the beech trees, which were on unsuitable soil, and a few firs that were stolen at Christmas. In 1932 when Warren was again stationed in Shanghai, Jack went on planting trees alone. He also supervised a scheme for draining the area below the lake, known as the swamp, and for giving the lake a controlled overflow so that it would not be stagnant. On Warren's return, their "public works" included making a good path from the lake up through "the jungle" to the crest of the hill. They also constructed a "soaking machine," a little patch sheltered from the wind and the outside world where they could sunbathe unobserved.

In those days both brothers loved the estate almost ecstatically. Warren called it "a veritable garden of Eden, a lotus island in a faerie land, or any other term that will express sheer loveliness." Jack loved to wander through the woods during every season of the year and always wrote about the estate idyllically. Thus one January he wrote to Arthur of a most glorious storm with howling in the chimneys and "trees plunging like terrified but tethered horses." He lay in bed "revelling in it." During February he and Warren carried out a program of tree planting, and he wrote of his enjoyment of primroses in the early spring sunlight with birds "thrilling and chuckling in abundance." That June he wrote of the delights of the pond in which he bathed before breakfast most mornings. It looked dirty, but he came out "perfectly clean." He entered the water from a punt. He wished Arthur could have been with him as he pushed it out from "under the dark shadow of the trees into the full glare of the open water," disturbing the moorhens and their chicks, which hurried into the shelter of reeds, half swimming and half flying "with a delicious flurry of silver drops." There among his favorite birch trees he loved all seasons, but autumn best with "its still, windless days, red sunsets, and all the yellow leaves still on the trees." He often felt that he had more pleasures than anyone could deserve.[8]

During the school year, except on weekends, Jack usually stayed at his Magdalen College rooms. His scout would call him with tea every morning at a quarter after seven. After bathing and shaving, he would walk for a few minutes along Addison's Walk, praying, praising God, and contemplating the beauty of nature. By eight he would be in the college chapel for the short service known as "Dean's Prayers." Then he would go with the other worshipers to breakfast in the Common Room. By a quarter to nine, he would be in his rooms, opening letters and notes and, as far as possible, answering them. His first pupil would come at nine, and others would come every hour until one, except on Tuesdays and on days when he was giving lectures in the buildings on Oxford's famous High Street. At one o'clock, he would hurry to the entrance of the college, where he would find Maureen or Paxford waiting for him with the car. After lunch at the Kilns, he would take a spade or a saw and set out past the pond into the woods, enjoying on his way the scurry of waterfowl or the rich scent of fallen autumn leaves. Sometimes, especially if there was a friend with him, he would go for a brisk walk. At a quarter to five, he would be driven back to the college for two more hour-long tutoring sessions. Dinner in hall was a leisurely meal that began at a quarter after seven. He thought himself lucky if he had two evenings a week free after dinner. Once a week, there was an Anglo-Saxon class in his rooms. Another evening might be taken up by reading Dante with another university teacher. Then there would be meetings of the college literary society and invitations to dine in other colleges, invitations that he was bound to reciprocate. By convention, these would take up a whole evening, including dinner, wine in the Common Room, and late-night talks. The guest might not leave until after midnight.

On Saturdays he had no pupils after one and usually ate lunch with two other dons and quite often went for a country walk. The other exception to his routine was on Mondays, when he had no pupils at all. He spent much of this time preparing lectures, correcting work done by those who were taking higher degrees, and reading some of the literature on which he had told his other pupils to write essays. It soon became a regular custom for Tolkien to drop in on Monday mornings "and drink a glass." This was one of the most pleasant times in Jack's week. "Sometimes we talk English school politics; sometimes we criticise one another's poems; other days we drift into theology or 'the state of the nation.' . . ."[9]

Certainly, he found his extensive tutoring hard work, but he was much happier in it after his reception into the Church. Now that he had a firm standpoint, he found teaching much easier, and, while he would never have thought of trying to convert his pupils to Christianity, he now had a strong sense of the usefulness of his job. In a letter written in 1932 to Bede Griffiths, a former pupil, he explained that he had now "very little doubt" that his work of lecturing and tutoring was worth doing. The terms of his appointment and the recent nature of his conversation prevented him from teaching the most important things such as the Christian faith. But there was plenty of work to be done on a lower level, "eradicating false habits of mind" and teaching his pupils to reason correctly. For this English Literature was as good as any other subject. He was very glad that he had not been able to do what he had at first wanted and become a research fellow with no pupils. As it was, nearly every generation of pupils produced someone who became his permanent friend. Indeed, as all his pupils of the 1930s will testify, his teaching consisted largely of making us aware of and debunking our absurdities, inconsistencies, and false sentiments.

He did his research mainly during vacations when he had no pupils, keeping the same hours as during the term and usually working in his rooms at Magdalen. The products of this early research were his series of lectures on medieval thought and the first of his two great works of literary history and criticism, *The Allegory of Love.*

His lectures were lively. Handled by anyone else, the subject matter would have seemed dull, but he so enthusiastically discussed such topics as medieval cosmology and astrology and rhetoric and theories that we became converts to his view of the Middle Ages. Those of us who later became schoolmasters often referred to his lectures in the courses we taught. None of us could have ever forgotten his account of the melancholic, phlegmatic, sanguine, and choleric man, or of the influences of the planets. How enthusiastic he was about the jovial man, a type all too rare; how much the jovial man he himself seemed as he spoke, his voice rich, his face full of vitality and delight.

The lectures were learned, fresh, and entertaining, but it was *The Allegory of Love* that made Oxford scholars realize that Lewis was a great literary critic. The subject of the book had been suggested by his English tutor, F. P. Wilson, in about 1925. Jack began the work in 1927 and worked most intensely on it between 1933 and 1935, usually in his rooms or in the Duke Humphrey room of the Bodleian Library. He sent the manuscript to Clarendon Press on September 18, 1935, and heard on October 29 that the press wanted to publish it. By Christmas it was in proof. The original title, "The Allegorical Love Poem," was altered to *The Allegory of Love* on the advice of Charles Williams who had been asked to read the book in proof and "to write something about it for travellers and booksellers and people." He "fell heavily" for it and wrote enthusiastically to Jack at almost the same time as Jack wrote to him praising his novel, *The Place of the Lion*.[10]

The book was published on May 21 and, without exception, highly praised by reviewers, some of whom recognized its greatness. Thus Professor Ifor Evans wrote in *The London Observer*: "Out of the multitude of volumes on literary history there arises once or twice in a generation a truly great work. Such I believe is this study by Mr. C. S. Lewis." The reviewer of *The London Sunday Times* agreed that it was a great book. In *Criterion*, Vera Fraser described the chapter on allegory as "most profound" and noted that, "apart from its argument, the book becomes an anthology of beauty," an allusion, I suppose, to Lewis's gift for quoting and to his qualities as a translator. There were some criticisms. Albert Guerard, of *New York Herald Tribune Books*, described it as "two books—both excellent, but each vitiating the other." He preferred the literary criticism to the history.

The book produced such excitement at Oxford that for a time it was difficult to find anyone who cared or dared to question its main conclusions. Since then, it has been under attack. Some Oxford tutors described it as brilliant but misleading. However, when closely examined, their criticisms turned out to concern only small sections of this massive work, mainly his view of the origins of courtly or romantic love, his summary of the attitudes of the church fathers toward sex and passion, the importance he gives to Andreas Capellanus, and his overemphasis on morality at the expense of purely literary criticism. These criticisms, even if entirely justified, are minor. All his literary criticism—his profound treatment of allegory, exciting critique of the *Roman de la Rose*, original thoughts on Chaucer, the Scottish Chaucerians, and Spenser—is highly regarded. He hardly mentions an author, no matter how minor, without saying something fresh and illuminating about him. Take, for instance, a comment on Alexander Montgomerie's *Cherry and the Slae:* "In Montgomerie we seem to hear the scrape of the fiddle and the beat of dancing on the turf: in Googe, the ticking of a metronome."[11] His poet's gift for language is impelled by a real enthusiasm for his subjects. He is the kindest of critics, always open to what is praiseworthy in his authors and never bored by them. His enthusiasm often has the effect of inspiring his audience to read the works for themselves. As some Oxford booksellers may remember, the publication of *The Allegory of Love* produced a sharp upsurge in sales of otherwise unpopular medieval works.

The courtly love poetry of the thirteenth century and the allegory of the *Romance of the Rose* seem remote from the way we live now. Nevertheless the poetry that they inspired in great poets such as Spenser and Shakespeare has altered our society's view of marriage through their presentation of spouses who treat each other as romantic lovers. Lewis finds Spenser most notable in this regard: "In the history of sentiment he is the greatest among the founders of that romantic conception of marriage which is the basis of all our love literature from Shakespeare to Meredith." He observes that "the whole conception is now being attacked" and goes on to present the correct understanding of Spenser, whose values he regards as exciting ideas for which it is well worth crusading. "What once was platitude should now have for some the brave appeal of a cause nearly lost."[12]

In his study of Spenser's *Faerie Queene,* he contrasts the Bower of Bliss and the Garden of Adonis, thus revealing the distinctions between kinds of love that are moral, fruitful, and life-enhancing and others that are sterile and life-destroying. This theme is important in the novels on which he soon began working.

Whether they agree with Lewis or not, almost all later writers on Spenser make use of *The Allegory of Love*. Thus Graham Hough speaks for many in writing: "By far my greatest debt in general criticism of *The Faerie Queene* is to the writing of Professor C. S. Lewis. Like so many others I found my first real guide to the reading of the poem in *The Allegory of Love*. . . ."[13]

Now, fifty years after its first publication, *The Allegory of Love* has a more solid reputation than ever. During the period of its composition, almost no one in Oxford knew anything about the subject. Since then European and American scholars have treated it extensively, yet *The Allegory of Love* remains the number one book on the subject. Lewis's moral approach to literary criticism is appropriate in dealing with writers whose attitudes were basically moralistic. He is unrivaled in excellence of style and in his ability to choose quotations that characterize his authors, and he writes of them more securely, accurately, and memorably than any other twentieth-century critic. On the strength of *The Allegory of Love* and of his *English Literature in the Sixteenth Century*, there can be no doubt of his greatness as a literary historian.

Jack always delighted in taking long walks. The few vacation days he allowed himself each year were spent on walking tours through villages and countryside. He usually took his vacation during the first week of January because Maureen would be home from school and could keep her mother company and because he thought the weather was usually good then. His letters vividly describe these vacations as important events.

In 1931 Warren accompanied Jack for the first time on a tour. Jack did not know whether Warren would enjoy it or "whether his selfish habits would really accommodate themselves to the inevitable occasional difficulties." But all went well. They took the train to Chepstow and after dinner went out for a moonlight stroll, seeing the castle there almost as if in a vision, huge and brightly lit. "'What is this?' said I. 'A witches' Sabbath,' said he. Imagine all this under a cloudless moon and the grass stiff with frost, crunching under our feet." The next day they walked to Monmouth through the woods, stopping to see Tintern Abbey on the way. Jack perceived the divine in both the scenery and in this ruined building that had been blessed by time: "Anything like the *sweetness* and peace of the long shafts of sunlight falling through the window on this grass cannot be imagined. All churches should be roofless. A holier place I never saw."[14]

Writing that it did him good to be with Warren, he took a charitable view of Warren's drunken escapades, "because while his idea of the good is so much lower than mine, he is in so many ways better than I am. I keep on crawling up to the heights and slipping back to the depths, he seems to do neither."[15]

Warren could not walk with him the following year because he was by then again in Shanghai in command of the Royal Army Service Corps depot there. After his retirement in December 1932, he and Jack celebrated their reunion by another January walking tour. They also continued their ambitious program of "public works" on the estate, after which they took an Easter vacation with Mrs. Moore and Maureen. They went to Hambledon in the Chilterns, where the brothers attended a Passion Play in Fingest Church on Good Friday and the early communion service on Easter. That day Jack first conceived the idea for a religious book, which ten years later would develop into one of his finest, *The Great Divorce*.

In August Jack and Warren took a longer vacation, one they had often talked about, a cruise to Scotland. The high point there was a glorious hour they spent in the mountains at a "golden brown stream, with cataracts and deep pools. We spread out all our [sweat-sodden] clothes to dry on the flat stones, and lay down in a pool just under a little waterfall, and let the foam come down the back of our heads and round our necks. Then when we were cool, we came out and sat naked to eat our sandwiches, with our feet still in the rushing water."[16] Jack's enjoyment of such scenes was as great as that of the most romantic of the romantic poets.

Their ship, the *Eddystone*, took them to Belfast where they gazed at Little Lea and then went inside Saint Mark's to look at the window they had had installed in memory of their parents. "I am profoundly glad," Warren wrote, "that we spent the money on what is a real addition to the stock of first-class modern stained glass."[17]

They then sailed down the Irish Channel and docked at Waterford. Their comments on Ireland reveal important differences in their characters and view of nature. Warren wrote in his diary: "There is something wrong with this country . . . a vague sense of something mean and cruel and sinister. . . . The natives were as depressing as their landscape: during the whole morning I did not see anyone of any age or either sex who was not definitely ugly: even the children looked more like goblins than earthborns." Sailing down the river out to sea, he saw "a long succession of big houses, all very shut in and desolate."[18]

On Jack the scene made a very different impression. He enjoyed the view of the river which he described as "peppered with v. early Norman castles," but the next three hours as they sailed out to sea were even better. The sea and the sky were flat French gray in color. In between them there was "a long fish-shaped streak of pure crimson, about twenty miles long." Then there were mountains, three or four of them, that seemed perfectly transparent and "so extraordinarily spiritualised that they absolutely realised the old idea of Ireland as the 'isle of the saints.'" It was "more calm and spacious and celestial" than anything he had ever seen.[19]

Jack's view of nature was essentially mystical. He often saw in it "the signature of all things." Warren's experience was visionary in a different way. "I wonder," he wrote, "can it be possible that a country which has an eight hundred year record of cruelty and misery has the power of emanating a nervous disquiet? Certainly I felt something of the sort." They argued on this subject, Jack "contending that not to like *any* sort of country argues a fault in oneself: which seems to me absurd."[20]

Their holidays continued until the war began. In 1934 they walked up the Wye Valley deep into Wales, stopping at Aberystwyth. In 1935 they were in the Chilterns, in 1936, Derbyshire, in 1937, Somerset, and in 1938, Wiltshire. They visited Malvern in 1939 and then walked on into Herefordshire and toward Wales. They were so attracted by Malvern that they even thought of retiring there. "Every time I visit Malvern," Warren wrote, "I like it better, not only for old sentimental relations, but for its peace and quiet, and the way it preserves so much of the atmosphere of a vanished age: J feels the same and that we might do worse than spend our declining years there. Today it was looking particularly lovely, with the Priory tower standing up gaunt and grey against the snow sprinkled hills. . . ."[21] This was their last walking holiday together.

For years no regular event delighted Jack more than the Thursday evening meetings of the little group of friends called the Inklings. His was the second group to use this name. Its predecessor was founded in about 1930 by a University College undergraduate named Tangye Lean. Members met in each other's rooms to read aloud their poems and other work. There would be discussion, criticism, encouragement, and frivolity, all washed down with wine or beer. Lean's group consisted mainly of students, but a few sympathetic dons were invited to join, including Tolkien and Jack, who may have been Lean's tutor. Lean graduated in June 1933, and that autumn Jack first used the name the Inklings to describe the group that had already begun to meet in his rooms.

It was always utterly informal. There were no rules, no officers, and certainly no agenda. To become a member, one had to be invited, usually by Jack. Nearly all members were his friends.

The first was J. R. R. Tolkien, elected Bosworth Professor of Anglo-Saxon in 1935. He was forty-two and full of energy. Coming from Leeds, he found the Oxford English School disappointing because it seemed to him that too much time was given to Victorian and modern literature and far too little to Anglo-Saxon and Middle English language and literature. He set out to remedy this with a remarkable energy and practicality. He also encouraged the study of Icelandic literature by forming another group of dons, called the Coalbiters, to read and translate the Sagas and Eddas. Most members of this group had a good knowledge of the language, but a few beginners, including Jack and Nevill Coghill, were invited to join. Tolkien presided and corrected everyone's mistakes.

Jack's first impressions of Tolkien were not entirely favorable, but he found the meetings of the Coalbiters exciting. He loved both the language and the literature, and the study revived his taste for "northernness" and brought back "the old authentic thrill" he had experienced as a child. Tolkien was a rather diffident and private person. He was a domestic man, deeply concerned with his home life and growing family. He was also a most gifted philologist and an inspired storyteller, combining these talents in the languages and people he invented for such books as *The Silmarillion*. A conservative Roman Catholic, he was rather quick to draw his sword if he thought his faith was under attack. He kept the best of himself for his own secret creative world as a storyteller, of which few indeed had any idea in the 1930s.

Although Jack studied Icelandic literature under Tolkien every few weeks, he did not realize until December 3, 1929, that they shared a taste for "northernness" and a delight in Norse mythology. Jack invited Tolkien to come back to his rooms after a Coalbiters meeting for a chat and some whiskey. He stayed for three hours, "discoursing of the gods and giants of Asgard." The visit was longer than Jack had intended, but "who could turn him out, for the fire was bright and the talk good."[22]

This discussion was the germ of the Inklings and the beginning of one of the most important literary friendships of the twentieth century. A few days later, Tolkien asked Jack to give his opinion on two poems, lyrical versions of some of the stories later published as *The Silmarillion*. Jack wrote encouragingly and suggested improvements. Although Tolkien did not care for many of these, he was delighted by Jack's genuine interest and suggested that they might meet once a week so that he could read the rest of *The Silmarillion* to Jack.

The duo became a trio in 1933 by the addition of Warren, who had been collecting books on the age of Louis XIV since World War I and was probably considering how to approach the study he hoped to write for publication. Although he did not begin his "doggerel history of the reign" until June 1934, meetings of the Inklings were for him among the high points of the week.[23] He brought to the sessions a keen mind, an experience of army life at home and overseas, and a knowledge of a large number of unusual subjects.

In 1934 Hugo Dyson and Dr. Robert E. Havard made it a group. Dyson, a lecturer at Reading University, was volatile, exuberant, and eccentric, a quick-witted comedian; Jack enjoyed his sort of humor. Dyson's encounter with Councillor Brewer, a man of vast bulk, in an Oxford pub is typical. Hugo addressed him with an almost servile deference, "You will pardon the liberty, sir.

I trust you don't think I presume, but I shall call you Fred." Then, gazing intently at his full pale face, broke in again, "You'll excuse me, sir, but am I looking at your full face or your profile?" The Councillor, still smiling determinedly, turned to his friend and began to reminisce about their having rowed together in the Teddy Hall boat the year Teddy Hall was bottom of the river. But we had never heard the story. "Bottom? Bottoms?" said Hugo. "Admirable things if ample enough, but you, sir, of course, could have no difficulty about that!" He much preferred talking to listening, and he disliked *The Hobbit* and *The Lord of the Rings*. For these reasons, people sometimes found him irritating.

Dr. Havard (always called Humphrey, a name given to him by Dyson) was Jack's and Warren's doctor from 1934 on. Although he was too busy to write much, he was well-read and keenly interested in the processes of literature and in theology. Havard did much to encourage Jack in the writing of the Narnia stories, the first of which was dedicated to his daughter. He was an entirely delightful man and much respected for his concern with the whole person, rather than just the physical body. I remember a reminiscence of Tolkien's that illustrates this point. "I told him that I was feeling depressed, so depressed that I hadn't been to Mass for a couple of weeks. I wasn't sleeping well either. He said I didn't need drugs, what I needed was to go to Confession. He was at my house at 7:30 the following morning to take me to Confession and Mass. Of course I was completely cured. Now that's the sort of doctor to have!"

Nevill Coghill, who read light verse, and Charles Wrenn, who tutored Jack's third-year pupils in Old English, sometimes came to the group, as did Owen Barfield and other friends of Jack's who happened to be in Oxford on Thursday evenings.

After the arrival of Charles Williams from London at the start of the war, still others joined the Inklings. Membership required the group's general agreement. As Warren put it, "We all knew the sort of man we wanted—and did not want." The latter included dogmatic men who relied, not on evidence, but on cliché—"The sort of fellow," Jack would say, "who uses language not to communicate thought but *instead* of thought."

The ritual never varied. When most of the expected members had arrived (and maybe only three or four would come), Warren would brew a pot of strong tea, the smokers would light their pipes, and Jack would say, "Well, has nobody got anything to read us?" If no one else produced a manuscript, Jack might read something of his own. This was not a mutual admiration society. "Praise for good work was unstinted but censure for bad, or even not so good, was often brutally frank."[24] To read could be a formidable ordeal.

Warren has left an account of the meetings in 1946, which he describes as a vintage year:

> . . . [W]e had at most meetings a chapter of what I call "the new Hobbit" from Tolkien; this being the book or books ultimately published as "The Lord of the Rings." [O]n 30th October . . . there was a long argument on the ethics of cannibalism, and on 28th November Roy Campbell read his translation of a couple of Spanish poems and John Wain won an outstanding bet by reading a chapter of "Irene Iddesleigh" without a smile. At our next meeting David Cecil read a chapter of his forthcoming book on Gray.
>
> Sometimes, but not often, it would happen that no one had anything to read to us, and on these occasions the fun would grow riotous, with Jack at the top of his form and enjoying every minute—"No sound delights me more," he once said, "than male laughter." At the Inklings his talk was an outpouring of wit, nonsense, whimsy, dialectical swordplay, and pungent judgements. . . . [25]

The same company used to meet on Tuesdays (later Mondays) for an hour or two before lunch at The Eagle and Child (a pub that was always referred to in University circles as "The Bird and Baby"). This particular inn was chosen partly because of its small back room, but mainly because of the character of its landlord, Charles Blagrove, who had "endless stories of an Oxford which is as dead as Dr. Johnson's . . . an Oxford in which it was not uncommon for undergrads to *fight* a landlord for a pint of beer: both would strip to the waist, have a mill in the backyard, and then the battered undergrad would throw down a sovereign and depart." Blagrove had begun life as a cab driver. He remembered undergraduates who were so fastidious that they would give him their new suits if they did not fit perfectly. He could talk about the lavish tips he had received for driving "what he used to call 'fancy goods' to secluded spots; of the people who used to hire his cab to be taken 'somewhere where they could find a fight'; of rags, dinners, that general reckless extravagance and panache which prevailed when the security of the upper classes was still absolute, and England ruled the world. . . ."[26]

Jack held meetings of the Inklings in his rooms for fifteen years, until one horrible Thursday in October 1949 when nobody turned up. What were his motives? In his brilliant book, *The Inklings*, Humphrey Carpenter suggests that he sought to protect himself through the formation of a circle of friends against the powerful inner circle that seemed to him to dominate Magdalen and university politics. This seems to me to be true. He felt isolated during his early years at Magdalen and under dialectical attack during the later ones. For reassurance, he needed fairly frequent meetings with his friends, men who held similar views. Though few who met him casually would have guessed it, he was beneath the surface plagued by Celtic melancholy and a streak of pessimism, qualities the Inklings held at bay. He loved his friends and liked to think that he was of service to them in their literary careers. Meetings of the Inklings made him utterly happy.

Jack wrote his first space-travel novel, *Out of the Silent Planet,* in 1937. He had been a fan of the space-travel thriller since boyhood and regarded such books so highly that after his father's death he brought his copies of *The First Men in the Moon* and *The War of the Worlds* from Little Lea to the Kilns. He was most impressed by the possibilities of the genre after reading David Lindsay's *Voyage to Arcturus.* Arthur Greeves had recommended it to him two years before, but he had only just managed to find a copy. He wrote to Ruth Pitter of his excitement in reading it. From it he learned that in fiction spiritual adventures were what planets were really good for. Only these could satisfy our imaginative cravings. He was deeply indebted to Lindsay for showing him the "terrific results" which could come from combining the spiritual adventures of the Novalis of the sort by George MacDonald and James Stephens with the planetary adventures of the sort written by Jules Verne and H. G. Wells.

Nevertheless, he disagreed with Lindsay's philosophy, which he described as being "on the borderline of the diabolical . . . [and] so Manichaean as to be almost satanic." This feeling no doubt aroused in him the desire to write a very different sort of space-travel novel, a Christian novel like the spiritual thrillers of Chesterton and Charles Williams. Concerned that such books were rare, he made a proposal to Tolkien: "We shall have to write books of the sort ourselves. Supposing you write a thriller that's a time-journey—you have such a strong sense of time—and I write one that's a space-journey."[27]

Each took the bargain seriously. Tolkien wrote the first part of a story called "The Lost Road," and Jack wrote *Out of the*

Silent Planet. The publishers were discouraging. Allen and Unwin, publisher of the fairly successful *Hobbit*, returned Tolkien's "Lost Road" with the comment that it did not seem likely to become a commercial success. J. M. Dent and Sons turned down *Out of the Silent Planet*, as did Sir Stanley Unwin of Allen and Unwin, to whom Tolkien had sent the manuscript on Jack's behalf. The publisher's reader had commented on the book: "Mr. Lewis is quite likely, I dare say, to write a worthwhile novel one day. This one isn't good enough—quite." He described the creatures met in Malacandra as "bunk."[28] Sir Stanley sent this report to Tolkien, who defended the book (with reservations) in an elaborate letter. Sir Stanley then suggested that he pass it on to the Bodley Head, another publishing house of which he was the chairman. Lewis agreed, and it was accepted by them.

Published in the autumn of 1938, *Out of the Silent Planet* initially received about sixty reviews, quite a large number for a book by a little-known writer. Only two reviewers showed any awareness of the book's Christian theology. It was typically regarded simply as science fiction, and Lewis was sometimes compared with Wells. *The Times Literary Supplement* of October 1, 1938, thought Wells more dramatic and better in characterization, "other-worldly exposition and vivid incident. . . . Alas! and alas! that Mr. Lewis, who is a capable writer with an excellent basic notion, did not learn more from his evident teacher."

The reviewers' failure to see the point of the book gave Jack the idea that would be basic to all his children's stories: ". . . [I]f there was only someone with a richer talent and more leisure I think that this great ignorance might be a help to the evangelisation of England; any amount of theology can now be smuggled into people's minds under cover of romance without their knowing it."[29] At this stage in his career, he was not often so explicit about his intent, because he was only gradually coming to realize that he had the power to evangelize through the writing of popular books in which Christianity was implicit. We have a more clearly formed statement of his view in a paper on the subject of Christian apologetics that he read to a group of Anglican priests and youth leaders in 1945. He pointed out that the difficulties of the Christian writer or lecturer arose from the fact that the culture was not at all Christian. This meant that the influence of a Christian lecture or article would be undermined very quickly by the influence of films, newspapers, and novels in which an opposing point of view was taken for granted. This made it impossible for the Christian writer to achieve widespread success. What was wanted was not more "little books about Christianity," but more books by Christians on other subjects in which the Christianity was *latent*.[30] All his fiction is of this sort, as are his philological books and works of literary criticism.

In spite of the favorable reviews, *Out of the Silent Planet* did not sell well until a few years later, when Jack had become famous through *The Screwtape Letters* and his broadcast talks. It is now established on both sides of the Atlantic as a modern classic. A myriad of critical books and articles explore its significance, and it has frequently been used in high school and college classes.

Jack wanted the moral and spiritual significance of his works of fiction to be assimilated subliminally, if at all, and he was annoyed when his publisher outlined the theme of *Out of the Silent Planet* in the blurb on the dust jacket. Over and over again in talking about his fiction, he would say, "But it's there for the story."

Nevertheless, he took seriously criticism of the book's significance, notably the attack on "Westonism." He had created the character Weston in response to such horrifying ideas as those presented in W. Olaf Stapledon's *First and Last Men*, a novel that describes the invasion of Venus by human beings who destroy the planet's inhabitants and have the intention, not only of preserving the human race, but also of creating a superior being. Weston is the personification of these ideas. He certainly intended the danger to be real. The motive of writing the book came from the discovery that one of his pupils took the dream of interplanetary colonization quite seriously, and that for very many people the meaning of the universe depended upon the hope of improving and perpetuating the human race. In other words the *scientific* hope of conquering death was a real rival to Christianity.[31]

Critics sometimes complain that Weston and Devine are cardboard characters, but Lewis, it is important to realize, never intended them to be fully human. Their beliefs and attitudes are dehumanizing and have the effect of destroying their personalities. However, this otherwise magnificent piece of science fiction does suffer by the weak characterization of Ransom, from whose perspective the story is told. Ransom is the one character who ought to be real, yet he never quite comes alive. He has no faults or idiosyncrasies, and we are told little of his spiritual life and intimate thoughts. There are three probable reasons for this thin characterization. One is that Ransom is, to some extent, a self-portrait, and that Lewis was at this time shy of writing about his own spiritual or private life, except to his most intimate friends. Another is that he did not want to put people off by making the book explicitly Christian or sectarian. Finally, he may have felt that a more detailed characterization would have slowed the story down.

The most remarkable parts of the novel are the descriptions of the scenery of Malacandra. Vivid, evocative, and astonishingly credible, they provide the sensitive reader a genuine imaginative experience.

The success of *The Allegory of Love* encouraged Jack to send two more scholarly works to the Oxford University Press in 1939, *Rehabilitations* and *The Personal Heresy*.

Rehabilitations is the only important book of his that has never been reprinted. It is a collection of essays on literary or linguistic subjects, written mostly in defense of the values he deemed important and the authors he loved. The essays on which he worked hardest, "Shelley, Dryden and Mr. Eliot" and "William Morris," were also the ones most highly rated by critics.

The former attempts too much. It sets out to show that Shelley is a more classical poet than Dryden, that he is "superior to Dryden by the greatness of his subjects and his moral elevation. . . . and in the production of poetry appropriate to its subjects.[32] The essay criticizes Dryden, especially for vulgarity, and also includes a sustained attack on T. S. Eliot's essay on Dryden, published in Eliot's *Selected Essays* of 1932. At the time that Jack wrote his essay (and until he was delighted by a performance of *Murder in the Cathedral*), he thought that, particularly with *The Waste Land*, Eliot had done more than any other writer of free verse to corrupt other poets and to lead the British poetry-reading public astray. Traditional English poetry had been so destroyed that it was now almost impossible for a traditional poet to achieve popular success. He thought Eliot's poetry was almost worthless and his literary criticism superficial and unscholarly.

Now these are subjects for short books or at least for separate essays. They cannot be properly dealt with in an essay of only thirty-one pages. Not surprisingly, "Shelley, Dryden and Mr. Eliot" suffers more from imbalance and exaggeration than almost anything else he wrote. Yet it contains fine things. The six or seven pages on *Prometheus Unbound* are among his finest pieces of literary criticism. He reveals Shelley's greatness as no other critic has ever done and carries us away with his own enthusiasm and delight. He also writes finely on the nature of myth, stating that the theme of *Prometheus* is rebirth and regeneration. "Like all great myths its primary appeal is to the imagination: its indirect and further appeal to the will and the understanding can therefore be diversely interpreted according as the reader is a Christian, a politician, a psychoanalyst, or what not. Myth is thus like manna: it is to each man a different dish, and to each the dish he needs."[33]

The essay on Morris has more serious defects. Morris had been a favorite author of his ever since he had first come across his romances while a pupil of Kirkpatrick's. He knew that he liked Morris without knowing why, and the reasons he gives in this essay seem artificially concocted and, as the reviewer J. B. Leishman once pointed out, a piece of special pleading. It is not convincing to be told that the purpose of the vagueness in Morris's scenery descriptions is to give us the opportunity to paint the landscapes ourselves. Those who are repelled by Morris's affected and archaic style must be astonished when told that his writing "consistently departs from modern prose in the direction of simplicity"[34] and that, if there are words we do not understand, we should take pleasure in looking them up. As an example of Morris's style, he quotes with approval: "All this while he durst not kiss or caress her save very measurely, for he deemed that she would not suffer it."[35]

Defending the medievalism of an author for whom "the real interest of the Middle Ages—Christian mysticism, Aristotelian philosophy, Courtly Love—mean nothing"[36] is a difficult task. Yet no essay of Lewis's is likely to be without merits. This one includes an excellent exposition of Morris's romantic socialism and its contrast with the materialistic socialism of the modern Left. He also shows here his appreciation of Morris's passion for immortality ("wild, piercing, orgiastic and heartbreaking") and of his belief in the values of simple work ("to mend the sails, or launch the boat, or gather firewood").[37] Of course, these quotes reveal as much about himself as about Morris.

Of the other essays in *Rehabilitations*, the most interesting are those on the Oxford English School. Oxford colleges, he tells us, should be places, not for teaching, but for the pursuit of knowledge. "The student is, or ought to be," he writes, "a young man who is already beginning to follow learning for its own sake, and who attaches himself to an older student, not precisely to be taught, but to pick up what he can. From the very beginning the two ought to be fellow students."[38] This was always his attitude toward his best pupils. He delighted in learning from them and generously praised them when he found something they had written or said at all illuminating. It happened quite often.

He believed that, as far as possible, the study of English should be a study in depth. The student should not be distracted by a course that contains "little bits of various subjects."[39] However, the whole range of English literature is too much and must therefore be pruned, not just of minor authors, but of modern literature, with which the student will need the least help. The origins of the English language, on the other hand, are essential to include. English cannot be fully understood, he maintained, without some knowledge of how Old High German, Old French, and, to some degree, Latin contributed to the development of Old English. But other languages were not to be included in this syllabus.

In this essay and in the one entitled "The Idea of an English School," which he read to a joint meeting of the classical and English associations, he was attacking the proposal of some Oxford English dons that some Greek, Latin, and French classics should be included in the syllabus of the Oxford English School.

He was convinced that their inclusion would not leave time for the study of a sufficient number of the great English writers, and he distrusted a syllabus abbreviated by fashion. Students should not have their course reduced to the study of what "a committee of four or five dons, brought up in a particular tradition, happened to think the best."[40]

Although J. B. Leishman described the essay as "of really first-rate importance,"[41] it aroused much disagreement among Oxford teachers. But perhaps because of its influence, Oxford persevered for many years with a syllabus that ended with the death of Keats. A paper on later writers was included, but this was voluntary. When I expressed interest in this paper, Jack responded coldly, "Remember that it won't influence the class of degree that you get, except by distracting you from working as hard as you should on the compulsory papers. You ought to be able to read most nineteenth-century writers without my help. Indeed, I doubt if I can spare the time to read them with you." Of course, I gave way. And he made up for it. We often discussed nineteenth-century books in later years.

Oxford University Press published *The Personal Heresy* by Lewis and Tillyard in the spring of 1939. Jack's part is an attack on the increasing role of biography in literary criticism and on the idea that literature is an expression of the writer's personality. It was the fruit of thirteen years of teaching, during which Jack often found that his pupils wrote essays about the lives or personalities of their authors instead of about their works. In fact, his dislike of biographical criticism was lifelong. While still an undergraduate he had begun an address to a society by congratulating himself on his entire ignorance of biographical detail. In one of the last essays he ever wrote, "The Genesis of a Medieval Book,"[42] he reiterated his view that "all criticism should be of books not authors." What made him think that he should do more than reprimand individual pupils was E. M. W. Tillyard's book *Milton*.[43] It was read by most of Jack's pupils, several of whom quoted Tillyard's view that the real subject of *Paradise Lost* is "the state of Milton's mind when he wrote it." Jack attacked the view in an article published in *Essays and Studies*.[44] The poet, he maintained, does not express his personality—he transcends it. "The mind through which we see the objects of poetry is not the poet's"; it is a mind "greatly beyond the human."

Tillyard wrote a reply for the next issue of *Essays and Studies*, and then the controversy was expanded into a book of six essays. The longer the discussion continued, the closer the two became in their views. Probably Tillyard found he could accept Jack's statement of the value of poetry: ". . . [A]n utterance, besides entertaining, charming or exciting us for the moment, should have a desirable permanent effect on us if possible—should make us either happier, or wiser, or better. . . . The only two questions to ask about a poem, in the long run, are, firstly, whether it is interesting, enjoyable, attractive, and, secondly, whether this enjoyment wears well and helps or hinders you towards all the other things you would like to enjoy or do, or be."[45]

Reviewers were quick to point out that by "personality" Lewis and Tillyard meant different things. Most reviewers agreed that the increasingly biographical approach to literature was regrettable, but most also pointed out that understanding something of an author's personality could be a pleasure.

Although the book never sold well, the idea it presents has had an important influence on the teaching of English literature. Henceforward, boys and girls who had hardly heard of C. S. Lewis were liable to be severely reprimanded if they served up biography in the guise of literary criticism.

The Second World War broke out within a few months of the publication of *Rehabilitations* and *The Personal Heresy.* Jack was then a man of forty. He had published seven books, of which only two were moderately successful. No one could have guessed that within a few years his would become a household name.

14

War Work

Jack was horrified by England's declaration of war on Germany, but he had no doubt of its rightness. He was a Christian, but not a pacifist, and he believed that England had no other honorable alternative. In a talk he once gave entitled "Why I Am Not a Pacifist,"[1] he clearly expressed his views on war.

The talk opens with a consideration of the meaning and nature of conscience. He believed that conscience must always be followed, but not before thoroughly examining the factors on which the conclusions of conscience are based—that is, on one's experience, the facts, certain basic moral intuitions, and human and divine authority.

One's experience, he said, can never reveal whether a particular war will do more harm than good, and historical facts do not support the pacifist position that all wars do more harm than good. This pacifist belief, he said, "involves the proposition that if the Greeks had yielded to Xerxes and the Romans to Hannibal, the course of history ever since would have been better, but certainly no worse than it actually had been. . . ."[2]

Moral intuitions cannot be argued, he felt, and must be obeyed. Love is good and hatred is bad; helping people is good and harming them is bad—these are basic intuitions. But we can't help everyone; we must help some people rather than others. Thus, if A is wrongly attacked by B, our helping A may involve "doing some degree of violence to B."³ When applied to nations, this argument involves an admission of the lawfulness of war, since an army or a whole nation cannot be restrained from doing what it wants except by war.

He countered the argument that to abolish war we need to increase the number of pacifists in all nations by pointing out that only liberal nations tolerate pacifists. A great increase in the number of pacifists in a liberal nation would cripple the state, he said, and put it at the mercy of its totalitarian neighbor.

The longest section of the lecture is devoted to a discussion of human and divine authority. Human authority, that of the people around us, of the society to which we belong, is certainly not pacifist. But what of the authority of God? The Christian case for pacifism rests on such sayings as "Resist not evil: but whosoever shall smite thee on thy right cheek, turn to him the other also" (Matt. 5:39). Jack maintained that this saying would have been regarded by individuals in Jesus' time as a guideline for handling the frictions of daily life, not war. He interpreted this verse: "In so far as you are simply an angry man who has been hurt, mortify your anger and do not hit back." All churches, he said, "have constantly blessed what they regard as righteous arms." Saint Thomas Aquinas ruled that princes have a duty to defend their land "by the sword from enemies without."⁴ Saint Peter and Saint Paul approved of the magistrate's use of force. And without reservation the Lord praised the Roman centurion.

Jack, therefore, did everything in his power to assist the war effort. He expected the next few years to be ghastly, but he had no doubt that, if rightly used, England's suffering could be for her ultimate good. It would probably be for his own good, too. "I daresay," he wrote to Arthur Greeves, "for me, personally, it has

come in the nick of time: I was just beginning to get too well settled in my profession, too successful, and probably self
complacent."[5]

After Warren, who was on the army reserve list, had been
called up some weeks before war was declared, Jack thought that
he might have to follow him. He was only forty, and the official
proclamation stated that men between the ages of eighteen and
forty-one were liable for military service. In any case, he supposed there would be no work for him in Oxford. His college
would probably be taken over by the army, and even if it weren't,
there would be few young men to teach. Upon the announcement
that New Buildings would be taken over for government work,
Jack obediently spent two or three exhausting days moving all his
books down to the cellar. A few weeks later, when it was
announced that New Buildings would remain in the hands of the
college after all, he spent another two or three days carrying his
books back. It now seemed that there would be undergraduates
aged eighteen to twenty, and teaching them would count as a
reserved occupation.

But Jack did not want to be just a teaching fellow in a safe,
reserved occupation. He wanted to be active for his country. So
he went to the recruiting office and volunteered to be an instructor of cadets. His offer was declined. It was suggested that he
should instead join the Ministry of Information. Since this would
involve creating propaganda and telling lies, he decided that the
best thing for him to do would be to join the Oxford City Home
Guard Battalion, a body of part-time soldiers being recruited to
repel German troops landing from the air.

His spell of duty began at half past one every Saturday morning. On the first occasion, since there was no sense in going to
bed on Friday evening, he invited Hugo Dyson and Humphrey
Havard to dinner and to a small Inklings meeting. He waited

until his friends had gone home and then walked to the Home Guard meeting place, munching his sandwiches on the way. He was joined there by two much younger men, both of whom he liked and found intelligent. They were "neither too talkative or too silent." He was pleased to find that he was allowed to smoke and that their tour of duty included an admirable place for a soak, the verandah of a college cricket pavilion, with a view over playing fields to the distant railway line. The three hours during which he was on duty passed quickly. He would have regarded them as pleasurable if he had not had to lug a heavy rifle around with him all the time. They broke up at 4:30. He found the walk home through the dawn twilight really beautiful and was in bed by five.[6] The pleasure decreased as time went on. He wrote to Arthur in December that he had spent "one night in nine mooching about the most malodorous and depressing parts of Oxford with a rifle."[7]

But he had much other war work to do. There were a dugout to be made in the garden of the Kilns, blackout curtains to be put up every evening and taken down every morning, and logs to be sawed for the fires, because coal was rationed. The house now contained extra people. Until the war was over, Jack and Mrs. Moore put their house at the disposal of children evacuated from London and other cities thought vulnerable to German bombing. Although their presence meant extra work, particularly since their staff of maids had dwindled, Jack enjoyed these children. "Our schoolgirls have arrived," he wrote to his brother, "and all seem to me—and what's more important, to Mint—to be very nice, unaffected creatures and all most flatteringly delighted with their new surroundings. They're fond of animals, which is a good thing (for them as well as for us)."[8] Having children in the house benefited Jack immensely. He had been shy and ignorant of them, but he now gradually acquired the knowledge and affection for them that made it possible for him to write the Narnia books. Without their presence, it is unlikely that he would even have had the impulse.

In spite of the vast amount of work, Jack was unfailingly cheerful throughout the war. "I have as little to complain of," he wrote to Arthur, "as anyone in England."[9] Some of the things that most people disliked, Jack enjoyed. Gas rationing, for instance, meant fewer cars on the city streets, which made them all the better for walking. From the top deck of the double-decker bus that he rode to and from the college, he was able to see much of the city. He enjoyed even the blackout because it gave him the simple pleasure of glimpsing Oxford by moonlight.

The war also held its sorrows for Jack, although even his closest friends heard little or nothing about them. Warren's call to service distressed him. On September 1, 1939, the day Warren left for the army camp in Yorkshire, Jack ended a tutorial early in order to see him off. But somehow he missed Warren, although he had arrived at the station just before Warren's train pulled out. The letter he wrote the next day has an unusually emotional ending: "God save you, brother."[10] He was no doubt concerned about Warren's habit of drinking heavily when under stress. Warren himself was miserable at being called up. He believed in his country's cause and wanted to serve creditably, but he was unfit and overweight and felt quite inadequate. He had been a binge drinker for years, and it was not unlikely that he would disgrace himself through drunkenness while on active duty. Even if the worst—a court-martial—did not happen, he might behave in a way that he would regret for the rest of his life.

Not much is known about what happened to Warren during his eleven months of active duty. Until being discharged in August, he was in and out of hospitals with some illness, but what exactly was wrong with him, we do not know. His letters mention high fevers, but he never spoke about his experiences in the Second World War, and his silence suggests deep shame. Certainly he was drinking heavily then. Jack wrote a long letter to him every week, probably to distract him from his troubles and to give him the positive task of answering.

As the war went on, Jack had a growing feeling that he was living in enemy-occupied territory. In his view, the enemy was not, however, limited to Hitler or the Germans, but included all the violently anti-Christian forces threatening to destroy the Europe that he knew and loved. He always disliked the black-and-white view of the war, that England was right and Germany wicked and wrong. "The sins of the democracies," he once said to me, "are very great. But very likely those of the totalitarian states are even greater." The general atmosphere of struggle, strain, and crisis that surrounded him gave his work an urgency that it would never have had in peacetime.

He wrote *The Problem of Pain* during the first autumn and winter of the war. It had been commissioned by the publishing firm of Geoffrey Bles as one title in The Christian Challenge Series of popular theological books. Ashley Sampson, the editor of the series, had read and liked *The Pilgrim's Regress* so much that he invited Jack to contribute a book on pain and suffering. Jack read chapters to the Inklings before the book was published and dedicated it to Havard and Tolkien, who had provided many suggestions. When it came out in October 1940, *The Problem of Pain* received many favorable reviews and was a best-seller from the start. It was reprinted twice in 1940, four times in 1941, and three times in 1942 and 1943. To this day, it is one of Jack's most popular books.

This very short text is far more than a treatise on pain. It is a brilliant exposition of Christian belief as a reasonable and humane system. Jack sets out to restore the reader's faith in

Christianity before addressing the subject of human pain. In his charmingly modest preface, he writes that he "believed himself to be restating ancient and orthodox doctrines" and that he had "tried to assume nothing that is not professed by all baptised and communicating Christians." Although he did not suppose himself able to teach fortitude and patience, he held the conviction "that when pain is to be borne, a little courage helps more than much knowledge, a little human sympathy more than much courage, and the least tincture of the love of God more than all."[11]

He wrote the book in plain, everyday language, partly to communicate with ordinary lay people and partly because he did not think that one could understand a philosophical or theological idea until one had translated it into plain language. In a letter to Chad Walsh, a critic who later wrote *C. S. Lewis: Apostle of the Skeptics*,[12] Jack wrote: "Any fool can write *learned* language. The vernacular is the real test. If you can't turn your faith into it, then either you don't understand it, or you don't believe it." His approach is fundamental. He begins with basic religious experience—the experience of the numinous—asking the reader, in one of many brilliant analogies, how he would feel if someone told him that there was a ghost in the next room. The combination of his genius for analogy, logical approach, and plain style in which every word is used precisely makes all his religious writing effective. Yet he rarely oversimplifies. He presents us with a "Christianity, true, as always to the complexities of the real."

The chapters on Hell and animal pain reflect his original thoughts. Hell is something that we are free to inflict on ourselves, if we insist and if we utterly reject God's wish to have us with him. Hell is the logical end of the freedom that God has given to man, the freedom to reject Him. Thus, if Hell has any inhabitants, they are self-enslaved.

The chapter on animal pain is delightful. In it we see the Jack Lewis who loved and understood domestic animals. He regards the personality that tame animals seem to have as being largely the gift of man—they are "reborn to soulhood in us as our mere soulhood is reborn to spirituality in Christ,"—and through us they may attain a sort of immortality.[13]

In his letter to Warren of July 20, 1940, he describes an idea for a book that became *The Screwtape Letters*. He had been unwell and overtired for some time and had had a bad fall that bruised his hip. For these reasons, he had been resting on Sunday mornings. On July 15, he went to Holy Trinity Church in Headington Quarry for the first time in many weeks. Ordinarily, he attended the eight o'clock communion service because he disliked almost all church music, and few hymns were sung at this service. But on this occasion he had slept late, having "considered himself invalid enough to make a midday communion." The sermon was preached by the Reverend T. E. Bleiben, whom he nicknamed "Blanchette" and whose sermons usually bored him. On this occasion, perhaps during the sermon and certainly before the service was over, he was struck by an idea for a book that could be both useful and entertaining. The first title he thought of for it was *From One Devil to Another.* It would be a book of letters of advice from an elderly devil to a young one who has just started work on his first "patient." The first thing to do was to undermine the patient's faith in prayer. This should be easy and often happens almost of its own accord if the prayer is not answered. Even if it is answered, it should be possible, for instance, to suggest that any moral improvement is the result of self-hypnosis or that other apparent results of prayer would have happened anyway. In this work of undermining faith, the younger devil should avoid arguments. They can only give rise to counterarguments. The important thing is to try to encourage in the patient the "unreasoning *feeling*" that the doctrines of the Christian faith are the sort of thing that can't really be true.[14]

He wrote *The Screwtape Letters* quickly, completing one letter in just a few hours each week. In February 1941, after all thirty-one letters had been written, he sent them to *The Guardian*, a Church of England weekly and the only paper to which he subscribed, because its editor had already agreed to publish his essay "Dangers of National Repentance." The letters came out weekly from the beginning of May until the end of November 1941, and *The Guardian*, not a rich paper, paid him £62 (about $1,500) for the whole lot. Jack instructed the editor to send the money to a charity for the widows of Church of England clergymen. He had resolved, I think, even before the publication of *The Pilgrim's Regress*, to give to charity the money he received from the writing of religious books, and he kept to this undertaking even at times when he was short of money, as during the early years of the war.

The letters were an immediate success. Many people who had never heard of *The Guardian* before sought it out just for the letters. Ashley Sampson read the first two or three, took them to Geoffrey Bles, and pointed out excitedly that, if the firm could buy the book rights before other publishers made offers, they might have a real bestseller on their list. And it was so.

Having never learned to type, Jack wrote all his books in longhand and had Warren type final drafts. He then ordinarily destroyed the original handwritten manuscripts because he hadn't the room to store them. After sending the only typewritten copy of *The Screwtape Letters* to Bles, he planned to burn the original manuscript, as was his custom. However, because he was concerned that heavy bombing by German aircraft might destroy the typewritten copy in Bles's office and that it might even be difficult to assemble the series run in *The Guardian*, he sent the handwritten manuscript to his friend Sister Penelope, a nun of the Community of Saint Mary the Virgin at Wantage. He asked her to keep it until the book was printed, after which it could be used to "stuff dolls or anything."[15]

The book came out in February 1942, but even before then letters, nearly always of appreciation, poured in. The correspondence was far more than Jack could cope with, and he enlisted Warren to handle routine correspondence and type lectures and other short pieces, paying him a small salary for this work. After the publication of *Screwtape*, Jack became almost dependent on Warren. He came to dread the mass of correspondence when Warren was away. The two had a close understanding. Warren answered many of the letters without bothering Jack at all. His letters were, in fact, nearly as lively and far more businesslike than Jack's. He also kept an appointment book for Jack and reminded him of upcoming engagements. Things sometimes went wrong when Warren wasn't there to help. There was, for instance, an important London lecture, an address to the Royal Society of Literature, for which Jack failed to turn up.

Screwtape was a success from the start. The first edition of 2,000 copies sold out before publication, and it was reprinted eight times by the end of the year. It was as great a success in the United States when it was published there the following year. Since then it has been translated into many languages and has sold at least two million copies worldwide.

If the book were praised in Jack's presence, he would often say that writing it had given him little pleasure and had, in fact, been painful. He thought it was bad for his character to imagine himself a devil, thinking about how to tempt and pervert those around him. Perhaps worries of this sort had something to do with the decision he made in October 1940 to go to the Cowley Fathers (the Church of England priests of the Society of Saint

John the Evangelist) to ask to be given a spiritual director to whom he could make auricular confession and from whom he could receive advice. He continued the practice for many years and had no doubt that it helped him to understand himself and the temptations he suffered.

Screwtape brilliantly combines spiritual profundity and a remarkable psychological understanding. Both qualities exist in the eighth letter on free will, for instance, and there is more truth about prayer in the fourth letter than in most books on the subject. Profound is the twelfth on the devil's policy of cutting Christians off from real pleasures and positive activities, so that when they arrive in Hell they realize that they spent their lives doing neither what they ought to have done nor what they enjoyed doing. Letter thirteen continues this discussion of pleasure. There is about real pleasures "a sort of innocence and humility and self-forgetfulness," which makes them always partly and often entirely good. Fourteen is a subtle essay on the distinction between true humility, which leads to self-forgetfulness, and false humility, which is a kind of pride and leads to a falsely low view of one's self and one's fellow creatures. The next letter makes the profound point that God wants our concern to be with eternity, or with the present, "obeying the present voice of conscience . . . giving thanks for the present pleasure." Screwtape wants us to think about the future, for the future inflames hope and fear, and is "of all things, the least like eternity." All the letters on the vices are valuable, perhaps particularly those that, like seventeen on gluttony, deal with habits hardly recognized nowadays as vices at all. Over and over again Lewis demonstrates their traditional importance and present-day relevance. The letters on love, lust, and marriage are so easy to read that their profundity can pass unnoticed.

The satire and humor remain surprisingly relevant. Take letter sixteen about the low church vicar and Father Spike. There are still people who wander around looking for churches and ministers who suit them; there are still vicars and priests who water down the faith to such an extent that they shock their parishioners, and others who cannot bring themselves "to preach anything which is not calculated to shock, grieve, puzzle or humiliate."[16] How admirable is the attack on what he calls "party churches"! And how sharp the piece of diabolical fun about working up hatred between those who call it 'mass' and those who say 'holy communion,' when neither party has any clear idea of the theological differences between Hooker's doctrine and Thomas Aquinas's.[17]

While there is some falling off in wit and invention in the later letters, the narrative interest is well maintained. The last letter is a great piece of visionary prose, soaring, as it does, to that world "where pain and pleasure take on transfinite values, and all our arithmetic is dismayed."

Although Jack felt at times that the writing of *The Screwtape Letters* tended to corrupt him, no reader can ever have felt endangered by it. The effect of the book is to clarify thought, to sharpen our knowledge of the distinctions between good and evil, to increase our desire to be virtuous, and through much practical advice to make it easier for us to become so. It is a truly devotional work.

15

Preacher and Broadcaster

About six months before *The Screwtape Letters* was published, Jack received a letter from Dr. James Welch, the director of religious broadcasting at the British Broadcasting Corporation (BBC), thanking him for the personal help he had received from *The Problem of Pain* and asking him to help in the work of religious broadcasting. Jack detested the radio, as later on he would detest television, but because he realized that through radio he would be able to reach people who would never think of reading his books, he accepted. He told Welch that he wanted to talk about the law of nature, or objective right and wrong, because in modern England the New Testament's assumption that people believed in natural law and knew that they had disobeyed it was no longer accurate. The first step, therefore, was to help people recover a sense of guilt. Welch liked the idea and engaged Jack to give four fifteen-minute talks every Wednesday during August 1941.

Broadcast live from the London studio of the BBC and billed in the *Radio Times* as "Right and Wrong: A Clue to the Meaning of the Universe?," they were a great success. His rich voice, educated yet earthy, came across perfectly. The extraordinary vitality that was characteristic of his best Oxford lectures made an unforgettable impression on almost everyone who listened, Christians and unbelievers alike.

I remember being at a pub filled with soldiers on one Wednesday evening. At a quarter to eight, the bartender turned the radio up for Lewis. "You listen to this bloke," he shouted. "He's really worth listening to." And those soldiers did listen attentively for the entire fifteen minutes.

Long before the talks were over, Jack had received a great number of letters mostly forwarded by the BBC. When he asked what he should do about them, Dr. Welch suggested giving another talk to answer some of his listeners' questions and objections. But this talk, given on September 6, had the opposite result. More letters than ever arrived. For the rest of his life, he had an enormous amount of correspondence, including "many [letters] from serious inquirers whom it was a duty to answer fully."[1] His system was to reply to these in longhand and to get his brother to type more or less standard letters to the others. But even with Warren's help (and this was invaluable), his correspondence was a great burden. Nevertheless, he responded to many complete strangers with letters that were minor masterpieces of good counsel and clear English.

Given the success of the first talks, the BBC naturally asked him to give another series of talks, collectively entitled "What Christians Believe." These talks were a marvelously compact exposition of Christian theology, that is, of the beliefs common to almost all Christians. He was most anxious in them, and in all his religious writings, to avoid inter-church controversy, to present a body of doctrine that would be acceptable to Protestants as well as Catholics, and to Baptists as well as Greek Orthodox. He succeeded wonderfully in this endeavor. Another outstanding feature of the talks was their rational character. In the popular mind, Christian belief tended to be identified with the emotional and irrational. But Jack's presentations flowed naturally and rationally. His approach was ideal for reaching the general public.

His first two lecture series were published together in July 1942 under the title *Broadcast Talks*, which became an immediate bestseller. Two months after its publication, the BBC broadcast a third series, entitled "Christian Behaviour." Remarkably positive in tone, these talks were far more concerned with Christian virtues, such as faith, hope, charity, and forgiveness, than with sins and vices. The advice given is practical, because it is based on Jack's personal experience, rather than on books or tradition. Thus, on the subject of the influence of moods on faith he tells us that it is his experience that moods will change however deeply one reasons. He has moods now that he is a Christian in which the whole thing seems extremely improbable. To combat this, the first step is to accept the fact that our moods do change. The next thing to do if one has accepted Christianity is deliberately to hold some of its main doctrines before one's mind for some part of every day. The need to do this explains why religious reading, daily prayers, and going to church are necessary to the Christian life.[2]

Three of his final series of seven talks for the BBC, originally entitled "Beyond Personality: The Christian View of God," were prerecorded on gramophone records late in 1943 and broadcast in February, March, and April 1944. He did not much like the process of prerecording or of being under the producer's constant scrutiny, but the talks were nevertheless effectively presented. Well-written and deeply profound, this series is generally recognized as the climax. In his last talk, "The New Men," he soared into an eloquence rare in broadcasting. He is explaining that our real new selves, which come from Christ and are our own real, higher personalities, will come only when we are searching for Christ. One principle runs through all life from top to bottom. "Give up yourself and you'll find your real self." Submit every day to the "death of your ambitions and favourite wishes" . . . "submit with every fibre of your being and you'll find eternal life. Keep nothing back. Nothing that you have not given away will ever be really yours. . . . Look for yourself, and you will find in the long run only hatred, loneliness, despair, rage, ruin and decay. But look for Christ and you will find Him, and with Him everything else thrown in."[3]

Hundreds of people wrote to the BBC asking for more talks, but Jack refused for two reasons. He had said about all that he could usefully say to a broadcast audience, and even with the help of his brother he could not handle another increase in the number of letters.

For many years, these series of talks sold well as separate books. The final series was published in *Beyond Personality*, and all the talks were later published together in a single volume entitled *Mere Christianity*. The reaction of professional reviewers to the books was more mixed than that of the general public. *The Times Literary Supplement* wrote of *Beyond Personality* that "Mr. Lewis has a quite unique power of making theology attractive, exciting and (one might almost say) uproariously funny."[4] J. H. Homes wrote in the *New York Herald Tribune Weekly Book Review* that "his clarity of thought and simplicity of expression have a magic about them which makes plain the most abstruse problems of theological speculation."[5] But many reviews were tepid or hostile. He was accused of being vague, pantheistic, and not wholly orthodox, and in one American review he was referred to as a "pious paradox-monger and audacious word-juggler."[6] One of the most hostile reviews was that of Alistair Cooke, who attributed Lewis's popularity to the uncertainties of wartime, and who considered his view of sex and marriage as puritanical and his apparent logicality as pat oversimplification.[7]

Such reviews have never influenced the popularity of the series. Today they read as freshly as ever and are firmly established as classics of popular theology. At the time of their publication, *Broadcast Talks* and *Beyond Personality* did much to encourage and sustain the morale of both servicemen and civilians. Jack's contemporary at Malvern, Air Chief Marshal Sir Donald Hardman, wrote to me:

> It astonished me that he should have become an author of uplifting religious books. Their nature and influence astonished me more. It was a time of strain and difficulty for all of us. The war, the whole of life, everything tended to seem pointless. We needed, many of us, a key to the meaning of the universe. Lewis provided just that. Better still, he gave us back our old, traditional Christian faith so that we could accept it with new confidence, with something like certainty. Without ever being political, military or jingoistic, I am sure that he did, perhaps without meaning to, a great deal for what is called the war effort. For this reason alone I am sure that he deserved the high decoration that was offered to him by Winston Churchill after the war.

In the winter of 1941, after the success of the first series of broadcast talks, Jack received an invitation to address the Royal Air Force (RAF) from the Chaplain-in-Chief, the Reverend Maurice Edwards. Jack doubted his ability to talk to servicemen, but he was quite prepared to try. He explained that he thought that he might be drafted. Edwards assured him that this was extremely unlikely, especially if he was already doing what could be classed as "war work."

He certainly regarded his talks to the RAF as war work, although his object was to convert men to Christianity or to make them better Christians. While he was not in the least concerned with making them better fighting men, he thought that this could follow from their being better, braver Christians. He offered to lecture during weekends since his teaching responsibilities were lighter than they had been before the war. His traveling expenses were to be paid, and in addition he would receive a small fee for giving the talks. This he accepted most gratefully as he was then extremely short of money.

Edwards sent a circular to the chaplains of various RAF stations announcing that Lewis was available and suggesting that they might invite him to talk to their men. He considered his first talks, which were at the RAF station near Abingdon, a complete failure. Fewer than a dozen men turned up, and none of them showed any desire to ask questions at the end. He was more successful at the bigger stations, where his audience often included men of real intellectual ability, but it is fair to say that he made a deep impression on only a few. Many of the men may have been put off by his tendency to lecture (he knew nothing at the time of leading a discussion group), but some were also put off by his cool, rational approach, by the lack of emotional and obvious devotional content. To him, of course, feelings were unreliable, transient things, and there was little to be gained by making people feel better.

All through the summer vacation, he was away every weekend at RAF camps, "away," he wrote to Arthur Greeves, "for 2 or 3 days at a time and then home for 2 or 3 days." He found continual traveling in crowded trains extremely tiring. "One felt all the time as if one had just played a game of football—aching all over."[8] And so it went on for years, especially during the summers. Fortunately, Warren was at home and able to confirm lecture engagements and to look up railway timetables. Warren had always taken a great interest in such matters and now took on with great pleasure his job as Jack's lecture and tour manager. Although he spent some of the summer months on the River Thames in his motorboat, the *Bosphorus*, as part of a Home Guard naval squadron, he sometimes accompanied Jack. They both enjoyed seeing different parts of the country for the first time, especially mountainous areas such as Perthshire, Cumberland, and central Wales.

Jack was often away on speaking engagements during the school term. If he weren't addressing the RAF, he might be preaching a sermon at St. Mary's University Church or giving a talk at a girl's school or a convent. But he would always have to be back in Oxford on Mondays, partly for tutoring and partly because of a very important meeting.

From January 1942, his Monday evenings were devoted to meetings of the Oxford Socratic Club, of which he was president and for which he was responsible to the university. The idea evolved from a conversation between a Somerville College undergraduate and Stella Aldwinckle, who was spiritual counselor at the college. The student complained that there did not seem to be anyone with whom one could discuss the sort of doubts and difficulties agnostics raise about God. Miss Aldwinckle at once put up a notice announcing a meeting in the Junior Common Room and inviting "all atheists, agnostics, and those who are disillusioned about religion or think they are" to come to it. Churches and religious societies came under strong attack at this meeting, and it was decided that Oxford badly needed an "open forum for the discussion of the intellectual difficulties connected with religion and with Christianity in particular."[9]

The Oxford Socratic Club was formed for this purpose. Because Jack was thought to have been at one time an atheist, he was invited to be the president and also the senior member of the university responsible for the club's good behavior and without whom permission to form the society would not be granted.

He accepted the role with great enthusiasm ("This club is long overdue," he told its initiator) and joined with Stella Aldwinckle and Dr. L. F. Grensted, former Nolleth Professor of the philosophy of the Christian religion, in devising a policy and a program for the first term. It was to be honestly concerned with the pros and cons of the Christian religion. "Here a man could get the case for Christianity without all the paraphernalia of pietism and the case against it without the irrelevant *sansculottism* of our common anti-God weeklies."[10]

At each meeting, a paper would be read either by a Christian or an unbeliever. A speaker who held the opposing view would reply. The meeting was then thrown open to general discussion, which Jack usually began by delivering, with enormous gusto, an attack on some of the unbeliever's propositions. Club members had to be led by logical and impartial argument that "has a life of its own, Jack maintained. . . . We expose ourselves and the weakest of our party to your fire no less than you are exposed to ours. . . . The arena is common to both parties and cannot finally be cheated; in it you risk nothing, and we risk all."[11] Jack's contributions were usually the high points of the evening. Most of the people there had come to hear him address the opposition with logic, quick wit, and his great gift of repartee. Often eighty to a hundred undergraduates would be present, as well as some senior members of the university. As the second-largest society at the university, the Oxford Socratic Club attracted some of the best and best-known speakers in the country, including Charles Williams, Iris Murdoch, Konrad Lorenz, Dorothy L. Sayers, J. Bronowski, and J. B. S. Haldane, to mention only a few who spoke while Jack was president.[12]

Unfortunately, the club's importance depended too much on Jack's genius. After his move to Cambridge in 1954, the membership gradually declined, although the club was not finally disbanded until the summer of 1972. For many who had been at Oxford during Jack's tenure there, Monday evenings were the most exciting events of their university careers. As one former member put it in a letter to me, "If I have an adult Christian faith that is a rational one, I owe it to the meetings of the Socratic society. I never realised before I went there that Christianity could be defended logically, and that most of the arguments used by its opponents could be shown to be irrational."

The policy of counterattack adopted by Lewis at these meetings and on many other occasions (but never in his tutorials) was something new in twentieth-century Oxford. For many years, Christians had been passively on the defensive. You might encounter a man frequently without ever knowing that he was a Christian. It was unlikely that in ordinary conversation he would uphold Christian principles and almost unheard of that he would make a vigorous, logical attack on nonbelievers from a Christian standpoint. Skepticism, tolerance, and even indifference were commonly thought to be the proper attitude toward Christianity. But for the time being Jack changed all that. He expressed his views, not only at the Socratic Club, but also at dinner and in the Senior Common Room afterward. This policy made him many enemies.

Although he had transgressed an unwritten code, he persisted in behaving in a way that was intolerable and incorrect by the standards of Oxford society. The Oxford Senior Common Room was a men's club. Its conventions obliged a man to behave in certain ways with his fellows. His table manners must be those of a gentleman. (At one time, it was said that before a man was elected to a fellowship at Magdalen, he would be invited to a dinner of, say, sole on the bone and cherry pie. Only if he dealt with the bones and stones neatly, but without too much obvious care, would he be elected.) The conventions of conversation were also important. A man who taught English or French literature might discuss academic questions with another specialist in the same subject, but it would be wrong for him to give his opinions on the classics or theology. Jack was resented by many for having written *The Pilgrim's Regress*, which satirized some philosophies and divisions of the Christian church. Harry Weldon, a philosophy professor, thought that the book should not have been written (although he once said to one of Jack's students, "The man is not as bad as his books"[13]). Weldon was not alone in his views. It was commonly thought that a man's belief is a private affair and should not be written about or published. It was thought unsociable and a breach of the conventions for members of the Senior Common Room to attack others for their beliefs or, worse still, to try to convert them. Also regrettable were his broadcast talks ("a professional theologian would not have been so popular," the Reverend Victor White once said to me) and his interest in writing fiction. Jack's colleagues thought that his proper work was teaching and writing scholarly books, such as *The Allegory of Love* (but even that was too moralistic for them). They especially could not forgive the fact that the man was serious in wanting to convert others.

Some men, such as Adam Fox, Colin Hardie, and Tom Stevens, shared Jack's views, but they had neither his gift of repartee nor his combative spirit. If they had, they might have transformed the spiritual life of the country. As it was, however, Jack tended to feel increasingly isolated when dining at the college. His dislike of what he saw as the negative anti-Christian machinations of some of his colleagues developed little by little into almost an obsession and compelled him to write *That Hideous Strength*. But this remarkable novel was merely one prong of a sustained counterattack against the anti-Christian forces that he found around him.

16

Writing, Writing, Writing

The Christian counterattack was carried on by a barrage of books, articles, and letters, as well as over the air. Considering his other activities, Jack's output during those remaining war years was astonishing. Between 1942 and 1946 he published *A Preface to Paradise Lost, Beyond Personality, Perelandra, That Hideous Strength, The Abolition of Man,* and *The Great Divorce.* In addition, he wrote a draft of *Miracles* and contributed articles to such publications as *The Guardian, The Spectator,* and *Time and Tide.* He also wrote letters on important subjects to the editors of *Theology, The Listener, The Times Literary Supplement,* and other papers, as well as to many individuals. Additionally, he wrote and preached a few magnificent sermons. All this in spite of, as Mrs. Moore put it, being "as good as an extra maid" at the Kilns.[1] He played his part, too, in entertaining the evacuated children, and he spent many hours trying to teach a mentally retarded boy to read and write. He was also working full-time as a tutor and lecturer.

To relax, he spent time with his friends. Meetings with them now became ever more important, providing him with good talk, the stimulus of new ideas, and one sort of love. These friends who most influenced him during the war years were Tolkien and, particularly, Charles Williams. He regarded the evacuation from London of the Oxford University Press, for which Charles Williams worked, as the war's great gift to him. Jack's enthusiastic letter to Williams about his novel *The Place of the Lion* had led to occasional meetings, and from September 1939 until Williams's death in May 1945 they met regularly, usually twice a week with other Inklings members at Magdalen, and very often on Tuesday mornings at the Eagle and Child pub.

Charles Williams was a man of extraordinary literary and theological genius. He was of humble background and always spoke with a lower middle-class London accent that Jack thought of as cockney. Since 1908, he had worked at Oxford University Press, for sixteen years as a proofreader, and then as an editor. He was as fluent and industrious as Jack; he wrote poetry, plays, novels, biographies, and literary criticism, but only his novels achieved even modest success. They are spiritual thrillers, altogether wilder and more mystical than those of Chesterton, and they show Williams's interest in both black and white magic, in the occult, and in Rosicrucianism. Jack was conscious of their serious faults, but nevertheless rated them highly, probably because at the time he himself was trying to write a novel that would be imaginative, profoundly Christian, and yet popular. But he rated far more highly the sequence of Arthurian poems that Williams was writing at the time of his move from London to Oxford in September 1939.

Those who liked Williams usually liked him very much (young women were particularly drawn to him). In a letter to Arthur Greeves, Jack described him as "ugly as a chimpanzee but so radiant (he emanates more love than any man I have ever known) that as soon as he begins talking he is transfigured and looks like an angel."[2] Jack delighted in his talk; in his speculative, far-ranging ideas; in the world that Williams called the Way of Affirmation; and in his theory of substitution, by which one could offer suffering for the welfare of another. He shared Williams's passion for the poetry of Wordsworth and Milton and strongly approved of his incantatory way of declaiming it. He thought Williams was a great poet, or at least the author of a great verse sequence, which he felt compelled to make better known. He liked Williams and was influenced by him more than by anyone else during the war.

Jack's friendship was of great value to Williams. Jack introduced him to a number of brilliant literary men, arranged for him to give lectures at the examination schools (an unusual invitation since Williams had never earned a university degree), and above all was enthusiastic about Williams's poems (which almost everyone else found impenetrably obscure). He advised Williams on how to improve his work, although his advice was rarely followed; arranged for him to have a book published in the Christian Challenge Series, of which his own *Problem of Pain* was part; encouraged him to write *The Figure of Beatrice*, a book on Dante; and, with other Inklings members, helped him to revise what is perhaps his finest book, *All Hallow's Eve*, in spite of what he called its "pseudoculture." Williams was far happier in Oxford than he had been in London, and he hoped that through Jack's influence he might obtain a readership in English or even be elected professor of poetry. However by May 1945, the month in which he died, he had given up hope of these appointments and had been preparing to return to work in his old office in London.

His death was a painful blow to Jack. For a few days afterwards he had a strong sense of Williams's presence around him. He experienced Williams as being in a state of bliss, yet still caring about his friends on earth. In a letter to Mary Neylan, an old pupil, he described Williams as "friend of friends, the comforter of all our little set, the most angelic man." Yet he found that his faith had actually been made stronger. He found, too, that those who said that death had made someone feel closer to them than before were speaking the truth. He couldn't put the experience into words, but it felt just like that. He seemed to be living in a new world, "lots, lots of pain, but not a particle of depression or resentment."[3]

He makes a similar point even more strongly in the moving preface he wrote to *Essays Presented to Charles Williams* and in a letter to Mrs. Williams. His friendship was not ended. He was left believing in life after death far more strongly than before. Just as our Lord was taken away from us, so our friends go in order to be in a new way closer to us than before.

These feelings of Williams's presence faded slowly, but they often recurred in later life, especially on the anniversaries of his death. It was not until he met Joy Davidman Gresham, the woman he would later marry, that he found anyone to take Williams's place in his heart.

The influence of Williams on Jack's writing is not evident, except in *That Hideous Strength*, but Jack discussed all his books with Williams. Jack often experienced a conflict between his intuitive and rational sides, and Williams helped him to gain confidence in his intuition. Williams also confirmed many of Jack's ideas. In dedicating *A Preface to Paradise Lost* to Williams, Jack wrote that his lecture "partly anticipated, partly confirmed, and most of all clarified and matured what I had long been thinking about Milton."[4] One is surprised here only by the word *anticipated*. His ideas on Milton seemed to his pupils clearly expressed as far back as the 1930s; indeed, they eventually caused almost a revolution in the teaching and interpretation of Milton. Jack was too modest. It was his book, not Williams's lecture, that marked the "recovery of a true critical tradition after more than a hundred years of laborious misunderstanding."[5]

The conception of hell and purgatory in the brilliant *The Great Divorce* may owe something to the discussions the two had together, but that book is indebted more to Dante and MacDonald than to anyone else. Williams influenced Jack most deeply in the writing of *That Hideous Strength*, primarily by sharing his vision of the world. Both men held a vivid awareness of evil and a profound understanding of its nature, which Williams called "the blackness of things," an understanding through self-awareness of evil in the psyche, as well as in the world and in the universe. As sensitive men, they found this awareness extremely painful. Jack had drawn on it in *The Screwtape Letters*, a book he found taxing to write. In *That Hideous Strength*, he presents both a psychological and cosmic experience of evil. He might have found this book even more painful to write if the evil were not balanced by visions of great, even supreme, good.

His perverted Belbury scientists, who rely upon black magic, remind one of some of the evil characters in Williams's *War in Heaven* and *Many Dimensions*. And the introduction of Merlin is certainly due to Williams's influence. Perhaps the delightful Fellowship of Saint Anne's also owes something to Williams. It may be based on a group of young women who joined together before the war as fans of Williams, calling themselves "the Household" or "the Companions of the Coinheritance" and pledging themselves to follow his wishes.

At the time that Jack wrote *That Hideous Strength*, he was already at work on a study of Williams's Arthurian poems, which, "for the soaring and gorgeous novelty of their technique and for their profound wisdom," he thought among the "two or three most valuable books of verse produced in the century."[6] In the spring of 1945, when Jack learned that Williams had decided to return to London, he organized six Inklings members to produce the book *Essays Presented to Charles Williams*. It was published by Oxford University Press in 1947. Though it contains only about 150 pages, it is an important and delightful collection that includes a fine essay by Dorothy L. Sayers on Dante, Tolkien's long and brilliant essay "On Fairy Stories," Jack's essay "On Stories," and learned contributions by Gervase Mathew, Owen Barfield, and Warren.

Jack acted as editor and contributed a preface that is a moving tribute to Williams. His description of the man is vivid:

> In appearance he was tall, slim, and straight as a boy, though grey-haired. His face we thought ugly . . . but the moment he spoke it became . . . like the face of an angel—not a feminine angel in the debased tradition of some religious art, but a masculine angel, a spirit burning with intelligence and charity. . . . No man whom I have known was at the same time less affected and more flamboyant in his manners: and also more playful. . . . [H]e threw down all his barriers without even implying that you should lower yours.[7]

There is a description, too, of the sort of men's discussions that Jack enjoyed almost more than anything else:

> That face—angel's or monkey's—comes back to me most often seen through clouds of tobacco smoke and above a pint mug, distorted into helpless laughter at some innocently broad buffoonery or eagerly stretched forward in the cut and parry of prolonged, fierce, masculine argument and "the rigour of the game."
> Such society, unless all its members happen to be of one trade, makes heavy demands on a man's versatility. And we were by no means of one trade. The talk might turn in almost

any direction, and certainly skipped "from grave to gay, from lively to severe": but wherever it went, Williams was ready for it. He seemed to have no pet subject. Though he talked copiously one never felt that he had dominated the evening. Nor did one easily remember particular "good things" that he had said: the importance of his presence was, indeed, made clear by the gap that was left on the rare occasions when he did not turn up. It then became clear that some principle of liveliness and cohesion had been withdrawn from the whole party: lacking him, we did not completely possess one another. . . . Before he came I had passed for our best conduit of quotations; but he easily outstripped me. He delighted to repeat favourite passages, and nearly always both his voice and the context got something new out of them.[8]

Jack was devoted to all his friends, but he loved Williams the most. Their friendship perfectly fulfilled the ideals that Jack would later describe in *The Four Loves*. They shared a common purpose and vision, romanticism and Christianity, and a love of both orthodoxy and wild speculation. For the rest of his life, Jack regarded Williams as a model of goodness. When in doubt or temptation, he would often try to imagine what Williams would do in the same situation. The thought of Williams and obedience to his theory of substitution would inspire him to offer himself as a substitute when his wife Joy was in great pain and dying of cancer.

Jack explained in his dedication of *A Preface to Paradise Lost* to Charles Williams that he was much indebted to Williams's short preface to Milton in the World's Classics series and to his lectures, especially the one on *Comus*. In this Williams had given to the virtue of chastity the importance it would have had in the minds of sincere Christians of Milton's day. This gave Jack the idea of doing the same for *Paradise Lost* but on a larger scale. He would not only expound the theology, of which many readers were in his experience ignorant, he would explain the characteristics of epic poetry, especially its style. The importance he attached to it is shown by the stages through which it went. He gave eleven lectures on the subject at Oxford in the Michaelmas term 1939, and then two years later a revised version as the Ballard Memorial Lectures at University College, North Wales. The book published by the Oxford University Press in 1943 consists of these lectures, further revised and enlarged.

The Preface is divided into two sections, chapters one through eight dealing with epic form and style, and nine through eighteen dealing with the subject and characterization of Milton's poem. The first section is the defense of the grandeur and artificial quality of Milton's verse. He looks at Milton's models, especially Homer, for poetry composed to be recited or read aloud to a group, and Virgil, for poetry written to be read by an individual. Both are deliberately grand and artificial; both are rhetorical in that they set out to influence us by working on our conventional emotional responses. It is unfair to attack *Paradise Lost* for sharing these qualities. If we do so, we are attacking it for being just what it sets out to be—an epic poem. But our ability to appreciate the poem is hindered by the fact that some of our conventional emotional responses are no longer the same as those of men and women of Milton's day. To give examples, pride was then thought a deadly sin and chastity a positive virtue. Modern readers need to be reeducated.

They need to accept or at least to understand the Christian doctrine of the creation and the fall then taken for granted. God created everything and made it good. Bad things are good things perverted by the sin of pride, which causes creatures to be disobedient to the will of God. They need also to accept the principle of a hierarchy in which we are all required to accept a subservient place. Satan's fault was that he refused to do so. This made him not a hero, but an egotistical tyrant.

In the last lecture he suggests that *Paradise Lost* is a personally relevant poem even for those who do not accept its Christian theology. It then embodies in mythical form "the great change in every individual from happy dependence to miserable self-assertion and thence either, as in Satan, to final isolation, or, as in Adam, to reconcilement and a different happiness."[9]

The publication of *The Preface* provoked hostility from many of Jack's fellow academics. Even twenty-three years later Dr. Helen Gardner wrote: "It is marred by an obsessive concern with the reader's morals, which turns *Paradise Lost* into a vast cautionary tale and tract for the times. It is the least satisfactory and the least attractive of Lewis's critical works, smelling both of the lecture room and the popular pulpit."[10] She is mostly right. Jack did regard the poem as a tract for the times, and in this and most of his books he is concerned with our morals. In spite of academic hostility, it remains the most widely read book on its subject.

Between *Out of the Silent Planet* and *That Hideous Strength*, Jack wrote *Perelandra*, the space-travel novel he liked best and of all his books the one most essentially his own. Ransom learns, in his last conversation with Oyarsa in *Out of the Silent Planet*, that the earth is "not so fast shut as was thought." There are even angelic creatures ("eldils") who descend into the air, "into the very strongholds of the bent one," who controls the earth.[11] The assault Ransom forecasts by the good eldils on the bent one who controls the earth is the subject of *That Hideous Strength*. *Perelandra* is about the interlude before the assault.

The story is very much that of Genesis or *Paradise Lost*. One theme is that human beings can only be happy if their wills and all other aspects of their nature are in a state of happy submission to God. The book describes a gloriously beautiful world and an unfallen woman who is exposed to temptations subtler than those of Milton's Eve. She is contrasted with an utterly rebellious, and therefore utterly miserable, creature.

Published in March 1943, *Perelandra* received largely enthusiastic reviews, though some reviewers thought it was too theological. Alan Pryce-Jones wrote in *The Observer* that "he should read more Verne and less Aquinas."[12] *The Times Literary Supplement* praised his rare power of inventive imagination. Leonard Bacon of *Commonweal* thought it was the result of "the poetic imagination at full blast" and praised the writing, noting "whole passages of prose poetry—that inevitably suggest the sweep of Dante and of Milton."[13] But Kate O'Brien of *The Spectator* thought the subject asked too much of prose and was only suitable for "verse at its most immense."[14]

Written with a confident virtuosity not to be found in *Out of the Silent Planet*, it conveys a rich flow of visual enchantments—floating islands, ever-growing and bursting bubble fruits, a green lady, a pure rose-red valley surrounded by glowing peaks—with imagination and sensuality. The descriptions of things convey a mythological, spiritual, or sacramental quality. Take, for instance, the description of the first thunder—"the laughter rather than the roar of heaven"—or of Ransom's first experience of the bubble baths that grow on the trees. He is tired and irritated by the little heraldic dragon nudging him on, when he sees the green bubble overhead. Moved by an impulse that is both supernatural and natural (in this novel the two are inseparable), he touches it. "Immediately his head, face and shoulders were drenched with what seemed (in that warm world) an ice-cold shower bath. . . . When he opened his eyes . . . all the colours about him seemed richer and the dimness of that world seemed clarified. A re-enchantment fell upon him. The golden beast at his side seemed no longer a danger or a nuisance."[15]

Jack was interested all his life in colors and their symbolism. His feeling for color enriches his description of Ransom's approach to the enchanted place where he is to meet the newly appointed king and queen. "He went on. Little by little the peaks and the tableland sank and grew smaller, and presently there arose beyond them an exquisite haze like vapourised amethyst and emerald and gold, and the edge of the haze rose as he rose, and became at last the horizon of the sea, high lifted above the hills."[16] The numinous quality of this passage comes from the religious associations and rareness of the precious stones, the sense of mystery produced by the haze, and the suggestion of a rising that is a spiritual as well as a visual experience.

Perelandra contains some delightful animals, such as the dolphinlike fish on which the few humans can ride through the warm seas, and the little froglike creatures that leap head-high and are as brightly colored as kingfishers. The most exciting for us are the singing beasts and the little golden dragon that Ransom first saw curled round a heraldically colored tree and recognized as the tree of the mythical garden of the Hesperides. Jack's idea is that the myths and mythological figures of our world may represent in corrupted form spiritual realities to be found in a purer form in planes less fallen than ours.

The characterizations in *Perelandra* are more successful than in the other space-travel novels. This is partly because there are fewer of them. There are only three characters, each presented in detail. Eve is delightful, and Weston is one of the most powerful and convincing representations of demonic possession in European literature. The characterization of Ransom is more complex because we are told his thoughts and feelings. Our knowledge of his secret fears and doubts and his ability to laugh at himself humanize him and make it easier for us to accept his heroic behavior. His great virtues are humility, which makes it possible for him to be open to spiritual promptings, and Christian obedience, which is often emphasized in Jack's works.

There is a close parallel between Ransom and Jesus Christ. Ransom offers his body and mind so that Perelandra can be saved. He undergoes a laceration of the flesh and a symbolic death. He descends into the underworld and, after a lapse of time that may be three days, rises again. In spite of fear, pain, and agony, he is open to the promptings of the Spirit and obedient to them. At the end of the book, he is rewarded and transformed by the sight of the great eldils and the Great Dance itself: "[A]nd a simplicity beyond all comprehension, ancient and young as spring, illimitable, pellucid, drew him with cords of infinite desire into its own stillness."[17]

One's appreciation of *Perelandra* depends upon how much of Christian doctrine the reader accepts. For many Christians, this is likely to be the most rewarding of his novels.

At the Socratic Club, Jack often found himself as a Christian crusader fighting two erroneous views. The first was that there is no such thing as an objective morality, that all values either are subjective or spring from the social and economic conditions of society. The second was that the Christian religion is fundamentally a moral or ethical system. To the latter view, Jack would reply that Christian ethics were far from unusual and, in fact, were common to most religions and embraced by most high-minded men in all civilizations. He maintained that Christianity is not a new ethic, but a way of obeying the old traditional ethic.

He spent a good deal of time in 1942 studying the ethics of other religions and philosophical systems. At about this time, he also learned from some of his students of the existence of school textbooks that taught that all literary and moral values are subjective. By coincidence, he had recently been sent a copy of *The Control of Language* by two schoolmasters, Alec King and Martin Ketley, which horrified him. Such a view seemed to him to destroy all human stability and to dehumanize man as a rational being. He therefore jumped at the opportunity to campaign against this view when he was invited to give three lectures at Durham University. The lectures are too closely argued to make for easy listening, and it seems that few members of his audience understood them. Nor were they well received when they were published as a pamphlet by Geoffrey Bles late in 1943. A second edition was not issued until 1946, and it was not published in the United States until 1947. None of the few reviewers of the first edition seem to have realized its importance. They must have been put off by the title: *The Abolition of Man: Reflections on Education with Special Reference to the Teaching of English in the Upper Forms of Schools.* Now, however, it is generally seen as his most important pamphlet and the best existing defense of objective values and the natural law, which he referred to as the Tao.

He tells us that, until quite modern times, all people believed in a universe in which there were appropriate and inappropriate emotional reactions to various situations. Furthermore, almost all people in almost all civilizations have agreed upon the appropriateness of these reactions and on the objective values that arouse them. Emotions, he says, are indispensable links between intellect and instinct, which must be trained to help the intellect control the body. "Without the aid of trained emotions the intellect is powerless against the animal organism," he says. "The head rules the belly through the chest—the seat . . . of Magnanimity, of emotions organised by trained habit into stable sentiments."[18] The teaching of views such as those held by King and Ketley will atrophy the chest, he says, and produce beings who lack stability and full humanity. The emotions must be trained to accept and act in harmony with stable values, those of practical reason or natural law, those of duty, justice, mercy, love, kindness, and so on. There are no other values, he maintains, and he supports this thesis by an appendix that illustrates the Tao, which is the generally accepted ethical code from the most varied sources, including Chinese, Sanskrit, Babylonian, Roman, Greek, American Indian, and Australian aboriginal philosophies and religions. The choice, he says, is really between accepting this thesis or doing without the Tao altogether. "Having mastered our environment, let us master ourselves and choose our own destiny," he urges. "Let us decide for ourselves what man is to be and make him into that: not on any grounds of imagined value, but because we want him to be that."[19]

The third lecture considers the case where groups seek to impose, without respect for the values of the Tao, the systems that they like, perhaps forms of scientific planning. Because of the advance in scientific techniques, he says, it really will be possible for posterity to be shaped and conditioned to an arbitrary pattern and for "the power of some men to make other men what they please."[20] Furthermore, man's conquest of nature could lead to the abolition of the human race. In the last pages of the pamphlet, he stresses that he is attacking, not science itself, but a science that rejects traditional values. He believed that the defense against the dangers he was describing might actually come from scientists who knew the value of knowledge rooted in the Tao and who would therefore remember the whole while speaking of the parts.

Nevertheless, the prospect of a civilization dominated by scientists intent on conquering nature filled him with horror, and out of this vision he wrote *That Hideous Strength*, the last of his space-travel novels. In his own college he knew men of the sort. He imagined what it and the whole university would be like if they got the power they wanted. Pictures of the result came into his mind and with them the setting and plot for this novel. It is peopled with men whose science, as suggested in *The Abolition of Man*, is tainted with magic and, opposing them, a delightful little company under the leadership of Ransom, who in some ways resembles Charles Williams. Also at work in this novel are immensely potent supernatural powers, including those of Merlin, who is at last awake after a thousand years of slumber.

That Hideous Strength contains many of Jack's likes and dislikes. There is his hatred of "the inner ring," or the small, elite group that assumes power in a school or other organization, and his disdain for "the progressive element." He had seen both in action in college meetings. The characters Lord Feverstone, Busby, and Curry are thinly disguised portraits of progressive colleagues who rigged meetings and held traditional values in contempt. Jack uses this book to attack the sterile and artificial—modern architecture, demolition crews, sadistic secret police, vivisection, experiments on mental patients and criminals, scientific planning—contrasting it with the fertile, productive, and natural. Tortured animals are contrasted with animals that are loved; Belbury, a tyrannical place with no room for nonconformists, is contrasted with Saint Anne's, a place of healing that welcomes all individuals. In the character of MacPhee, Jack pays a loving and amusing tribute to Kirkpatrick.

The book was not well received by the critics, although it is an overstatement to say, as Jack did in a letter, that it was unanimously damned. Several reviewers criticized the construction, finding it too moralistic and objecting to the mixture of imaginative worlds. George Orwell, reviewing it as a crime story, found it spoiled by the presence of the supernatural. Critics still attack the book for these reasons. To Margaret P. Hannay, it is a sprawling novel nearly sunk by "the heavy weight of dogmatic exposition" and "as a whole structurally weak, with too many heterogeneous themes and motifs."[21] Professor Chad Walsh finds it "intellectually overstuffed" and thinks it would be a stronger novel if the entire Arthurian element were eliminated.[22]

But the public has not agreed with the critics. *That Hideous Strength* has for some time been the most popular of his four novels. Perhaps because of the reviewers' criticisms, Jack agreed to his publisher's suggestion that he should produce a shortened version for the American market. This was entitled *The Tortured Planet,* and, although the characterizations suffer from brevity, the book has sold quite well.

Jack was writing more than ever at this time. Even before he had completed *That Hideous Strength*, he began to write *The Great Divorce,* for which he had had the idea since 1933. Warren had described it in his diary: "J has a new idea for a religious work, based on the opinion of some of the Fathers, that while punishment for the damned is eternal, it is intermittent: he proposes to do a sort of infernal day excursion to Paradise."[23] The prospect was thrillingly attractive because it enabled him to present in a single setting a miniature paradise, purgatory, and inferno. The book is a dream vision of Heaven in which the narrator meets several people who are on holiday from Hell. If they find that they prefer Heaven to Hell, they are free to stay there, but to do so, they must give up something, some vice that comes between them and the experience of real joy. Jack introduces George MacDonald as a guide, rather like Beatrice was to Dante.

Originally entitled *Who Goes Home? or the Great Divorce,* this short book is perhaps the most profound and nearly perfect

of all his works. It was first published in fourteen weekly install-
ments in *The Guardian*, from November 10, 1944 to April 14,
1945. When Geoffrey Bles published it in book form in
November, the title was changed to *The Great Divorce: A
Dream*. The title refers to the all-important division between
those who choose to obey God's will and those who follow their
own. "There are only two kinds of people in the end: those who
say to God, 'Thy will be done,' and those to whom God says, 'thy
will be done.'"[24]

The Great Divorce is Jack's tribute to his master, George
MacDonald. The very structure is designed to show off some of
MacDonald's ideas. MacDonald was what is known as a
Universalist, or almost one. He believed that before or after
death, usually after, everyone, or practically everyone, would
eventually surrender to the love of God. This would involve a surrender of their self-will and self-centeredness. Jack's difficulty was
to reconcile this view, which he did not hold himself but thought
a possibility, with various orthodox Christian ideas such as pre-
destination, purgatory, and a judgment that takes place immediately after death. He did this brilliantly by two simple means. He
made Hell and purgatory the same place. It is Hell for those who
are determined to stay there, purgatory for those who want to
leave and are prepared to make the necessary sacrifice of self.
Second, a supernatural bus service links Hell-purgatory with
Heaven or the High Countries (MacDonald's phrase). Those who
make the journey will be bombarded with love. Hell for
MacDonald and Jack is not a place of punishment; it is a place
where the Almighty is trying to convert free creatures, who are
obstinately clinging to the miseries of the demon self, to a life of
joy. We are shown one success—the man obsessed by lust who
makes the decision to give up forever his sordid pleasure. He is
immediately transformed by his surrender to Christ. The lizard,

which symbolizes lust, becomes a stallion. The victory influences the earth, woods, and waters so that they sing, "Overcome us that, so overcome, we may be ourselves: we desire the beginning of your reign as we desire dawn and dew, wetness at the first of light."

Another basic idea of MacDonald's is also illustrated. The love we receive from the Father, if passed on, will transform others. Sarah Smith, a socially humble person on earth, did just this. As a result boys and girls went back to their parents loving them more. Married men became truer to their wives. Every beast and bird that came near had its place in her love. Jack has MacDonald comment, "There's joy enough in the little finger of a great saint such as yonder lady to waken all the dead things of the universe into life." For those sensitive to it, the book itself has this devotional effect.

In the summer of 1943, Jack began a book on the subject of miracles. Many people had told him that they could not accept the Gospels because of the number of miracles recorded in them. As far as they were concerned, miracles were an obstacle to belief. He found this book difficult to write, probably because when he began it, his own ideas about miracles were not quite clear. He was still working on it during the long vacation after Charles Williams's death. Although there is no sign of Williams's influence in the book, Jack once said that his feeling that Williams was nearby had helped him to finish it.

Miracles was published by Bles in 1947. Although it is the most philosophical of his books and, after *Dymer*, the most carefully considered, it is one of the least successful, primarily because its main argument is suspect. The argument is based on a distinction between naturalism and supernaturalism. In the naturalist system, everything is caused by and dependent on everything else. Such a system, therefore, has no such thing as free will or free reasoning. Jack argued that, if human reasoning is invalid or, neither valid nor invalid, but determined in a context in which validity has no meaning, then all belief in science and philosophy is also invalid. Likewise, belief in the naturalist system is invalid, and naturalism is, therefore, self-contradictory. What we call reason makes it possible for us to alter nature. But human reason cannot be explained by rational or naturalistic causes; rather, it must come from a self-existent reason, a supernatural reality that can be called God. Similarly, moral judgments can have no validity if they are part of a naturalist system in which there is no free will. They are based on human conscience, which is an incursion into nature of a self-existent moral wisdom.

His argument for the existence of God soon got him into trouble. At a meeting of the Socratic Club on February 2, 1948, Elizabeth Anscombe, who later became a professor of philosophy at Cambridge University, read a criticism of Jack's argument that naturalism is self-refuting. Jack replied, and an exciting debate followed. The audience disagreed about who had won the debate, but Jack thought that he had been defeated, and he was still unhappy about the evening when he spoke to me about it during Easter vacation. He told me that he had been proved wrong, that his argument for the existence of God had been demolished. This was a serious matter, he felt, because in the minds of simple people the disproof of an argument for the existence of God tended to be regarded as a disproof of the existence of God. He wanted to mount a counterattack, but he thought that it would be dangerous to do so unless he were quite sure of its validity.

When told years later of the effect of the discussion on Jack, Professor Anscombe was surprised and upset. "Oh dear! I had no idea that he took it so seriously. As a matter of fact I don't think I agree that I won. All that I was doing was to argue as a modern philosopher, academically. I was not expressing my deepest beliefs."

The debate had been a humiliating experience, but perhaps it was ultimately good for him. In the past, he had been far too proud of his logical ability. Now he was humbled. He had been cheered on by the crowd of admirers at the Socratic Club, often young women who regarded him as the great defender of Christianity, almost like a knight of the Round Table. But he saw that he had underrated the difficulty of taking on the new school of Oxford philosophers, that the study of philosophy had changed very much since he had taken first-class honors. The Hegelians of his youth were now completely out of fashion. "Logical positivism" was the current mode, and "linguistic analysis" was gaining popularity. The former held that all statements about moral or religious values are scientifically unverifiable and therefore meaningless; the latter, that all philosophy should involve the criticism of language, and that the most important philosophical question to ask is why a particular word or expression is used. Jack could not cope with such developments and really had no desire to. They made what he regarded as philosophical thinking almost impossible. "I can never write another book of that sort," he said to me of *Miracles*. And he never did. He also never wrote another theological book. *Reflections on the Psalms* is really devotional and literary; *Letters to Malcolm*, published after his death, is also a devotional book, a series of reflections on prayer, without contentious arguments.

The attack on *Miracles* came at a time when Jack was experiencing great difficulties at home. The evacuees had gone, leaving Mrs. Moore exhausted and in broken health. The varicose veins in her legs made walking increasingly difficult for her, so much so that she spent most of 1947 in her bedroom. She did not give up running the house, but she did depend heavily on Jack, calling for him many times a day. He would leave his work, go upstairs and do her bidding, and then return to his writing. There were two maids in the house, but they quarreled with each other and sometimes with Mrs. Moore, too. Jack's role was to try to make peace, over and over again. Under these conditions, he began to write the best-known and most widely loved of all his books.

17

Into Narnia

The thought that he might write a children's story occurred to Jack in September 1939, but he did not complete his first one, *The Lion, the Witch, and the Wardrobe*, until almost ten years later. The evacuated children staying at the Kilns provided his original inspiration. One of them showed an interest in an old wardrobe, asking if she could go inside and if there was anything behind it. Her request triggered his imagination. Perhaps he was reminded, too, of a story he had read as a child, *The Aunt and Amabel*, by E. Nesbit, in which a magic world is entered through a wardrobe in a spare room. He had read and loved the books of Edith Nesbit, but had given them up when he went away to prep school for fear of seeming childish. Now he thought of writing a story for and about the evacuated children, because he was concerned about how poorly developed their imaginations were and how little they read.

His method of writing stories was to assemble the pictures that appeared in his mind. As he explained in a lecture to the Library Association, "With me the process is much more like bird-watching than like either talking or building. I see pictures. Some of the pictures have a common flavour, almost a common smell, which groups them together. Keep quiet and watch and they will begin joining themselves up. If you were very lucky

(I have never been so lucky as all that) a whole group might join themselves so consistently that there you had a complete story; without doing anything yourself. But more often (in my experience always) there are gaps. Then at last you have to do some deliberate inventing. . . ."[1]

Since he was sixteen he had had a picture in his mind of a faun carrying parcels and an umbrella in a snowy forest. Other pictures came to him during the war years, and in 1948 he set about filling in the gaps and turning them into a continuous story. He was also helped by his pupil and friend, Roger Green, who had written a story called *The Wood That Time Forgot*, which Jack read excitedly and criticized in detail and from which he took elements to incorporate in *The Lion, the Witch, and the Wardrobe*.

After he had written a good deal of the book, he got the idea of the lion Aslan, who "came bounding into it." Jack had been "having a good many dreams of lions about that time . . . [and] once he [Aslan] was there he pulled the whole story together, and soon he pulled the other six stories in after him."

The story was largely finished by the end of the Christmas vacation in 1948. Two months later, Jack read it to Tolkien. Jack had always been constructively helpful and sympathetic with Tolkien's writing, and he probably expected similar treatment. He was hurt, astonished, and discouraged when Tolkien said that he thought the book was almost worthless, that it seemed like a jumble of unrelated mythologies. Because Aslan, the fauns, the White Witch, Father Christmas, the nymphs, and Mr. and Mrs. Beaver had quite distinct mythological or imaginative origins, Tolkien thought that it was a terrible mistake to put them together in Narnia, a single imaginative country. The effect was incongruous and, for him, painful. But Jack argued that they existed happily together in our minds in real life. Tolkien replied, "Not in mine, or at least not at the same time."

Tolkien never changed his view. He so strongly detested Jack's assembling figures from various mythologies in his children's books that he soon gave up trying to read them. He also thought they were carelessly and superficially written. His condemnation was so severe that one suspects he envied the speed with which Jack wrote and compared it with his own laborious method of composition.

Jack had a high opinion of Tolkien's judgment and was distressed and disconcerted by his harsh response, especially since he himself had little confidence in the merits of his story. Were it not for friends who praised it highly, he might never have published it. There was his doctor, Humphrey Havard, and Havard's daughter, Mary Clare, to whom the book was eventually dedicated. More important, there was Roger Green, an old pupil and a man of infectious enthusiasm in whose judgment Jack had faith. Although Green shared Tolkien's dislike of the introduction of Father Christmas, on the whole he liked the story. Jack once said that, without Green's encouragement, he probably would not have completed the book.

Most people who knew Jack were astonished that he had written a children's story. His publisher, Geoffrey Bles, doubted that it would sell and feared that it might even damage Jack's reputation and the sales of his other books. Bles advised that, if it had to be published, it should be the first of a series of children's stories.

Almost at once, Jack began a second story about the beginnings of Narnia and how the lamppost came to be standing at its edge. There is a delightful account of a boy named Digory, who understands the speech of animals and trees until he cuts off a branch from an oak tree to help Polly, the little girl next door, build a raft. But Jack got stuck in the writing soon after the arrival of Digory's godmother, Mrs. Lefay, a woman skilled in magic. He felt she didn't come off, and Green verified this feeling. So he put the story aside, thinking that he might later rework it, and instead began to write a story about children drawn across space and time by magic and told from their point of view, rather than from that of the magician. The theme is described by the original title, *Drawn into Narnia*. The writing went quickly and well, so that it was finished by the end of 1949 and eventually published as *Prince Caspian*.

Jack considered illustrating the stories himself, but decided that even if he had the skill, he would not have the time. Tolkien enthusiastically recommended Pauline Baynes, the young illustrator who had done the drawings, paintings, and other embellishments for his story *Farmer Giles of Ham*, which had just been published. Although Jack liked her art for its wit and fantasy, he wondered if she could manage a more realistic style. When sample drawings suggested that she could, he invited her to have lunch with him at Magdalen College on December 31.

He was delighted by her and by her enthusiasm for the magic world of his imagination. But because he had distinct tastes, he was a difficult author for an artist to please. He loved the drawings of Arthur Rackham in *Undine* and *The Ring*, those of Charles Robinson in *The Secret Garden*, those of Kemble in *Huckleberry Finn*, and, although he found them cramped, those of Arthur Hughes in George MacDonald's books. He loathed illustrations in which the children had vapid, empty faces and hated even more the grotesque style that derived from Walt Disney's cartoons. Some of Pauline Baynes's illustrations of his books pleased him, such as the frontispiece and most of the full-page drawings in *Prince Caspian*. But he often found the faces of her children empty, expressionless, and too alike. Although he

thought she improved in this respect, he was never entirely satisfied. Her most serious weakness was her drawing of animals.
More than once he said to me, "She can't draw lions, but she is
so good and beautiful and sensitive that I can't tell her this."

The title adopted, *Prince Caspian*, was suggested by his publisher. Jack was reluctant to accept it, as it did not in any way suggest the theme of the book. But he had to be content with a
subtitle, *The Return to Narnia*.

The Lion, the Witch, and the Wardrobe was published in the
autumn of 1950, in time for the all-important Christmas gift market. Thereafter, one Narnia book was published each year until
1956. Some were very quickly written: *The Voyage of the Dawn
Treader*, in two months by the end of February 1950; *The Horse
and His Boy*, which was originally called *Narnia and the North*,
by the end of July; and *The Silver Chair*, which he originally
thought of calling *The Wild Waste Lands*, begun during the
Christmas vacation and finished by the beginning of March
1951. *The Magician's Nephew* and *The Last Battle* were written
more slowly. Jack showed manuscripts of all these books to
Green, who made many suggestions for small improvements,
although he helped his former tutor more with enthusiasm and
encouragement than in any other way. "I did not always agree
with him," Jack once said to me. "Perhaps I more often disagreed. But sympathetic criticism of his sort is for a writer one of
the rarest and most precious of things."

With few exceptions, the reviews of the Narnia books were
cautious. Occasionally, they were hostile. At the time the books
appeared, the real-life children's story was in fashion. It was commonly believed then that stories should help children to understand and relate to real life, that they should not encourage them
to indulge in fantasies, and that fairy stories, if for any children
at all, should only be for the very young. Some reviewers disliked

the Narnia books for their Christian content, perhaps finding the parallels with the gospel story embarrassing, and further objected to the "indoctrination" of children. Of course, for many there was too much moralizing. Others attacked them because they contained "unnaturally unpleasant children" and too many violent and frightening incidents.

Hostile reviews may have curbed initial sales of the books, but only temporarily. From the very beginning, despite all the reviewers' apprehensions, children loved the Narnia stories. Left to themselves, almost all children who read the books enjoyed them just as stories, without being aware of their Christianity. They usually enjoy the supposedly frightening incidents and are not embarrassed or put off by the moralizing. More than any other stories that I can think of, they appeal to all sorts of children. It is easy to find children who are left cold by *Alice in Wonderland* and *The Wind in the Willows;* it is rare to find those who enjoy reading and yet are not delighted by the Narnia stories.

Jack's main object was, of course, to write good stories. He was also concerned with the atmosphere of separate adventures and incidents and with fidelity to the complex world of his imagination. As the series developed, he gained confidence in his imaginative vision and delighted in the rich medley of human, animal, and mythological beings that he was creating. His idea of Heaven was of a place where all sorts of people could come together to celebrate, dance, and sing with fauns, giants, centaurs, dwarfs, and innumerable and very different animals. Some of this joyous, festive vision is perceived by many children who read the books. It extends and develops not merely their delight in the real world but in a vision of the created world permeated with the world of myth and imagination.

The natural beauties of Narnia are set against the background of the supernatural and eternal. The apple tree at the beginning of *Prince Caspian* is no ordinary apple tree. The ruined castle in chapter two gives Lucy and Peter a queer feeling; this interpenetration of the natural by the supernatural runs throughout the whole series and has much to do with the characteristic atmosphere. We are in Aslan's country usually without knowing it.

The most precious moments to Jack in his ordinary life were those when he did know it, when he was aware of the spiritual quality of material things, of the infusion of the supernatural into the workaday world. His success in translating these moments into his fairy stories gives the series a haunting appeal; simultaneously it gives its readers "a taste for the other."

Modern children are often thought of as rebellious and anarchistic, yet those who read the Narnia stories accept without opposition a hierarchical society. Aslan is not a believer in equality and is of course supreme over all. Below him there may be kings and queens and princes to whom respect and obedience should normally be given.

After telling Prince Caspian of his true identity, Doctor Cornelius drops down onto one knee and kisses his hand. People are not equal; among them, some are meant to serve, others to command. Animals are below people and perhaps have their own hierarchy.

The Narnia stories show a complete acceptance of the Tao, of the conventional and traditional moral code. Humanity, courage, loyalty, honesty, kindness, and unselfishness are virtues. Children who might perhaps object to the code if they were taught it in churches and schools accept it easily and naturally when they see it practiced by the characters they love. They are learning morality in the best and perhaps only effective way.

It is possible to extract from the Narnia stories a system of theology very like the Christian. Thus the theological content of *The Magician's Nephew* is the story of the creation. Aslan sings it into being. The temptation in the Garden of Eden and the Fall are there. In the story he wrote next we have death, judgment, Hell, and Heaven. But the author almost certainly did not want his readers to notice the resemblance of the Narnian theology to the Christian story. His idea, as he once explained to me, was to make it easier for children to accept Christianity when they met it later in life. He hoped that they would be vaguely reminded of the somewhat similar stories that they had read and enjoyed years before. "I am aiming at a sort of pre-baptism of the child's imagination."

Nevertheless, he did not, as is sometimes supposed, begin with a worked-out theological scheme in his head and write the stories to exemplify and inculcate it. The actual process was less calculating; he wrote the stories because he enjoyed writing stories and always had. The characters and their actions were of course influenced by his conception of morality and theology. It was in the course of writing, as a result of brooding over the events in the stories, that his ideas developed. They grew less intellectual, more integrated with feeling. Like many of his other books, the Narnia stories were important to his own spiritual growth.

Children and grown-ups often differ about the stories that they like best. Adults usually prefer the last two, *The Magician's Nephew* and *The Last Battle*, the latter of which was awarded the Carnegie Medal for the best children's book published in 1956. But the children often like the earlier stories best, and for a long time *The Lion, the Witch and the Wardrobe* was the one that sold the most copies. But all are bestsellers and, along with Tolkien's *The Lord of the Rings*, represent a remarkable phenomenon of postwar publishing. The Narnia stories have liberated the children's story from its bondage to realism. Since their publication, magic, myth, fairy tale, and fantasy stories have been written, but none with such inherent theological depth and mythic quality.

The whole series has classic status. The rather ordinary style and simple characterization to which some of the early reviewers objected are virtues in the children's point of view. These qualities make it all the easier to be swept along by the story. Complex characterization often puzzles, and a literary style distracts inexperienced readers. All the evidence suggests that the Narnia stories will be read at least as long as anything else that Jack wrote.

The Narnia stories reveal more about Jack's personal religion than any of his theological books, because he wrote them more from the heart than from the head. The character of Aslan is his supreme achievement, the apex, as Paul Ford puts it, "of his literary, mythopoeic, and apologetic gifts."[2] Bede Griffiths has eloquently expressed this point: "The figure of Aslan tells us more of how Lewis understood the nature of God than anything else he wrote. It has all the hidden power and majesty and awesomeness which Lewis associated with God, but also all the glory and the tenderness and even the humor which he believed belonged to him, so that children could run up to him and throw their arms around him and kiss him. There is nothing of 'dark imagination' or fear of devils and hell in this. It is 'mere Christianity.'"[3]

No wonder that my little stepdaughter, after she had read all the Narnia stories, cried bitterly, saying, "I don't want to go on living in this world. I want to live in Narnia-with Aslan."

Darling, one day you will.

18

Escape

That the Narnia stories are full of laughter and breathe forth joy does not mean that the years of their writing were happy for Jack. What it does mean is that his faith had taught him how to cope with difficulties and to rise above miseries that would have overwhelmed most men.

There were difficulties at the Kilns, largely Mrs. Moore's illness and Warren's alcoholism. Mrs. Moore's varicose veins had caused her more and more pain as the war went on. She had far less domestic help than she had been accustomed to, tended to quarrel with the maids she was able to get, and also found it difficult to get along with Vera Henry, a distant relative on whom she depended heavily for household help. Her temper worsened, and she was often autocratic and difficult. Economizing to the greatest extent possible was, she thought, her patriotic duty. Therefore, the Kilns would be run as a self-sufficient estate.

The plan to economize met with Jack's approval—for patriotic reasons and because he had begun to fear that he might go bankrupt—and with Paxford's cooperation because he loved making do simply for its own sake. Nothing was repaired or replaced unless absolutely necessary. To avoid the expense of buying them, vegetable seeds of all varieties were saved. Wood from the grounds was used for fuel, and no fires were allowed except those that Mrs. Moore considered necessary. There were some winter days when Jack did not have a fire in his work room.

Of course, there was some excuse for these economies. Coal was rationed, and the Kilns was an expensive and laborious house to heat. In 1944 the need to economize in fuel as part of the war effort intensified. Fires were rarely lit in the dining and drawing rooms, with the result that they became extremely damp, the wallpaper discoloring and coming away from the walls. As an economy the rooms were not repapered. The old paper was simply stripped off and the walls left in the stained and dreary state that astonished visitors to the house until the late 1950s after Joy moved into the house. Vera Henry complained bitterly about the condition of these rooms, but Jack had little difficulty in rising above the squalor. Such detachment was an ascetic practice as well as a patriotic duty.

For the same reasons Jack rarely had a hot bath in the house, and the boiler that heated the water was often left unlit. He gradually became accustomed to taking cold-water sponge baths and used hot water only for shaving.

But Warren was not an ascetic. He suffered from the lack of heat and hot water. He liked to think that he was living the life of a gentleman and that he had at least some of its amenities. He detested the domination of the household, especially of his brother, by the ailing Mrs. Moore. Except at the very beginning, theirs had never been a happy relationship. Mrs. Moore objected to his alcoholism and to his refusal to help in the house. He had a remarkable objection to performing ordinary household tasks. As Paxford said of postwar life at the Kilns, "Mr. Jack worked himself to the bone, but the Major hardly did a thing. He didn't like work."

Warren's drinking binges became more and more frequent at this time and frequently led to his being hospitalized. This added to Jack's difficulties, for he had come to rely on Warren's services as his secretary. Without Warren, the letters piled up, the bills remained unpaid or were paid twice, and important university business was neglected.

In 1944 Jack had been engaged to write *English Literature in the Sixteenth Century*, one volume of *The Oxford History of English Literature*. He did an immense amount of reading for this project because he refused to give an opinion on a book he had not read. As he expresses on the first page of this book, he found many of these authors extremely dull. "Their prose is clumsy, monotonous, garrulous; their verse either astonishingly tame and cold or, if it attempts to rise, the coarsest fustian. In both mediums we come to read a certain ruthless emphasis; bludgeon-work. Nothing is light, or tender, or fresh. All the authors write like elderly men."[1]

He did much of his reading in the Duke Humphrey room of the Oxford Bodleian Library. Sometimes when he read a book from his own library, he marked the end with the date that he finished it. Once or twice he added in his neat, fine script, "Never again" or "n.a."

Yet it wasn't all a chore. He enjoyed debunking current or fashionable concepts and presenting new insights. And in conversation he enjoyed startling his friends by concise summaries of his ideas. Thus, he summarized for us the first chapter, "New Learning and New Ignorance": "I think I have succeeded in demonstrating that the Renaissance, as generally understood, never existed. . . . There was nothing whatever humane about humanism. The humanists were intolerant and Philistine. There is no humanist philosopher of any importance. . . . I have given only five pages to Donne. His place is that of a minor poet."

The study begins with a startling and controversial general survey. In the early part of the sixteenth century English poetry was dull, monotonous, and drab. Then suddenly it seemed reborn, and by the end of the century it was rich in fantasy, paradox, color, and incantation, just the qualities we find in the sonnets of Shakespeare. Literary historians before Jack had given credit for this to the Renaissance. He disagreed. The Renaissance in his view was brought about by the humanists. They recovered, edited, and wrote commentaries on the classics of Greece and Rome, but they were pedantic scholars. They crushed the romance out of the classics with an exaggerated concern for form, polish, and exactness of language. They killed Latin by refusing to let it develop and grow. They produced a literature remote from the senses and the soil. They hated the Middle Ages, particularly chivalrous romance and scholastic philosophy. Humanism was a Philistine movement. "The new learning created the new ignorance."[2]

After his crusade against the humanists—and it amounted to that—Jack tells us that our view of the Puritans is wrong. The Protestant doctrine of salvation by grace is not gloomy or terrifying; it is joyous. The Puritans praised the marriage bed; it was the Catholics who exalted virginity. As for Calvin, his "was the creed of progressives, even of revolutionaries. . . . The fierce young don, the learned lady, the courtier with intellectual leanings were likely to be Calvinists. He was a dazzling figure, a man born to be the idol of revolutionary intellectuals."[3] All this and much more come in the first sixty pages. The controversy provoked by their brilliance has not yet died down.

The rest of the book consists of a review of all the major and many minor writers of the period. Over and over again we are swept away by his enthusiasms and the quotations he has found to illustrate them. There are new discoveries, such as Tyndale as a great prose writer. He quotes: "Where the spirit is there is always summer. Who taught the eagles to spy out their prey?

Even so the children of God spy out their father. That they might see love and love again." In his comparison of Tyndale and More Jack writes: "In More we feel all the smoke and stir of London; the very plodding of his sentences is like horse traffic in the streets. In Tyndale we breathe mountain air."[4] From Richard Hooker, another discovery, he does not quote much, "for very few of Hooker's beauties can be picked like flowers and taken home: you must enjoy them where they grow—as you enjoy a twenty acre field of ripe wheat."[5]

In his splendid chapter on the Scottish followers of Chaucer, he invites us to share his enthusiasm for Gavin Douglas and William Dunbar, to whom he attributes real greatness. Of an uncharacteristic poem of Dunbar's he writes: "it is speech rather than song, but speech of unanswerable and thunderous greatness. From the first line to the last it vibrates with exultant energy. It defies the powers of evil and has the ring of a steel gauntlet flung down."[6]

He is splendid on old favorites such as Edmund Spenser and Sir Philip Sidney and as fresh on Shakespeare's poems as if no one had written on them before. It is no exaggeration to say that there is wit and humor on every page. "Shakespeare's Venus is a very ill-conceived temptress. She is made so much larger than her victim that she can throw his horse's reins over one arm and tuck him under the other, and knows her art so badly that she threatens, almost in her first words, to 'smother' him with kisses. Certain horrible interviews with voluminous female relatives in one's early childhood inevitably recur to the mind."[7]

The account of John Donne has none of the sustained polemic of his famous 1938 essay published in a book of *Seventeenth Century Studies Presented to Sir Herbert Grierson*; it is an attempt at a balanced estimate. These pages show his independence of fashion and the views of others. He was that rare critic, one who trusted his own judgment and was fearless in attacking idols, cant, and trendiness.

The first draft was probably finished by 1952. Revising the text and compiling the chronological table and extensive bibliography took him another year. The book, bound in the dark blue cloth characteristic of the Clarendon Press, was published in the autumn of 1954. He was disappointed by the reception, although many of the reviews were favorable (perhaps his poor health at the time influenced his judgment of them). Reviews in the popular papers tended to be positive. A. L. Rowse described it in *The Sunday Times* as a magnificent work, with "such intellectual vitality, such sweep and imagination, such magnanimity." John Wain wrote in *The Spectator* that "Mr. Lewis, now as always, writes as if inviting us to a feast." M. B. Charlton of the *Manchester Guardian* considered it outstanding in judgment and style. B. Ifor Evans thought that by "some miracle" Lewis had produced a brilliant and interesting book on the period, "as great a tour de force in criticism as I have seen in this generation." But other reviewers, especially academics, objected to the radical approach. They disliked his reassessment of humanism and regarded his division of poetry into two categories—drab and golden—as a gross oversimplification. Yvor Winters made an extreme comment: "Lewis simply has not discovered what poetry is." The doubt and the controversy continue. In a letter written to me after Lewis's death, Tolkien described it as "a great book, the only one of his that gives me unalloyed pleasure." Some Oxford tutors still warn their pupils that it is "unsound but brilliantly written." Nevertheless, or perhaps partly because of this warning, it outsells all the other volumes in the series.

In 1955 *Surprised by Joy: The Shape of My Early Life* was published. Jack had been writing it off and on since 1948 in what little spare time he had had. For students of Lewis, it is a fascinating book, but as an autobiography it is unsatisfactory. There is not a word about his relationship with Mrs. Moore or about the part that writing played in his childhood. The account of his misery at school takes up a third of the book. Why is it so exaggerated? An answer is suggested in his letter to Bede Griffiths of February 1956—he simply wanted to be free of the past: "I feel the whole of one's youth to be immensely important and even of immense length. The gradual *reading* of one's own life, seeing a pattern emerge, is a great illumination at our age. And partly, I hope, getting freed from the past as past by apprehending it as structure." He wanted to be free of his father and, above all, of a near obsession with his school days and the memory of the sexual and sadistic obsessions that accompanied them. The way to freedom for him was through writing. His work on *The Pilgrim's Regress* and *That Hideous Strength* had decreased his anxiety about the past. Now it was very important that these obsessions be expunged from his imagination because he wanted it to be fresh and open, clear and clean for his work on the Narnia stories. This necessarily unbalanced autobiography helped him to prepare for this task.

Writing *Surprised by Joy* enabled him to see quite clearly the pattern of his past life. Even his most unpleasant experiences were honest guides. He could not explore them very deeply without longing to overcome the evil in his own heart and seeking the help of Christ. In many of the incidents and emotional encounters of his life, he was able to see the deity shaping and guiding him.

Jack was personally pleased with the imaginative freedom that resulted from writing *Surprised by Joy*, so much so that he hardly cared about the public reaction. Reviewers were inevitably disappointed, however, because it was neither an autobiography nor a book written to convert others to Christianity. The reviewer for *The Nation* complained that it was disappointing as a guide to the non-Christian. *New Statesman*'s reviewer was misled to such an extent as to declare that Jack was not equipped for apologetic writing and that his reasoning was feeble. Indeed, one would have to have known him very well to penetrate the smoke screen. As his friend Humphrey Havard remarked in a letter to me, it could have been titled "Suppressed by Jack." Nevertheless, *Surprised by Joy* has for many years been one of the bestsellers among his books.

The number of students reading English at Oxford vastly increased after the war. Whereas during the war Jack had easily been able to tutor all Magdalen English students as well as some from other colleges, spending one hour alone with each student every week, he now found that he needed help. Even when another tutor was appointed to take over some of the syllabus, he found himself busier than ever. Like most other Oxford tutors, he began to take his pupils in pairs, but he never ceased to prepare for the tutorials by reading some of the material that was the subject of each student's essay. In spite of his great knowledge and prodigious memory, he believed that such preparation was essential to good teaching.

It soon became clear to his friends that his work load was excessive. They suggested that a professorship would be less demanding than tutoring. Because Mrs. Moore and Warren could not be expected to move, it would have to be at Oxford. When a Merton professorship of modern English literature became available, Tolkien, who was a Merton Professor of English and, therefore, an elector, rallied to Jack's support, hoping to achieve what had been a prewar ambition, of having Jack and himself installed as the two Merton Professors. He suggested this to his fellow electors, H. W. Garrod, C. H. Wilkinson, and Helen Darbishire and found to his surprise that all three were against Jack. They felt he had not produced a sufficient amount of scholarly work, pointing out that his most successful books were three novels and some popular religious or theological books. They thought his election would lower the status of the professorship and even discredit the English School. They also objected to his dislike of higher degrees and research in English literature. Jack considered the subjects of most of these theses obscure and trivial and the theses themselves dull and without merit. He was fond of saying that there were three kinds of literacy at Oxford: the literate, the illiterate, and the B. Litterate, and that personally he preferred the first two.

When he realized that it would be impossible for Jack to be elected, Tolkien supported the election of another friend, Lord David Cecil, but he, too, seems to have been insufficiently scholarly to satisfy the other electors. Jack's former tutor, F. P. Wilson, was eventually elected to the professorship. Jack was generous in his praise in a letter to me. "Oh, I owe a great deal to him. Incidentally I wonder if anyone will notice in his lectures the sources of some of my Literary heresies." Nonetheless, Jack was disappointed, if not surprised. As time passed, he became more and more critical of the electors' literary standards. The election for the Goldsmiths' Professor of English Literature was made soon afterward. This went to Lord David Cecil, a friend and fellow Inkling whom Jack would not have wanted to oppose. But this generosity gave him no relief from his excessive work load.

In the summer of 1949, Warren returned to the Kilns after a weekend at Malvern to find an ambulance at the door waiting to take Jack to the Acland Nursing Home. The symptoms were a high temperature, delirium, a splitting headache, a sore throat, and swollen glands. Dr. Havard had diagnosed "a severe infection" and had ordered him to go to the Acland because there were no facilities for nursing him at the Kilns. Mrs. Moore, who had looked after him very well during his many bouts of flu in earlier days, was distressed that she could not help him now.

Warren's letter of June 15 to my wife describes what happened:

> I can hardly imagine a greater contrast than that between the peace and happiness of Malvern and the anxiety and misery I have found here. Jack was taken ill on Sunday night with a high temperature and is now in the Acland having injections of penicillin every three hours. Thank God he is now out of danger. But it has been a serious illness for a man of his age. Humphrey says that the real trouble is exhaustion brought on by overwork and that he must have a long holiday away from the Kilns (the real source of the trouble). I think I have arranged this.

The arranging took the form of getting Mrs. Moore's agreement. To Warren's surprise this was not difficult. Indeed she soon came to think that it was her idea that Jack should go away for a month.

Jack spent a week at the Acland Nursing Home. He always enjoyed times of convalescence because they provided him an opportunity to read for pleasure. On this occasion, he read Masefield's *Captain Margaret* and Haggard's *People of the Mist* and Chesterton's *The Flying Inn*. He was anticipating a month-long holiday in Ireland, which, had it come off, would have been his first vacation, except for the walking tours, since about 1933.

When he got back from the Acland to the Kilns, he wrote to Arthur Greeves that he had been ill and was ordered to have a real change. He intended to cross over to Belfast in the first week of July and to stay in Ireland for a month. Of course, he wanted to see as much of his friend as possible. He asked Arthur to find a "nice little hotel (or decent rooms)" near his own cottage. For part of the time he wanted them to go off together to somewhere else, such as Ballycastle or Hilltown. He looked forward eagerly to Arthur's reply. For once he would be free. In his next letter he sounded even happier, for he had made definite arrangements to cross from Heysham to Belfast on the night of July 4 and to stay in Ireland until August 4.[8]

But it was too good to be true. Even as he was writing, Warren was starting to drink again heavily, to assuage his feelings of guilt because he could not bear the thought of staying in the Kilns alone and looking after Mrs. Moore while Jack was in Ireland. Jack wrote on July 2 to tell Arthur about it. The doctor had begged Warren to go into a nursing home, a treatment which had been effective in ending previous bouts of drinking. But Warren refused until it was too late, and he was so uncontrollable that the nursing home could not keep him. The mental specialist who was called in said that he would have to be moved to a mental hospital. Jack hoped it would be only for a short stay, but even so, there would be "no question of an Irish jaunt" for him that year.[9]

In fact, Warren recovered so quickly on this occasion that by the middle of July Jack was again planning a holiday in Ireland, although a considerably shorter one. But again almost as soon as it was planned, Warren showed signs of the irritability and insomnia that were the usual preludes to his bouts of drinking. "It wd. be better," Jack wrote to Arthur, "that the door of my prison had never been opened than if it now bangs in my face! How hard to submit to God's will."[10] This is almost the only clear expression of the strain under which Jack was then living. He rarely discussed his suffering—his exhaustion from overwork, his bad health, his worry about Mrs. Moore and Warren. Normally, he drew spiritual and physical refreshment from the unspoiled countryside, especially that of his homeland, Northern Ireland.

But this was now denied him. Soon after, it was decided that Warren should go to Ireland alone. "But I have (faint) hopes of another year," Jack wrote. "He has been completely tee-total now since he came out of hospital."¹¹ Yet, when he was on board the cross-channel boat, Warren went straight to the bar and ordered a stiff drink.

The best Jack could do in the way of a holiday was to go away for one or two weekends. I think he visited the Barfields and remember clearly his visit to Malvern. He was physically out of condition. Halfway up Midsummer Hill, he suddenly said, "I can't go on. I must stop." We sat down while he smoked a cigarette. But I'm sure all that was wrong was that for months he had not been able to find time for much exercise. A full week in Malvern would have put him right.

From this time on, he spoke freely to me and to other friends about Warren's alcoholism. In the past, he had usually spoken of the causes of Warren's ill health as "insomnia or nerves." But it now seemed certain that Warren's drinking problem would be a permanent part of his life and one that he would be unable to conceal from his friends. Perhaps, too, he wanted our advice. He was devoted to his brother and deeply worried about his future. Yet, except through prayer, he was powerless to help. There seemed to be no clear course of action, no straightforward expert advice on how best to help Warren. Was it necessary for him to stop drinking altogether, or could he try to limit himself to a single glass? Was it a moral or a medical problem or both? He once asked me if I thought he should "show his teeth" to his brother. "There is nothing I should dislike more," he said. "But it might work. The knowledge that he causes vast expense and upsets the entire household influences him not at all."

Warren was away from August 14 to September 27, 1949. When he returned, he spent the first two weeks of October dealing with the backlog of Jack's correspondence, after which he came to stay with my wife and me at Malvern. The account he gave of life in the hospital was full of praise ("just the place to go for a serious illness"), and he seemed well, as if he were not drinking heavily. But he was a deceptive drinker and, like many alcoholics, was able to appear sober even when he was not. We did not know then that his assumption of an air of superiority and his concern about who was and was not a gentleman was a sign that he was drinking heavily, and after he left, we were surprised to find two empty whiskey bottles on the top of the wardrobe in our spare room.

Jack was also unwell that autumn. The apparent collapse of the evening meetings of the Inklings was yet another depressing event. But there was good news. Maureen, who had been giving violin lessons at Malvern College during the previous few years, and her husband, Leonard Blake, the director of the Music School there, announced the birth of their second child, Eleanor. Everyone was delighted by this news. Jack and Warren always regarded Eleanor and her brother Richard as model and well-brought-up children.

The second helpful event was the death of Mrs. Moore's elderly dog, Bruce, in January of 1950, about which Warren wrote in his diary: ". . . the penultimate gate of poor Jack's prison is down at last."[12] Lately Bruce's little walks had become an obsession with Mrs. Moore and consequently an almost intolerable burden for Jack.

One night late in April, Mrs. Moore fell out of bed three times. On the doctor's insistence, she was taken by ambulance to Restholme, a north Oxford rest and nursing home where Warren had already been a patient (they had succeeded in keeping him there and thus preventing him from buying liquor by the simple expedient of hiding his trousers).

Jack had again been planning a holiday in Ireland and looked forward to it as "an enormous liberation," but he now cancelled it because he was worried by the "crushing expense" of keeping Mrs. Moore in a nursing home. It would cost ten guineas a week, well over £500 a year. What would he do if "poor Minto" was still alive when he had to retire in nine years time? It was essential that he should economize stringently. Such things as an Irish holiday were "fantastically out of the question . . . cancel all." He felt in a whirl with "relief, pity, hope, terror and bewilderment." He asked for Arthur's prayers.[13]

Jack visited her almost every day that she was at Restholme. He had no doubt that this was his duty and that his visits did something to relieve her misery. But he rarely enjoyed them, for by this time she was senile. He did not mind the occasions when she was childish or incoherent. But there were distressing occasions when she grumbled, blasphemed, and stormed against people they knew. Sometimes she cried. I think Jack prayed for her almost continually, and he certainly asked his friends to pray for her.

Warren sometimes took Jack's place on afternoon visits to Mrs. Moore, so that Jack could take weekend trips. When he came to Malvern, Jack appeared more lighthearted than he had been for a long time. On our walks, he was as uninhibited as a schoolboy. One hot afternoon while we were walking by Leigh Brook, he suddenly said, "I'm going to bathe," took off his clothes, and flopped in. The stream became cloudy with the mud he stirred up, which deterred me from joining him, but he seemed to enjoy it, even ladling the water over his face and head.

In the early part of January 1951, we were walking in the southern part of the Malvern Hills. Our way lay through a farm and past a field in which there were a number of pigs. We leaned over the fence, talking about them. Just on the other side of the fence was a sow. Jack rubbed her back with a stick, saying, "I'm afraid I've no food for you, but perhaps like most human beings, you will enjoy having your back scratched."

Just then a younger or at least smaller pig came over with a bundle of hay it had carried from the far part of the field. It laid the hay down in front of the sow and stood a few feet away watching her eat. Jack was astonished. "George, this animal has been transformed. It has been touched by grace and raised to a higher level. What unselfishness! It must be hungry, too! George, we are witnessing something extraordinary. We are witnessing the birth of the first pog." Then he addressed the pog in courtly language, welcoming him into "this corrupt world and beseeching such blessing as you are able to give." Strangely, the pog looked at us and grunted apparently in answer. Then Jack said, "George, let us move on before the spell be broken or lest we offend his honor by our vulgar staring."

He talked about the incident for most of the rest of the day. What story, what poem could he write about the first pog? What other transformations would follow? Could it be made into a new sort of animal story? His talk was lighthearted, but I am sure that for him divinity was at work in a special way that day in the southern part of the Malvern Hills.

Mrs. Moore died of influenza on January 12, 1951. Warren celebrated the event by drinking just enough to make it impossible for him to go to the funeral. His diary entry of the seventeenth is one of the longest and most interesting of all. He was bitter about the way in which Jack's friendship with her had prevented them from taking long holidays together. He forgets that had Jack married, there would have been the same result. Perhaps, too, he was thinking of his bouts of heavy drinking when he went on holiday alone and blaming Mrs. Moore for preventing his brother from saving him from them. His diary contains a long entry in which he rails about the vast amount of time that Jack spent in household duties. He fails altogether to see that Jack also gained from the relationship. If Jack had lived the cloistered existence of a bachelor don, his writing would have suffered from a loss of warmth, humanity, and the understanding of pain and suffering.

Even before her death, Jack began to ask people to stay at the Kilns, which, despite its shabbiness, he described in a letter to Arthur as "now a house less horrible to stay in than I know it was before."[14] He once again began to take regular walks and sometimes went swimming at Parson's Pleasure. As a result, his health improved immensely.

He once wrote of the year that lay ahead as the happiest of his life, but it began with another academic disappointment. The professorship of poetry, which had fallen vacant, was to be filled through an election in which all senior members of the university could vote, and several of Jack's friends had nominated him. The other candidates were Edmund Blunden and Cecil Day Lewis. But several English teachers did not want Jack on any account. They had not forgiven him for having made Adam Fox professor of poetry years earlier; they feared and disagreed with his attitude toward advanced studies in English; they objected to his career as a popular writer and especially to his preaching of Christianity. Some were certainly jealous of his success.

Yet it was not easy to see how he could be defeated. His friends and many Christian graduates inside and outside the university would vote for him. If two candidates stood against him, the vote against him would be split. To defeat Jack it was essential that one of them should be coaxed to withdraw. This delicate piece of diplomacy was negotiated by Enid Starkie, the most important of C. Day Lewis's supporters. She was a flamboyant and rather eccentric woman from southern Ireland and a fellow of Somerville College who disliked Jack as much for his northern Irish background as for his opinions on literature. She campaigned against him with skill and vigor. Edmund Blunden was persuaded to withdraw, and C. Day Lewis was promoted as a successful practicing poet. (Ironically so was Jack Lewis, but most of his poems had been published anonymously, so no one knew it.) In spite of the efforts of canvassers on both sides, less than four hundred of the thousands of senior members voted, and C. Day Lewis won the election by nineteen votes.

Warren recorded the event in his diary: "J took it astonishingly well, much better than his backers. The only remark Jack has made is that he thinks votes were cast on the political issue on both sides. . . . I confess I'm astonished at the virulence of the anti-Xtian feeling shown here. . . ."[15] Jack was naturally disappointed, but not seriously, for he was looking forward to a year in which he intended to enjoy himself.

By the end of January, he was already planning a spring holiday in Ireland with Arthur. In March he suffered an attack of flu and a painful swelling of the salivary glands, but these did not change his plans. He had not been alone with Arthur for many years and was somewhat apprehensive about seeing him. What would he be like? Would he be a Unitarian, a member of the Bahai faith, or a Christian Scientist? How would they get along? When I asked him afterward how their visit had been, he said, "The first day or two were difficult. Then it was wonderful. Not for years have I been so happy."

He stayed at the seventeenth-century inn in Crawfordsburn, the village where Arthur had a cottage. It is a pretty village not far from the sea on the Ards peninsula ten miles east of Belfast. For Jack it was home. Holywood and Glenmachan were not far away. It was rapture for him to walk again in the countryside that he had known as a child. For the first time since his boyhood, he was free from serious worry, or at least from no worry worse than his brother's alcoholism. "I know now," he wrote, "how a bottle of champagne feels when the wire has at last been taken off the cork and it's allowed to go POP!"[16]

Almost as soon as he was back, he planned another holiday, this time with Warren for part of the time—four days in Crawfordsburn and two weeks in southern Ireland. Then he planned to stay two weeks alone in Crawfordsburn. The jaunt in southern Ireland with Warren included a short stay at the Golden Arrow, a seaside bathing establishment arranged along the beach at Anagassan, a little place on Dundalk Bay on the east coast. Two complete railway coaches, joined by a porch, faced the sea, and a third joined the porch at right angles to the other two, making a letter T fronting the beach. There were beds for about sixteen people and two comfortable sitting rooms. Both enjoyed the bathing, though it was not of their favorite sort. One had to walk quite a long way out to get into deep water and there were no "real" waves.

The following year Jack went on a motor tour of Ireland with Arthur. They stayed at Portsalon in Donegal, Ireland's wildest, most barren and northerly county, at Rathmullen, also on Lough Swilly, and then at the little hamlet of Inver on the Atlantic coast.

The following year he went for two summer jaunts in Ireland, again one with Warren in the south and one with Arthur at Inver and Rathmullen. These were happy years. In 1954 and 1955 he was much bothered by ill health and by worry about Warren's drunkenness. Nevertheless he found health, relaxation, and relief in similar holidays. He left the arrangements largely to Arthur. "Shall we," he wrote to Arthur in June 1955, "stay a night longer at Rathmullen or will you book me a room at the C'Burn Inn for the night of the19th? Which you please . . . a crust, a cup of cold water and a bed of straw, or even a rug shared with you on a summer night is enough for me!"[17]

They were very different men. How did they pass their time? I suspect much in the same way as Jack did with his other friends when on holiday, much as he did when he visited me in Malvern.

I think he came gladly to Malvern partly because he knew it already. The memory of his unhappy school days did not put him off. He loved to revisit places already familiar and stayed in Malvern with Lady Dunbar as well as with me.

My wife invited him whenever school holidays coincided sufficiently with university vacations, and he came once or twice a year from 1946 on, but I think he came only once during the period of his marriage. When he came, he was always our only guest. He would have disliked it if he had been shown off as a distinguished friend, or if we had invited anyone else to meet him or walk with us. His replies to invitations were by letter or postcard, for he never telephoned unless he had to. They were usually brief and often amusing:

> The 24th. Usual time and train. Bless you both. I want to see that POG again. Wot larx!
>
> Jack.

> 15/8/1951
>
> Dear George and Moira,
>
> You are treasures. Yes, I'd love to. The 15th Sept. weekend (i.e., arrive 14th) if I may. Lovely. I've just been having mumps. Humphrey kept on quoting bits out of *The Problem of Pain*, which I call a bit thick. Love and deep thanks to both.
>
> J.

Except once or twice when I happened to be in Oxford and could drive him over, he always came by train. His method of traveling was unusual. He always arrived very early at Oxford station, partly because he never had a watch. "They never seem to go on me," or "I always forget to wind them up" were the reasons he gave. I think also that he disliked the idea of spending so large a sum of money on himself. Once at the station, he would walk up and down the platform, saying his prayers, and then take the first slow train to Malvern. I remember well the surprise of porters and ticket clerks when he asked for a slow train. He liked the leisurely pace and the time it gave him to look at the countryside. Most of all, he liked to sit in the very front of the little rail motorcars that stop at every station on the Oxford-Worcester line. If the weather was fine, he would just enjoy the scenery. Otherwise he would read the book he had brought with him. He never bought a newspaper. There were better things with which to occupy the mind. "You don't need to read the news. If anything important happens, far too many people are sure to tell you about it."

He always seemed dressed in much the same way when he stepped off the train at Malvern Link station: an old gray Harris tweed jacket, often with leather patches on the elbows, baggy trousers of thickish gray flannel or brown corduroy, stout brown walking shoes, an old hat, and a walking stick. All the luggage he brought with him was contained in a simple, much-stained khaki rucksack that looked old enough to have been in his possession when he was a boy before World War I. He always called it "the pack"; later in the visit, it would be used to hold the food, raincoats, and anything else we took with us on the walks that would be our main activity during his stay.

He wanted always to begin our first walk as soon as possible. My wife would have sandwiches, perhaps some ham, some cheese ready. We might then ask her to drive us somewhere, perhaps the British Camp on the Malvern Hills, from which we would walk home.

The Malvern Hills consist of a single ridge about ten miles long that falls away very steeply on either side. Because of its isolation and steepness, it produces the impression of a range of far greater height. It commands one of the longest and best views in England with the Welsh mountains on one side, Bredon, the Severn valley, and the Cotswolds on the other. Jack loved the long views. As soon as he had climbed to the crest of the hill, he would stand drinking it in, with a serene, happy look, almost of ecstasy, on his face.

The routine of the walk was always the same. One of us would shoulder "the pack." We would walk for half an hour. If it was warm enough, and somehow it usually was, we would then have a "soak." This meant lying or sitting down while Jack smoked a cigarette. As soon as the cigarette was finished, we would get up, the other man would take the pack, and we would walk for another half hour or so before another soak. This continued for as long as the walk lasted. "Turn and turn about," as he put it.

The route would be determined by the need to arrive between 12:30 and 1:30 at a pub that we both liked. Fortunately we had much the same taste, a taste that I am sure Arthur Greeves also shared. The pub had to be small, simple, old, and preferably in the black-and-white style. It must serve what would now be called "real ale," that is, bitter beer drawn from wooden casks, not ale pasteurized and stored under pressure in metal drums as is now common in England. Jack and his brother would not drink this latter kind, and both disliked bottled, and even more, canned beer. The interior of the pub could not be "tarted up"; the furniture had to be traditional with wooden tops to the tables, preferably polished with wax. If it were at all cold, a coal or wood fire burned in the grate. If there was music, such as a switched-on radio, Jack would want to leave. Fortunately television, jukeboxes, and fruit machines were menaces not to be found in the country pubs of those days. With our pints of beer we ate our sandwiches. Then Jack smoked a cigarette and often had a second pint of beer.

Ideally he liked to be back at our house by five in the evening. If this was not possible, we would look for a cottage where we could have a pot of tea—nothing to eat, just tea, but tea made strong in the Irish way. Without tea at this time of day he felt rather unhappy, perhaps a little faint.

When we got home, he would go to his bedroom and wash thoroughly. He rarely had a bath when he was staying with me, and I think less often still at the Kilns. If there was not already one in his room, he would then ask for a Bible "in any translation" and say his prayers. He found this the best time of day for them. If he left them till later, he was usually too sleepy. We dined at half past seven or a quarter to eight, so at about seven Jack came down to sip a glass or two of dry sherry over a cigarette and, unless she was in the kitchen (to which he rarely penetrated), to recount to my wife the events of the day's walk. He invariably managed to make them most entertaining.

His taste in food was for the plain, the solid, and the traditional. He liked roast meat of any sort, hot or cold, served with the conventional trimmings. I don't think he appreciated in the least the rather subtle French recipes that my wife, who tended to be bored by plain food, often followed, and he liked still less the cooking of the excellent Italian girl that we at one time had as home help. He took no interest in vegetables apart from new potatoes, in puddings, or in fruit, but he enjoyed good cheese, especially ripe Stilton or cheddar.

What made him a difficult guest at the dinner table was the

tremendous speed with which he ate. If allowed, he would often have finished a second helping before my wife and I were halfway through our first. He was well aware of the fault ("I'm afraid I gobble"), which he sometimes explained as hereditary. Once he began to eat, his main idea seemed to be to finish the meal so that he could smoke a cigarette. With us he sometimes even asked if he could smoke between the courses.

He liked to drink a couple of glasses of red wine with his dinner. We preferred claret, but generally gave him burgundy, which he considered a far superior wine. He rarely drank white wine, though I can think of an occasion when he enjoyed a bottle of hock, but he would take still cider or draught beer with pleasure.

During dinner and until the tea or coffee had been cleared away (he preferred tea), he regaled us with brilliant talk—literary, anecdotal, fantastic, usually lighthearted, and nearly always amusing. (One of the great regrets of my life is that I did not act like Boswell by trying each evening to write up as much as I could remember of it.) But after dinner he liked to settle down for an hour or two of silent reading. He would choose a book from my shelves, usually a novel I could recommend or a book that he wanted to reread (he held strongly to the view that the qualities of a good book could not be exhausted at a first reading). He read very fast and if the book was a humorous one, he would often chuckle or laugh aloud.

An exception to this routine could occur when he was alone with a friend. They might then read aloud together. He was convinced of the value of reading aloud. One person read a page or two, more if it was a novel, and then passed the book to the other. I read with him in this way some of Wordsworth's *The Prelude*, some Dante, and some Ruskin. On one occasion he read to me some Sappho and Pindar.

At about half past ten he liked to be brought another cup of tea, after which he went to bed, falling asleep almost at once. He usually woke early. I think he was always awake when I took him a cup of tea at half past seven, and I think he was usually praying. He dressed and shaved very quickly and then liked, if it was fine weather, to go out in our garden or for a short walk before breakfast. I think he spent the time drinking in the beauty of the morning, thanking God for the weather, the roses, the song of the birds, and anything else he could find to enjoy.

When we first knew him, he ate a full breakfast, that is, eggs, bacon, toast, and marmalade, but he came to prefer bread to toast, and in his later years he was put on a diet that allowed him only tea and crisp bread (which he detested). I don't think he always kept to this diet when at home at the Kilns.

In walking in the countryside my own interests are partly architectural and archeological. I like exploring old churches and buildings of almost any sort. I enjoy gardens, too. Jack did not share these interests at all. He never wanted to go inside a village church and cared nothing for looking at castles. His pleasures arose from the scenery and from our adventures.

We sometimes walked the ridges and valleys of the Black Mountains on the borders of England and Wales. We once arrived at the Abbey Hotel at Lanthony without a packed meal and asked if we could have lunch. We were both poorly dressed, especially Jack. "I cannot have you in the dining room," replied the landlady, "for I have gentry staying in the house, but if you will go to the back kitchen and have money in your pockets, I'll see if I can find you a plate of cold meat. And mind you wipe your feet well before coming in." Jack took it like a lamb. He actually took his shoes off before entering and made me do the same. Over the cold meat and what he maintained was home-brewed ale, he whispered, "You know I enjoy being ordered about like this. What would the psychologists make of it?"

And once when we were walking on Bredon Hill, we met a bedraggled and exhausted fox. "Oh, poor thing," Jack said. "What shall we do when the hunt comes up? I can already hear them. Oh, I know—I have an idea." He cupped his hands and shouted to the first riders, "Hallo, yoicks, gone that way," and pointed in the direction opposite to the one the fox had taken. The whole hunt followed his directions. There followed a long discussion about when lying was morally justifiable, but he boasted delightedly later to my wife that he had saved the life of a poor fox and showed no trace of guilt.

Although he loved nature, he was rather ignorant of natural history, but he enjoyed learning, or at least being given the information. He was deeply interested when I showed him specimens of the poisonous or intoxicating fungi *Amanita phalloides* and *muscaria*. He at once began to plan a story that made use of the latter. He was delighted by the look of it. He was interested, too, in a mandrake plant and wanted to dig it up to see if the root was really forked. I particularly enjoy the scents of the garden and countryside and enjoyed introducing them to Jack. I remember getting him to smell honeysuckle, pinch mint and wild thyme between finger and thumb, and in the garden break off and taste little bits of rosemary, rue, and lemon balm. He was fascinated and said at once that his experience of pastoral poetry was enriched. To the end of his life he loved to acquire, especially from a friend, little scraps of (preferably) out-of-the-way knowledge.

Of course, we talked a great deal while walking and drinking our beer. Much of his conversation was literary. If he had discovered books that he had not known about and found interesting or exciting, he would tell me about them with the object of sharing the pleasures of discovery. He would talk, too, about books he had just reread and about which his views had changed. From others, such as the essays of Montaigne, he would produce odd bits of information and odd opinions, just the sort of things he knew would delight me.

He would also talk about some of his private worries, very often about his brother. He mentioned only those of his friends I already knew. (I did not know even of the existence of Arthur Greeves.) If he had met any interesting or amusing people since we had last been together, he would describe them. He described his meeting with Konrad Lorenz, the great German zoologist. They had dinner together, after which Lorenz was due to lecture. Over the coffee, Lorenz leaned over and said, "I have eaten too much to lecture well. I shall now go out to make myself vomit." And he did.

Jack did most of the talking, but he was also a very good listener. He would want to be told about the books I had been reading and of the events in my private life. If I was in any sort of difficulty, he would give sympathetic and carefully considered advice. He was in all respects the perfect walking companion.

19

Surprised by Joy

The death of Mrs. Moore gave Jack the freedom to do many things. Not only could he go away for holidays, but it was also now possible for him to be on terms of close friendship with women, to marry, and to accept a professorship in another university.

Ruth Pitter was one of the very few modern poets whose work he admired. His writing to her of his appreciation developed into a witty and profound correspondence and occasional meetings between them. Even after he was free, however, it was not easy for him to meet her. She and a friend, a Miss O'Hare, earned their living by painting papier-mâché trays for Harrods, and they lived in a somewhat inaccessible village in Buckinghamshire. Neither they nor Jack had a car. So he sometimes asked friends to drive him over. I did it three times between 1953 and 1955, though on one occasion Ruth was not there—I don't think he ever wrote or phoned to tell her that we intended to come.

It was obvious that he liked her very much. He felt at ease in her presence—and he did not feel relaxed with many people. In fact, he seemed to be on intimate terms with her. The conversation was a mixture of the literary and the domestic. They discussed Eddison's romances and the poems of R. S. Thomas and

Andrew Young. Each suggested amusing and improbable books for the other to write. Herbs were pinched and tasted in the cottage garden. Homemade drinks were sampled. She asked for the recipe of my moselle-like elder-flower wine. We also discussed marmalade. Jack did not contribute much to this domestic conversation, but it was clear that he enjoyed it. He even offered to help gather elder flowers for the winemaking and recalled, apparently with pleasure, the occasions when he had helped Mrs. Moore peel and slice oranges for marmalade. It was clear that he enjoyed both the idea and the reality of domesticity.

After one visit in 1955, he remarked that, if he were not a confirmed bachelor, Ruth Pitter would be the woman he would like to marry. "One could have with her the kind of relationship described by Patmore in *The Angel in the House*," he said.

"It's not too late," I commented.

"Oh yes it is," he said. "I've burnt my boats." Then he began to talk about something else. At the time, I did not know what he meant, and I am unsure now. Like most of his friends, I had not yet been told the status of his relationship with Joy Gresham.

The death of Mrs. Moore no doubt encouraged Joy to cross the Atlantic in September 1952, obviously with the intention of getting to know Jack. She had been born Joy Davidman in New York City in 1915. Her parents were Jews from Eastern Europe, but both had lost their faith. Her father was a Fabian socialist and an atheist; her mother practiced Judaism to the minimum extent. She liked talking to Joy about village life in the Ukraine, where ritual laws governed almost every action and religious practice was a matter of outward observance. As a child, Joy read rapidly and widely and was encouraged in this by her parents, who were both teachers. The desire to please her father and the influence of Wells's *Outline of History*, which she read at the age of eight, made her an atheist. She rejected all morality and saw nothing to live for except pleasure, and yet she had supernatural or mystical experiences rather like Jack's own. But hers was not a happy childhood. She was always frightened of her father, who had a hair-trigger temper. She found it hard to communicate and was socially unsure of herself, but she hid her insecurity under a mask of callous indifference. Her idealism came out only in the poetry she wrote in her teens and in her passion for stories of the supernatural.

She took her B.A. degree at Hunter College, New York, in 1934 and then her M.A. in English literature at Columbia University when she was still only twenty. Afterward she taught English in various New York high schools, joined the Communist Party and became an energetic party worker, and continued to write poetry. Her *Letter to a Comrade*, a book of free verse written in a style similar to that of Auden and McNeice, won the Yale Poetry Award for 1938, the year of its publication, and was widely praised. Its success gave her the confidence to give up teaching for full-time writing. Her next book, a novel called *Anya* that was published in 1940, gives a vivid account of Jewish village life in the Ukraine before the First World War. The heroine is a shopkeeper's daughter who rebels against narrow conventions by her search for free love. Joy became film critic and poetry editor of the Communist paper *New Masses* and contributed as a free-lancer to other left-wing papers. She also worked for a short time in Hollywood as a junior scriptwriter for Metro-Goldwyn-Mayer.

In 1942 at a Communist Party meeting, she met William Lindsay Gresham. He was six years older than her and also an atheist. He had been a nightclub singer and a newspaper reviewer. He had gone to Spain to fight on the Communist side, but had spent over a year there without firing a shot, and came home depressed and suicidal. Psychiatric treatment helped to restore his self-confidence, but he remained an alcoholic. When Joy met him, he was the editor of a fiction magazine. He had already been married and divorced and was undoubtedly a womanizer. His great charm gave him the ability to make people, especially women, feel sorry for him. They were soon married and had two children, David, born in 1944, and Douglas, born in 1945. Both Joy and William eventually became disillusioned with communism.

Father Victor White, a friend of Joy's, described Bill to me as "a very bright lad, cram-full of ideas. He could do almost anything, but one could never guess what he would do next. He carried around the *I Ching* and often consulted it for guidance." He wrote a thriller, *Nightmare Alley,* which brought them a period of affluence when it was made into a film that starred Tyrone Power. But he was reckless and extravagant and could not handle money. To protect herself and the children, Joy got him to buy a farm with the proceeds of the film. It seems that she ran it while he continued to edit magazines in New York. One day he phoned from his office to say that he was going mad and did not know what to do. He could not bear to stay in the office, and he could not come home, he said. Then he hung up. Joy and the children were stranded in the house. She did everything she could to find out where he was, but failed in this effort. She felt helpless. As she later expressed it in an article describing her conversion: "All my defenses—the walls of arrogance and cocksureness and self-love behind which I had hid from God—went down momentarily. And God came in." She felt that God was there in the room with her as a person, "a person so real that all my previous life was by comparison mere shadow play."[1] When the vision was over, she found herself on her knees praying. She knew that God cared about her and loved her.

When Bill eventually came home, Joy described this experience to him. He was profoundly moved by it, and the two began to study theology together. In 1948 he began to pray that he might be rescued from his alcoholism, which he realized he was powerless to resist. For the next three years, he did not drink at all. They began to attend the Presbyterian church near their farm. Both contributed accounts of their conversion to a Protestant anthology, *These Found the Way*, published in 1951. For the rest of her life, Joy was deeply Christian.

In 1949 Father Victor White was lecturing in New York on the relationship of psychology, particularly Jungian psychology, and religion. Joy went to one or two of the lectures and talked to him afterward. Father White told me, "She wanted to know if I knew C. S. Lewis. Told me that she was fascinated by him, and wanted to hear all I could tell her about him. She asked how difficult it would be to meet him. I told her pretty difficult. I suggested she might write. It was said that he answered all letters that seemed to come from people who needed help or advice."

In the latter part of the same year, Chad Walsh, a friend of the Greshams, published *C. S. Lewis: Apostle of the Skeptics.* Joy talked with Walsh about what she owed to Lewis's writings and said that she would like to know the answer to some of the points raised by Lewis. Walsh also suggested that she might write to him.

Her first letter to Jack arrived at the Kilns in January 1950. Both Jack and Warren found it unusually amusing and well written. Jack was stimulated to write a reply that was, according to Warren, "rather brilliant." The correspondence that followed intensified Joy's feelings and led Jack to want to meet her.

Joy began to consider how she could visit Oxford without much expense and without making her main motive crudely obvious. She acquired a pen pal, Phyllis Williams, who lived in

London, and received an invitation to stay with her for some of the time that she was in England.

At this point, her relationship with Bill was deteriorating. His conversion to Christianity had not made him more stable. Indeed, it is doubtful that he really was a Christian. He became an enthusiastic convert to Dianetics, the early form of Scientology invented by Ron Hubbard, and later became feverishly interested in Zen Buddhism. He also used tarot cards, practiced yoga, and began once again to consult the *I Ching* before making decisions. He was still irresponsible with his money and still a womanizer, worst of all, one who boasted of his conquests to his wife.

For her there was the problem of the children. She could not leave them alone with Bill. This problem was solved when early in 1952, her cousin Renée Pierce came from Florida to live with them. Renée, who was five years younger than Joy, had also married an alcoholic from whom she was seeking refuge. She brought her two young children with her and readily agreed to look after Bill, David, and Douglas while Joy was away.

Joy desperately wanted advice from Jack about her marriage. She also wanted to discuss with him the book she was writing on the Ten Commandments. She wrote to him from London and invited him to have lunch with her and Phyllis Williams early in September. He returned the invitation by inviting her and Phyllis Williams to lunch in his Magdalen College rooms. The fourth member of the party should have been Warren, but he withdrew, and I was asked to take his place.

The party was a decided success. Joy was of medium height, with a good figure, dark hair, and rather sharp features. She was an amusingly abrasive New Yorker, and Jack was delighted by her bluntness and her anti-American views. Everything she saw in England seemed to her far better than what she had left behind. Thus, of the single glass of sherry we had before the meal, she said, "I call this civilized. In the States, they give you so much hard stuff that you start the meal drunk and end with a hangover." She was anti-urban and talked vividly about the inhumanity of the skyscraper and of the new technology and of life in New York City. Even in the countryside, she said, it was hardly possible for a woman to go for a walk without being molested. She attacked modern American literature, finding that most of it had had its reputation manufactured by publishers' publicity departments. Her view of modern America was even lower than his. "Mind you, I wrote that sort of bunk myself when I was young." Small farm life was the only good life, she said. Jack spoke up then, saying that on his father's side he came from farming stock. "I felt that," she said. "Where else could you get the vitality?"

Of course, Jack liked this. It fitted in with his own anti-American prejudice. I remember his saying to me when I was his pupil, "What are you doing, going around with Americans?"

After the meal, she asked to be taken around the college. Her enthusiasm, interest, and many impudent questions made us roar with laughter. I suppose the quantity of good wine that we had drunk contributed to our hilarity.

Jack asked me to stay behind for a minute after his other guests had gone. He had asked Joy to stay at the Kilns, and he wanted my advice. Should he and Warren behave in their usual holiday fashion, walking, drinking beer, and eating bread and cheese in pubs? Or should they try to be more conventional hosts? I said that they should do as they usually did on holiday, and later I heard from Warren that the visit was a great success. "We treated her just as if she were a man. She loved the pubs, walked fairly well considering that she was not used to it, drank her pints of beer and often made us laugh." Her ability to make him laugh was one thing that Jack enjoyed about her. Another was her flow of sharp, almost outrageous comments. He had not met anyone like her before. She, of course, would have been utterly happy with him no matter what they were doing.

It seems that they did not meet again until December 6 in London as soon as the Oxford term had ended. The evidence of their meeting is found in a copy of *Preface to Paradise Lost*, which he apparently gave to her. In the book (which I now have) Joy has written:

> *I read it over fish and chips*
> *And now I read it with my beer—*
> *Of wandering Trojans and their ships*
> *And lightless hell aflame with fear;*
> *As Housman said there's power in malt*
> *And likely it's not Milton's fault—*
> *But Jack can do more than Milton can*
> *To justify God's ways to man!*
>
> Joy Davidman

At that meeting, December 6, 1952, he invited her to spend Christmas at the Kilns. She stayed two weeks, cooked a turkey dinner on Christmas, and went with him on long walks and to some of his favorite pubs. At one pub, much to Joy's astonishment, Jack lustily sang the choruses of some popular songs, just as he would have done in the Belfast music halls of his boyhood. She read some of his unpublished work, and he read the draft of her newest book, *Smoke on the Mountain*, told her how to improve it, and wrote an introduction that ensured its success.

Just before she left, a letter from Bill arrived. "Renée and I are in love and have been since the middle of August," he wrote, and then suggested a divorce, after which Joy could be married "to some really swell guy, Renée and I to be married, both families to live in easy calling distance so that the Gresham kids could have Mommy and Daddy on hand." It would be better for him to be married to Renée, he wrote, because, unlike Joy, Renée's "only interest is taking care of her husband and children and making a home for them." He asked for her "cooperation in this ideal solution."[2]

Joy discussed the letter with Jack, who advised her to divorce her husband, but it seems that she was opposed to this on theological grounds. He was horrified by what he knew of Bill's behavior and thought that it was out of the question that the children should be left with him. Yet how was Joy to support them? It is quite likely that Jack offered to help her if she decided to live with her children in England, as she wanted to. Yet it is unlikely that a woman as proud as she was would have accepted this offer without a commitment on his part. On Christian grounds, he could not have offered to marry her once she was free of Bill. She knew that. She would probably have been satisfied if he could have said that he loved her, but without this understanding she would simply have to try to earn a living and bring the boys up in the United States, even if it meant living in the same house as Bill and Renée.

She returned to the United States, only to discover that Bill was drinking again and that Renée was Bill's sexual partner. She wrote about her miseries to Jack, and by the end of February she came to agree with Bill that they should be divorced, presumably on condition that she should have custody of the boys and that he should contribute to their support. The problem now became one of money. They had hardly enough for necessities, let alone the legal expenses of divorce. Renée stayed with them until she had saved enough money to go to Florida and file for divorce. Joy stayed on after her departure in order to help pay off their debts and to save for lawyer's fees and, presumably, the cost of the trip to Europe. Perhaps she was helped by her parents, with whom she was now on better terms than at any other time in her life.

After arriving in Liverpool, she went straight to London, arranged lodging for herself and the boys, and secured places for them at Dane Court, a prep school in Surrey. It was an expensive school that she could not afford on her income from royalties and the maintenance money Bill sometimes sent her. No doubt Jack helped with the cost and later on paid all the expenses. Warren and, as far as I know, all Jack's friends were kept in complete ignorance of this arrangement. When I asked Warren how Joy managed to pay her way, he replied that she was "a very clever journalist, easily able to support herself and the boys." The bills from Dane Court were probably paid by the charitable trust that Jack had had set up and into which he paid a considerable part of his literary earnings. It was, of course, an entirely proper and legitimate use of the funds, and the existence of the trust must have made it easier for Joy to accept her dependent position.

Jack invited Joy and her children to spend four days at the Kilns in the middle of December 1953. He enjoyed their visit, but found it tiring. He wrote to one of his American correspondents: "Last week we entertained a lady from New York for four days, with her boys aged nine and seven respectively. . . . It however went swimmingly, though it was very, very exhausting. The energy of the modern American boy is astonishing; this pair thought nothing of a four mile hike across broken country as an incident in a day of ceaseless activity, and when we took them up Magdalen tower, they said as soon as we got back to ground, 'Let's do it again.' . . ."[3] Joy wrote to Bill that "both boys were a big success with the Lewises" and mentioned "long walks through the hills, during which Jack reverted completely to schoolboy tactics and went charging ahead with the boys through the thorniest, muddiest steepest places. . . ."[4] Before they left, Jack gave the boys a typescript of *The Horse and His Boy* and told them that he was going to dedicate the printed version to them.

Joy and Jack do not seem to have seen very much of each other in the period between December 1953 and August 1955, when she moved into a house at Headington. Once or twice he came to London, and she was invited a few times to Oxford, where he gave her lunch and introduced her to some of his friends, most of whom did not like her. Her abrasive New York manner and the sharp speech masked her essential kindness and generosity. She was far too shy to reveal that she was deeply Christian and a mystic. They did not find her attractive, but, most of all, they feared for Jack. Wasn't there a risk of her moving into the Kilns and dominating him? I do not think that they knew anything at this time about the boys or the breakup of her marriage. Even Jack may not have known how difficult she found it to make ends meet in London. She did not want to receive any money from him except for the Dane Court fees, although she let him pay her, since he was most insistent, for a book that she typed for him.

In 1954 Jack left Oxford for a teaching position at Cambridge. With his increasing age and with his vast and ever-growing correspondence, he had been finding his work as a tutor more and more burdensome. He disliked and distrusted the way in which the syllabus of the English School seemed to be developing. The younger dons were clamoring for the inclusion of more modern literature and, to make room for it, a reduction in the amount of time given to earlier literature, especially the study of Old English. The principles of the syllabus for which he and Tolkien had fought before the war now seemed to be supported by very few. He was now not even sure of Tolkien's support, and this hurt him deeply.

When some of his friends and admirers at Cambridge learned of his dissatisfaction, they raised the matter at a meeting of the university English faculty. As a result, the professorship of medieval and Renaissance studies was created just for him. The kind offer almost overwhelmed him with joy, but he was initially reluctant to accept it because of his love of Oxford, his natural dislike of change, and, far more serious, his fear of what might happen to his brother if he moved to Cambridge. He considered buying a house in Cambridge and moving there with Warren, but soon gave up that idea as impractical. To fund such a purchase they would have to sell the Kilns, which they could not do because they only had a life interest in it. Though for Warren the pleasure of living in the Kilns had been lessened by his disagreements with Mrs. Moore during her later years, he could think of nowhere else in which he could continue to work on the French seventeenth century.

Jack's friends at Cambridge suggested a compromise. He should reside at Cambridge only from Monday to Friday. Weekends, including Monday morning, and the whole of each vacation could be spent at Oxford or wherever else he wished. Jack agreed to this arrangement.

Although he did not move to Cambridge until January of 1955, he gave his inaugural lecture as professor on November 29, 1954. It was an extraordinary occasion. The hall was so crowded that a party of his friends and old pupils from Oxford could find nowhere to sit and ended up on the platform behind him. The lecture was a brilliant performance acknowledged by an ovation rarely given to an academic. Its subject developed from his assertion that the great divide in culture and civilization had taken place between the period of Jane Austen and the present day. He cited examples from politics (rulers had been replaced by leaders), the arts ("the Cubists, the Dadaists, the Surrealists, and Picasso" had introduced the "shatteringly and bewilderingly new abstract art"), and religion (the decline of Christian belief had cut people off from the past). But the greatest change of all, he said, had come from the machine, which "alters man's place in nature" and gives us a new myth—that the new is better. He went on to describe himself as a member of the old order. "I read as a native texts what you must read as foreigners," he said. ". . . In order to read Old Western Literature aright you must suspend most of your responses and unlearn most of your habits you have acquired in reading modern literature." If his audience wanted to understand the past, specimens of old Western man should be useful to them, he said. "That way, where I fail as a critic, I may yet be useful as a specimen. I would even dare to go further. Speaking not only for myself but for all other Old Western Men whom you may meet, I would say, use your specimens while you can. There are not going to be many more dinosaurs."[5] One undergraduate commented to me, "We were overwhelmed by his vitality and enthusiasm. I had never heard a lecture anywhere near as exciting. We discussed it until far into the night. For weeks afterwards you heard people describing themselves as 'dinos.'"

Jack was given rooms at Magdalene College, Cambridge, that were richly panelled but less spacious than his rooms at Magdalen College, Oxford. He dreaded the move into them. It "looms large and black," he wrote to Arthur Greeves on December 4, "all the things to see to and all the decisions to make."[6]

The move to Cambridge brought Jack closer to Joy. She had made some suggestions about what to take to Cambridge when she and the boys had visited the Kilns during the summer holidays. She now came to help him with the move. The rooms at Oxford had to be cleared. He took the minimum number of books to Cambridge, and all the rest were sold or taken to the Kilns, where a bedroom had to be converted into a second library. A cook was engaged to prepare meals for Warren between Tuesdays and Fridays, and he and Jack planned to have lunch together on Monday and to go out on weekends.

Jack's Cambridge rooms were depressingly bare and uncomfortable. He had bookcases, two tables, and three or four hard chairs, but no armchair or sofa. My wife offered to lend him a comfortable chair, but he declined the offer. He cared little for the appearance of furniture or even for comfort. Tables and chairs which gave him a place to eat, read, and write were almost the only pieces of furniture that he needed. Of course, a bed was essential, but he hardly seemed to care if even that was comfortable. Again, I think that there was in the back of his mind a desire to practice the ascetic life.

He liked many things about Cambridge. The town was smaller, quieter, and less industrial than Oxford; the fellows of his new college more friendly and courteous; and the atmosphere relaxed. He missed some things about Oxford, but they were of little importance. What really worried him during his early months at Cambridge was that, now that he had all the time in the world to write, he had dried up. For the first time in his life, he had no ideas for books. No pictures came into his mind. he had nothing to say. And this is where Joy gave him invaluable help.

It happened all in one week. My wife and I had asked Jack and Warren to dinner in Oxford. Jack replied in a letter to us dated April 2, 1954: "By bad luck Mrs. Gresham (our queer, Jewish, ex-Communist, American convert) and her two boys will be here all next week. So we can't come and dine. But cd. you both come in on the Tue. or Wed. and meet at the Eastgate at 11 for an hour or more's talk? She's a queer fish and I'm not at all sure that she's either yours or Moira's cup of tea (she is at any rate not a bore). But it wd. be a v. bright spot for W. and me. Do." The meeting was uneventful. Joy drank whiskey, asked my advice about public schools, and talked about American novels of fantasy and science fiction. Moira sensed that she was in love with Jack but anxious to disguise the fact. She also thought that he was very fond of her. The important remark came from Jack at the end of the meeting, "And, by the way, I've at last got a really good idea for a book."

When Joy learned that Jack had run out of ideas, she had set out to help him. They settled down in comfortable chairs, "kicked a few ideas around until one came to life. Then they bounced it back and forth between them. By the following evening, Jack had written the first chapter. She criticized it; he "did it over and went on with the next."[7] By the end of the month *Till We Have Faces* was about three quarters finished. No doubt Joy read it, criticized it, and typed it. She thought that her real gifts were, not those of the original writer, but those of the editor-collaborator. To judge from *Till We Have Faces,* she was right. Her part in the book, and there is so much that she can almost be called its joint author, put him very much in her debt. She stimulated and helped him to such an extent that he began to feel that he could hardly write without her.

We do not know how often they met before 1955. We know that she and the boys stayed at the Kilns in the summer and Christmas holidays of 1954, the year that her divorce was final (Bill divorced her on the grounds of desertion and incompatibility). In 1955 she and the boys moved into a three-bedroom, semidetached house at 10 Old High Street in Headington, not far from the Kilns. Jack leased the house and paid the rent. Lyle Dorsett has suggested that she may have tricked him into renting the house for her,[8] but it is not clear how, and the evidence is that Jack took advantage of her proximity to get her to help him with his writing. At this point they were meeting nearly every day that he was in Oxford.

A little incident in which my wife Moira was involved gave us a good idea of the closeness of their relationship. It is worth including because it illustrates Joy's possessiveness, jealousy of Jack's friends (especially if they were women), and lack of emotional self-control. I had been invited to the confirmation of a former pupil who was a member of the university. I took Moira with me, and we invited Jack to lunch at the Eastgate Hotel. Afterward Moira asked if, instead of going to the confirmation ceremony, she could spend the afternoon reading at the Kilns. We both felt that Jack was embarrassed by the request, but he agreed. He showed her into the room at the Kilns that he called the Common Room, found for her a story by George MacDonald that she had not read, and then said that he was going into the "fourth dimension." Before long Joy came in whistling loudly and carrying some laundry. "Who the ____ are you and what the ____ are you doing in this house?" she exclaimed, apparently not recognizing Moira.

Moira flared up, "We've met before. I'm Mr. Lewis's guest. I have as much right to be here as you."

Joy swore and went off, slamming the door. Moira said that Jack was quite miserable when, later on in the afternoon, she conveyed a softened version of what had happened. When they next met, both women behaved with cautious politeness, as if the incident had never occurred.

During his holiday in Ireland in September 1955, Jack discussed with Arthur his relationship with Joy. He was already considering whether to marry her in a civil ceremony, just to enable her and the boys to stay permanently in England. He did not, of course, think of it as a "real" marriage. "The 'reality' wd. be," he wrote, "from my point of view, adultery and therefore mustn't happen (an easy resolution when one doesn't in the least want it!)."[9]

In April of 1956, Jack told me that Joy's permit to live and work in England would not be renewed and that the only way she could stay in England would be to marry an Englishman. It would be utter misery for her and tragic for the boys to go back to the United States. Her ogre of a husband still wrote charming letters, he said, hoping that she would return with them. Jack had decided, therefore, to go through a civil ceremony of marriage with her. Purely legal marriages were common, he said, and he had no objection to helping her out in this way. He was not going to tell more people than necessary because many would misunderstand. The marriage would never be anything more than a formality, he said, and it should be kept secret.

I raised objections. A civil marriage with Joy could not possibly be a formality, I said, but would, in fact, make him legally responsible for maintaining the boys if Joy were unable to earn enough to do so. And what if Joy wanted to contract a real marriage with someone else? Jack answered that in the eyes of the church she could not marry anyone else since she was already married. I asked if her marriage to Bill had been a Christian marriage. Had she and her husband been baptized? Did they accept the Christian view of marriage? Had Jack told me that Bill had already been married, my case would have been stronger. But he did not agree with my view of marriage, and he contended that the civil marriage would make no difference at all to his relationship with Joy. He liked her and admired her in a number of ways, but he was not in love with her, and this would not be a real marriage.

When we met over the summer holidays, he told me that the marriage had taken place. He indicated that it was making no difference to their relationship, but, in fact, I think that Joy was putting considerable pressure on him to allow her and the boys to live at the Kilns. It would not be easy to extend the lease of the

Headington house, and his frequent visits there, she pointed out, were compromising her and would be likely to cause a scandal.

Jack told me that he was positively not in love with Joy at this time, but in his biography of Joy, Lyle Dorsett states otherwise, citing as evidence a remark she made to her friend Bel Kaufman, that even if marriage were impossible, "the most wonderful ecstasy came from just holding hands and walking on the heather."[10] I frankly don't believe that this can be taken literally. It would have been utterly out of character for Jack to hold hands with a woman he did not think he could marry in the Christian church. This remark reveals only Joy's feeling for Jack, not his feeling for her.

He was extremely kind to the boys. He taught David Latin and helped him with his Greek and gave Douglas a horse, which was tethered and stabled on the estate. But I do not think he enjoyed their company. During holidays, which they spent at the Kilns, they came between him and Joy. He could not talk with her about theology or the book he was writing if they were there. They were only eleven and twelve in 1956, too young to be left on their own without supervision. He probably visited her so frequently at night just because the boys would be sleeping then.

In June Joy began to suffer from severe pains in the upper part of her leg, back, and chest that made it difficult for her to walk much or keep house. The illness was diagnosed as fibrositis. This seemed to be another reason for her to move into the Kilns, at least for a time. But in late October, an event occurred that entirely altered their relationship. Joy fell in her house and found herself lying in great pain unable to get up. She managed to attract the attention of a neighbor, and at the same time her friend Katherine Farrer, who had had an intuition that something was wrong, arrived. She was taken by ambulance to a hospital. X-rays showed clearly that she was suffering from cancer of the left femur, which, weakened by the disease, had broken in her fall. There was also a malignant tumor in her left breast, which was thought to be the primary site of the cancer, as well as secondary sites in her right leg and in one shoulder. The following month, she underwent three operations. The cancerous part of the femur was cut out, and the bone was repaired. The tumor in her breast was cut out, but she was spared a mastectomy. Her ovaries were also removed.

Her illness intensified Jack's affection for her. From this time onward, he was certainly aware of loving her. As he wrote to one friend: "Never have I loved her more than since she was struck down." But I think he would still have said that he was not *in love* with her. "The prospects," he wrote to Arthur, "are 1. A tiny 100th chance of ultimate cure. 2. A reasonable probability of some years more of (tolerable) life. 3. A real danger that she may die in a few months." He added: "It will be a great tragedy for me to lose her." The letter continues: ". . . [I]f she gets over this bout and emerges from hospital she will no longer be able to live alone so she must come and live here. That means (in order to avoid scandal) that our marriage must shortly be published. W. has written to Janie and the Ewarts to tell them I am getting married, and I didn't want the news to take you by surprise."[11]

But when Warren came to stay with us early in December, he said nothing of the distress that Joy's illness must have been causing Jack or of any plans to move Joy into the Kilns. He did say that he thought they would have to look after the boys until she recovered and that the prospect alarmed him. He was drinking heavily at the time, and he complained that he was seeing almost nothing of Jack.

On Christmas Eve of 1956, the following notice appeared in *The Times:* "A marriage has taken place between Professor C. S. Lewis of Magdalene College, Cambridge, and Mrs. Joy Gresham,

now a patient in the Churchill Hospital, Oxford. It is requested
that no letters be sent."

We received from Warren the following letter dated
January 2, 1957:

My dear Moira and George,

Here we are, on the surface once more; or more or less,
for after sixty the annual attack of flu is not so easily shaken
off as it was thirty years ago. One is left limp, and gets up saying like Jeremiah, "would it were night." And to the normal
depression of the state is added a special one. For tragedy is
fallen upon us. In the autumn Jack was quietly married to Joy
Gresham whom you have met. . . . At the time she was suffering from what appeared to be fibrositis, which got so bad
that she had to go into the Wingfield with it—where her complaint was diagnosed as a neglected cancer. . . .

Now what follows is at Jack's request, and is absolutely
sub sigilio; you are the only people except Jack, myself, and
(presumably) Jack's confessor, who know it. Joy is a divorcee
with a living husband and two small sons at prep school; and
Jack feels that you would both—very rightly—be very
shocked if you learnt that he of all men had married a woman
in Joy's situation. So he asks me to tell you that the marriage
was purely a nominal one, contracted for the purpose of giving Joy English nationality, for she is passionately anxious
that her two boys grow up English, and was also dreading for
herself a compulsory return to America. If she is to die, it will
at least be with the consolation that she leaves the two boys
to a man who will see them through Public School and give
them a start in life.

But not a word, and above all, not a hint to Maureen. . . .
J has written to her by this post and gave a bare outline of
the story, viz. the marriage to "a Mrs. Gresham" (*suggestio
falsi* I fear), and Mrs. G.'s illness, prospects etc. I said noth-

ing about the boys. I should dearly like to convalesce at Hamewith, but cannot do it just now; we have the two boys staying with us and you can imagine—with no resident servants—how exhausting this is. I couldn't with any decency, especially after my own illness, leave the whole task to Jack. They are nice kids as boys go, but need constant supervision; have no idea of time, are invariably late for meals; shockingly untidy; and of course noisy. And they won't get up in the morning. By the way, George, their mother has set her heart on their going to Bryanston; If you've any confidential information about the place, Jack would be most grateful for it. . . .

If the existence of the boys was meant to be a secret, it was one for only a short time. Lady Dunbar (Maureen) drove over to Oxford, called at the Kilns, and discovered them. On January 5 I had another letter from Warren saying that she had most generously offered to take charge of "the Bowery boys" for the rest of the Christmas holidays and for the Easter holidays as well. Warren called her offer "truly heroic" considering that she had a young family of her own.

All along, Joy had been worried that her marriage to Jack was only a registry office affair. But by now Jack had come to agree that, if possible, it should be solemnized by an ecclesiastical ceremony. Perhaps he had come to hold the view of the Roman Catholic church that Joy's marriage to Bill was no marriage at all, because Bill's wife had been alive at the time it took place, and that, therefore, Joy was free to marry. But this was and is not the official attitude of the Church of England, which regards every legal marriage as valid. The bishop of Oxford, Dr. Carpenter, discussed the position with Jack. Although he was full of sympathy for the difficult position that Jack and Joy were in, he was not able to give permission for one of his priests to marry them.

They were rescued from this agonizing situation by the kindness of an old pupil of Jack's, the Reverend Peter Bide. Jack had heard that Bide was a healer. He wrote and asked him to come and lay his hands on Joy and pray for her recovery. When he arrived at Headington, the question of Joy's marriage was discussed. Jack stated his view that Joy's marriage to Bill was not really a marriage and that she was, therefore, free to marry him. For the church to deny this, he said, was to try to have it both ways. It was impossible to maintain that the marriage with Bill both was and was not a Christian marriage. Bide agreed and said he would perform the ceremony the day after he had laid his hands on her and prayed for her recovery. "At 11 A.M.," Warren wrote in his diary, "we all gathered in Joy's room at the Wingfield—Bide, J., sister, and myself, communicated, and the marriage was celebrated. I found it heart-rending, and especially J's eagerness for the pitiable consolation of dying under the same roof as J.; though to feel pity for anyone so magnificently brave as Joy is almost an insult. She is to be moved here next week and will sleep in the common room, with a resident hospital nurse installed in Vera's room. There seems little left to hope but that there may be no pain at the end."[12]

But in the event, there was joy.

20

Surprised by Marriage

In fact, Joy lived to enjoy three years and four months of married life with Jack. Although they were often both in great physical pain, it was the happiest period of their lives. Prayer made this possible. Prayer and sacrifice. During those early weeks of 1957 after Joy came to the Kilns presumably to die, Jack prayed for long periods of time, not only for her, but also for the ability to be a substitute, to take some of her pain on himself. The occasions when Charles Williams had talked to him of his theory of substitution were often in his mind.

The results were astonishing. She came home in April, but by the end of the month, she was able to move about the house. By midsummer it was he who was in great pain, according to Paxford, "screamin' and 'ollerin' and no sleep without dope." His disease was diagnosed as osteoporosis, a weakening of the bones caused by a serious reduction in their calcium content. "The intriguing thing," he said later to a friend, "was that while I (for no discernible reason) was losing the calcium from my bones, Joy, who needed it much more, was gaining it in hers. One dreams of a Charles Williams substitution!"[1]

He suffered much pain all that summer. He could hardly walk at times and was fitted with a surgical brace or support to protect his weakened spine from fracture.

That August, the news from Warren, who had gone to Ireland, added to his worries. First there was a message from the landlord of the White Horse Hotel at Drogheda, saying that Warren had been found "dead drunk." Jack at once asked for him to be taken to the hospital of Our Lady of Lourdes. A few days later, a letter from Warren arrived. It was not reassuring. He had a heart complaint, he wrote, that would kill him in a year. Although Jack knew that in his state Warren could imagine anything, he feared that Warren's claim might be true, and he wrote to the Reverend Mother. She informed him that "the trouble is slight and curable; it was a by-product of acute alcoholism and pneumonia."

Early in April, Joy received an upsetting letter from Bill. "Naturally" he wrote, "I shall want them [Doug and Davy] to be with me in the event of your death." In response Jack penned the two strongest letters that he ever wrote, both on the same day. He told Bill that he had "tortured one who was already on the rack" and that there was nothing she dreaded so much as a return of the boys to their father's charge. They remembered him as a violent character, he wrote, "a man who fired rifles throu' ceilings to relieve his temper, broke up chairs, wept in public, and broke a bottle over Douglas's head." It would be agony for them as well as for Joy, "coming on top of the most appalling tragedy that can happen to childhood."[2] If Bill did not relent, Jack would place every legal obstacle in his way. But Bill did relent. He really did love the boys and want them to be happy. He seems to have accepted Jack's statement that, absolutely without any propaganda from Joy, they were made miserable by the prospect of returning to America. Joy and he continued to write more or less friendly letters to each other until shortly before her death over two years later, and when he visited the boys after her death, he did not try to persuade them to go back with him.

Jack was sustained at this time by the marvelous improvement in Joy's health. She became more and more active in the house and was able to take over the secretarial work while Warren was away. In September and October, Jack began to respond to treatment with strontium lactate tablets and steroids. At the beginning of the autumn term, rather than taking the train, he was driven by car to Cambridge because he could not otherwise manage his luggage. When I visited him at Magdalene in November, he explained that the pain "didn't matter." "All that matters is that I'm in love," he said. "At times I'm tempted to think it's a double miracle. Recovery for her, and for me the love that passed me by in youth and middle age."[3]

He told a friend on November 27, "I am no longer in pain. I wear a surgical belt and shall probably never be able to take a real walk again, but it doesn't somehow worry me." On the same day, he told Arthur Greeves that Warren was well "and busily writing." Joy was helping here, too. Much to his astonishment, Warren found that she was interested in seventeenth-century France and knew quite a lot about it. He was delighted to have someone in the house with whom he could discuss, say, the Chevalier de Gramont. In the last year of her life, she actually began work on a section of one of his books. She appreciated his sense of style, especially when it was crisp and caustic. Apart from encouraging him to be industrious, she improved the tone of his books, reducing the pleasure he seems to have taken in cruelty in some of his earlier works—*The Splendid Century*, for instance.

Throughout 1958, Joy was wonderfully well. Although she walked with a limp (and always would, for one leg was now shorter than the other), she could walk for a mile. She explored the estate and had the borders around the house dug, weeded, and planted with flowers. She persuaded a slightly resentful

Paxford, who did not much care for flower gardening, to raise plants in the greenhouse for this purpose.

She also made improvements on the house. The outside was repainted, the inside redecorated. The boiler was made to work, or perhaps a new one was bought, and the radiators were reconnected. It was now possible to have a hot bath and to sleep on a comfortable mattress. They ate well, too—Mrs. Miller cooking the lunches and quite often Joy cooking the evening meals. To Paxford's delight, far greater use was made of his garden vegetables and fruit.

In spite of these improvements, the house was not in the least luxurious. Joy wanted to bring it up to the level of ordinary middle-class standards by buying new curtains, carpets, and perhaps some new furniture, but Jack prevented her from doing so because he feared bankruptcy. He was not mean; he was just unused to spending large sums of money on the house. His scale of expenditure had remained the same since before the war, and he was accustomed to living extremely economically. Joy's medical treatment and the boys' education were heavy expenses. Besides, Jack was simply insensitive to elegance in furniture. He disliked the idea of replacing tables and chairs that had been in the house for a long time, unless they were so broken down that they could not be mended. Even after Joy's improvements, first-time visitors to the Kilns were often surprised by the lack of taste and quality.

By the end of April, Jack's osteoporosis was so much better that he could walk a mile without tiring. He asked his doctor if it were possible for a man of his age and state of health to have sexual intercourse. The doctor replied that it was certainly possible "if you are careful and sensible." There can be little doubt that their relationship became that of a complete and consummated marriage at this time. Joy told a correspondent that Jack was a "wonderful lover" and that she was glad she had not had a mastectomy, because he very much enjoyed caressing her breasts.[4] At Cambridge that summer, he told me that he missed her very much, but he had much work to do, and he enjoyed thinking of the delights of the weekend that had passed and of that which was to come.

He had hoped for a long time to be able to show her his homeland, and that summer they flew to Ireland. It was his first airplane flight. He had wanted to travel by sea, as he had always traveled, but the doctor advised against it. If the sea were rough, either might possibly suffer a fall, and in each case this would be calamitous. He was nervous about flying, and the takeoff terrified him. It seemed to him that the aircraft was out of control and would crash. He prayed until the plane was off the ground, and then the rest of the flight was an experience of pure ethereal beauty. He often spoke afterward of the enchanting new world of the cloudscapes, the delight of floating above the clouds and their brilliance when seen from above, the excitement of peering down the great rifts between them to catch glimpses of the Welsh mountains, and the mystery of wondering where one was. He was excited by the first glimpse of the Irish coast, "brilliantly sunlit and standing out like a bit of enamel."

Arthur met them at the airport and drove them to the hotel at Crawfordsburn, where they stayed a few days to explore County Down in Arthur's car. Then they went to Donegal, the bleak, northwestern county that Arthur and perhaps Jack liked most of all. The weather was perfect, and they "returned drunk with blue mountains, yellow beaches, dark fuchsia, breaking waves, braying donkeys, peat smell, and the heather just beginning to bloom."[5]

A holiday with the boys would not be much of a holiday for Jack, yet children need to get away, too. So Joy arranged to take them on a holiday in an inn at Solva in Pembrokeshire where, as she put it, "the beds are soft and the drinks are strong." Jack wrote to me on August 15, 1958: "From about August 30th to September 6th—W. in Ireland and Joy taking the boys away for a jaunt—I shall be a grass widower, grass stepfather, and grass brother. Any chance of your coming up for a couple of nights or so? Humphrey also will be a very grass etc. And you can have your choice of several bedrooms, all now with new mattresses! Do."

Of course, I did. Even before I got to the front door, I was struck by the new paint on the house, the neater appearance of the garden, and the flowers. Joy had not yet left. It was the first time I had seen her since her operations. She had gained weight and her face had become rather puffy. Her conversation was sensible and practical, not witty, but often direct and abrasive. "Tell me, isn't it less like a tenement in the South Bronx?" she asked of the improvements in the house. "Tell him that he won't go broke." She explained that Jack could easily earn far more than he did. He could, for instance, write articles for top American publications, such as the *Saturday Evening Post*. He was a wonderfully quick and fluent writer whose work Americans loved, she said. In some ways, Warren wrote just as well. But neither he nor Jack knew how to sell their work.

Just before she left, she said, "There are village boys in our wood again. I'm going up with my gun. Come with me." She limped awkwardly, but with determination past the pond and up the steep path, helped by a stick. She was carrying a shotgun. Most of the estate had been recently fenced, but it seems that village boys still got in. She fired a couple of times into a tree. "That'll scare 'em," she said. "Pity I didn't get a pigeon." Then, "Are you a sentimental bird-lover?" She went on to say that she wasn't shooting just for sport. She would eat any pigeons she killed. Nevertheless, I think Jack disliked the activity.

In the evening, Humphrey Havard arrived in his car with Tolkien as passenger. He drove us out to Studley Priory, which was at the time Jack's favorite country hotel. While Jack was paying the bill after a hilarious dinner, we talked a little about his health. Tolkien was gloomy about the terrible strains and anxieties Jack was suffering: Warren's drunkenness, two rather difficult boys, and "a strange marriage" to "a sick and domineering woman." It turned out that what worried him most was that she was a divorcee. He did not accept my argument that she could not have been divorced since as a Christian she had never been married. However, the reappearance of Jack forestalled a discussion of this question.

After a couple of days at the the Kilns, we drove to Malvern, where it became quite obvious to my wife and me that Jack was very happy as a married man. He thought it was wonderful to be in love with someone whom he could unreservedly admire. She had a very fine mind—"intellectually I often feel her inferior," he said. But her style of conversation often caused people to regard her as hard and unfeeling. He said that some of the people he had invited to meet her had failed to appreciate her directness and concern for integrity. She was, anyway, too shy and diffident to be at her best with people she did not know.

In 1959 I stayed for another night or two at the Kilns. There was some good-humored banter, an art at which Joy could be nearly as proficient as Jack. But what impressed me most about their marriage was its natural quality. There was no striving to be something they were not, to be clever or even good. They just were. They accepted each other simply, naturally, without fret or fuss. They were kind to each other and unusually quick to grasp the nuances of each other's thoughts.

It was amusing to find Jack talking like the most conventional of fathers about school uniforms and pocket money. The boys' clothes must be entirely correct, that is, just the same as those worn by others. They must have the average amount of pocket money. They must not suffer as he and Warren had done from the shame of not being able to afford things commonly bought by their schoolmates.

After supper they settled down to play Scrabble, which surprised me (the game was not then as highly regarded in England as it was in America). Another surprise was to find Jack doing *The Times* crossword puzzle with Joy. If Jack could not think of the word immediately, he would make fantastic comments, often about the state of mind and character of the author of the puzzle.

They were both worried about Warren. Joy told me that when he came to Malvern, we should give him "dry ginger with nothing in it. Let him imagine the alcohol." (We tried this. It did not work.) Jack had always been extremely gentle with Warren, but he doubted that any of his appeals had influenced him at all. Joy, who had had plenty of experience living with a drunkard, thought it might help if he "got tough" or at least "acted tough." However, I doubt if this policy was ever adopted.

In March 1959, Jack had written to Arthur that lack of money would prevent them from taking an Irish holiday. "We have just been financially knocked by a huge surtax on royalties earned two years ago, which was a bumper year, long since forgotten and of course spent. I think we shall weather it alright, but we shall have to go very carefully—not perhaps for always but certainly for eighteen months or so."[6] This was typical of the financial anxieties that Jack and Warren seem to have inherited from their father. Jack's mathematical skills never got much beyond simple addition and subtraction; I doubt if he ever really understood the difference between gross and net income. As usual, it turned out that there was no crisis at all. They went to Ireland again in June and July, spent a week at Crawfordsburn and another week at Rathmullen with Arthur. Once again they took the boys into Wales for a summer holiday. Joy now seemed almost completely well and went happily and confidently into the hospital for a routine check. The result plunged them both into depression: "[C]ancer has returned in several parts of her skeleton."[7] She was at once given drug therapy and X-ray treatment. "The doctors say there is some hope," Jack wrote to me in November 1959, "of her being able to live without pain for a year or two. Well, we've enjoyed the fruits of a miracle. I'm not sure it would be right to ask for another. Nor do I think it would be given if I did. They tell me that there is no example on record of anyone who was granted the same miracle twice."

In spite of the unpleasant side effects of the therapy and a certain amount of pain from the disease itself, Joy went on living her normal active life with great courage and cheerfulness. She even went on an eleven-day holiday to Greece during the Easter vacation of 1960. It had always been one of her great ambitions to go there. Their friends, Roger and June Lancelyn Green, had gone on a group tour in April, 1959. When they later told Jack and Joy about the trip, Joy said she would like to have been with them. Roger at once suggested that they should all go together on a similar tour the following year. He would make the arrangements.

The trip is described in the diary that Roger kept and that was later printed in *C. S. Lewis: A Biography*, which he wrote with Walter Hooper.[8] It is a marvelous tribute to the ability of the human spirit to rise above pain. The flight was exhausting by modern standards. There were three landings for refueling, so they did not arrive in Athens until after midnight. They rested the following morning, but in the afternoon climbed the Acropolis and sat in the sun enjoying the beauty of the Parthenon. That evening, as on every other evening during their trip, they ate dinner together, laughed, talked, and drank wine. They took a day trip to Mycenae, where they were awed by the ruins, and another to the Gulf of Corinth, where they found classical castles and lovely scenery. "I had some ado," he wrote to Chad Walsh, "to prevent Joy (and myself) from lapsing into paganism in Attica! At Delphi it was hard not to pray to Apollo the Healer. But somehow one didn't feel it would have been very wrong—would only have been addressing Christ *sub specie Apollonis.*"9

At Rhodes, which he told me was "simply the Earthly Paradise," they went to the Greek Orthodox cathedral for part of the Easter service. Jack was moved by it and by a village wedding ceremony they went to. Thereafter, whenever the subject came up between us, he said that he preferred the Orthodox liturgy to either the Catholic or Protestant liturgies. He was also impressed by Greek Orthodox priests, whose faces, he thought, looked more spiritual than those of most Catholic or Protestant clergy.

They spent three days in Heraklion, the busy, uninviting capital of Crete. The restaurant to which they went on the first evening had an extremely noisy band and slow service. Joy, desperately bored, began flicking bread pellets at the nearest musician and to Jack's delight scored at least one hit. Jack does not seem to have been much impressed by Sir Arthur Evan's famous restorations at Knossos, but they very much enjoyed excursions through the still unspoiled Cretan countryside to less developed sites. Their meals, wherever they went, were filled with laughter. Green records that, at Phaistos, Jack "was the life and soul of the party, 'keeping the table in a roar.'"10

Both Jack and Joy enjoyed the trip immensely. Jack, who had always been sensitive to natural beauty, was enraptured by this spring visit to the Mediterranean. His head was full of the classics, and he enjoyed seeing places about which he had been reading for fifty years. Joy was delighted for the same reasons. The fact that they were both unwell and that Joy was in pain and certainly dying made the trip more precious.

On their return, they found that "there was a heavy price to pay in increased lameness and leg-pains."[11] Joy often had to go to the hospital for treatment. A reappearance of cancer in her right breast, the primary site of the disease, was soon discovered. The subsequent breast surgery went much better than had been expected, and she was able to go home on May 2.

She came back "radiant" and still took an active part in running the house, although she could now only move around in a wheelchair. Sometimes Warren took her out into the front garden. She enjoyed the roses and especially the flowers that she herself had planted two years earlier. On Sundays they sometimes went to Studley Priory for lunch. Early in June, she seemed even better. Mrs. Miller and her husband took her out for a drive after supper on June 11, and she did not seem at all tired when she returned. Three days later, she asked Warren to push her up as far as the pond, "with stops to inspect her favorite flower bed." Afterward, they went to the greenhouse, "where she got out and looked at her plants." But on June 20, she was taken to the Acland Nursing Home, vomiting "or at least trying to vomit all the time." The following day, Warren wrote in his diary: "Joy is dying. . . ."[12] The doctors now thought she had secondary sites of cancer in her liver and gallbladder. Douglas was sent for at his school in Wales.

But even then, Joy did not die. Every extra day or hour that she could spend with Jack was immensely precious to her, as she knew it was to him. She was in love with him, as he with her, and knew that, almost as long as she was conscious, she could rise above the pain and discomfort so that they could be happy together. She "made fools of the doctors and nurses"[13] by coming back to the Kilns on June 27, looking and saying that she felt better than she had for a long time. On July 3, she went out for dinner with Jack at Studley Priory and the following day for a drive in the Cotswolds with her nurse.

The end came suddenly on July 11. "At quarter past six on Wednesday morning," Jack wrote, "my brother, who slept over her, was awakened by her screaming and ran down to her. I got the doctor who fortunately was at home, and he arrived before seven and gave her a heavy shot. At half past one I took her into hospital in an ambulance. She was conscious for the short remainder of her life, and in very little pain, thanks to drugs; and died peacefully about 10:15 the same night."[14] One of her last recorded remarks was typical of her, "Don't get me a posh coffin. Posh coffins are all rot." Her most profound words are enshrined in the last three sentences of A Grief Observed: "She said not to me but to the chaplain, 'I am at peace with God.' She smiled but not at me. *Poi si torno all eterna fontana.*"[15]

Few marriages can have been more Christian. She had loved and revered him rather as the Church loves Christ, and in loving her he learned that the ideas he had met in Coventry Patmore over twenty-five years earlier were true in practice: Woman "is both Heaven and the way." "Heaven becomes very intelligible and attractive when it is discerned to be—Woman." She is a reflection of the divine and has the power to make evident to man truths that he would miss without knowledge of her body. Yet the wisdom of married love consists not in "high aspirations," but in the "sweet and regular use" of what is good in husband and wife. The "right life" is known by the joy it brings.[16] There is no conflict between duty and delight. Lovers can make the degree of their delight the test of the morality of their actions. They will obtain no satisfaction from disobeying God's law.

Jack felt that he had achieved full maturity and manhood

only through marriage. In one of his most profound sonnets he
wrote:

> *And everything you are was making*
> *My heart into a bridge by which I might get back*
> *From exile and grow man.*[17]

In living with Joy, he was being himself. There was no need to
posture and play at different roles, except for fun. With her, he
was free from self-doubt and introspection. He could speak ideas
just as they arose and receive back from her answers or arguments that would stimulate still more interesting ideas in his
mind. They were a most blessed and richly gifted pair.

21

Inspired by Joy

The books inspired by Joy are four, the novel *Till We Have Faces*, *The Four Loves*, *Reflections on the Psalms*, and *A Grief Observed*, the heart-rending little book that Joy never knew.

Till We Have Faces is based on the myth of *Cupid and Psyche*, which Jack first came across in Smith's classical dictionary while at Malvern College and then read in the sophisticated version of the second-century Roman writer Apuleius. While still an undergraduate, he made at least three attempts at writing the story, one in couplets, another in ballad form, and the third as a masque or play. About seventy lines of couplets survive, enough to show that he had invented for Psyche a brother called Jardis and a sister called Caspian, names that he used in other books. We know too from a diary entry for September 9, 1923, that he already had the idea of making Psyche's palace invisible to ordinary mortal sight. But he could not see how to construct the novel or how to give it the necessary new twist.

The technical success of the novel comes from the invention of a new character, Orual, queen of Glome, who is the narrator of the story. Sister to Psyche, she is ugly but passionate, unloved, longing to love and be loved. She could have been tender and true, but her love is spoiled by jealousy and possessiveness. What such love cannot stand is to see the beloved, in this case Psyche, "passing into a sphere where it cannot follow."[1] The story is largely that of her redemption. Early in the story she puts on a veil so that no one can see how ugly she is and also so that she may deceive herself about her own nature. At the end she is forced to remove the veil and to see herself as she really is. The result is a surprise, redemption and joy, the work of the self-sacrificing Christlike sister she has come to hate.

After it had been edited and typed by Joy, the book was sent to publisher Geoffrey Bles under the title of *Bareface*. The publisher objected to the title ("it might be mistaken for a Western"), probably, Jack thought, before he had read the book. Jack and Joy liked *Bareface* as a title and thought it suggested the theme admirably, but Jack was remarkably humble in taking the advice of the publisher on the subject. After much thought he suggested *Till We Have Faces*. The phrase comes from a speech of Orual at the beginning of the last chapter. The Fox has just told her that the whole art of words is to say what you really mean. She replies:

> A glib saying. When the time comes to you at which you will be forced at last to utter the speech which has lain at the centre of your soul for years, which you have, all that time, idiot-like, been saying over and over, you'll not talk about joy of words. I saw well why the Gods do not speak to us openly, nor let us answer. Till that words can be dug out of us, why should they hear the babble that we think we mean? How can they meet us face to face until we have faces?"[2]

When the book came out in September 1956 in England and in the following January in the United States, it sold surprisingly poorly, perhaps because of the unattractive title. Yet it had been favorably reviewed, although often found difficult. An American reviewer, Anthony Boucher, described it as "a masterwork," and

Jack's "major work to date . . . as a story, as a fantasy, as a study in human psychology, as a grappling with spiritual dilemmas, above all as work of art this book is magic."[3] *The Times Literary Supplement* treated it as a profound allegory. *The New York Times Book Review* stated that "love is quite literally given wings again."[4]

No myth wears its meaning on its sleeve. Different interpretations of *Till We Have Faces* are to be expected. In this case interpretation is made more difficult by the construction, which is that of a perfect periodic sentence. The meaning is not apparent until almost the end. (Perhaps the memory of the hundreds of times that he explained periodic sentences to his pupils had influenced Jack in the planning.)

The subject is love. All meanings of the word are illustrated from primitive carnality to divine love: affection, friendship, jealous love, the possessive love that turns to hatred if it does not get its own way, unselfish, sacrificial love, and mystical union. In particular there is a contrast between redeemed and unredeemed love. The setting is on the fringes of the Greek world among a people whose religion is still dominated by primitive superstition and animal sacrifice, though the influence of Greek rationalism is becoming important. There are none of the descriptions of scenery that are among the highlights of his other novels, for nature does not much interest Orual. Her concern is with rites (the temple of Ungit is wonderfully vivid) and above all with people.

Some, like Humphrey Carpenter, think of Orual as a self-portrait, supposing that the hearty manly mask that Jack wore brought him success but made it difficult for him to understand himself or to express his deeper feelings.[5] No matter how much he talked, and prayed, underneath he often felt himself at the mercy of anger and other negative and antisocial emotions.

Some, who knew Joy better than I, think that Joy has much in common with Orual. But there is no sense in considering which of the two she resembles most—we all of us have some of Orual in us. We too may have seen our love for someone turn to something near to hatred when we cannot possess the person we think we love. We may have known the feeling of resentment when the person we love is swept away by a faith or a vocation that we cannot share or even understand. Similarly we can be helped, as perhaps Jack and Joy were, toward self-knowledge and an understanding of the nature of love by meditating on the book. Perhaps Jack, through writing it, liberated himself from painful obsessions, confusions, and inhibitions. It was a preparation for a complete and successful marriage.

Jack sometimes said that he thought *Till We Have Faces* was his best novel, and sometimes he thought *Perelandra* was. But the two are so different that it is pointless to compare them. If *Till We Have Faces* were published anonymously, few would recognize it as being written by C. S. Lewis. Style and characterization as well as subject are quite different, but both are masterpieces, two of the most profound novels written in this century.[6]

In *Till We Have Faces* Affection, Friendship, Eros, and Charity are depicted in action; in *The Four Loves* they are analyzed. This book had a curious origin. In 1957 Jack was asked by a Christian organization called the Episcopal Radio-TV Foundation of Atlanta, Georgia, to make some tape recordings for broadcasting in the United States. They could be on any subject of his choice, but of course the foundation would want to know for programming and advance publicity what the subjects would be. He discussed the invitation with Joy and chose a subject of which his mind at the time was full. He wrote to Dr. H. I. Louttit, the bishop of South Florida who was acting as intermediary, that he had chosen as the subjects of his talks the four loves:

storge, philia, eros, and *agape.* It seemed to him that this would "bring in nearly the whole of Christian ethics."[7] But he found the writing rather laborious, so the scripts for the talks were not finished until the summer of 1958. The actual recording was done on August 19 and 20 in a London studio. Mrs. Caroline Rakestraw, executive director of the Radio-TV Foundation, flew over to supervise it and to take the tapes back to America. Jack said that he was far less happy and confident during this recording than in the broadcasts of fifteen years before.

Once the tapes were in the United States, the Radio-TV Foundation launched a really big publicity campaign. I do not suggest that there was any intention to deceive, but certainly many of Jack's admirers had the impression that he was coming in person to deliver a series of broadcasts. Several letters expressing rapturous delight at the prospect arrived at the Kilns. Then came the surprise. The tapes were not going to be broadcast widely at all because they were apparently too frank for some sectors of the American public. Certain bishops of the church in America had listened to the tapes or read the transcripts and, it seems, disapproved. These would shock many American Christians. Mrs. Rakestraw and a friend came over to explain this to Jack. Although astonished and indignant at the time, he later enjoyed telling the story of their meeting.

Mrs. Rakestraw said, "The trouble, Professor Lewis, is that you have several times brought sex into your talks on *Eros.*"

He replied, "My dear Mrs. Cartwheel, how can anyone talk about *Eros* without bringing it in?"

Of course, I burst out laughing. "Was her name really Mrs. Cartwheel?"

"I can't remember. But whatever it was, I don't think I got it right. The woman she was with had a name like Clara Bootlace. They were very nice. But isn't it incredible that the inhabitants of a country so used to every sort of pornography should object to my most circumspect discussion of married love? The wonder is that many admirable Christian people manage to live there."

"What's going to happen?"

"I don't know. I said that I wasn't going to alter the talks or do them again. She said that she would go back and try to get them accepted."

And so it turned out. They were never broadcast widely at all, but twelve years later *Four Talks on Love*, an album by C. S. Lewis, was put on sale. The recordings are not an impressive performance. For one thing, they are spoken too fast. For another, they sound like they are being read. There is little of the admirable broadcasting technique of years before, which made every listener feel personally addressed. We never feel that he is talking directly to us.

It was agreed that he should be free to use the radio script as the basis of a book. He completed this by midsummer 1959, and it was published in March 1960 as *The Four Loves*. There are important differences between the text of the book and that of the talks, always to the advantage of the book. It was favorably reviewed in the United States, and no one seems to have been the least surprised or shocked by the treatment of sex. Edmund Fuller, writing in the *Chicago Sunday Tribune*, spoke for many when he described it as "extremely good and fresh, often funny, on the troubled issue of Eros."[8] Father Martin d'Arcy hailed it as "a minor classic": "Lewis combines a novelist's insight into motives with a profound religious understanding of our human nature."[9]

Several reviewers wrote as if they did not realize that *The Four Loves* was more than anything else a religious and apologetic work. The fact that God is love, and genuine gift-love is most likely to occur in men and women who are close to Him, is one of the main themes. Another is that love "begins to be a demon the moment he begins to be a god." All the lower forms of love (affection, friendship, and *eros*) can be and often are distorted by need or selfishness. This will often happen if the individual is not at the same time concerned with a higher form of love, his or her relationship with God.

The most personal and, for those who knew Jack, the most interesting section is that on friendship. It is plainly based on his own experience with friends such as Arthur Greeves and Owen Barfield.

He may well have been thinking of his relationship with Joy when he wrote that a friendship between two people of different sexes who "discover that they are on the same secret road" may very easily pass, even in the first half-hour, into "erotic love." Indeed, that is almost certain to happen unless they find each other physically repulsive or "have loves elsewhere."[10]

How characteristic is the word *secret*. Jack never ceased to be secretive. How many of this Oxford friends even knew of the existence of Arthur Greeves? To how many was his relationship with Joy a great surprise? Who knew that he and Joy were on the same secret road? Surprising too is his comment, ". . . [W]e do not want to know our friend's affairs at all. . . . You become a man's friend without knowing or caring whether he is married or single or how he earns his living." This was true for him. No man was less likely than Jack to ask personal questions of his friends. Nor did he care for the company of a man or woman who tried to probe him about his own private life. Such a one would not have been a friend.

Jack describes vividly the golden delights of the best of his walks. After a hard day's walking, the four or five friends come to their inn. With their slippers on, they sit in front of the blazing fire, their drinks at their elbows. Then as they talk, "the whole world, and something beyond the world, opens itself to our minds. . . . Affection mellowed by the years enfolds us. Life—natural life—has no better gift to give."[11]

He is amusing on the cultivated woman who tries to bring her husband up to her own cultural level: "It often does surprisingly little harm. The middle-aged male has great powers of passive resistance and (if she but knew) of indulgence: 'Women will have their fads.'"[12]

Friendship he tells us "is the sort of love one can imagine between angels." "The survival of Christianity depended on it." "The little pockets of early Christians survived because they cared exclusively for the love of 'the brethren.'"[13] And at the end of the section: "Christ . . . can truly say to every group of Christian friends, 'You have not chosen one another but I have chosen you for one another.' . . . It is the instrument by which God reveals to each the beauties of all the others."[14] Because he believed this, Jack regarded his friendships as friendships for life.

The conviction of the usefulness of *The Four Loves* toward an understanding of the psychology and value of love has grown steadily among the leaders of different Christian churches. Thus for some years quotations from it have been appearing in the sermons and addresses of Pope John Paul II. In an interview with Walter Hooper, the Holy Father, who had read with admiration several of Jack's works, spoke of it as one of his favorite books.

Reflections on the Psalms, published in 1958, was Jack's first religious work since *Miracles* (1947) and the humiliation that he thought he had received from argument with Elisabeth Anscombe. It was suggested to him by his friend, the theologian Austin Farrer, at a time when he was barren of ideas for a book and worried by Joy's illness and his own poor health. Farrer assured him that there was a great need for a book dealing with the things that worried people when they read the Psalms. Joy warmly supported the idea and offered to edit and type the book, if she was well enough. Much of it was discussed with her and Austin Farrer during the long vacation of 1957. In a letter to Arthur Greeves dated November 27, Jack wrote: "I have been writing nothing but academic work except for a very unambitious little work on the Psalms, wh. is now finished and ought to come out next spring."

He was correcting the proofs in the spring, but, in fact, it did not come out until the autumn of 1958. Such was Jack's popularity at the time that in Great Britain alone no less than 11,000 copies were sold before publication, in those days a very large number for a religious hardback.

However the first reviews were tepid. The book was attacked for not being a work of scholarship. Yet in the introduction he had stated that it was not meant to be: "I write as one amateur to another, talking about difficulties I have met, or lights that I have gained. . . . I am comparing notes, not presuming to instruct." He was sure most of the reviewers hadn't even read the introduction.

The first few short chapters deal with those aspects of the Psalms that repel modern readers: the way they welcome the day of judgment; the frequent cursings and their delight in the slaughter of the enemies of Israel; the lack of any belief in a life after death; and their self-righteousness. He is clear and helpful on these stumbling blocks, but probably better in the chapters that follow. He describes the pleasure that he personally gets from reading them. "The most valuable thing the psalms do for me is to express that same delight in God which made David dance."[15] He contrasts the pleasure one gets from them in church with "the merely dutiful church-going and laborious saying our prayers to which most of us are, thank God not always, reduced."[16] He enjoys their gusto or appetite for God. He writes of the beauty of God's law and the way in which the psalmists revel in it. He explains their attitude toward nature—they are practical farmers, but can rejoice in nature because they know that they, animals, and plants are all creations of the one God.

Though it is a very short book, there are a number of near digressions—one on the significance for Christians of the pagan myths, one on the risks of connivance with evil men, and one on marriage and sexual union as symbols of the union between Christ and the Church. The book ends with a discussion of the suitability of certain psalms for great feasts of the church such as Christmas, Whitsun, and the Ascension. There is an introduction on meter, structure, and form, and scattered throughout praise of the poetry, especially in Coverdale's translation.

He was delighted to be asked, not long after the publication of the book, to join the committee of seven that the Convocations of Canterbury and York were appointing to revise the translation of the Psalms that appeared in the Church of England's *Book of Common Prayer*. He was reticent about discussing what happened at committee meetings—I think he thought them confidential. He was surprised to find T. S. Eliot, his old "enemy," on the same committee, and pleased to discover that he now rather liked and respected him. A small number of revised psalms appeared in 1961, presumably to find out the reactions of churchgoers to the revision. The complete version appeared in 1963 as *The Revised Psalter*. This was not the end of Jack's scriptural work. He was consulted about various points of translation in the New Testament section of the New English Bible, which came out in 1961. The reason why he enjoyed meeting distinguished Biblical scholars was that he usually learned something from them. He would then pass the information, most often about a long-standing mistranslation, on to his friends.

Of all his books, *A Grief Observed* is the most personal and the one that tells us most about his relationship with Joy. After her death in July 1960, he felt both paralyzed and obsessed. He was unable to pray in his own words. He was reduced to repeating conventional or "infantile" prayers. He was quite unable to write. No ideas came; certainly no pictures. He was obsessed by thinking of Joy and their life together. But he realized the dangers of this—it could become a blockage to his spiritual development. To liberate himself, he did what he had done in the past—he wrote a book about it, a book that is very short and desperately truthful. It is not fiction at all. In it he is trying to understand himself and the nature of his feelings. It is analytical, cool, and clinical.

He describes clinically the state of anxiety in which he found himself after Joy's death. Through understanding his state he becomes better able to control it. He feels Joy gradually slipping away from him. But after the pain of the most intense grief has been dulled, he recovers her. She is now in a way more real to him than in life. He is now in contact with her essence. He believed that bereavement is a normal and inevitable part of the experience of love that is felt by the dead as well as by the living. It follows marriage normally. It is a phase of marriage, "not the interruption of the dance, but the next figure." "We are taken out of ourselves," raised to a higher level of consciousness, "by the loved one while she is here." In this tragic part of the dance, "we must learn still to be taken out of ourselves though the bodily presence is withdrawn, to love the very Her. . . ."[17]

This mystical experience of knowing and loving the Her, the essence of Joy, was his on and off for the rest of his life. It is quite different from remembering her as she was. It is not an enshrining; it is a developing spiritual marriage. Somehow it reopens to him his relationship with God and deepens his faith. He can think of her good qualities and turn from her to Him who made her.

In a beautiful passage he likens her to "a nest of gardens wall within wall, hedge within hedge, more secret, more full of fragrant and fertile life, the further you entered. . . . Then up from the garden to the Gardener . . . to the life-giving Life and the Beauty that makes beautiful."[18] In each case he must be prepared for shocks and surprises, for he relates to potent realities, not to his static ideas of Joy and of God.

He was surprised one night by an experience of Joy that was "just the impression of her *mind* momentarily facing my own." There was no emotion. Instead "there was an extreme and cheerful intimacy." This led to a sort of spring cleaning in his mind. Perhaps it has helped him to see that there is no practical problem for him at all. "I know the two great commandments and I'd better get on with them."[19]

The book is so intimate and personal that it had to be published pseudonymously or anonymously. He would have found unbearable the correspondence that would have followed publication under his own name. It was published only because he thought it might perhaps help others who had suffered bereavement, a hope in my experience that was justified. The firm chosen for the publication was Faber and Faber, probably because T. S. Eliot was one of its directors and was probably in on the secret of its authorship. Of his friends, as far as I know, only Green knew of it. When he gave me a copy, because he thought it might help my wife who had just lost her father, he said, "It is by a man I know." I had no doubt of the identity of the pseudonym, N. W. Clerk, for I knew that he had published poems under the initials N. W. There was a perceptive review in *The Times Literary Supplement,* but few copies of the book were sold until it was reissued under his own name in 1964.

A handful of good poems, the best that he had written since *The Pilgrim's Regress*, were directly inspired by Joy. They were published a year after his death in a volume edited by Walter Hooper and titled *Poems*. Most of the poems in the book are ones he wrote for publication in *Punch, The Spectator, The Month, Time and Tide, The Oxford Magazine,* and *The Cambridge Review* in the 1940s and 1950s. All are short, many are light, and some are humorous. He had long ago given up his early ambition of achieving fame as a poet. Quite apart from the fact that he disliked and did not want to write in the free verse manner still dominant, he felt that he no longer had the power. The verses he now wrote were not carefully worked over. They were written in odd moments, in trains and during boring committee meetings. He did not rate them highly. Perhaps this is why they were published under the pseudonym "N.W.", an abbreviation of "Nat whilk" ("I do not know whom"). He was nevertheless delighted to find a market for them and particularly happy in his relationship with what he called "the club that runs *Punch*." "Almost the only literary honor I am tempted to covet," he once said to me, "is to be a member of that. It seems to be a luncheon or dining club as well as an editorial committee. I am sure that there would be good talk there."

Most of the other poems were found by Walter Hooper among his papers. Their range is considerable. There is an exquisite epitaph:

> *Lady, to this fair breast I know but one*
> *Fair rival; to the heart beneath it, none.*[20]

and the robustly witty:

> *Erected by her sorrowing brothers*
> *In memory of Martha Clay.*
> *Here lies one who lived for others;*
> *Now she has peace. And so have they.*[21]

There are the fine stanzas of *Infatuation*, a poem in the manner of *Dymer*. There's a magnificent late lyric, I think the fruit of his relationship with Joy:

> *Love's as warm as tears,*
> *Love is tears . . .* [22]

and the splendid sonnets, surely addressed to Joy, to which Walter Hooper has given the titles, "Joys That Sting," "Old Poet Remembered," and "As the Ruin Falls." These three poems, poignant and deeply felt, almost justify Thomas Howard's description of them in *Christianity Today* as "the glorious best of Lewis." [23]

22

Life After Joy

For about eleven months after Joy's death, Jack's way of living seemed outwardly to follow the pattern of previous years. He spent his academic terms at Cambridge, traveled home every weekend, and met his friends each Monday morning at the Lamb and Flag or Eagle and Child. But there were differences. He was more dependent on his friends than in the past and far more likely to accept their invitations. He did not often go to their houses because he did not really want to see their wives, but he enjoyed going out to lunch or dinner with them or for a drive in the country. He looked forward to his friends' visits in Cambridge or at the Kilns (where, as he would tell them, there was a choice of bedrooms and far more luxury than in the past). He was pleased when Roger Green left Cheshire to visit him and on the great occasion when Arthur Greeves came over from Belfast. On Sundays when Mrs. Miller was not there, Humphrey Havard often drove him out to Studley Priory for lunch. Sometimes he took the slow train to Cambridge, but more often he was taken there by Alfred Morris, his usual and favorite taxi driver.

His correspondence was now greater than ever. Warren wrote the routine letters, but during weekends Jack spent much time writing long personal letters to people who seemed in need of advice or help and to far-off friends. This arrangement worked only as long as Warren was sober. When he was drunk, Jack had to let the letters pile up.

At Cambridge he continued to write on academic subjects. In fact, in the months after Joy's death, he wrote one of his best books of literary criticism, *An Experiment in Criticism*. He had been discussing the subject with friends for years. As a working schoolmaster, I had often spoken to him of the importance of shielding students from literary criticism until they had made a personal response to the books they were studying. Some might be so dominated by the writings of literary critics that primary experience would be no longer possible for them. He said that the same thing was happening in the universities. Honors students and even those taking higher degrees tended more and more to see books "wholly through the spectacles of other books."[1] The system tended to be self-perpetuating. University students practiced evaluative criticism themselves, and taught their pupils to practice it, and on it went.

Then on one of his visits to Malvern he announced in some excitement that he had thought of a possible way out—to look at books from the reader's point of view. We discussed this for most of his stay, talking about good and bad readers, and the books that had enriched our own lives. A good reader is one who reads and rereads a book, fully entering into the experience and perhaps being permanently enriched or altered by it.

A little later we heard that he had written a short book on the subject. *An Experiment in Criticism* was not well reviewed in 1961, the year of its publication, but within five years it was referred to as "a now classic broadside." Though the least combative of Jack's critical books—he became notably gentler after Joy's death—it is the most influential. His respect for the actual tastes of readers and condemnation of critics who often do harm "by preventing many happy unions of a good reader with a good book," has attracted a considerable following, especially in America, and is already useful in moderating the influence of academic literary criticism.

The book ends with a most eloquent statement of a great critic's final view of the value of literature:

> Literature enlarges our being by admitting us to experiences not our own. They may be beautiful, terrible, awe-inspiring, exhilarating, pathetic, comic, or merely piquant. Literature gives the entree to them all. Those of us who have been true readers all our life seldom realize the enormous extension of our being that we owe to authors. We realize it best when we talk with an unliterary friend. He may be full of goodness and good sense but he inhabits a tiny world. In it, we should be suffocated. My own eyes are not enough for me. Even the eyes of all humanity are not enough. Very gladly would I learn what face things present to a mouse or bee.
>
> In reading great literature I become a thousand men and yet remain myself. Like the night sky in a Greek poem, I see with a thousand eyes, but it is still I who see. Here, as in worship, in love, in moral action, and in knowing, I transcend myself: and am never more myself than when I do.[2]

It was written at a time when he was suffering from intense grief, yet it shows no loss of power. His thesis is original and soberly presented. It reads like the work of a man at the height of his powers and who has an important and productive literary career ahead of him. So it might have been were it not for an event that took place in June 1961.

Even in his thirties, Jack was in the habit of passing water far more frequently than most men. He thought the reason was the large amount of beer and tea that he drank and the lack of early training. He liked to quote Montaigne, who wrote that, though he was an old man, he could stand all day without passing water. Warren might follow this remark with a discourse on how long courtiers were expected to stand in the presence of Louis XIV. Even his friend and doctor, Humphrey Havard, who was well aware of the habit, did not suspect a problem.

But early in June 1961, he noticed that he had difficulty in passing water. He felt no real pain, only slight discomfort. Although he began to feel unwell, he did not see a doctor, probably because he was looking forward to spending two days with Arthur Greeves, who planned to visit him on June 21 and 22. Arthur noted later that "he was looking very ill." After Arthur had gone back to Belfast, Jack saw Humphrey, who diagnosed a seriously enlarged prostate, booked a room for him at the Acland Nursing Home, and briefed a surgeon. In the meantime, Jack was shown how to use a catheter.

The surgeon soon came to the conclusion that Jack was not fit enough to withstand the operation. His kidneys were infected, and as a result he was suffering from toxemia, which caused, among other symptoms, cardiac irregularities. A semipermanent catheter was inserted, draining into a bag, and antibiotics prescribed. He was put on a low-calorie diet with a minimum of protein. He was told not to go to bed at night, but rather to sleep upright in a chair. When I visited him in September, he looked unwell. He must have been suffering a good deal of discomfort. The future seemed glum. He had been told that he could not go back to Cambridge for the autumn term. Nevertheless, he was wonderfully brave and cheerful. He told me that the doctors had told him not to smoke, but he was not going to obey them. "If I did, I know that I should be unbearably bad-tempered. What an infliction on my friends. Better to die cheerfully with the aid of a little tobacco, than to live disagreeably and remorseful without."

He never lost his sense of humor. Indeed, the worse he became, the more he valued this quality as one of the greatest of God's gifts. Thus, during the following months, when his kidney trouble became acute and he had to go to the Acland Nursing Home for blood transfusions, he wrote: "For the first time I feel some sympathy with Dracula. He must have led a miserable life."[3] But a gradual improvement in his condition came in January 1962 and seemed to continue until July 1963.

His great consolations were his religious experiences, his feeling of closeness to Joy, and his reading. He read voluminously. When I visited him in January, he said that he had just reread Ruskin's *Praeterita* and for the first time had gone right through *Modern Painters*. He commented to me that "there is no writer who achieves so perfectly the synthesis of the scientific with the poetic or romantic. Some of his descriptions of nature are the most satisfying that I know." He had also "reread *The Prelude* for the umpteenth time," he said, adding, "I find that I mind the dull stretches less and find the bad patches less frequent." He warmly welcomed visitors, especially if they were old friends who had cars and could take him for a drive. He still wrote a few letters, but Warren, who was having a sober year, in spite of being denied his Irish summer holiday, efficiently handled most of his correspondence at this time.

Jack never quite stopped writing. He now spent a good deal of time compiling or revising his texts, "Did you ever go to my *Prolegomenon to Mediaeval Studies?*" he asked me. "I'm making a book out of the lectures. It'll be a good deal shorter. People in Cambridge can't stand a great deal of that sort of thing." And: "I'm getting a good deal of fun putting together various talks, lectures, and sermons that I have been asked to give at various times. I now wish I had been more careful about keeping papers. I seem to have lost one or two of the best, and I'm not sure how many of the others are worth printing." Again: "What do you think of *A Slip of the Tongue* as a title for a book of talks and papers? Almost the most difficult part of a book is finding a title that will satisfy one's friends *and* the publisher." He said that he was not writing anything new, that the power and the pictures in the mind had gone. Perhaps they would come back with improving health, but he doubted that he would ever be really well again. He was not unhappy. In fact, much of the time he enjoyed being an invalid.

By April he had recovered sufficiently to be able to return to Cambridge. I drove him there one Monday, and for fun we stopped on the outskirts of the Duke of Bedford's great Woburn estate and entered the woods by a small gate. Almost nervously law-abiding, he was rather unwilling to do this because it was marked "Private," but I assured him that trespassing was no crime in English law, that the trespasser must simply leave when asked to and could only be sued for any damage done. We walked with some hesitation along a narrow path through a wood and suddenly found ourselves in a glade surrounded by a number of miniature deer. Jack was entranced. "You know, while I was writing the Narnia books, I never imagined anything as lovely as this," he said. We sat on a fallen tree trunk, and Jack gazed radiantly at the elegant little animals and adored the God who had created them. "Pure white magic," he said when we had returned to the car. "Wonderful. I never even thought of wanting to smoke."

On another occasion, I drove him back from Cambridge, again via Woburn. We went in through the same private gate, but there were no deer this time. "Well," said Jack, "as I found once before, you can't expect the same miracle twice."

His health continued to improve, but he began to realize that he would probably never be well enough for the prostate surgery.

Because of difficulties with what he called "the plumbing," he underwent a minor operation and had to go to the Acland quite often for checkups. Nevertheless, he seemed almost fully himself again by the spring of 1963. He was as amusing and full of fun as he had ever been, and as witty. But he was also now more tolerant than he had ever been. There had been times in the past when David and Douglas had, according to Paxford, "reduced him to tears." Now I heard a good deal to their credit.

Supposing that Jack was well enough to be left on his own, Warren planned to leave in June for his Irish holiday. Jack suggested to Douglas that they should go together to Ireland at the end of July. Douglas would act as porter, carrying the luggage. They would meet Arthur Greeves and go off together to the seaside, either in Arthur's car, or, if Arthur did not feel well enough to drive, in a hired car. It seems that Arthur thought it would be too exhausting to go to Donegal, as they had done before Jack's illness. Instead, they would go to a small place on the north coast. Arrangements were not easy to make because berths on the cross-channel boats and beds in the Irish seaside hotels were usually booked up four or five months in advance. "How difficult it is to do anything," Jack wrote to Arthur.[4] But arrangements were eventually made.

When I met him late in June, he seemed well but very easily tired. He took a long rest each afternoon, went to bed early, and was slow in going upstairs. Nevertheless, he was looking forward to the Irish holiday. He was convinced that he had what he called a "weak" or "groggy" heart, but when I asked Humphrey about it, I was told that the heart symptoms were still those of renal failure. Jack had permanently damaged his kidneys by "sitting on a prostate" two years before. He would need to live with great care for the rest of his life.

But in the second week of July, he became breathless and

unsteady on his feet. Humphrey asked the Acland to take him in
for a blood transfusion. Walter Hooper visited him at the Kilns
on July 15 and found him looking exceedingly ill, hardly able to
sit up or hold a teacup. On the following day, he was admitted
into the Acland, where he had a heart attack at about five o'clock
and went into a coma. It was thought that he was dying. The next
morning, his theologian friend Reverend Austin Farrer and his
wife, Kay, who had been close friends of Joy's, prayed by his bed-
side. At two o'clock, the Reverend Michael Watts, a curate at the
Church of Saint Mary Magdalen, gave him the sacrament of
extreme unction. Just after he had been anointed, an extraordinary thing happened. He awoke from his coma, opened his eyes,
and asked for a cup of tea. He supposed that it was early morning and that he had just awakened from a good night's sleep. He
looked and felt refreshed, his heart was steadier, and for the time
being he seemed out of danger.

But there was one restriction that made him miserable. When
I called on him three days later, I found him standing up nervously. He was wearing pajamas and a dressing gown. He walked
forward, clutched me, and said, "Thank God, a friend. You see
a dying man. For God's sake, and as you value our friendship, go
and get me some cigarettes and matches. And don't, on any
account, let them see you bring them in. I did as he asked, intend-
ing to let him have only one cigarette out of the pack. He smoked
it greedily, inhaling deeply. He then said that he had been made
Charles Williams's literary executor. Because of the attitude of
Mrs. Williams, this was giving him a lot of trouble. Charles had
left unpublished a manuscript of the very greatest importance,
and it was his duty to prepare it for publication. The trouble was,
he said, that Mrs. Williams would not let him have the
manuscript unless he paid her £10,000. She kept it under her

mattress. There would have to be a lawsuit if he were to get possession of it.

I did not know what to make of this, until he made a reference to Mrs. Moore as if she were still living, and I saw that he was suffering from delusions. He then asked me if I had met Walter Hooper. "I've engaged him as my secretary," he said. "I want you to like him. I want all my friends to like him. He is a young American. Very devoted and charming. He is almost too anxious to please, but no fool. Certainly not a fool. I must have someone in the house when I go home. Warnie has deserted me and David and Douglas have gone away. There will be hundreds of letters. I must have a secretary."

I was not quite sure that Walter Hooper was a real person, but I readily agreed that he must have a secretary. When I next visited him at the Acland, Humphrey assured me that Walter was real and said that he was very glad about his existence. He could not have agreed to Jack's going back to the Kilns unless someone else was there with him at night.

On this visit, Jack talked about Warren. "I have not had a word from him since he went to Ireland, except a note from the hospital at Drogheda to say that they had taken him in, as usual, drunk. I don't suppose he reads any letters. How am I to let him know what has happened to me?"

I volunteered to go to Ireland and try to get Warren to come back. But I found that Warren was not at the hospital of Our Lady of Lourdes at Drogheda during the day, or at least during the day on which I called. He was in Dublin. I discussed his alcoholism with the sister in charge and with his doctor, who told me that he was free to do what he liked during the day but had to be back in time for an evening meal at the hospital. "Sure, this keeps him from damaging his health. It's gently that does it. As usual, he'll be fighting fit by sometime in September."

At present, they said, he was not fit to travel, and he would certainly drink himself insensible if he were told that his brother was dangerously ill. They did not think that he knew much about what had happened to Jack in Oxford because he had not opened any letters with Oxford postmarks. They undertook to break it to him gently so that by the time he was fit to travel, he would know about Jack's coma. And that was how I left it.

The nuns were plainly very fond of him. The Warren they knew seemed rather different from the Warren we knew in Oxford. "Very devout in a simple way," one sister said. "Certainly a Catholic in the heart," said another. "If it had not been for his brother, he would be a full practicing member of the church," said still another, who thought that at one time or another he had made a confession to the convent chaplain. I was surprised to hear that he had gone as far as this.

The hospital was a curiously happy place. Warren had often said to me, "If you know you are going to have an operation or a serious illness, go there at once, and you'll enjoy it." Certainly it was his spiritual and happiest physical home.

Jack was disappointed that I did not bring Warren back with me. "Deserted!" he said. "I thank God that Walter Hooper is going to go on helping with the letters. They say that I shall have to have a nurse for a few days when I go home." And he did have a nurse, Alec Ross, in case he should be taken ill at night when he went back to the Kilns early in August. He now slept on the ground floor and lived a very quiet life.

He usually had a good night's sleep—the toxemia that had resulted from the renal failure tended to make him drowsy. In the morning, he spent most of his time writing letters with Walter Hooper, who proved to be an admirable secretary. Lunch was cooked and served by Mrs. Miller, who also did the housework. Although he was supposed to be on a low-protein diet, he appeared to eat a lot of high-protein foods, such as chicken, cheese, and eggs. After lunch he usually took a nap until about four, when he had a cup of tea. Then he read or wrote until dinner time. He went to bed at about ten o'clock. Although his doctors had advised him to quit, he was still smoking in September and October. They would probably have also disapproved, had they known, of the large quantities of strong tea that he drank. Unfortunately, he was as addicted to tea as to tobacco.

Although he seemed to be recovering in September, he did not expect to live long. He wrote to Cambridge early in August resigning his professorship of medieval and Renaissance literature and his fellowship at Magdalene College. His books were sent from Cambridge and piled on the floor or pressed into the already crowded shelves at the Kilns. Partly to make room for them, and partly to give mementos to his friends, he took some of us into a room that had been turned into a second library and asked us to choose a book. It was a poignant moment. Unfortunately, I made the embarrassing mistake of asking for the *Unspoken Sermons* of George MacDonald. He remarked a little sadly, "Well, that's three books." I hastily withdrew my choice and asked to be allowed to have something else.

Late in September, Walter Hooper had to go to the United States to wind up his affairs there and to teach for one more term before coming back to act as Jack's permanent secretary. There was a short gap between his departure and Warren's arrival from Ireland, a few days during which Jack felt lonely and depressed. Would Warren show up, or would he really have to spend his dying days without the company and consolation of the person who was almost a wayward wife to him, his brother and best friend?

Jack now spent his days rereading some of his favorite books: the *Odyssey* and *Iliad* and a little Plato in Greek; the *Aeneid* in

Latin; Dante's *Divine Comedy;* Wordsworth's *The Prelude;* and works by George Herbert, Patmore, Scott, Austen, Fielding, Dickens, and Trollope.

Warren did return, but it was painful and difficult for him to accept the role of companion, secretary, and nurse to his slowly dying Smallpigiebotham. They had seen little of each other for many years. Now, at last, they were again companions. "The wheel had come full circle," Warren wrote. "Again we were together in a new 'little end room,' shutting out from our talk the ever-present knowledge that as in the Black years of Belsen, the holidays were drawing swiftly to a close and a new term fraught with unknown possibilities awaited both of us."[5]

They talked of the past, "cheerfully reminiscent, but not such as will bear repetition for it was only of long-forgotten incidents in our shared past. When such were recalled the old Jack, whimsical, witty, laughter-loving, would for a minute or two come back to life again and we would be almost gay together. In fact, these were more often than not pleasant days, for as the end drew nearer, more and more did we recapture our old schoolboy technique of extracting the utmost from the last dregs of our holidays. It was only when I went to bed that the horrible fear recurred each night—shall I find him alive in the morning?"[6]

"Don't think I am not happy," Jack wrote in a letter. "I am re-reading the *Iliad* and enjoying it more than I have ever done."[7] And in another letter he wrote, "Yes, autumn is really the best of the seasons: and I'm not sure that old age isn't the best part of life. But, of course, like autumn it doesn't last."[8]

One fine autumn afternoon, I drove him along the London Road, up Beacon Hill to the crest of the Chilterns, then along the crest past Christmas Common. The beech trees had colored marvelously, and, although the sun was shining, there was that slight sharpness in the air that he loved and described in some of the most moving passages of his books. We stopped, opened the windows of the car, and he gazed, rapt. He was praying, praising God, and adoring nature's beauty. He got out of the car once and said, "I'd like to take more of the air." Then he said, "I think I might have my last soak of the year," and he sat on a fallen tree and smoked a cigarette. We came back along country roads through Garsington and Chistlehampton. The light was fading, and the moon and a bright star were rising. We stopped again and gazed. I said, "Venus or Hesperus."

He quoted in Greek an epitaph of Plato's, and when I asked him to translate, quoted (or slightly misquoted) Shelley:

> *Thou wert my morning star among the living,*
> *Ere thy fair light had fled;*
> *Now, having died, thou art as Hesperus giving*
> *New splendour to the dead.*[9]

When I saw him for the last time in the middle of November, he was far less well. I think he had gotten up especially in order to have lunch with me and found it a great strain. His face was ominously puffy. He no longer smoked, but several times helped himself instead to some boiled sweets that were on the table. After lunch he fell asleep, and I tiptoed quietly away. This was the last time I saw him.

Roger Green spent the night of November 15 at the Kilns and was worried at the way Jack kept falling asleep after dinner, "and for alarming intervals apparently ceasing to breathe at all."[10] Not surprisingly, when he left next morning, he had the feeling that he would not see Jack alive again. Nevertheless, on Monday, November 18, Jack seemed much better, well enough to be driven to the Lamb and Flag for the usual Monday morning Inklings meeting.

During the next few days, Warren noticed that his brother

was finding it difficult to keep awake, even at times of the day when he was normally active. He does not seem to have realized that this was a danger signal, a sign that his brother was suffering from uremia, a result of his renal insufficiency. He did not, therefore, phone the doctor or take any action. Warren has recounted the events of November 22:

> [F]inding him asleep in his armchair after lunch, I suggested that he would be more comfortable in bed. He agreed and went there. After four o'clock I took him in his tea and had a few words with him, finding him thick in his speech, very drowsy, but calm and cheerful. It was the last time we ever spoke to each other.
>
> At five thirty I heard a crash in his bedroom, and running in, found him lying unconscious at the foot of the bed. He ceased to breathe some three or four minutes after. The following Friday would have been his sixty-fourth birthday.

On the same day, President Kennedy was shot in Dallas, and Aldous Huxley died in California. The worldwide shock of the former event meant that Jack's death was only briefly reported. Perhaps this explains why few people came to his funeral at Headington Quarry Church on November 26. They were nearly all close personal friends. I remember Barfield, Harwood, Tolkien, Colin Hardie, Lawlor, Peter Bayley, Maureen and Leonard Blake, Douglas, David, the Millers, and Paxford.

Warren was not there. He could not bear to face the funeral or life without his beloved SPB. He escaped in his usual way, lying in bed all that day, more or less unconscious. In the absence of any blood relative, Maureen, David, and Douglas followed the coffin out of the church.

We clustered around to see the coffin lowered into the grave. It was the sort of day Jack would have appreciated, cold but sunlit. It was also very still. A lighted church candle was placed on the coffin, and its flame did not flicker. For more than one of us, that clear, bright candle flame seemed to symbolize Jack. He had been the light of our lives, ever steadfast in friendship. Yet, most of all, the candle symbolized his unflagging pursuit of illumination.

Afterward, Barfield invited a few of us into the house and then into the common room for the reading of the will. I think the old-fashioned side of Jack would have appreciated the formal way in which it was done. The executors were named as Arthur Owen Barfield and Alfred Cecil Harwood. They were also appointed trustees of the estate. After a few legacies, all the remaining assets were left in trust for the completion of the education of David and Douglas, then in trust to Warren for life, and after his death, to David and Douglas. The value of the estate was given later in the probate as £37,772 net. It was so little because during his lifetime Jack had given away most of his literary earnings. And, of course, he had been only the life tenant of the Kilns.

The one surprise was the size of the legacy to Paxford, a mere £100. "Well, it won't take me far, wull it?" Paxford said. "Mr. Jack, 'e never 'ad no idea of money. 'Is mind was always set on 'igher things."

AFTERWORD

This biography was first published in 1988. Since then the readership of C. S. Lewis's books (over a million and a half copies sold every year) and interest in him as a man have continued to increase. Any book about him gives rise to an almost embarrassing amount of correspondence. One of the things I am going to try to do in this short introduction is to answer some of the questions that I am often asked.

Since Lewis throughout his academic life attacked what he called "the personal heresy" (the idea that the study of a writer's private life is valuable either in itself or in helping us to understand and appreciate his books), it is sad to have to record that most of the questions are about the man.

There is more interest than ever in Lewis's relationship with Joy Gresham. I see no reason at all to modify my account of it. In his biography of Lewis, A. N. Wilson presents us with the idea that the relationship was consummated before the Christian marriage in the Churchill Hospital. This is a most serious charge. If it is true, it destroys Jack's credibility as an honest man and a Christian moralist. For Lewis not only taught and believed that sexual intercourse outside marriage was utterly wrong for the Christian, he told his brother and a few of his closest friends (I had the honor to be among them) that the registry office marriage was a formality to enable Joy to stay permanently in England and that any living together as man and wife was out of the question.

All of us who knew him had no doubt that he was an honest man who practiced what he preached.

To support his theory of Lewis's adultery, Wilson tells us that Douglas Gresham in an oral interview taped at Wheaton College states that in 1955, when he was only eight, he surprised his mother and Lewis in a compromising position in her bedroom. But Gresham has stated in writing that he never made this statement, and I have it on his authority and on that of the former curator of the Wade Center, Lyle Dorsett, that the statement is not on the tape or in the typescript that was made from it.

Wilson also uses to support his theory the account given in this book of a conversation I had with Dr. Humphrey Havard years later soon after the publication of the Green-Hooper biography. I asked Dr. Havard if he thought the marriage had been consummated. Dr. Havard recollected that some time after the Christian marriage, Lewis asked him if it was possible for a man of his age and state of health to have sexual intercourse. Wilson quite without justification places the conversation before the Christian marriage. But in my account I make it quite clear that the conversation took place in 1958, a year after the marriage in the Churchill Hospital. Lewis would never have asked Havard after the marriage about his ability to have sexual intercourse if he had been having intercourse with her before. Wilson also quotes a statement made by Father Bide who performed the ceremony of Christian marriage in the hospital: "Joy desperately wanted to solemnize her marriage before God and to claim the grace of the sacrament before she died." But this does not mean, as he supposes, that, smitten with guilt because of her adultery, she had not been receiving the sacrament of the Eucharist. It means rather that she desired to receive another sacrament, that of matrimony. It therefore offers no support for Wilson's theory. His theory is also psychologically improbable. If they had been living as man and wife after the registry office marriage, Joy, a strong self-assertive character, would never have tolerated the situation. She would have clamored for her rights and insisted on being given her proper status as Mrs. C. S. Lewis.

Wilson and some other recent writers on C. S. Lewis have presented him as a rather unhappy, introspective, guilt-ridden creature, obsessed with sadomasochistic fantasies, who often sought relief from his inner conflicts and uncertainties in over-dogmatic faith, in bullying argument and at times even in heavy drinking and bawdy talk.

I do not think that anyone who knew him holds such a view. Indeed I should not recognize such a character as the C. S. Lewis I knew for twenty-nine years. The sexual fantasies were only a problem for him in the early part of his life. Overcoming them was one of the blessings he owed to his conversion. "That sort of thought," he once said, "can be fairly easily overcome by prayer and fasting."

I agree with his friend Owen Barfield that in his maturity he was not introspective at all. He was usually cheerful and took a spontaneous, almost boyish delight in many things. He was great fun, an extremely witty and amusing companion. He was courteous and considerate to those he was with and seemed more concerned with the welfare of his friends than with himself.

Although he enjoyed lively hammer-and-tongs argument, and in the heat of the argument could be insensitive to the feelings of others, I never knew him to bully. He would often refrain from attacking a man whom he thought could not stand up to him. I will give one example. He went to a lecture by the well-known poet and critic (Sir) Herbert Read, with whose ideas he strongly disagreed. I invited him to meet Read afterwards over a glass of port or a cup of tea. I expected a lively argument. But there was nothing, only pleasant small talk. "I didn't say what I thought," he said later, "because I thought he looked unwell. It would have been unfair."

I did not much care for his end-of-term parties, but in my day they were not, as Wilson states, events at which the object was to get drunk. Nor do I remember obscenities. It was hard to be much in Lewis's company without being aware of his goodness, even holiness. It was nourished by prayer—he meditated daily on verses from the New Testament—by his openness to mystical experience, and his habit of communing with nature. He took his religious duties seriously, though without ever losing his glorious sense of humor. As one of these duties:

> . . . *Christes lore, and his apostles twelve,*
> *He taughte, and first he folwed it himselve.*

Wilson's book on Lewis shows the influence of modern Freudian psychology. David Holbrook's *The Skeleton in the Wardrobe* goes much further in this direction. Indeed it includes something not far from a full-scale psychological study of *The Lion, the Witch and the Wardrobe*. Holbrook does not like Lewis or believe in the spiritual world and religious realities that Lewis writes about. To him the "other world" is the world of the unconscious. Many of the elements of the children's stories are derived from events in Lewis's early life, such as the loss of his mother, his supposed hatred of his father, his cruel and sadistic prep school headmaster, and his own sadistic fantasies during adolescence. Thus according to Holbrook, the wardrobe represents the womb, and the passage through it the journey into the dead world where the mother has gone. Since Lewis himself is immature and perverted, the Narnia stores are likely to have a bad influence on children. The characters set up for their admiration are cruel, authoritarian, belligerent, and sexist. Perhaps the most important thing to say about Holbrook's attack on Lewis is that he fails to take into account or even to understand or believe in Lewis's spiritual development. As I have shown in this book, Jack was psychologically wounded as an adolescent and young man. But he went through a process of conversion that altered him radically, so that in his maturity he practiced none of the vices mentioned by Holbrook.

But whatever he was as a man is irrelevant to the reader of his books, as irrelevant as the private life of Wagner is to the enjoyment and understanding of *Die Meistersinger*. "By their fruits ye shall know them." The Narnia stories have been read by millions of children and are firmly established as classics. Where are those who have been corrupted or in any way damaged by reading them? The stories were written to be read with delight by children, not taught and analyzed by academics. Grown-ups sometimes object to the amount of moralizing—children never.

Some people have read or been told that Lewis lost his faith after the death of Joy. This idea may have come from *Shadowlands*, an excellent short biography of Lewis by Brian Sibley which contains a particularly full treatment of his relationship with Joy. The same title was used for a most successful play and for a film, both mainly about the life together of Jack and Joy. Many people who have seen the film have been left with the impression that, as a result of Joy's death, Jack lost his faith in God.

Brian Sibley is in no sense to be blamed for this. In fact, he provides a simple and clear account of what actually happened. Lewis suffered intense and paralyzing grief after Joy's death. He found it impossible to believe in the goodness of God or perhaps in any God at all except a cruel and even sadistic one. "What chokes every prayer and every hope is the memory of all the prayers we offered and all the false hopes we had." Then gradually he began to realize that he and Joy in their praying were telling God what to do; they were putting themselves first. In the exercise book in which he described these experiences he wrote: "These notes have been about myself, and about Joy, and about God, in that order. The order and the proportions are exactly what they ought not to have been."

This realization gradually altered his spiritual life and opened the way to a new relationship with God. The fact that God gave no answer to his questions about the reasons for his misery did not mean that He was uncaring. It was "a rather special sort of 'No answer' . . . more like a silent, certainly not uncompassionate gaze. As though He shook His head, not in refusal, but waiving the question. Like, 'Peace child; you don't understand.'"

Gradually Jack's attitude to bereavement altered so that he was able to see that it really is a "universal and integral part of our experience of love." He saw it as part of the divine plan. In this way he came to acquire a faith in God more logical and firmly based than the one he had before. The loss of Joy was a terrible experience for him, but it did not destroy his faith; it strengthened it. With the object of helping those in similar distress he wrote about his feelings of grief and their development in a little book called A Grief Observed. He gave copies away to a few recently bereaved people.

The film Shadowlands is inaccurate as a picture of life at the Kilns. I think that the author of the script, William Nicholson, makes Lewis lose his faith for dramatic effect. When the film was first shown by the BBC, Nicholson wrote an article in which he stated that none of the dialogue spoken by his characters was historical. He was perhaps not much concerned with accuracy; his main object was to write a powerful and successful TV play. The film goes some way towards dispelling the idea that Lewis was a misogynist. I don't know how it came into being, and certainly I can't think of an educated and well-read woman who knew him and held this view about him. I have written "educated and well-read" because he was bored by very much ordinary social conversation about such matters as clothes, shopping, household improvements, and the schooling of children. This sort of conversation bored him just as much if it came from a man as if it came from a woman, but he was more likely to experience it from a woman. He would try to avoid or to cut short such conversation, if he politely could. He may have sometimes given the women concerned the impression that he did not like them.

It is worth remembering that an important part of his work, from the writing of his great academic masterpiece *The Allegory of Love* to *Till We Have Faces*, was a celebration or glorification of femininity and romantic love. A misogynist could hardly have written these books, nor could he have appreciated, as Lewis did, the writings of Coventry Patmore, the supreme poet of married love.

Some people are uneasy at the use made of what they call the occult, that is of magic and witches, in the Narnia stories. People who are worried in this way are taking the stories far too literally. These are entirely fictitious. Thus the fact that Lewis included witches certainly did not mean that he believed in their power in real life. The main theme of the stories is the conflict between good and evil; characters such as the white witch represent the forces of evil. The stories are not meant to teach Christian doctrine. They are written first as stories that children could wholeheartedly enjoy, and secondly as stories in which some of the imaginary episodes rather resemble the true events of the Christian faith. He did not want the resemblances to be pointed out by adults, nor even did he expect them to be noticed by more than a few children. His hope was that when, at an older age, the child came into contact with the real truths of

Christianity, he or she would find these truths easier to accept because of reading with pleasure and accepting stories with similar themes years before.

I am surprised that few of those interested in C. S. Lewis's personality and way of life have read his brother Warren's diaries. Excellently edited by Clyde Kilby and Marjorie Lamp Mead, the volume is entitled *Brothers and Friends*. Jack owed a great deal to the help of Warren ("Warnie"), whom he thought of as his best friend. Warren acted as his secretary while they were living together at the Kilns, handling his vast correspondence, and often writing letters on his behalf. Jack was happy for him to do this as Warren was an admirable letter-writer and prose stylist.

More important still, Warren provided companionship. Jack tended to feel lonely if alone for long. He liked country walking and thought a good walk almost every afternoon important for his health. But he did not like walking alone. Warnie was for him the perfect walking companion. They enjoyed the same scenery, though they often had different impressions of it, and both relished the halts for bread and cheese and beer in old-fashioned pubs. It is a mistake to think that in their conversation Warnie was always the junior partner. He often took the lead, for he had a far greater experience of ordinary life than his brother and was probably shrewder in his assessments of character. Both enjoyed listening to music, but Warnie had a far greater knowledge. His conversation was sometimes enriched by references to life in the French seventeenth century, a subject of which he had made a life-long study. His series of books, of which *The Splendid Century* is the first, are remarkable for their readability and elegance of style. He was a modest author, but his books are for the general reader perhaps the best of all introductions to that period of history.

Unfortunately, he was an alcoholic, liable to bouts of really heavy drinking. When he was himself, as he often was for many weeks at a time, he was the most charming and courteous of men. John Wain once said of him that he had the best manners of any man he knew. The high praise was well deserved.

I am sometimes asked why C. S. Lewis did not become a Roman Catholic or how close his position was to that of the Roman Catholic church. There is a full discussion of this in a book by an old pupil, Christopher Derrick, C. S. Lewis and the Church of Rome. I have little to add. I always had the impression that he wanted very much to avoid what he thought of as sectarian controversy and the bitterness that often went with it. He was concerned with the central beliefs of Christianity, those which were accepted and shared by most men of all churches. He thought that the few ideological divergences were subjects for discussion by theologians and other highly trained experts. They were not important for laypeople. I remember Dr. Havard saying, "Jack, most of your friends seem to be Catholic. Why don't you join us? Aren't you tempted?"

Lewis replied that the important thing was to make one's submission to a Christian church. Which branch of the Christian church one chose was far less important. And he said he was not tempted to share what he called "your heresies."

"Heresies! What heresies, Jack?"

"Well, here are two—the position you give to the Virgin Mary and the doctrine of papal infallibility." But he refused to discuss them. He attributed his prejudice against the Roman church to his upbringing in Northern Ireland. If it had not been for him, Warren would almost certainly have been received into the Roman church. At the time Warren was a patient in the hospital of Our Lady of Lourdes, run by a remarkable order, the Medical Missionaries of Mary. When he wrote that he was shortly to be received, Jack immediately traveled to the hospital to prevent it. He argued not only with Warren, but also at length with the parish priest. In describing the event to me, Warnie commented, "Jack did not always get the best of it." Warnie also remarked that he had hardly ever seen his brother so upset. We should not assume that his objections were mainly doctrinal. I think his rather violent reaction was caused by the fear of anything that might come between him and his beloved brother. All the time I knew him, Jack was about as nonsectarian as it is possible for a devout Christian to be. I cannot think of any occasion when he attacked another Christian church, or indeed another religious faith. He was also nonliturgical and seemed to take little interest in the High Church/Low Church, Anglo-Catholic/Evangelical conflicts common in the Church of England. He went regularly to a church in Headington with "high" services, not because of any preference but because it was the parish in which he lived. This practice was for him a matter almost of obedience. He thought it was a mistake for a Christian to shop around looking for an eloquent vicar or a pleasing service. I agree with Derrick that Lewis was nearest to becoming a Roman Catholic in about 1950, but I do not regret that he did not. I think that it would have limited his influence, especially among evangelical Christians.

I am sometimes asked about his friendship with Ruth Pitter. On one occasion when I was staying with him at the Kilns, he asked me if I would drive him to visit a friend who lived in Long Crendon, a Buckinghamshire village. He talked about her on the way. He began by saying that if he were a marrying man, it was Ruth Pitter he would have chosen. He went on to describe her as a delightful and witty woman and a true poet. I enjoyed the visit and liked her very much. She was a pleasant-looking woman of the same age as Jack, rather plump but energetic. She made shrewd and amusing remarks about George Orwell and

Dylan Thomas. She spoke admiringly of Eddison, R. S. Thomas and Andrew Young, but most of her conversation was sensible, down to earth, even homey. Long Crendon is a large and attractive village with many fine old houses. Her cottage was not one of these and was distinguished only by a fine garden of over two acres. She particularly enjoyed cultivating vegetables and fruit, but was concerned at the waste. She sold some of the surplus but not always enough. I suggested homemade wine, a hobby of mine. This led to a long conversation and a correspondence. I gathered that she shared the cottage with a woman called Kathleen O'Hara, who was also her partner in the business of making and painting decorative trays, which were sold at high prices by Harrods. "Working with one's hands is the most satisfactory way of earning a living. It rests and refreshes the mind." But during the war there was no demand for trays. She was forced to do factory work. While Jack was out of the room, she told me that she was rescued from severe depression by Jack's broadcast talks and by the letters he wrote to her. They guided her conversion to the Anglican faith. In her company Jack seemed unusually quiet and peaceful, very happy together.

Ruth did not like Joy and saw very little of her during the period when Joy was mistress of the Kilns. After Joy's death Jack "came back to her" (to quote Ruth's friend, Mary Thomas) and confided in her. If he had been in better health, they might still have married.

NOTES

The following abbreviations are used for frequently cited sources:

LP—"The Lewis Papers: Memoirs of the Lewis Family, 1850-1930," 11 vols. Leeborough Press. A typescript of the original is in the Wade Collection, Wheaton, Illinois.

WHL Biog.—Warren Hamilton Lewis, "C. S. Lewis: A Biography" unpublished typescript in the Wade Collection, Wheaton.

Letters —W. H. Lewis, ed. *The Letters of C. S. Lewis* (London: Bles, 1966).

SJ—C. S. Lewis, *Surprised by Joy: The Shape of My Early Life* (London: Bles, 1955).

TST —Walter Hooper, ed. *They Stand Together: The Letters of C. S. Lewis to Arthur Greeves* 1914—1963 (London: Collins, 1979).

PREFACE

1. G. K. Chesterton, *The Ballad of the White Horse*, bk. 2, v. 32.
2. *Ibid.*, bk. 7, v. 50.

CHAPTER ONE: *Very Different Strains*

1. *TST*, 292.
2. *LP*, 2:57.
3. *Ibid.*, 59.
4. *Ibid.*, 61.
5. *SJ*, 11.
6. *Ibid.*

7. Roger Lancelyn Green and Walter Hooper, *C. S. Lewis: A Biography* (London: Collins, 1974; New York: Harcourt Brace Jovanovich, 1974), 17.
8. *LP*, 2:149.
9. *Ibid.*, 155.
10. Flora Hamilton to Albert Lewis, 14 November 1886, *LP*, 2:159.
11. Albert Lewis to Edie Macown, draft, n.d., *LP*, 2:14.
12. *Ibid.*
13. *Ibid.*, 62.
14. Flora Hamilton to Albert Lewis, 26 June 1893, *LP*, 2:248.
15. Flora Hamilton to Albert Lewis, 5 July 1893, *LP*, 2:251.
16. *LP*, 2:281-82.

CHAPTER TWO: *Good Parents, Good Food, and a Garden*

1. *Mrs. Beeton's Household Management* (London: Ward Lock, n.d.), 20.
2. *SJ*, 13.
3. *SJ*, 18.
4. *Ibid.*
5. WHL Biog., 3-4.
6. 3 May 1900, *LP*, 2:298.
7. 19 August 1900, *LP*, 2:309.
8. WHL Biog., 4.
9. Letter to Albert, 8 May 1900, *LP*, 2:300.
10. Letter to Albert, 14 July 1901, *LP*, 2:327.
11. Flora Lewis to Albert Lewis, 24 July 1901, *LP*, 3:2.
12. *Letters*, WHL Memoir, 1.
13. *Ibid.*, 62.
14. *Ibid.*, 2.
15. *SJ*, 50.
16. *Letters*, WHL Memoir, 3.
17. WHL to his parents, 5 June 1905, *LP*, 3:45.
18. CSL to WHL, n.d., *LP*, 3:76.
19. *LP*, 3:89.
20. *LP*, 3:102.
21. *LP*, 3:230.
22. *LP*, 3:82, and *Boxen: The Imaginary World of the Young C. S. Lewis*, ed. Walter Hooper (London: Collins, 1985; New York, Harcourt Brace and Jovanovich, 1985). Letter of 4 September, Warren Lewis to his father.
23. Flora Lewis to Albert Lewis, 11 September 1907, *LP*, 3:83.
24. WHL Biog., 151.
25. *LP*, 3:120.

CHAPTER THREE: *Into Bondage*

1. Letter of 27 October 1904, *LP*, 3:25.
2. *Ibid.*, 26.

3. *SJ*, 123.
4. *LP*, 3:25–26.
5. *LP*, 3:35.
6. *LP*, 3:36.
7. *LP*, 3:37.
8. *LP*, 3:40.
9. *Ibid.*
10. *SJ*, 39.
11. C. S. Lewis's Wynyard Journal, 1909, *LP*, 3:194.
12. *SJ*, 39.
13. *LP*, 3:42.
14. See *Letters to an American Lady*, 120.
15. Albert Lewis to WHL, 13 November 1910, *LP*, 3:222.
16. *Norman May's Guide to Malvern* (1908), 142–44.
17. *LP*, 3:227.
18. *SJ*, 70.
19. *SJ*, 69.
20. *SJ*, 70.
21. *LP*, 3:230ff.
22. *Boxen*, 4 September (n.d.).
23. WHL Biog., 127–28.
24. *LP*, 4:266–70.
25. W. H. Lewis, "Malvern in My Time," *The Beacon* (Malvern College, 1953), 84–89.
26. *LP*, 3:286–87.
27. *LP*, 3:298.
28. Albert Lewis to C. S. Lewis, 7 December 1912, *LP*, 3:313.
29. From the documents collected by R. B. Porch, Jack's house tutor.
30. Richard Wagner, *Siegfried and the Twilight of the Gods*, trans. Margaret Armour (New York: Doubleday, 1911).
31. *SJ*, 77.

CHAPTER FOUR: *Malvern College*

1. WHL Biog., 29–31.
2. *Ibid.*
3. *SJ*, 101.
4. December 1913, *LP*, 4:112.
5. *TST*, 47.
6. *Letters*, 4–5.
7. *SJ*, 107.
8. C. S. Lewis to Albert Lewis, 29 September 1913, *LP*, 4:77.
9. Donald Hardman to the author, 10 June 1979.
10. Donald Hardman to the author, 12 October 1979.
11. *TST*, 47.
12. *Loki Bound* has not yet been published. See *LP*, 4:215ff.
13. *SJ*, 115.

14. A. F. Lace to the author, 10 June 1980.
15. W. T. Kirkpatrick to Albert Lewis, 14 May 1914, *LP*, 4:172.
16. W. H. Lewis to Albert Lewis, 29 March 1914, *LP*, 4:156.
17. Albert Lewis to W. H. Lewis, 29 March 1914, *LP*, 4:159–61.
18. W. T. Kirkpatrick to Albert Lewis, April 1914.

CHAPTER FIVE: *Great Bookham*

1. 6 October 1915, *TST*, 53.
2. C. S. Lewis, *That Hideous Strength: A Modern Fairy Tale for Grown-Ups* (London: Lane, 1945).
3. *SJ*, 129.
4. *SJ*, 133.
5. *LP*, 4:240.
6. *SJ*, 137.
7. 26 September, 1914, *TST*, 50.
8. W. T. Kirkpatrick to Albert Lewis, January 1915, *LP*, 4:131.
9. *LP*, 3:303.
10. *Ibid.*
11. *LP*, 4:181–82.
12. *SJ*, 129.
13. H. A. Grueber, *Myths of the Norsemen* (London: Harrap, 1908), xv.
14. 20 October 1914, *TST*, 56–57.
15. Charlotte M. Yonge, *The Trial* (London: 1895).
16. 4 November 1914, *TST*, 59.
17. *TST*, 64.
18. *TST*, 75.
19. 20 February 1917, *TST*, 170.
20. *SJ*, 33.
21. W. B. Yeats, *Poems*, 3rd ed. (London: T. Fisher Unwin), pref., xi–xii.
22. 7 March 1916, *TST*, 92.
23. *SJ*, 169.
24. George MacDonald, *Phantastes* (London: Fifield, 1905), 108.
25. *SJ*, 169.
26. *TST*, 150.
27. *TST*, 112.
28. *TST*, 150.
29. *LP*, 5:106–30.
30. *TST*, 124.
31. 12 October 1916(?), *TST*, 135.
32. *TST*, 136-38.
33. *LP*, 5:74–75.
34. *LP*, 5:78.
35. *LP*, 5:79.
36. 21 July 1916, *LP*, 5:113.
37. *LP*, 5:176.
38. *LP*, 5:156.

39. W. T. Kirkpatrick to Albert Lewis, 15 December 1916, *LP*, 5:162–63.
40. C. S. Lewis to Albert Lewis, postmarked 8 February 1917, *LP*, 5:185.
41. *LP*, 5:179 and *Letters*, 33.
42. *LP*, 5:197–98.
43. *Ibid.*
44. Albert Lewis to W. H. Lewis, 16 April 1917, *LP*, 5:202–3.
45. W. T. Kirkpatrick to Albert Lewis, 18 April 1917, *LP*, 5:202–3.
46. *LP*, 5:204–5.

CHAPTER SIX: *Into Battle*

1. W. H. Lewis to Albert Lewis, 23 March 1914, *LP*, 4:156–58.
2. 28 April 1917, *TST*, 179.
3. April 1917, *TST*, 180.
4. C. S. Lewis to Albert Lewis, 2 May 1917, *LP*, 5:208.
5. 6 May 1917, *TST*, 181.
6. 13 May 1917, *TST*, 183.
7. Postmarked 3 May 1917, *TST*, 185.
8. Albert Lewis to W. H. Lewis, 30 April 1917, *LP*, 5:207–8.
9. Albert Lewis to W. H. Lewis, 7 May 1917, *LP*, 5:209.
10. 13 May 1917, *TST*, 183.
11. 27 May 1917, *TST*, 187.
12. Albert Lewis to W. H. Lewis, 12 June 1917, *LP*, 5:222–23.
13. C.S. Lewis to Albert Lewis, n.d., *LP*, 5:212–13.
14. 27 May 1917, *TST*, 5:187.
15. 27 August 1917, *LP*, 5:231–32.
16. 24 September 1917, *LP*, 5:233.
17. 23 October 1917, *LP*, 5:237–38.
18. *LP*, 5:239.
19. *LP*, 5:242.
20. *LP*, 5:243.
21. *LP*, 5:256-57.
22. 16 February 1918, *LP*, 5:285–86.
23. 8 April 1918, *LP*, 5:304.
24. *LP*, 5:302.
25. *LP*, 5:311.
26. *LP*, 5:309.
27. *LP*, 5:316.
28. *Ibid.*
29. 30 May 1918, *LP*, 5:320–21.
30. 20 June 1918, *LP*, 5:330–31
31. *LP*, 5:330-31.
32. n.d., *LP*, 6:17–18.
33. *Ibid.*
34. *Ibid.*
35. 1 October 1918, *LP*, 9:44–45.
36. *TST*, 230.

37. Quoted by Walter Hooper in his Preface to *Spirits in Bondage* (San Diego: Harcourt Brace Jovanovich, 1984).
38. *LP*, 6:54.
39. *LP*, 6:62.
40. *LP*, 6:64–65.
41. *LP*, 6:66.
42. *LP*, 6:68–69.
43. *LP*, 6:74–75.
44. *LP*, 6:79.

CHAPTER SEVEN: *Spirits in Bondage*

1. *Letters*, 46–7, and *LP*, 6:82–83.
2. *LP*, 6:85–86, and *Letters*, 47.
3. *LP*, 6:82–83.
4. *LP*, 6:85–86.
5. W. H. Lewis to Albert Lewis, 28 January 1919, *LP*, 6:84.
6. *TST*, 221.
7. Clive Hamilton, *Spirits in Bondage* (London: William Heinemann, 1919), 11. All quotations from *Spirits in Bondage* are from this edition. There is also a reprint with a preface by Walter Hooper (San Diego: Harcourt Brace Jovanovich, 1984).
8. *Ibid.*, 43.
9. *Ibid.*, 11.
10. *Ibid.*, 43.
11. *Ibid.*, 17.
12. *Ibid.*, 23.
13. *Ibid.*, 30.
14. *Ibid.*, 31.
15. *Ibid.*, 41–42.
16. *Ibid.*, 86.
17. *Ibid.*, 86–87.
18. *Ibid.*, 89.
19. *Ibid.*, 98.
20. 28 January 1919, *LP*, 6:84. Quoted in *Spirits in Bondage*, xxxvii–xxxviii.
21. C. S. Lewis to Albert Lewis, 5 March 1919, *LP*, 6:96.

CHAPTER EIGHT: *Mrs. Moore*

1. *LP*, 6:118.
2. 20 May 1919, *LP*, 6:122–23.
3. 25 June 1919, *LP*, 6:145–46.
4. 29 August 1919.
5. 4 April 1920, *LP*, 6:183.
6. 1 May 1920, *LP*, 6:197.
7. 25 July 1920, *LP*, 6:195–96.
8. 6 June 1921, *LP*, 6:189.

9. 22 November 1920, *LP*, 6:208.
10. 11 January 1921, *LP*, 6:225.
11. 26 January 1921, *LP*, 6:221.
12. 28 March 1921, *LP*, 6:269–70.
13. 19 January 1921, *LP*, 6:226.
14. C. S. Lewis, diary entry of 12 March 1921, *LP*, 6:286.
15. CSL to Albert Lewis, n.d., *LP*, 7:20–21.
16. 9 July 1921, *LP*, 7:33.
17. *LP*, 7:39.
18. 28 July 1921, *LP*, 7:51.
19. *LP*, 7:49–50, and *Letters*, 70.
20. *LP*, 7:150.
21. This account of life with Mrs. Moore, Maureen, and friends is based on CSL's diary, *LP*, 7:168–204.
22. *Letters*, 12.
23. Roger Lancelyn Green and Walter Hooper, *C. S. Lewis: A Biography* (London: Collins, 1974; New York: Harcourt Brace Jovanovich, 1974), 66.
24. Humphrey Carpenter, *The Inklings: C. S. Lewis, J. R. R. Tolkien, Charles Williams, and Their Friends* (London: Allen Unwin, 1979), 10.
25. *LP*, 7:50, 153.

CHAPTER NINE: Into Poverty

1. CSL to Albert Lewis, 15 October 1922.
2. *Ibid.*, and *Letters*, 82.
3. Milton, *Samson Agonistes*, ll. 80-82, 1669–71.
4. Nevill Coghill in *Light on C. S. Lewis*, ed. Jocelyn Gibb (London: Bles, 1965), 55.
5. *LP*, 8:76ff.
6. 29 February 1924, *LP*, 8:188–89.
7. *LP*, 8:41–42.
8. *Ibid.*
9. 11 May 1924, *LP*, 8:225–26.
10. Diary 18 May 1924, *LP*, 8:229–30.
11. 21 May 1924, *LP*, 8:231.
12. 23 May 1924, *LP*, 8:232.
13. 21 and 24 June 1924, *LP*, 8:247.
14. Diary 15 October 1924, *LP*, 8:263.
15. C. S. Lewis to Albert Lewis, 28 August 1924, *LP*, 8:260.
16. C. S. Lewis diary, 6 February 1925, *LP*, 8:273.
17. C. S. Lewis diary, 10 February 1925, *LP*, 8:273.
18. C. S. Lewis diary, 29 July 1925, *LP*, 8:255.
19. C. S. Lewis diary, 30 July 1925, *LP*, 8:257–58.
20. 20 May 1925, *LP*, 8:290.
21. C. S. Lewis to Albert Lewis, 26 May 1925, *LP*, 8:291–92.
22. C. S. Lewis diary, 18 July 1925, *LP*, 8:301.

CHAPTER TEN: *Fellow and Tutor*

1. CSL to Albert Lewis, 21 October 1925, *Letters*, 104.
2. *Letters*, 103–4.
3. *Letters*, 104.
4. *LP*, 9:124.
5. C. S. Lewis to author in conversation.
6. C. S. Lewis to W. H. Lewis, 19 November 1939.
7. *LP*, 9:98.
8. November 1928, *LP*, 10:94.
9. *LP*, 10:94.
10. *LP*, 9:148.
11. John Lawlor, "The Tutor and the Scholar" in *Light on C. S. Lewis,* ed. Jocelyn Gibb (London: Bles, 1965).

CHAPTER ELEVEN: *Dymer*

1. Canto 1, vv. 3, 6. All quotations from *Dymer* are from the first edition (London: Dent, 1926; New York: Dutton, 1926).
2. Canto 1, v. 10.
3. Canto 2, v. 29.
4. Canto 2, v. 33.
5. Canto 3, v. 12.
6. Canto 5, v. 2.
7. Canto 5, v. 27.
8. Canto 6, v. 16.
9. Canto 7, v. 31.
10. Canto 9, v. 4.
11. Canto 9, v. 13.
12. Marjorie Mack, "Dymer, Myth or Poem?" *The Month*, September, 1952.

CHAPTER TWELVE: *The Pilgrim's Regress*

1. WHL Biog., 231.
2. *Ibid.*, 232.
3. *Ibid.*
4. *Ibid.*, 233.
5. Richard I. Aaron, "Epistemology," *Encyclopedia Britannica* (1974).
6. *SJ*, 197–98.
7. *SJ*, 207.
8. *LP*, 9:144.
9. *SJ*, 194.
10. Shelley, *The Cenci*, act 2, sc. 2, ll. 8–13.
11. C. S. Lewis, conversation with the author; see also *SJ*, 202.
12. Character in "Determined to Be a Villain" modeled on T. D. Weldon, *LP*, 10:123.
13. C. S. Lewis, conversation with the author; see also *SJ*, 211.
14. C. S. Lewis to W. H. Lewis, 29 September 1929, *LP*, 10:194–95.

15. 1 October 1931, *TST*, 425.
16. *SJ*, 223.
17. C. S. Lewis, *The Pilgrim's Regress: An Allegorical Apology for Christianity, Reason, and Romanticism* (London: Sheed and Ward, 1944), 13.
18. *Ibid.*, chap. 5, last paragraph.
19. *Ibid.*, 183, 205.
20. 18 August 1930, *TST*, 379.
21. December 1935, *TST*, 474–75.

CHAPTER THIRTEEN: *The Kilns*

1. Clyde S. Kilby and Marjorie Mead, eds., *Brothers and Friends: The Diaries of Major Warren Hamilton Lewis* (New York: Harper & Row, 1982), 39.
2. WHL Biog., 222.
3. 4 December 1934, W. H. Lewis diary, *Brothers and Friends*, 165.
4. 26 May 1931, W. H. Lewis diary, *Brothers and Friends*, 81.
5. 17 January 1931, *TST*, 404.
6. 29 February 1931, *TST*, 408.
7. 26 June 1931, *TST*, 415.
8. 5 September 1931, *TST*, 419.
9. C. S. Lewis to W. H. Lewis, 22 November 1931, WHL Biog., 145.
10. Charles Williams to C. S. Lewis, 12 March 1936.
11. C. S. Lewis, *The Allegory of Love: A Study in Medieval Tradition* (Oxford: Clarendon Press, 1936), 259.
12. *Ibid.*, 360.
13. Graham Hough, *A Preface to the Faerie Queen* (1962).
14. 10 January 1931, *TST*, 400–1.
15. *Ibid.*
16. 17 August 1933, *TST*, 450.
17. 8 August 1933, W. H. Lewis diary.
18. 29 August 1933, W. H. Lewis diary.
19. 17 August 1933, *TST*, 458.
20. 9 and 10 August 1933, W. H. Lewis diary.
21. 5 January 1939, W. H. Lewis diary.
22. 3 December 1929, *TST*, 317.
23. 3 June 1934, W. H. Lewis diary.
24. *Brothers and Friends*, 220. Warren delighted in telling droll stories of Dyson.
25. *Letters*, WHL Memoir, 13.
26. *Letters*, WHL Memoir, 14.
27. 24 May 1948, W. H. Lewis diary.
28. Stanley Unwin to J. R. R. Tolkien, 2 March 1938.
29. 9 July 1939, *Letters*, 167.
30. Church of Wales Assembly at Carmarthen, Easter 1945; printed in C. S.

Lewis's *Undeceptions: Essays on Theology and Ethics* (London: Bles, 1971).
31. 9 July 1939, *Letters*, 167.
32. C. S. Lewis, "Shelley, Dryden, and Mr. Eliot," *Rehabilitations and other Essays* (London: Oxford University Press, 1939), 14.
33. *Ibid.*, 29.
34. C. S. Lewis, "William Morris," *Rehabilitations*, 39.
35. *Ibid.*, 41.
36. *Ibid.*, 42.
37. *Ibid.*, 45, 47.
38. C. S. Lewis, "Our English Syllabus," *Rehabilitations*, 85.
39. *Ibid.*, 88.
40. C. S. Lewis, "The Idea of an English School," *Rehabilitations*, 76.
41. J. B. Leishman, review of *Rehabilitations* in *Review of English Studies* (January, 1940).
42. Published in C. S. Lewis, *Studies in Medieval and Renaissance Literature*, ed. Walter Hooper (Cambridge: Cambridge University Press, 1966).
43. E. M. W. Tillyard, *Milton* (Cambridge: Cambridge University Press, 1930).
44. *Essays and Studies* published by members of the Oxford English Association, vol. 19, 1934.
45. C. S. Lewis and E. M. W. Tillyard, *The Personal Heresy: A Controversy* (London: Oxford University Press, 1939), 119–20.

CHAPTER FOURTEEN: *War Work*

1. It is not known to whom the talk was given. CSL gave me a carbon copy, which I passed on to Walter Hooper for publication in *The Weight of Glory and Other Addresses*, revised and expanded edition, ed. Walter Hooper (New York: Macmillan, 1980).
2. *The Weight of Glory*, 40.
3. *Ibid.*, 42.
4. *Ibid.*, 48.
5. 15 September 1939, *TST*, 485.
6. C. S. Lewis to W. H. Lewis, 11 August 1940, unpublished in full.
7. 27 December 1940, *TST*, 487.
8. C. S. Lewis to W. H. Lewis, 2 September 1939.
9. 9 May 1940, *TST*, 485.
10. C. S. Lewis to W. H. Lewis, 2 September 1939.
11. C. S. Lewis, *The Problem of Pain* (London: Bles, 1940), viii.
12. Chad Walsh, *C. S. Lewis: Apostle of the Skeptics* (New York: Macmillan, 1949); also in *Undeceptions*, 83–84.
13. C. S. Lewis, *The Problem of Pain*, 129.
14. C. S. Lewis to W. H. Lewis, 20 July 1940.
15. 9 October 1941, *Letters*, 194.
16. *The Screwtape Letters*, (London: Collins-Fontana; New York: Macmillan), 16:83.
17. *Ibid.*, 16:84.

CHAPTER FIFTEEN: *Preacher and Broadcaster*

1. 23 December 1941, *TST*, 497.
2. C. S. Lewis, *Mere Christianity* (London: Bles, 1952), 111.
3. C. S. Lewis, *Beyond Personality: The Christian Idea of God* (London: Bles, 1944), 64; *Mere Christianity*, 171.
4. *The Times Literary Supplement*, 21 October 1944.
5. *The New York Herald Tribune Weekly Book Review*, 26 September 1945, sec. 6, p. 12.
6. Victor Yarros, review in *American Freeman* (December 1947).
7. Alistair Cooke, "Mr. Anthony at Oxford," *New Republic* 110 (24 April 1944).
8. 23 December 1941, *TST*, 491.
9. Stella Aldwinckle, *The Socratic Digest* 1 (1942–43):6.
10. C. S. Lewis, *The Socratic Digest* 1 (1942–43): pref.
11. *Ibid.*
12. A full list of speakers can be found in Walter Hooper's article, "Oxford's Bonny Fighter," in *C. S. Lewis at the Breakfast Table and Other Reminiscences*, ed. James T. Como (New York: Macmillan, 1979).
13. T. D. Weldon, conversation with Martin Moynihan.

CHAPTER SIXTEEN: *Writing, Writing, Writing*

1. Quoted by WHL in *Letters*, Memoir, 16.
2. 30 January 1944, *TST*, 501.
3. CSL to Mary Neylan, 20 May 1945, *Letters*, 206.
4. C. S. Lewis, *A Preface to Paradise Lost* (London: Oxford University Press, 1947), v.
5. *Ibid.*
6. C. S. Lewis, ed., *Essays Presented to Charles Williams* (Oxford: Oxford University Press, 1947), vi–vii.
7. *Ibid.*, ix.
8. *Ibid.*, x–xi.
9. C. S. Lewis, *A Preface to Paradise Lost*, 129.
10. Helen Gardner, "John Milton," lecture to the British Academy, 1966.
11. C. S. Lewis, *Out of the Silent Planet* (London: John Lane, The Bodley Head, 1938), 233.
12. Alan Pryce-Jones, review of C. S. Lewis's *Perelandra* in *The Observer*, 25 April 1943.
13. Leonard Bacon, review of C. S. Lewis's *Perelandra* in *Commonweal*, 8 April 1944.
14. Kate O'Brien, *The Spectator*, 14 May 1943.
15. C. S. Lewis, *Perelandra* (London: Lane, 1943), 52.
16. *Ibid.*, 221.
17. *Ibid.*, 253.
18. C. S. Lewis, *The Abolition of Man: Reflections on Education with Special Reference to the Teaching of English in the Upper Forms of Schools*,

Riddell Memorial Lecture, Fifteenth Series (London: Oxford University Press, 1943), 20.

19. *Ibid.*, 37–38.
20. *Ibid.*, 42.
21. Margaret Patterson Hannay, *C. S. Lewis: Modern Literature* (New York: Ungar, 1981), 104.
22. Chad Walsh, *The Literary Legacy of C. S. Lewis* (New York: Harcourt Brace Jovanovich, 1979), 120.
23. 16 April 1933.
24. C. S. Lewis, *The Great Divorce: A Dream* (London: Bles, 1945), 66–67.

CHAPTER SEVENTEEN: *Into Narnia*

1. C. S. Lewis, "On Three Ways of Writing for Children" in *Of Other Worlds: Essays and Stories*, ed. Walter Hooper (London: Bles, 1966).
2. Paul F. Ford, *Companion to Narnia* (San Francisco: Harper & Row, 1980), 12.
3. Dom Bede Griffiths, Letter of 26 November 1983 to *The Canadian C. S. Lewis Journal*, published in summer 1984 issue.

CHAPTER EIGHTEEN: *Escape*

1. C. S. Lewis, *English Literature in the Sixteenth Century Excluding Drama*, vol. 3 of *The Oxford History of English Literature* (Oxford: Clarendon Press, 1954), 1.
2. *Ibid.*, 31.
3. *Ibid.*, 43.
4. *Ibid.*, 193.
5. *Ibid.*, 462.
6. *Ibid.*, 96.
7. *Ibid.*, 498.
8. 21 and 23 June 1949, *TST*, 512–13.
9. *TST*, 514.
10. 27 or 29 July 1949, *TST*, 516.
11. *Ibid.*
12. 17 January 1950, W. H. Lewis diary.
13. 2 May 1950, *TST*, 517.
14. 15 June 1950, *TST*, 518.
15. W. H. Lewis diary, 8 February 1951, in *Brothers and Friends: The Diaries of Major Warren Hamilton Lewis*, ed. Clyde S. Kilby and Marjorie Mead (New York: Harper & Row, 1982), 239.
16. 23 March 1951, *TST*, 519.
17. *TST*, 533.

CHAPTER NINETEEN: Surprised by Joy

1. Joy Davidman, "The Longest Way Round," in *These Found the Way*, ed. D. W. Soper (Philadelphia: Westminster, 1951), 23.
2. Bill Gresham to Joy Davidman Gresham, December 1952.
3. C. S. Lewis to Vera Gebbert, 23 January 1953.
4. Joy Gresham to Bill Gresham, 22 December 1953.
5. C. S. Lewis, "De Descriptione Temporum," in *Selected Literary Essays*, ed. Walter Hooper (Cambridge: Cambridge University Press, 1969).
6. *TST*, 533.
7. Joy Gresham to Bill Gresham, 29 October 1954; quoted in Lyle Dorsett, *And God Came In: The Extraordinary Story of Joy Davidman, Her Life, and Marriage to C. S. Lewis* (New York: Macmillan, 1983), 116–17.
8. *And God Came In*, 113.
9. 30 October 1955, *TST*, 534.
10. *And God Came In*, 112.
11. 25 November 1956, *TST*, 542–43.
12. 21 March 1957, W. H. Lewis diary.

CHAPTER TWENTY: Surprised by Marriage

1. C. S. Lewis to Sheldon Vanauken; quoted in Sheldon Vanauken, *A Severe Mercy* (New York: Harper & Row, 1977), 227–28.
2. C. S. Lewis to Bill Gresham, 6 April 1957.
3. In conversation with the author, 27 November 1957.
4. Lyle Dorsett had this information from Howard Davidman, Joy's brother.
5. Letter to Mrs. Watt, 28 August 1958.
6. 25 March 1959, *TST*, 549.
7. C. S. Lewis to Chad Walsh, 21 October 1959.
8. Roger Lancelyn Green and Walter Hooper, *C. S. Lewis: A Biography* (London: Collins, 1974; New York: Harcourt Brace Jovanovich, 1974), 271–76.
9. C. S. Lewis to Chad Walsh, 23 May 1960.
10. C. S. Lewis, 275.
11. C. S. Lewis to Chad Walsh, 23 May 1960.
12. 21 June 1960, Clyde S. Kilby and Marjorie Mead, eds., *Brothers and Friends*, 248.
13. *Ibid.*
14. C. S. Lewis to Vera Gebbert, 15 July 1960, *Letters*, 293.
15. C. S. Lewis, *A Grief Observed* (London: Faber and Faber, 1961), 60.
16. Coventry Patmore, *The Rod, the Root and the Flower* (London: George Bell and Sons, 1911), 167.
17. C. S. Lewis, *Poems*, ed. Walter Hooper (London: Bles 1964).

CHAPTER TWENTY-ONE: Inspired by Joy

1. C. S. Lewis to Clyde Kilby, 10 February 1957, *Letters*, 274.

2. C. S. Lewis, *Till We Have Faces: A Myth Retold* (London: Bles, 1956; New York: Harcourt Brace Jovanovich, 1956), 294.
3. Anthony Boucher, *Magazine of Fantasy and Science Fiction* (12 June 1957).
4. *New York Times Book Review*, 13 January 1957.
5. See Humphrey Carpenter, *The Inklings: C. S. Lewis, J. R. R. Tolkien, Charles Williams, and Their Friends* (London: Allen & Unwin, 1979) 244–45.
6. See Thomas Howard, *The Achievement of C. S. Lewis: A Reading of His Fiction* (Wheaton, Ill.: Shaw, 1980); Evan Gibson, *C. S. Lewis: Spinner of Tales* (Washington, D.C.: Christian University Press); Donald Glover, *C. S. Lewis: The Art of Enchantment* (Athens, Ohio: Ohio University Press, 1981).
7. Quoted in Roger Lancelyn Green and Walter Hooper, *C. S. Lewis: A Biography* (London: Collins, 1974; New York: Harcourt Brace Jovanovich, 1974), 231.
8. *Chicago Sunday Tribune Magazine of Books*, 31 July 1960.
9. *New York Times Book Review*, 31 July 1960.
10. C. S. Lewis, *The Four Loves* (London: Bles, 1960), 79–80.
11. *Ibid.*, 85.
12. *Ibid.*, 87.
13. *Ibid.*, 93.
14. *Ibid.*, 104–5.
15. C. S. Lewis, *Reflections on the Psalms* (London: Bles, 1958), 45.
16. *Ibid.*, 46.
17. C. S. Lewis, *A Grief Observed* (London: Faber and Faber, 1961), 41.
18. *Ibid.*, 50.
19. *Ibid.*, 55, 57–58.
20. C. S. Lewis, *Poems*, ed. Walter Hooper (London: Bles, 1964), 133.
21. *Ibid.*, 143.
22. *Ibid.*, 123.
23. Thomas Howard, review of C. S. Lewis's *Poems*, *Christianity Today* (18 June 1964).

CHAPTER TWENTY-TWO: *Life after Joy*

1. C. S. Lewis, *An Experiment in Criticism* (Cambridge: Cambridge University Press, 1961), 128.
2. *Ibid.*, 140–41.
3. C. S. Lewis to Kathleen Raine, 25 October 1961.
4. 15 March 1963, *TST*, 564.
5. WHL Biog., 468–69.
6. WHL Biog., 469.
7. C. S. Lewis to D. H. Banner, 1 November 1963.
8. C. S. Lewis to Jane Douglass, 27 October 1963.
9. Shelley, *Epigram to Stella*, translation of the Greek of Plato. The original first line reads, "Thou wert the morning star . . ."

10. Roger Lancelyn Green and Walter Hooper, *C. S. Lewis: A Biography* (London: Collins, 1974; New York: Harcourt Brace Jovanovich, 1974), 300.
11. WHL Biog., 470.

BIBLIOGRAPHY

BOOKS BY C. S. LEWIS

[Clive Hamilton, pseud.]. *Spirits in Bondage: A Cycle of Lyrics.* London: William Heinemann, 1919. Reprint with an introduction by Walter Hooper. New York: Harcourt Brace, 1985.

[Clive Hamilton, pseud.]. *Dymer.* London: J. M. Dent, 1926; New York: E. P. Dutton, 1926. Reprint with a new preface. New York: Macmillan, 1950.

The Pilgrim's Regress: An Allegorical Apology for Christianity, Reason, and Romanticism. London: J. M. Dent, 1933; Sheed and Ward, 1935. Reprint with an important new preface on romanticism, footnotes, and running heads. London: Sheed and Ward, 1944; Grand Rapids, Mich.: Eerdmans, 1958.

The Allegory of Love: A Study in Medieval Tradition. Oxford: Clarendon Press, 1936.

Out of the Silent Planet. London: John Lane, 1938.

Rehabilitations and Other Essays. London: Oxford University Press, 1939. (Contents: Preface, "Shelley, Dryden, and Mr. Eliot," "William Morris," "The Idea of an English School," "Our English Syllabus," "High and Low Brows," "The Alliterative Metre," "Bluspels and Flalansferes: A Semantic Nightmare," "Variation in Shakespeare and Others," "Christianity and Literature.")

(With E. M. W. Tillyard). *The Personal Heresy: A Controversy.* London: Oxford University Press, 1939.

The Problem of Pain. London: Geoffrey Bles, Centenary Press, 1940.

The Screwtape Letters. London: Geoffrey Bles, 1942. Reprinted with a new letter and an additional preface, as *The Screwtape Letters and Screwtape Proposes a Toast.* London: Geoffrey Bles, 1961. The letters were first published in *The Guardian*, a Church of England weekly.

A Preface to Paradise Lost. London: Oxford University Press, 1942.

Broadcast Talks. London: Geoffrey Bles, 1942. Two series of broadcast talks ("Right and Wrong: A Clue to the Meaning of the Universe" and "What Christians Believe") given in 1941 and 1942, printed with some alterations.

Christian Behaviour: A Further Series of Broadcast Talks. London: Geoffrey Bles, 1943.

Perelandra. London: John Lane, 1943. Reprinted in paperback as *The Voyage to Venus.* London: Pan Books, 1953.

The Abolition of Man: Reflections on Education with Special Reference to the Teaching of English in the Upper Forms of Schools. Riddell Memorial Lectures, Fifteenth Series. London: Oxford University Press, 1943.

Beyond Personality: The Christian Idea of God. London: Geoffrey Bles, Centenary Press, 1944.

That Hideous Strength: A Modern Fairy Tale for Grown-Ups. London: John Lane, 1945. A version abridged by the author was published as *The Tortured Planet* (New York: Avon Books, 1946) and as *That Hideous Strength* (London: Pan Books, 1955).

The Great Divorce: A Dream. London: Geoffrey Bles, Centenary Press, 1945.

Miracles: A Preliminary Study. London: Geoffrey Bles, 1947. Reprint with a new version of chapter 3. London: Collins-Fontana Books, 1960.

Arthurian Torso: Containing the Posthumous Fragment of the Figure of Arthur by Charles Williams and A Commentary on the Arthurian Poems of Charles Williams by C. S. Lewis. London: Oxford University Press, 1948. Reprint with an introduction by Mary McDermott Shideler. Grand Rapids, Mich.: Eerdmans, 1974.

Transposition and Other Addresses. London: Geoffrey Bles, 1949. Published in the United States as *The Weight of Glory and Other Addresses.* New York: Macmillan, 1949.

The Lion, the Witch, and the Wardrobe. London: Geoffrey Bles, 1950.

Prince Caspian: The Return to Narnia. London: Geoffrey Bles, 1951.

Mere Christianity. London: Geoffrey Bles, 1952. This is a revised and amplified version of *Broadcast Talks, Christian Behaviour*, and *Beyond Personality.*

The Voyage of the Dawn Treader. London: Geoffrey Bles, 1952.

The Silver Chair. London: Geoffrey Bles, 1953.

The Horse and His Boy. London: Geoffrey Bles, 1954.

English Literature in the Sixteenth Century Excluding Drama. Vol. 3 of *The Oxford History of English Literature.* Oxford: Clarendon Press, 1954.

The Magician's Nephew. London: Bodley Head, 1955.

Surprised by Joy: The Shape of My Early Life. London: Geoffrey Bles, 1955.

The Last Battle. London: Bodley Head, 1956.

Till We Have Faces: A Myth Retold. London: Geoffrey Bles, 1956; New York: Harcourt, Brace and World, 1956.

Reflections on the Psalms. London: Geoffrey Bles, 1958.

The Four Loves. London: Geoffrey Bles, 1960.

Studies in Words. Cambridge: Cambridge University Press, 1960.

The World's Last Night and Other Essays. New York: Harcourt, Brace and Co., 1960. (Contents: "The Efficacy of Prayer," "On Obstinacy in Belief," "Lilies That Fester," "Screwtape Proposes a Toast," "Good Work and Good Works," "Religion and Rocketry," "The World's Last Night.")

[N. W. Clerk, pseud.]. *A Grief Observed.* London: Faber and Faber, 1961. Reprinted as by C. S. Lewis. London: Faber and Faber, 1964. Reprint, [N. W. Clerk, pseud.]. Greenwich, Conn.: Seabury Press, 1963.

An Experiment in Criticism. Cambridge: Cambridge University Press, 1961.

They Asked for a Paper: Papers and Addresses. London: Geoffrey Bles, 1962. (Contents: Acknowledgments, "De Descriptione Temporum," "The Literary Impact of the Authorised Version," "Hamlet: The Prince or the Poem?," "Kipling's World," "Sir

Walter Scott," "Lilies That Fester," "Psycho-analysis and
Literary Criticism," "The Inner Ring," "Is Theology Poetry?,"
"Transposition."

Letters to Malcolm: Chiefly on Prayer. London: Geoffrey Bles, 1964.
A selection of these letters, entitled *Beyond the Bright Blur*, was
published as a limited edition for Lewis's friends (New York:
Harcourt, Brace and World, 1963).

*The Discarded Image: An Introduction to Medieval and Renaissance
Literature.* Cambridge: Cambridge University Press, 1964.

Poems. Edited by Walter Hooper. London: Geoffrey Bles, 1964.

Screwtape Proposes a Toast and Other Pieces. London: Collins-
Fontana Books, 1965.

Studies in Medieval and Renaissance Literature. Edited by Walter
Hooper. Cambridge: Cambridge University Press, 1966.

Of Other Worlds: Essays and Stories. Edited by Walter Hooper.
London: Geoffrey Bles, 1966.

Christian Reflections. Edited by Walter Hooper. London: Geoffrey
Bles, 1967.

A Mind Awake: An Anthology of C. S. Lewis. Edited by Clyde S.
Kilby. London: Geoffrey Bles, 1968. Reprint. New York:
Harcourt, Brace and World, 1969.

Narrative Poems. Edited and with a preface by Walter Hooper.
London: Geoffrey Bles, 1969. Contains *Dymer, Launcelot, The
Nameless Isle,* and *The Queen of Drum.*

Selected Literary Essays. Edited and with a preface by Walter
Hooper. Cambridge: Cambridge University Press, 1969.
(includes "Donne and Love Poetry in the Seventeenth Century,"
"Hamlet: The Prince or the Poem?" "Shelley, Dryden, and Mr.
Eliot," "Sir Walter Scott," "William Morris," "The Literary
Impact of the Authorised Version," "The Vision of John
Bunyan," "Kipling's World," "Four-Letter Words" and other
essays.)

God in the Dock: Essays on Theology and Ethics. Edited and with
a preface by Walter Hooper. Grand Rapids, Mich.: Eerdmans,
1970. A paperback edition of the theological section was published as *God in the Dock: Essays on Theology* (London:

Collins-Fontana Books, 1979) and as *Undeceptions: Essays on Theology and Ethics* (London: Geoffrey Bles, 1971).

Fern-Seed and Elephants and Other Essays on Christianity. Edited and with a preface by Walter Hooper. London: Collins-Fontana Books, 1975.

The Dark Tower and Other Stories. Edited and with a preface by Walter Hooper. London: Collins, 1977; New York: Harcourt Brace Jovanovich, 1977.

The Joyful Christian: Readings from C. S. Lewis. New York: Macmillan, 1977.

On Stories, and Other Essays in Literature. Edited by Walter Hooper. London: Collins, 1982. New York: Harcourt Brace Jovanovich, 1982.

Boxen: The Imaginary World of the Young C.S. Lewis. Edited by Walter Hooper. London: Collins, 1985; San Diego: Harcourt Brace Jovanovich, 1985.

LETTERS OF C. S. LEWIS

For a list of some of the letters written by C. S. Lewis to newspapers, magazines, and individuals, see Walter Hooper, "A Bibliography of the Writings of C. S. Lewis," in *C. S. Lewis at the Breakfast Table and Other Reminiscences*, edited by James T. Como (New York: Macmillan, 1979). This admirable bibliography should also be consulted for a list of the books to which Lewis contributed introductions, his pamphlets, his prose, and verse contributions to various papers and other periodicals, and his book reviews.

There are valuable collections of letters in the Wade Collection at Wheaton College, Wheaton, Illinois, and at the Bodleian Library, Oxford. Many still remain in private hands. A list of his published letters follows.

Letters of C. S. Lewis. Edited and with a memoir by W. H. Lewis. London: Geoffrey Bles, 1966. (Many of these letters have, unfortunately, been abridged, and the names of some correspondents altered.)

Letters to an American Lady. Edited by Clyde S. Kilby. Grand Rapids, Mich.: Eerdmans, 1967. Reprint. London: Hodder & Stoughton, 1969.

They Stand Together: The Letters of C. S. Lewis to Arthur Greeves, 1914—1963. Edited by Walter Hooper. London: Collins, 1979.

Letters to Children. Edited by Lyle W. Dorsett and Marjorie Lamp Mead. New York: Macmillan, 1985. Contains ninety-seven of the letters in the Wade Collection, Wheaton College, Illinois, and a foreword by Douglas Gresham.

BOOKS ABOUT C. S. LEWIS

The family papers are a primary source of information for the C. S. Lewis scholar. Compiled by W. H. Lewis, the papers comprise eleven volumes, which were bound under the "imprint" of "Leeborough Press" and "printed" in an edition of perhaps three copies. "The Lewis Papers: Memoirs of the Lewis Family, 1850-1930," can be found on microfilm at the Bodleian Library, Oxford, and in its original state in the Wade Collection at Wheaton College, Illinois.

A list of valuable secondary sources on C. S. Lewis follows. For a more comprehensive list, see *C. S. Lewis: An Annotated Checklist of Writings about Him and His Works,* compiled by Joe R. Christopher and Joan K. Ostling, published by The Kent State University Press with the biographical supplement, and *Farther Up and Farther In: C. S. Lewis as Reflected in Recent Secondary Sources,* by Lois Larsen and D. W. Krummel, 1975. The manuscript of the latter is part of the Wade Collection at Wheaton College, Illinois.

Carpenter, Humphrey. *The Inklings: C. S. Lewis, J. R. R. Tolkien, Charles Williams, and Their Friends.* London: Allen & Unwin, 1979.

Christopher, Joe R. *C. S. Lewis* (Twayne's English Authors Series). Boston: G. K. Hall & Co., 1987.

Como, James T., ed. *C. S. Lewis at the Breakfast Table and Other Reminiscences*. New York: Macmillan, 1979. Contains Walter Hooper's invaluable bibliography and list of writings. Other contributors are Leo Baker, Peter Bayley, Derek Brewer, James Douglas-Grant, Jane Douglass, Austin Farrer, Adam Fox, Charles Gilmore, Roger L. Green, Bede Griffiths, A. C. Harwood, R. E. Havard, R. W. Ladborough, Eugene McGovern, Gervase Matthew, Clifford Morris, Luke Rigby, Erik Routley, George Sayer, Nathan Starr, John Wain, and Charles Wrong.

Gibb, Jocelyn, ed. *Light on C. S. Lewis*. London: Geoffrey Bles, 1965. Contributors include Owen Barfield, J. A. W. Bennett, Nevill Coghill, Austin Farrer, Stella Gibbons, Walter Hooper, John Lawlor, Kathleen Raine, and Chad Walsh.

Gilbert, Douglas, and Clyde S. Kilby. *C. S. Lewis: Images of His World*. Grand Rapids, Mich.: Eerdmans, 1973.

Green, Roger Lancelyn, and Walter Hooper. *C. S. Lewis: A Biography*. London: Collins, 1974; New York: Harcourt Brace Jovanovich, 1974.

Gresham, Douglas. *Lentenlands*. New York: Macmillan, 1988.

Griffin, William. *Clive Staples Lewis: A Dramatic Life*. San Francisco: Harper & Row, 1986.

Hooper, Walter. *Through Joy and Beyond: A Pictorial Biography of C. S. Lewis*. New York: Macmillan, 1982.

Kilby, Clyde S., and Marjorie Lamp Mead, eds. *Brothers and Friends: The Diaries of Major Warren Hamilton Lewis*. New York: Harper & Row, 1982.

Schofield, Stephen, ed. *In Search of C. S. Lewis*. South Plainfield, N.J.: Bridge Publishing, 1984. Contains interviews with Kenneth Tynan, A. J. P. Taylor, Malcolm Muggeridge, and others who knew Lewis.

Vanauken, Sheldon. *A Severe Mercy*. New York: Harper & Row, 1977. London: Hodder and Stoughton, 1979. Contains nineteen complete letters by Lewis.

BOOKS ON HIS FICTION

The number of critical books is already large. In this selection, I have marked with an asterisk those to which I am most indebted.

*Ford, Paul F. *Companion to Narnia.* San Francisco: Harper & Row, 1980.
*Gibson, Evan K. *C. S. Lewis: Spinner of Tales.* Washington, D.C.: Christian University Press, 1980.
*Hannay, Margaret Patterson. *C. S. Lewis.* New York: Ungar, 1981.
*Howard, Thomas. *The Achievement of C. S. Lewis: A Reading of His Fiction.* Wheaton, Ill.: Harold Shaw, 1980.
Karkainen, Paul A. *Narnia Explored.* Old Tappan, N.J.: Revell, 1979.
Kreeft, Peter. *C. S. Lewis: A Critical Essay.* Grand Rapids, Mich.: Eerdmans, 1979.
Purtill, Richard. *Lord of the Elves and Eldils: Fantasy and Philosophy in C. S. Lewis and J. R. R. Tolkien.* Grand Rapids, Mich.: Zondervan, 1974.
Sammons, Martha. *A Guide through Narnia.* Wheaton, Ill.: Harold Shaw, 1979.
Schakel, Peter J., ed. *The Longing for a Form: Essays on the Fiction of C. S. Lewis.* Kent, Ohio: Kent State University Press, 1977.
*Schakel, Peter J. *Reading with the Heart: The Way into Narnia.* Grand Rapids, Mich.: Eerdmans, 1979.
*Schakel, Peter J. *Reason and Imagination in C. S. Lewis: A Study of Till We Have Faces.* Grand Rapids, Mich.: Eerdmans, 1984.
*Walsh, Chad. *The Literary Legacy of C. S. Lewis.* New York: Harcourt Brace Jovanovich, 1979.

BOOKS ON HIS RELIGION AND RELIGIOUS WRITING

The reader should be warned that some of these books are sectarian. C. S. Lewis was not.

Christensen, Michael T. *C. S. Lewis on Scripture: His Thoughts on the Nature of Biblical Inspiration, the Role of Revelation, and the Question of Inerrancy*. Waco, Tex.: Word Books, 1979.

Cunningham, Richard B. *C. S. Lewis: Defender of the Faith*. Philadelphia: Westminster Press, 1967.

Hannay, Margaret Patterson. *C. S. Lewis*. New York: Ungar, 1981.

Holmer, Paul L. *C. S. Lewis: The Shape of His Faith and Thought*. New York: Harper & Row, 1976.

Hutter, Charles, ed. *Imagination and the Spirit: Essays in Literature and the Christian Faith Presented to Clyde S. Kilby*. Grand Rapids, Mich.: Eerdmans, 1971.

Kilby, Clyde S. *The Christian World of C. S. Lewis*. Grand Rapids, Mich.: Eerdmans, 1964.

Kilby, Clyde S. *Images of Salvation in the Fiction of C. S. Lewis*. Wheaton, Ill.: Harold Shaw, 1978.

Lindskoog, Kathryn Ann. *C. S. Lewis: Mere Christian*. Glendale, CA.: G/L Publications, 1973. Revised and expanded. Downers Grove, Ill.: InterVarsity Press, 1981.

Lindskoog, Kathryn Ann. *The Lion of Judah in Never-Never Land: The Theology of C. S. Lewis Expressed in His Fantasies for Children*. Grand Rapids, Mich.: Eerdmans, 1973.

Meilander, Gilbert. *The Taste for the Other: The Social and Ethical Thought of C. S. Lewis*. Grand Rapids, Mich.: Eerdmans, 1978.

Payne, Leanne. *Real Presence: The Holy Spirit in the Works of C. S. Lewis*. Wheaton, Ill.: Crossway Books, 1979.

Purtill, Richard C. *C. S. Lewis's Case for the Christian Faith*. San Francisco: Harper & Row, 1981.

Walsh, Chad. *C. S. Lewis: Apostle to the Skeptics*. New York: Macmillan, 1949.

White, William Luther. *The Image of Man in C. S. Lewis*. New York: Abingdon Press, 1969.

C. S. LEWIS PERIODICALS

CSL: The Bulletin of the New York C. S. Lewis Society. Hope Kirkpatrick, Secretary, 466 Orange Street, New Haven, Conn. 06511. Founded 1969.

The Chronicle of the Portland C. S. Lewis Society. Terri Williams,

Secretary, 1830 Northeast 141 Avenue, Portland, Oreg. 97230. Founded 1972.

The Lamp-Post of the Southern California C. S. Lewis Society. Marilyn Peppin, Secretary, 19 West Orange Grove Avenue, Sierra Madre, Calif. 91024. Founded 1974.

The Canadian C. S. Lewis Journal. Stephen Schofield, Secretary, Dunsfold, Godalming, Surrey GU8 4PF, England. Founded 1979.

Seven: An Anglo-American Literary Review. Barbara Reynolds, Editor, Wheaton College, Wheaton, Ill. Founded 1980.

Inklings-Jahrbuch für Literatur und Ästhetic. Gisbert Kranz, Editor, Verlag M. Claren, Werdohler Str. 11, D-5880 Lüdenscheid, West Germany. Founded 1984.

INDEX

9/691